RESURRECTING CANDRAKĪRTI

Studies in Indian and Tibetan Buddhism

This series was conceived to provide a forum for publishing outstanding new contributions to scholarship on Indian and Tibetan Buddhism and also to make accessible seminal research not widely known outside a narrow specialist audience, including translations of appropriate monographs and collections of articles from other languages. The series strives to shed light on the Indic Buddhist traditions by exposing them to historical-critical inquiry, illuminating through contextualization and analysis these traditions' unique heritage and the significance of their contribution to the world's religious and philosophical achievements.

Series Titles Previously Published

Among Tibetan Texts
History and Literature of the Himalayan Plateau
E. Gene Smith

Approaching the Great Perfection
Simultaneous and Gradual Methods of Dzogchen Practice in the Longchen Nyingtig
Sam van Schaik

A Direct Path to the Buddha Within
Gö Lotsāwa's Mahāmudrā Interpretation of the Ratnagotravibhāga
Klaus-Dieter Mathes

Foundations of Dharmakīrti's Philosophy
John D. Dunne

Freedom from Extremes
Gorampa's "Distinguishing the Views" and the Polemics of Emptiness
José Ignacio Cabezón and Geshe Lobsang Dargyay

Luminous Lives
The Story of the Early Masters of the Lam 'bras in Tibet
Cyrus Stearns

Mipham's Beacon of Certainty
Illuminating the View of Dzogchen, the Great Perfection
John Whitney Pettit

Reason's Traces
Identity and Interpretation in Indian and Tibetan Buddhist Thought
Matthew T. Kapstein

Scripture, Logic, Language
Essays on Dharmakīrti and His Tibetan Successors
Tom J.F. Tillemans

The Svātantrika-Prāsaṅgika Distinction
What Difference Does a Difference Make?
Edited by Georges Dreyfus and Sara McClintock

Vajrayoginī
Her Visualizations, Rituals, and Forms
Elizabeth English

Publisher's Acknowledgment

THE PUBLISHER gratefully acknowledges the generous help of the Hershey Family Foundation in sponsoring the publication of this book.

STUDIES IN INDIAN AND TIBETAN BUDDHISM

Resurrecting Candrakīrti

Disputes in the Tibetan Creation of Prāsaṅgika

Kevin A. Vose

Wisdom Publications • Boston

Wisdom Publications
199 Elm Street
Somerville MA 02144 USA
www.wisdompubs.org

Library of Congress Cataloging-in-Publication Data
Vose, Kevin A.
Resurrecting Candrakīrti : disputes in the Tibetan creation of Prāsaṅgika / Kevin A. Vose.
p. cm.
Includes bibliographical references and index.
ISBN 0-86171-520-9 (pbk. : alk. paper)
1. Candrakīrti. 2. Prāsaṅgika. 3. Buddhism–China—Tibet—Doctrines. I. Title.

BQ7479.8.C347V68 2009
294.3'92092—dc22

2008052230

ISBN 0-86171-520-9

13 12 11 10 09
5 4 3 2 1

Cover and interior design by Gopa & Ted2. Set in Diacritical Garamond Pro 10.5/13.

Wisdom Publications' books are printed on acid-free paper and meet the guidelines for permanence and durability of the Production Guidelines for Book Longevity of the Council on Library Resources.

Printed in the United States of America.

This book was produced with environmental mindfulness. We have elected to print this title on 30% PCW recycled paper. As a result, we have saved the following resources: 10 trees, 7 million BTUs of energy, 908 lbs. of greenhouse gases, 3,771 gallons of water, and 484 lbs. of solid waste. For more information, please visit our website, www.wisdompubs.org. This paper is also FSC certified. For more information, please visit www.fscus.org.

Contents

Acknowledgments

When an extraordinarily bored literature professor one day undertakes a study of "Acknowledgments" in American academic books, the unfortunate graduate student assigned to collect data on the Buddhist Studies genre will surely notice a striking correlation between works on Madhyamaka and the authors of those books appealing to the notion of "dependent arising" (*pratītyasamutpāda*) as a means to thank all those who contributed to the book's appearance in this world. It is an appealing concept. Reflecting on the many people, over many years, who play a role in the making of a book that in the end bears only one name on its cover can engender if not the realization of emptiness at least a strong sense of humility.

And so it is that I express thanks to Jeffrey Hopkins, whose guidance, vast knowledge, and enthusiasm for the intricacies of Buddhist philosophy shaped my understanding of the dynamics of Buddhist thought. Jeffrey's prolific scholarship on a great many topics continues to inspire and to serve as a model. Reading Tibetan Madhyamaka with Jeffrey, one senses that there is no end to his erudition. It is my hope that this present work can complement his great contribution to Madhyamaka and to the study of Buddhist doxography. I extend my mentor my deepest gratitude.

My readings of the Madhyamaka texts of Jayānanda and Chapa Chokyi Sengé (*Phya pa chos kyi seng ge,* 1109–69), which undergird this study, were enhanced through close consultation in Darjeeling, India, with Ken Rinpoche Ngawang Jinpa, among the last generation to complete his training at Loseling College of Drepung Monastery in Lhasa, Tibet. While he would heartily disagree with my presentation of Candrakīrti and Prāsaṅgika, his lively intellect and good humor deepened my understanding of many issues.

This book has greatly benefitted at various stages from the careful attention of others. Derek Maher's extensive comments on chapter 1 helped me clarify many points. John Dunne's feedback on an oral presentation of the ideas found in chapter 5 improved my thinking on those matters. David Germano, Bob Hueckstedt, and Karen Lang read an earlier version of this work and offered many good suggestions on the place of texts and institutions in

India and Tibet. Sincere thanks to Donald Lopez for reading through the entire manuscript and providing direction and suggestions for improvement. My appreciation goes to Helmut Tauscher for discussing with me particularly tricky passages in Chapa's text. I thank Christian Wedemeyer for sharing with me his pre-publication work that helps illuminate the relationships between the two (or three, or four) authors bearing the name Candrakīrti. Thanks to David Kittelstrom, the former editor of this series, for his thoughts on the manuscript. MacDuff Stewart, the current editor of the series, has shown great patience and guidance as the book took shape and aided the prose immensely. I express genuine gratitude to José Cabezón, co-editor-in-chief of this series, for sharing his extensive thoughts on the strengths and shortcomings of this book's central notions.

Finally, I wish to thank my family, whose love and support make this life enjoyable and, on a more basic level, possible. I thank Suzanne Bessenger, who reminds me that there is more to life than books, but not much more. This book is dedicated to Jakob, born the same year this project was first conceived.

Introduction

Among the most commonly held tenets of the Buddhist religion is the view that human suffering, indeed, the suffering of all sentient beings, arises due to delusion. A great deal of Buddhist training, then, is aimed at refining one's mind to overcome the fundamental misconceptions concerning ourselves, others, and the world around us that, in this view, characterize existence in saṃsāra. The centrality of human intellect in both suffering and liberation poses several crucial questions that many Buddhists across time and place have attempted to resolve: If fundamentally flawed, what value can the mind have in freeing us from suffering? Can the mind, imbued with delusion, have any knowledge of that state beyond suffering, nirvāṇa? Does enlightened mind bear any resemblance to our present delusional mind? How does nirvāṇa relate to the world of suffering in which we now live?

While competing camps of Buddhist philosophies have construed these issues variously, two Indian schools of thought came to dominate Tibetan Buddhist presentations of knowledge, transformation, and enlightenment. The Epistemological tradition stemming from Dignāga and Dharmakīrti provided Tibetans with a system of distinguishing falsehood from "valid cognition" (*pramāṇa, tshad ma*), a system that privileged direct experience over conceptual thought as the pre-eminent means to know reality. Various types of perception (*pratyakṣa, mngon sum*) and inference (*anumāna, rjes dpag*) produced valid knowledge of both the mundane world and its final nature. While Tibetans utilized Dharmakīrti's work to differentiate knowledge from delusion, the ultimate object of transformative knowledge came from a very different source. From the early introduction of Buddhism to Tibet, Nāgārjuna's Middle Way School championed emptiness (*śūnyatā, stong pa nyid*) as the final nature of reality, knowledge of which alone overcomes our ignorant belief in an existing self and yields liberation from suffering. While for many English readers, "emptiness" would seem to connote a vacuous eradication of all that exists, many Tibetan scholars understood Nāgārjuna's emptiness to be fully compatible with Dharmakīrti's "foundationalist" epistemology.[1] Wedding these two approaches became the formula for transformation, as one rode "the yoked necks of the lions of the Middle Way and Epistemology"[2] in order to make the passage out of ignorance and suffering to wisdom and nirvāṇa.

Of foremost importance in Tibetan presentations of emptiness is the seventh-century Indian Candrakīrti, whose writings form the basis for studying the Middle Way in many Tibetan monasteries. Candrakīrti is celebrated as offering the most thorough and accurate vision of Nāgārjuna's emptiness, which, in turn, most fully represents the final truth of the Buddha's teaching. Candrakīrti's idea of emptiness denies any existence to "nature" (*svabhāva, rang bzhin*), rejecting any enduring essence in ourselves or anywhere in the phenomenal world. In this view, our false belief in natures is at the root of our ignorance and the basis for all manner of emotional turbulence. For many Tibetan scholars, only Candrakīrti's Middle Way entirely overcomes our false belief in natures and, consequently, alone overcomes ignorance and proffers freedom from cyclic existence.

Candrakīrti frequently appears in Tibetan presentations of the Middle Way alongside Bhāvaviveka (c. 500–570), whose own version of emptiness followed Nāgārjuna's insights on the whole but, some maintain, failed to overcome all traces of belief in natures. Bhāvaviveka, according to some interpretations, held that no nature could be found anywhere, *ultimately*, but that conventionally the notion of natures proved quite useful in explaining the everyday world. Candrakīrti argued in his *Clear Words (Prasannapadā)* against Bhāvaviveka, despite their many commonalities as followers of Nāgārjuna. Candrakīrti's argument served as proof for many in Tibet that Candrakīrti's emptiness was the final explanation of reality, uniquely complete, and singularly capable of yielding liberation.

Candrakīrti's critique of Bhāvaviveka also formed the *locus classicus* for dividing the Middle Way into two camps, based on allegiance to or thematic similarity with the views of Candrakīrti and Bhāvaviveka. From an early period of the transmission of Buddhism, Tibetan scholars developed the genre of doxography (*grub mtha', siddhānta*) that, similar to Latinate compilations of Greek philosophers, organized important figures into perceived systems of thought. While Indian Buddhist authors composed similar texts, Tibetan doxographies uniquely divided the Middle Way into subschools centered round Candrakīrti and Bhāvaviveka.[3] In Tibetan estimations, Candrakīrti's subschool, Prāsaṅgika,[4] consistently ranks ahead of Bhāvaviveka's Svātantrika subschool at the pinnacle of all Buddhist viewpoints. Candrakīrti's unique view of emptiness accounts, in some interpretations, for his top ranking.

Additionally, Candrakīrti is lauded for his *method* of proving or ascertaining emptiness. Indeed, Prāsaṅgika takes its name from a logical method employed by Candrakīrti, that of *prasaṅga,* "consequence," in which one points out absurd and unwanted consequences of an opposing view in order to demonstrate that the view is untenable. While the precise rationale for the compatibility of *prasaṅga* reasoning with the ontology of emptiness has frequently been debated, Tibetan scholars nearly unanimously agreed that the Prāsaṅgika ("Consequentialist") method was ideally suited to a world that was, in the end, empty.

In contradistinction, Bhāvaviveka favored proving the validity of his own Middle Way position by means of formal inferences accepted in "one's own [mental] continuum" (*svatantra*), a position indebted to the logic of Dignāga and that warranted his brand of the Middle Way the appellation Svātantrika ("one who uses *svatantra* inference," or "Own Continuumist").[5] Despite Bhāvaviveka's overt courting of the Buddhist Epistemological tradition, many Tibetans believed that Candrakīrti and his Prāsaṅgika followers offered a more refined presentation of the processes by which one gains a reasoned understanding of emptiness than Svātantrika. Bhāvaviveka's reliance on formal inference reveals, at best, an "addiction to logic" (as Candrakīrti put it) or, at worst, a false belief in essences. Candrakīrti's superiority lies, in some presentations, in both his understanding of emptiness and in his method of moving beyond ignorance to realize it.[6]

Implicit in Tibetan doxography, and in a wealth of Tibetan doctrinal literature, is the generative and authoritative position of Buddhist India. For Tibetans, India remains the hallmark of authenticity for both literature and doctrine. Inclusion of a text in the Tibetan Buddhist canon, for example, was allowed only for Tibetan translations for which an Indian original could be accounted. The reach of Buddhist India's authority extends to presentations of the Middle Way such that Tibetan scholars maintain that Candrakīrti's superiority was affected in his own lifetime, in India, where he vanquished all competing Buddhist schools. Tibetan estimates of Candrakīrti's supremacy could be seen as a simple reflection of Indian Buddhists' own preferences.

However, the Indian textual record complicates Tibetan presentations of the Middle Way. The very notion that Candrakīrti and Bhāvaviveka formed separate schools of the Middle Way is dubious.[7] While it is beyond doubt that Candrakīrti took exception with Bhāvaviveka's insistence on formal inference, the superiority of Candrakīrti's views was not at all apparent to Buddhists of his day. As I argue in chapter 1, Indians took little notice of Candrakīrti's texts during his lifetime and in the three centuries following his death. Meanwhile, the mainstream of Middle Way thinking grew even closer to the logical program of Dignāga and Dharmakīrti than Bhāvaviveka's thought had been. The most successful Middle Way scholars of the eighth century were Śāntarakṣita and Kamalaśīla, whose blend of the Epistemological and Middle Way traditions strongly diverge from Candrakīrti's work. The discrepancy between Indian evidence and later Tibetan presentations becomes more pronounced when we recognize that Śāntarakṣita and Kamalaśīla were instrumental in establishing Middle Way scholarship in Tibet during the first promulgation of Buddhism across the Himalayas in the eighth century. Their brand of the Middle Way held pride of place in Tibetan doxographies of the eighth through eleventh centuries.

The question, then, is how did Candrakīrti come to be the Buddhist paragon of Tibet? And how did his views on emptiness come to be "yoked" with the Buddhist Epistemological tradition in order to form the dominant soteriological model for Tibetan monasticism? This book examines the rise and transfiguration of Candrakīrti, centuries after his death, from a marginally known, conservative commentator on Nāgārjuna to the darling of Tibetan Buddhist philosophy. Chapters 1 and 2 trace the historical ascent of Candrakīrti first in eleventh-century India and then in twelfth-century Tibet, showing that the shifting currents of late Indian Buddhism offered him his first glimpse of renown while the fractious and competitive world of the Tibetan "renaissance" provided him for the first time with a school of thought. The remaining chapters explore the philosophical issues that Candrakīrti's writings illuminated in this formative period of Tibetan Buddhism. By examining Candrakīrti's rise—over three hundred years after his death—this book takes strides toward explaining how and why Indian and Tibetan Buddhists revived Candrakīrti's major texts and reworked them over the centuries into Tibet's doctrine of choice. In short, this is an investigation into how Tibetan Buddhist doctrine took the shape that we recognize today.

The Twelfth-Century Candrakīrti

One of the central themes of this book is the difference in Candrakīrti's appearance upon his resurrection in the eleventh and twelfth centuries from his refined image in later Tibetan scholarship, an image that continues to appear in monastic curricula today. This early Tibetan portrait of Candrakīrti comes into focus through recent discoveries of Tibetan Middle Way texts from this period, previously believed to have been lost over time.[8] The twelfth-century portrait suggests the divergent concerns of Tibetan authors, and sometimes their Indian teachers and dialogue partners, from those of Tibetan authors in the fourteenth century and beyond. These later authors' texts have long been in scholarly circulation and have frequently served as sources of information about earlier, less documented times. Now that earlier Tibetan authors can speak for themselves, we find that the later authors were not always faithful to their predecessors, exhibiting a strong tendency to "restate" earlier authors' positions in the terms of their own philosophical concerns.[9] In some cases, sectarian polemics may be at work in these misrepresentations; in other cases, it is likely that the later authors simply did not possess copies of the earlier materials, which had already fallen out of circulation. In any case, the newly available literature warrants our reconsideration of the now accessible earlier period.

We additionally see that previous scholarly tendencies to trace direct lines from seventh- and eighth-century Indian authors to fourteenth-century Tibetan authors must be regarded with suspicion. In the portrayal of most Tibetan doctrinalists, the foundational figures of Indian Middle Way thought flourished between the second and eighth centuries of the common era.[10] While many Tibetan sources value later Indian authors, aside from Atiśa (c. 982–1054) these figures are rarely accorded authoritative status. The importance that many Tibetan scholars attach to Nāgārjuna, Bhāvaviveka, Candrakīrti, and Śāntarakṣita, combined with the absence of early Tibetan literature, can subtly influence our approach to Indian and Tibetan Middle Way philosophy. At worst, we can be led into the view that nothing interesting happened between the eighth and fourteenth centuries. Only slightly better, we can read fourteenth-century Tibetan interpretations of seventh and eighth-century Indian authors as the necessary or logical trajectory of the Indian authors, without appreciating the intervening centuries of development.[11] Newly available Tibetan sources and a renewed appreciation for long-available late Indian sources allow us to get a better sense of the development of Buddhist philosophy, of the creativity of these neglected periods, and of the importance of these authors for the better-known Tibetan works of the fourteenth century and beyond.[12]

Central to this present investigation into the historical rise of Candrakīrti is Helmut Tauscher's edition of a new-found manuscript of Chapa Chokyi Sengé's (1109–69) *Compilation of the Three Mādhyamikas from the East.*[13] While Candrakīrti's major texts have long been available to scholarly access, as have later Tibetan treatises that valorize Candrakīrti, missing from view have been extended critiques of his central ideas. Criticism is surely an important marker of success; it is difficult to imagine that Candrakīrti slipped silently into the role of philosophical pre-eminence without a dissenting voice raised.[14] Chapa's text provides this missing piece, taking to task Candrakīrti's most important concerns (as his eleventh- and twelfth-century champions presented them). Chapa's twelfth-century critique tells us when Candrakīrti's views gained sufficient acclaim to warrant rebuttal and gives us a good sense of the philosophical issues on which Candrakīrti's works were brought to bear in this period, issues that amounted to a litmus test for accepting or rejecting the authority of his works. By providing this critical perspective, Chapa testifies to when and how Candrakīrti became the dominant figure of Tibetan Buddhist philosophy.

Another significant piece of evidence for tracing the rise of Candrakīrti is the only known Indian commentary to any of his works, Jayānanda's massive exegesis of Candrakīrti's *Entrance to the Middle.*[15] Jayānanda's twelfth-century text was included in the Tibetan canon of "treatises" and consequently has long been available to scholarly access.[16] However, the size of the text (365 folios) and the somewhat hostile attitude of later Tibetan authors toward it have kept researchers at bay. While we may debate Jayānanda's fidelity to Candrakīrti's views, his text is of undeniable importance for understanding how Candrakīrti's ideas gained prominence in the twelfth century. Jayānanda traveled from his native Kashmir, where his partisan support of Candrakīrti's Middle Way may have formed part of a broader Candrakīrti revival, to Central Tibet, where he and his writings were among the keys to Tibetans' development of a Prāsaṅgika school. He and Chapa represent the primary interlocutors in this study. While they vehemently dispute the validity of Candrakīrti, the issues that each chooses to highlight from within his corpus align remarkably well. Taken together, they show us what that corpus meant to some of the first Buddhists to take a strong interest in it.

While Chapa's and Jayānanda's works offer the most extensive discussions of Candrakīrti in this period, a host of works from both sides of the Himalayas offer glimpses into the impact his views made in the eleventh and twelfth centuries. In India, we see citations of Candrakīrti's texts in both philosophical and tantric literature; we find two authors writing under Candrakīrti's name (one composing tantric works and the other a brief Middle Way treatise);[17] and we see some muted criticism from Abhayākaragupta (c. 1025–1125) and Ratnākaraśānti (eleventh century).[18] In twelfth-century Tibet, we see for the first time discussions of two schools of the Middle Way, one formed around Candrakīrti's views and the other formed in opposition. Unlike later presentations, we find no widespread agreement on which school was preferable.

Tibetan discussions appear in works by the second and third Sakya hierarchs, Sonam Tsemo (1142–82) and Drakpa Gyeltsen (1147–1216),[19] and by Mabja Jangchub Tsondru (d. 1185);[20] the former and latter were students of Chapa. While these Indian and Tibetan texts have long been available, Chapa's and Jayānanda's more thorough treatments help us to recognize less developed themes in the broader literature. Chapa's protracted critique of Candrakīrti casts light on more muted criticism of Candrakīrti's views, while Jayānanda's lengthy defense sets the stage for the Tibetan formation of a Prāsaṅgika school. When we appreciate the philosophical issues at play in Candrakīrti's ascension, we can see these issues in a range of contexts.

A text such as Chapa Chokyi Sengé's, then, contributes greatly to our understanding of a formative period in Tibetan Buddhism both for what it says and for what it can reveal in related literature. Many texts in the recent thirty-volume publication of early Kadampa (*bka' gdams pa*) masters' works are likely to have a similar impact on our understanding of early Tibetan Middle Way thinking.[21] Chapa's text utilized in the present work is of the "compilation" (*stong thun*) genre, in which Chapa extracts a number (*stong,* literally "one thousand") of key points (*thun,* literally "doses") from the Indian texts that Tibetans refer to as "the Three Mādhyamikas from the East," Madhyamaka treatises from Śāntarakṣita, Kamalaśīla, and Jñānagarbha. Included in the thirty-volume collection are Chapa's commentaries on each of these three texts, as well as his brief doxography. The collection also included a host of early commentaries (including Chapa's) on Śāntideva's (eighth century) *Engaging in the Bodhisattva's Practice,* a crucial text in the development of Tibetan Middle Way philosophy, and Patsab Nyimadrak's commentary on the foundational Middle Way treatise, Nāgārjuna's *Fundamental Treatise on the Middle.* As discussed in chapter 2, Patsab was the primary Tibetan translator of Candrakīrti's works; his would seem to be the earliest Tibetan commentary on Nāgārjuna and promises to increase our understanding of the creation of a Candrakīrti-centered school of Madhyamaka exegesis.

This wealth of newly available material from a formative era of Tibetan Middle Way philosophy reads very differently from better-known literature of later centuries, both in style and in substance. While a given author's arguments may at first (and, sometimes, at last) be impenetrable, as more early literature becomes known we can begin to glimpse the shared concerns of the day. A documentary impulse (What did these scholars write? What were their positions?) yields a broader appreciation of the common assumptions behind an author's discussion of particular arguments and issues. In Buddhist doctrinal literature, positions are stated as sparsely as possible with the presumption of a common background out of which a listener or reader could draw meaning. As our knowledge of eleventh- and twelfth-century issues grows, we will begin to share in these common assumptions. Already, the texts utilized herein reveal fundamental tensions in Buddhist trajectories of thought that either were not a concern for or were understood very differently by fourteenth-century authors.

The primary tensions that brought Candrakīrti to life in the eleventh and twelfth centuries centered on the validity of human knowledge in the pursuit of awakening. By the fourteenth century, Tibetan scholars nearly unanimously took Candrakīrti's views to be the superior interpretation of the Middle Way. As noted above, reconciling his philosophy with Dharmakīrti's Epistemological tradition became accepted either broadly (by Tsongkhapa and his Gelukpa followers) or reservedly (by most Sakya authors). In sharp contrast, in twelfth-century Tibet Candrakīrti's Middle Way connoted a radical rejection of Buddhist Epistemology, particularly of the validity of human consciousness. I suggest that for many Indian Buddhist scholars Candrakīrti represented such a rejection of epistemological norms that his views could not be taken seriously until new configurations of philosophy and practice—in the form of the final developments of Indian Buddhist tantra—gave him voice around the beginning of the second millennium. Twelfth-century Tibetans heatedly debated Candrakīrti's Middle Way under a shared assumption that his views opposed the Buddhist Epistemological tradition. Part of Candrakīrti's broad acceptance in Tibet consisted of a softening of his radical twelfth-century portrait, a process that began in the generation following Chapa.

The importance of coming to terms with Candrakīrti's twelfth-century portrait becomes acute when we appreciate the vibrancy and far-reaching importance of this formative period, which Ronald Davidson refers to as the "Tibetan Renaissance."[22] Davidson's valuable mapping of the resurgence of Tibetan Buddhism that began in the closing years of the first millennium mainly charts the role of tantric literature and practice, which would become the signature pursuits of most Tibetan orders. In the eleventh and twelfth centuries, new tantras flooded into Tibet; however, these were accompanied by new philosophical materials, most importantly newly composed Indian commentaries on Dharmakīrti's treatises and the major works of Candrakīrti, translated into Tibetan for the first time around the year 1100.

Dharmakīrti and Candrakīrti would become the twin foci of Tibetan scholasticism, elliptical though their union may be. Tibetan scholasticism—the textual, philosophical, and pedagogical practices developed around Indian texts—surely played as large a role as tantra in the success of Tibet's monastic Buddhism and took shape during this period.[23] In the twelfth century, the canonical status of Candrakīrti's texts and philosophy was very much in dispute, as was his place in the monastic curricula of the day. While we have only a rough sense of which Indian texts circulated and were taught in particular monastic academies in twelfth-century Tibet (as discussed in chapter 2), the recently available materials noted above allow us to examine philosophical aspects of early scholastic practice. In these materials, we can see the importance of harmonizing Buddhist Epistemology with the Middle Way, either by defending the venerable Indian union of these traditions embodied in Śāntarakṣita's and Kamalaśīla's work—Chapa's approach—or by developing strategies to harmonize the views of Dharmakīrti and Candrakīrti, as we see in the work of Mabja Jangchub Tsondru. Mabja's approach, novel in his day, of uniting the two kīrtis' seemingly antithetical philosophies would become a hallmark of Tibetan scholasticism.[24] Examining how this enduring, if problematic, union formed and developed furthers our insight into the success of scholastic Buddhism in Tibet.

The twelfth-century Candrakīrti, then, has much to say both to the seventh- and fourteenth-century Candrakīrtis. When we appreciate his belated popularity in India, we are in a better position to appreciate the obstinately conservative position he held in his own lifetime, which undoubtedly contributed to his marginal status for hundreds of years afterward. Removing the yoke that—centuries later—Tibetans used to join Candrakīrti to Dharmakīrti's epistemology, we can see that the most straightforward reading of Candrakīrti shows him critiquing and rejecting Dharmakīrtian philosophy.[25] So dominant was the epistemological turn in Indian intellectual life that Candrakīrti's philosophy would not be influential until constellations of thought and praxis realigned centuries after his death. Our appreciation for Candrakīrti's philosophy allows us to see how his champions, from the eleventh through twenty-first centuries, recast his views, sometimes faithfully and often times creatively. The portrait of Candrakīrti's seamless integration with Dharmakīrtian epistemology, familiar to us in Gelukpa sources from Tsongkhapa into the present, took shape gradually; it was sketched first in the twelfth century in the writings of Chapa's "lost student," Mabja Jangchub Tsondru, who abandoned Chapa's positions to embrace (and alter) Candrakīrti. Placing together the many images of Candrakīrti developed over the centuries in India and Tibet prevents us from flattening out the intellectual history, the making and remaking, of one of Buddhism's most influential figures.

School, Movement, Doxographical Category

Candrakīrti is often identified with the "school" of the Middle Way that he "founded," Prāsaṅgika. In view of his late success, his foundational role in a Prāsaṅgika school must be qualified in at least one of two ways. Either we can say that Candrakīrti's major texts exhibit the doctrinal features that would form the touchstone for the doxographical category "Prāsaṅgika," or we can say that Candrakīrti functions as the marker around whom a Prāsaṅgika school was—centuries after his death—created, refined, and debated. The first option provides us with a rather ahistorical category; when we notice strong similarities between a given author's philosophical positions and those of Candrakīrti, we can align that author with Prāsaṅgika, regardless of any historical connection between the figures. In this approach, we would not say that Candrakīrti "founded" a Prāsaṅgika school to which others subscribed but instead would acknowledge his philosophical importance in staking out a unique doctrinal position that helps us to trace similarities in the thinking of others.[26] This interpretation would not require us to attribute any great impact to Candrakīrti in his own lifetime. This option does, however, require us to offer a coherent interpretation of just what Candrakīrti's views were, and thus bleeds into the latter approach.

When we take the second approach, our attention shifts to how historical individuals understood the works of Candrakīrti. We could examine finely nuanced doxographical works from Tsongkhapa and his important Gelukpa interpreters, or from Sakya, Kagyu, or Nyingma authors of the fourteenth century into the present, and find how these authors portrayed Candrakīrti's positions and the manner in which they aligned Middle Way thinkers either with or against those positions. While any of these authors could provide us with fresh insights into Candrakīrti's work, in this approach we would of course be studying the author's interpretation of that work, regardless of how we understand the accuracy of that interpretation and whatever claims the author might make for its veracity. In dealing with this literature, we are operating in a world in which Candrakīrti's superiority is a given. The Tibetan "canonization" of doxographical categories that Cabezón discusses makes for a rigid hierarchy,[27] and by the fourteenth century, Prāsaṅgika frequently received top billing. However, these categories allow a great deal of interpretive room in characterizing the works that fit into them. In Gelukpa and Sakyapa sources, for instance, authors identify their own positions as Prāsaṅgika but disagree heatedly over just what constitute Prāsaṅgika views.[28] The mutual acceptance of Prāsaṅgika's superiority creates the possibility of polemics: to call an opponent's position "Svātantrika" is to denigrate that position's soteriological utility as something other and lesser than Prāsaṅgika.[29]

These two perspectives could yield very different interpretations of a given author's work. One might be tempted to say that Tsongkhapa's views, for instance, bear stronger resemblance to those of Śāntarakṣita than to Candrakīrti, and thus warrant his placement in the Yogācāra-Svātantrika subschool of Madhyamaka rather than in Prāsaṅgika. However, any consideration of Tsongkhapa's Madhyamaka writings makes abundantly clear that he identifies as Prāsaṅgika and is intensely concerned with demonstrating the superiority of Prāsaṅgika. Our attention to Tsongkhapa's construction of Prāsaṅgika again alerts us to the contested nature of these categories, which carry strong overtones of individual and institutional identity. Indeed, Tsongkhapa's critics who wish to construct a Prāsaṅgika at odds with his vision claim that his views are actually Svātantrika in disguise.[30]

Whether we examine Candrakīrti's texts for their quintessential statement of "Prāsaṅgika," to which we may align similar authors, or focus on how Tibetan authors understood Candrakīrti's texts as demarcating a "Prāsaṅgika" category, we are operating within a doxographical framework—in the latter case, Tibetan doxography and in the former case, our own. Twelfth-century Tibetan authors certainly utilize a doxographic approach to Candrakīrti, probably for the first time in Buddhist history, tracing out central features in Candrakīrti's writings that could define "Prāsaṅgika."[31] However, in the eleventh and twelfth centuries, "Prāsaṅgika" does not possess the aura of superiority: Candrakīrti's works certainly function as the marker of a doxographic category for twelfth-century authors, but without the presumption that Prāsaṅgika represents the highest and most correct view. That Prāsaṅgika was one option among many helps us to recognize that it acted as both doxographic category and burgeoning intellectual movement. Twelfth-century Tibetans did not argue (primarily) over whose Prāsaṅgika was most faithful to Candrakīrti, but argued over whether Candrakīrti should be taken as any kind of authoritative interpreter of Buddhist doctrine. This book attempts to tell the story of how the Prāsaṅgika movement grew in Central Tibet to where, perhaps within a century, it formed a nearly irreproachable standard of Tibetan Buddhism.[32]

Conceiving of "Prāsaṅgika" in its earliest usage as an intellectual movement allows us to trace Candrakīrti's resurrection, his introduction to Tibet, his gradual acceptance, and his triumphant ascendancy. It also points us to the institutional aspects in twelfth-century Tibet that accompanied his ascension: acceptance or rejection of Prāsaṅgika in some cases determined the monastic institute with which one affiliated. Just as "Prāsaṅgika" takes on more than doxographic meaning in this period, so too does its accompanying term, "school." When we typically speak of "schools" of the Middle Way, we refer to doxographical subdivisions of it; we identify Prāsaṅgika and Svātantrika schools, and often divide the latter into further "subschools." "School" here connotes an ahistorical category used to classify doctrinal positions. In reference to twelfth-century Tibet, we can speak of "schools" in a more basic sense as monasteries where particular texts and doctrinal interpretations were valorized and taught. A "Prāsaṅgika school" in this sense does not refer to a doctrinal position created by Candrakīrti to which others subscribed but to a monastic institute that, among other activities, advocated the new interpretation of the Middle Way created by Candrakīrti's eleventh- and twelfth-century champions. The number of monasteries adopting this doctrinal stance grew in the twelfth century as influential Tibetan scholars took up the Prāsaṅgika view.

In tracing the formation of these schools, chapter 2 examines important Tibetan translators, their work in creating Indian canonical bases for their Tibetan monastic academies, and the competition these translators engaged in when embedded within the wider networks of socio-political administration that their monasteries assumed. It is undeniable that Prāsaṅgika and Svātantrika are traditions invented by a few well-educated and creative individuals, standing amid the riptide of an Indian past quickly receding and a swell of translations sweeping into Central Tibet. However, the role of these individuals as abbots and important teachers in monastic academies requires our reflection on the communities in which these interpretations took root. A precise working out of the socio-political conflicts and patronage concerns that accompanied twelfth-century doctrinal disputes awaits a great deal of future research. A more modest attempt herein casts Middle Way debates in their monastic homes, suggesting how certain Tibetan monasteries became centers for the study of certain Indian Buddhist textual traditions and how the teaching and exegesis of these texts—when combined with tantric ritual and monastic behavioral codes—helped form early Tibetan monastic communities. That these communities were put into competition with other monasteries for legitimacy, patronage, and political control in this fractious and formative period implies that our attention to the development of doctrinal systems can yield insights into the development of religious institutions, and vice versa.

The uses of "Prāsaṅgika" and "school" that I suggest here move away from a strictly doxographic approach toward a historicist approach. While these two approaches are not mutually exclusive, we might identify a "doxographer's impulse" and a "historian's impulse" as the driving forces behind these approaches. As suggested above, the doxographer's impulse primarily utilizes synchronic doctrinal categorization; it represents an attempt to trace out affinities between the views of past thinkers, regardless of when they lived, that would suggest a shared vision or common philosophical project, perhaps warranting attribution of a "school" of thought. The historian's impulse attempts to trace the development of trends of thought, alternatively suggesting influence and opposition. To illustrate how these two approaches can take us in very different directions, we can look at two interpretations of the silent treatment that eighth-century Indian Middle Way authors gave to Candrakīrti.

As discussed in chapter 1, several prominent Middle Way authors—Avalokitavrata, Śāntarakṣita, and Kamalaśīla—had good reason to attack Candrakīrti's views, as they lived after Candrakīrti and held viewpoints similar to those Candrakīrti assailed. Instead, they say nothing. Some Tibetan scholars see this silence as evidence for those authors' recognition of the superiority of Candrakīrti's view. The Gelukpa scholar Ngawang Belden (*Ngag dbang dpal ldan,* b. 1797) ends a discussion of Candrakīrti's superiority over Bhāvaviveka's Svātantrika system by writing:

> No one—such as followers of Bhāvaviveka and so forth—in the country of Superiors [India] refuted this master within mentioning his name, whereas this very master made refutations within mentioning the names of the master Bhāvaviveka, the master Dharmapāla, the master Dignāga, and so forth, but no Proponent of the Middle or Proponent of Mind-Only was able to do as he had done even though they disagreed with him.[33]

Ngawang Belden notes that Candrakīrti named names; most importantly, he criticized Bhāvaviveka for his misappropriation of *svatantra* inference. Others whom doxographers categorically link to Bhāvaviveka—his Svātantrika "schoolmates"—could not single out Candrakīrti for critique, though they would have liked to. So stunning were Candrakīrti's arguments, in this assessment, no Indian could think of a response. Their silence admits defeat.

I, on the other hand, interpret this silence as evidence for Candrakīrti's marginal status during his life and in the ensuing centuries. Our differing conclusions point to differences between our two academic traditions.

Tibetan doctrinal scholarship of the thirteenth century and onward sought to give order to a massive array of translated Indian texts, all claiming canonical authority. In creating order, Tibetans developed a ranked harmony between "systems" of Buddhist thought, categorizing lower and higher systems that less and more closely presented the "true thought" of the Buddha's teaching.[34] Later scholars inherited these systems. While they began (and continue to begin) with fixed ends (*grub mtha', siddha-anta*), their training brings to attention myriad contradictions between the inherited system and the Indian texts it is based upon, as well as between the parts of the system itself. Rather than contradict the received system, or claim that the system contradicts itself, Tibetan scholars seek out new ways to interpret the texts and systems such that the original perceived order and harmony can be maintained. Scholars gain a deeper doctrinal knowledge by confronting contradiction and creatively endeavoring to resolve these conflicts.[35]

In contrast, when presented with a model (the existence and superiority of Indian Prāsaṅgika) that does not quite seem to fit the facts (little Indian interest in Candrakīrti until around the year 1000, and a thriving Madhyamaka system of interpretation that ignored Candrakīrti), I have sought an explanation that better matches the newly available historical data and that allows us to recognize the importance of previously neglected data. Where Tibetan scholars search out harmony and coherence, I see historical development. This is not to cast a firm divide between "history" and "doxography." Certainly, Tibetan doxographers have a strong sense of the chronology of important Indian authors; Ngawang Belden's point holds (for those who take it to hold) only in the acknowledgment that "Svātantrikas" like Śāntarakṣita post-date Candrakīrti. Also, my interpretation of Śāntarakṣita's silence vis-à-vis Candrakīrti assumes that the two authors belong to the same category; only because they both belong to the Middle Way is Śāntarakṣita's silence interesting. In spelling out the divergent aims embedded in our varying uses of "Prāsaṅgika" and "school," I suggest that our scholarly impetuses and goals play a significant role in generating our interpretations and, as such, deserve our consideration. In the present work, our attention to these impulses will help us to appreciate the evolving figure of Candrakīrti.

The construction of a Prāsaṅgika school out of the exhumed bones of Candrakīrti's corpus and the continued reassembly of those bones to form the towering figure that Candrakīrti came to be constitutes the main drama of the present investigation. Rather than an Indian Prāsaṅgika lineage that passed unchanged for hundreds of years and a Tibetan Prāsaṅgika that accurately (or inaccurately) reflected that Indian lineage, a picture emerges of a dynamic Indian tradition still developing in its final period and a Tibetan tradition that recast Indian texts in a unique social milieu and continued to develop those texts for hundreds of years. Candrakīrti's dominance must be seen as a peculiarly Tibetan development. However, from around the year 1000, we hear echoes of Candrakīrti's rise in the writings of several important Indian authors, centuries after his death. It is to the evidence for this ascension that we now turn.

1. The Indian Discovery of Candrakīrti

PROMINENT TIBETAN SCHOLARS of the fourteenth and fifteenth centuries uniformly speak of a Prāsaṅgika school of Madhyamaka ("Middle Way"), founded by the Indians Buddhapālita (c. 500)[1] and Candrakīrti (c. 570–640),[2] developed in India—in some accounts by a lineage of mostly unlettered disciples but always including such luminaries as Śāntideva (early eighth century) and Atiśa (c. 982–1054)—and later propagated in Tibet. The Tibetan systematizers likewise speak of clear differences between the Prāsaṅgika and Svātantrika interpretations of Madhyamaka and of the superiority of Prāsaṅgika in elucidating the "true thought" of Nāgārjuna (c. 200), the founder of Madhyamaka. In this vein, Candrakīrti is said to have "refuted" Bhāvaviveka (c. 500–570), the "founder" of the Svātantrika interpretation, and established the preeminence of Prāsaṅgika through writing his commentary on Nāgārjuna's *Fundamental Treatise on the Middle.*[3] While the precise nature of the Prāsaṅgika-Svātantrika division was debated in the Kagyu, Sakya, and Geluk schools throughout the fourteenth to eighteenth centuries and in the Nyingma school in the nineteenth century, there was no disagreement that just such a division accurately reflected Indian Buddhist developments of the sixth and seventh centuries.[4] Tibetan scholarship on this distinction, from the fourteenth century into the present, has influenced a great deal of contemporary scholarship that continues to speak of two schools of Indian, and then Tibetan, Madhyamaka.

However, the Indian textual record presents a remarkably different view than fifteenth-century Tibetan scholars' accounts. When we consider this record, we must conclude that Candrakīrti, rather than forming a school of Madhyamaka and triumphing over or refuting Bhāvaviveka, was in fact largely ignored in his day and for some three hundred years in both India and Tibet. Jayānanda (twelfth century)[5] is the only known Indian commentator on the works of Candrakīrti,[6] whereas there were eight Indian commentaries on Nāgārjuna's *Fundamental Treatise on the Middle* and twenty-one Indian commentaries on Maitreya's *Ornament for Realization*.[7] The lineage of Indian Prāsaṅgika disciples stretching from Candrakīrti through Śāntideva and extending to Atiśa, the supposed progenitor of Prāsaṅgika in Tibet, varies widely in the Tibetan accounts and rarely includes figures known elsewhere.[8] Furthermore, the argument from silence against Candrakīrti's importance in India is bolstered by the fact that none of these shadowy figures is known by Tibetan scholars to have written on Madhyamaka (or anything else). This absence of any reported texts strongly suggests that, unlike the many volumes known to Tibetan scholars to have existed in India or Tibet in the past but no longer accessible to them or to us,[9] no such texts by these figures ever existed. Rather, these figures would seem to represent Tibetan historians' acknowledgment of great gaps in the Prāsaṅgika "lineage" and their attempts to fill in these holes with names, if not writings.

One can infer that the very survival of Candrakīrti's writings down to the time of Jayānanda could only have been brought about by some kind of following, whether Candrakīrti's writings were preserved in monastic libraries or transmitted in scribal families.[10] Most strongly, we can imagine the existence of a marginal school of thought that did not champion Candrakīrti with new treatises (at least none that survived even until the time of Jayānanda) but studied and preserved his texts. It may have been this sense of a "lineage" that Tibetan authors imagined and attempted to enliven with names. A school, family, or library preserving Candrakīrti's writings furthermore provides a more coherent picture of how his texts could later be popularized.

While the ongoing search for Sanskrit manuscripts could one day turn up a treatise from an early member of a putative Candrakīrti following, recent discoveries strengthen the case that Candrakīrti's popularity arose long after his death. Studies of the recently recovered eighteen-folio *Lakṣaṇaṭīkā* show it to be a series of notes composed mostly in Sanskrit (with parts of four folios consisting of Tibetan notes) on three of Candrakīrti's compositions.[11] The colophons to the texts that the "*Lakṣaṇaṭīkā*" was bundled with lead Yonezawa tentatively to conclude that these comments stem from Abhayākaragupta (c. 1025–1125) through the pen of Nur Dharmadrak, who served as the scribe.[12] While attributing these comments to Abhayākaragupta will require a great deal of further investigation into this manuscript and comparison with his known writings, the dating of the text seems secure, given Nur Dharmadrak's role. A late eleventh- to early twelfth-century frame for these important notes on several of Candrakīrti's major writings aligns well with the surviving evidence for Indian interest in his work. Thus, at present we can deduce that Candrakīrti's writings did not spawn a literary tradition for many hundreds of years, with Jayānanda's commentary and the "*Lakṣaṇaṭīkā*" representing the earliest known works that take Candrakīrti as their subject matter.

The silence of Candrakīrti's supposed Middle Way adversaries rings even more tellingly. While Avalokitavrata (c. 700) in his subcommentary on Bhāvaviveka's *Lamp for Wisdom* mentions Candrakīrti in a list of Indian scholars who wrote commentaries on Nāgārjuna's *Fundamental Treatise on the Middle,*[13] he says nothing about Candrakīrti's lengthy criticisms of Bhāvaviveka. One can well assume that, in the Indian commentarial tradition, if Avalokitavrata deemed Candrakīrti's attacks damaging, it would have been incumbent upon him to respond. His silence, in an otherwise extensive treatise (spanning three volumes in Tibetan translation), suggests that he viewed Candrakīrti's criticisms as insignificant, not worthy of response, perhaps not even as serious philosophy.

Likewise, the important Mādhyamikas Śāntarakṣita (eighth century) and Kamalaśīla (c. 740–95) remained silent on Candrakīrti.[14] Their extensive use of the Buddhist epistemological tradition, to an even greater degree than Bhāvaviveka, would require their responses to Candrakīrti's attacks on that tradition, had they viewed his attacks to be damaging. Both authors, instead, were more concerned with Dharmapāla's critique—from a Yogācāra viewpoint—of the feasibility of joining epistemology with Madhyamaka ontology.[15] Furthermore, in Ichigō's analysis, Kamalaśīla worked to refine Bhāvaviveka's and Śāntarakṣita's views, arguing against subtleties in their writings[16] rather than concern himself with the widely divergent views of Candrakīrti. The wide success of Śāntarakṣita's and Kamalaśīla's Yogācāra-Madhyamaka interpretation, an interpretation well at odds with Candrakīrti's own, suggests Candrakīrti's insignificance during this time.[17] In contradistinction to what fifteenth-century Tibetan authors state, the textual evidence leads one to conclude that Candrakīrti was a marginal figure in his day and uninfluential in India until the close of the first millennium.

Tibetan evidence—translations of Sanskrit Madhyamaka texts and native Tibetan commentaries and doxographies—from the establishment of Buddhism in Tibet until 1000 show a similar disinterest in Candrakīrti. Whereas a wealth of important Madhyamaka texts by Nāgārjuna, Āryadeva, Buddhapālita, Bhāvaviveka, and Śāntideva were translated during the "early diffusion" (*snga dar*) of Buddhism into Tibet, Candrakīrti's major writings were not translated into Tibetan until the eleventh century. Only two of his commentaries, both on two of Nāgārjuna's texts, *Sixty Stanzas of Reasoning*[18] and *Seventy Stanzas on Emptiness*,[19] were translated in the "early diffusion." These commentaries would be likely candidates for translation as they represent the only Indian commentaries on these important Nāgārjuna texts.[20] In cases where Tibetans had a choice of commentarial tradition, for instance with Nāgārjuna's *Fundamental Treatise on the Middle*, Candrakīrti was left out.

As is well known, Śāntarakṣita and Kamalaśīla, both later categorized as Svātantrika-Mādhyamikas,[21] were instrumental in the early diffusion of Buddhism in Tibet, the former credited with creating the first monastery in Tibet at Samyé and ordaining the first Tibetan monks and the latter, his student, credited with establishing the orthodox "gradual path" at the purported Great Debate at Samyé. Their most important Madhyamaka texts were translated during the early diffusion, along with those by another key Indian author, Jñānagarbha, who blended components of Dharmakīrti's epistemology with Madhyamaka thought.[22] Not surprisingly then, the first Tibetan doxographies by Yeshé Dé (*Ye shes sde*) and Kawa Peltsek (*Ka ba dpal brtsegs*) in the eighth century esteem the Yogācāra-Madhyamaka synthesis created by Śāntarakṣita and Kamalaśīla as the highest Buddhist school of thought.[23] Bhāvaviveka's Sautrāntika-Madhyamaka is ranked second. Candrakīrti is not mentioned. No Prāsaṅgika school is identified nor do we see the appellation, "Svātantrika," which—as discussed in chapter 2—is first employed only in the twelfth century, in contradistinction to Candrakīrti's views. This earlier bifurcation of Madhyamaka into Yogācāra and Sautrāntika sub-streams, to the apparent exclusion of Candrakīrti's views, appears also in Rongzom Chokyi Zangpo's (*Rong zom Chos kyi bzang po*, eleventh century) three doxographical works, perhaps our earliest sources for the Madhyamaka of the "later diffusion" (*phyi dar*) of Buddhism in Tibet.[24]

The Indian and Tibetan evidence point to an eleventh-century resurrection of Candrakīrti's writings in India and a twelfth-century birth of the Prāsaṅgika movement in Tibet. In addition to detailing Candrakīrti's Indian rise, this chapter discusses the fragmented evidence that illuminates the philosophical and doctrinal issues (treated more fully in chapters 3 through 5) engendered by his writings that polarized Indian and Tibetan Buddhists in this period. The central issue around which Candrakīrti's fame grew was his perceived denial of "valid cognition"[25]—the epistemological enterprise foundational to Indian thought from at least the sixth century. As will be seen, both Candrakīrti's supporters and detractors saw his philosophy as denying the validity of ordinary human cognition in the project of reaching enlightening knowledge. This denial held far-reaching ramifications, extending from a low appraisal of the value of human intellect to the very nature of buddhahood.

Reviving Candrakīrti's Critique of Ultimate Valid Cognition

As mentioned above, fifteenth century and later Tibetan authors frequently group Śāntideva's writings with Candrakīrti's as "Prāsaṅgika" and place him in a lineage stretching from Candrakīrti down to these authors themselves. Śāntideva is the one figure in these lineage lists prior to Atiśa about whom we have literary information. However, Śāntideva's own writings make no reference to Candrakīrti nor to any other of the figures that Tibetan historians would place in a lineage between Candrakīrti and Śāntideva. Śāntideva's surviving writings, consisting of poetry and comments interspersing his collection of sūtra fragments,[26] allow a great deal of interpretive room. Several verses from the ninth chapter of *Engaging in the Bodhisattva's Practice* echo sentiments found in Candrakīrti's writings, especially the denial that ultimate truth is a referent of human intellect, the explanation of ultimate truth as "non-seeing," and the refutation of self-cognizing consciousness.[27]

Despite this seeming harmony between Candrakīrti and Śāntideva, it is important to note that this text was commented upon from a decidedly non-Prāsaṅgika standpoint both in the early diffusion of Buddhism in Tibet and during the later spread. Saito points to two Indian commentaries, likely the earliest, that treat Śāntideva's text from a Yogācāra-Madhyamaka perspective.[28] From the later diffusion, we see commentaries to the text by Ngok the Translator and Chapa, both of whom opposed Candrakīrti's views.[29] Furthermore, Śāntideva's text grew over hundreds of years: the version cataloged in the Den karma collection (c. 800) is 600 stanzas in length,[30] while that preserved in the Dunhuang caves (dated to before 950) contains 701.5 stanzas.[31] Both are far shorter than the present canonical version in 913 stanzas. The fact that Śāntideva's stanzas were important to Yogācāra-Mādhyamikas and the growth of the text heightens our uncertainty as to which views we may ascribe to the eighth-century Śāntideva.

While we thus cannot with any certainty show a historical link between Śāntideva and Candrakīrti, over two hundred years after Śāntideva wrote, his commentator, Prajñākaramati (950–1030), ties Śāntideva's views to Candrakīrti. Prajñākaramati cites Candrakīrti's *Entrance to the Middle* repeatedly in his commentary to Śāntideva's *Engaging in the Bodhisattva's Practice.*[32] Prajñākaramati relies particularly heavily on Candrakīrti in his comments on Śāntideva's proclamation of the two truths (*satyadvaya,* stanza IX.2), citing *Entrance to the Middle* four times (stanzas VI.23, 25, 28, and 29),[33] a lengthy sūtra passage found in *Entrance to the Middle,* and three sūtra passages found in Candrakīrti's *Clear Words.* The stongest link we may establish is not between Candrakīrti and Śāntideva but between Candrakīrti and Prajñākaramati. The latter is the earliest Indian author that we know of to express overt enthusiasm for Candrakīrti's writings.

Vibhūticandra (c. 1200) likewise employs stanzas from *Entrance to the Middle* in his comments on Śāntideva's stanza IX.2.[34] Vibhūticandra was part of the last entourage of Indian *paṇḍitas* to travel to Central Tibet in 1204; he traveled with Śākya Śrībhadra (1127/1145–1225/1243),[35] with whom the extremely influential Tibetan scholar Sakya Paṇḍita (1182–1251) worked. As will be discussed in more detail in chapter 2, Sakya Paṇḍita was the first to adopt the Prāsaṅgika position in the Sakya school.[36] Vibhūticandra, then, may have been partly responsible for this development within Sakya.

Śāntideva's brief stanza, in which ultimate truth is declared outside the realm of human intellect, reads:[37]

> It is asserted that there are two truths—obscurational and ultimate.
> The ultimate is not a referent of awareness; awareness is said to be obscurational.

Classical Indian aesthetics valued poetic brevity; elaborating on meaning was left to a commentator. So while Śāntideva may have meant his stanza to echo an important theme in Candrakīrti's writings that the ultimate "is just not an object of consciousness,"[38] Prajñākaramati makes the first certain connection between the two and is the earliest commentator to explicate this theme in either Candrakīrti's or Śāntideva's works. Prajñākaramati elaborates at some length, writing that Śāntideva's "awareness" means "all consciousness," that the ultimate "surpasses the sphere of all consciousness," and that it is "impossible to bring [the ultimate] within the sphere of awareness in any way."[39] He later notes, "All awareness, whether having an object or not having an object, has a nature of conceptuality and all conceptuality has a nature of ignorance."[40] Prajñākaramati also utilizes Candrakīrti's comparison of objects of consciousness to the flickering hairs seen by those suffering from eye diseases, suggesting that just as all awareness is flawed with ignorance, so all objects of awareness are unreal.[41]

In linking Candrakīrti's and Śāntideva's texts on the radical separation of human consciousness and the ultimate, Prajñākaramati establishes an important tenet of his interpretation of Madhyamaka and shows a lengthy pedigree of the tenet, drawing upon a sūtra in which the Buddha himself makes such a proclamation;[42] he establishes a tradition of exegesis, the beginnings of what would become a Prāsaṅgika interpretation of Buddhist philosophy. Furthermore, he posits a radical separation of ultimate truth and those things known by ordinary consciousness: what we call knowledge he calls ignorance. Such a vast divide between ordinary consciousness and knowledge of the ultimate runs directly counter to the epistemological project of establishing the valid foundations of all knowledge, conventional and ultimate, engaged in by Mādhyamikas since the sixth century. Indeed, Prajñākaramati concludes his discussion of ultimate truth by stating that only āryas—advanced bodhisattvas who realize emptiness directly—have valid cognition concerning the ultimate.[43] This conclusion, too, is lifted directly from Candrakīrti's *Entrance to the Middle.*[44] However, unlike in Candrakīrti's India, Prajñākaramati's great divide separating conventional knowledge from knowledge of the ultimate sparked debate among Mādhyamikas on both sides of the Himalayas. Candrakīrti's rejection of valid cognition in ultimate pursuits ran directly counter to the tenor of Indian philosophy that in his day was dominated by epistemological concerns across religious traditions. In such a religious climate, his separation could not be taken seriously. By Prajñākaramati's time, Candrakīrti's conservative bent could be recast as a unique and viable Madhyamaka interpretation.

As noted above, Atiśa (Dīpaṅkaraśrījñāna), a junior contemporary of Prajñākaramati, is commonly credited with establishing Prāsaṅgika in Tibet. His *Introduction to the Two Truths* twice praises Candrakīrti, once for Candrakīrti's presentation of the two truths[45] and once for Candrakīrti's understanding of ultimate truth. The latter passage reads:[46]

> Candrakīrti is the disciple of Nāgārjuna
> Who saw the truth of the final nature.
> The truth of the final nature is to be realized
> According to the instructions of his lineage.

Leading up to this stanza, Atiśa denied the validity of both forms of valid cognition accepted by Buddhists—direct perception and inference—to realize the ultimate and further rejected the ability of conceptual and nonconceptual consciousness to realize it.[47] Clearly, his praise of Candrakīrti's understanding of ultimate truth references Candrakīrti's denial that the ultimate can be known by human intellect.

In this same text, Atiśa refers favorably to Bhāvaviveka,[48] the supposed founder of the Svātantrika interpretation of Madhyamaka, over whom Candrakīrti's Prāsaṅgika supposedly triumphed. Atiśa also translated into Tibetan two of Bhāvaviveka's most important texts, *Heart of the Middle* and its autocommentary, *Blaze of Reasoning.*[49] These two texts were translated at the request of Ngok Lekpay Sherab,[50] whose monastic institute staunchly opposed Candrakīrti's views. Elsewhere, Atiśa lists Bhāvaviveka and Candrakīrti as authoritative interpreters of Madhyamaka, along with Nāgārjuna, Āryadeva, Śāntideva, and Atiśa's own teacher, Bodhibhadra.[51] We might conclude that Atiśa saw Candrakīrti and Bhāvaviveka as upholding equally valid positions. Ruegg notes that, "In Dīpaṅkaraśrījñāna's time and circle, Bhavya's and Candrakīrti's schools of the Madhyamaka were apparently not clearly differentiated by distinct designations and they were evidently being studied side by side."[52] Extending Ruegg's point, the very issues that would polarize Bhāvaviveka's and Candrakīrti's writings into separate schools of thought were only in Atiśa's day coming to be elucidated.

However, Atiśa's endorsement of Candrakīrti may be the earliest instance of an Indian author favoring Candrakīrti over Bhāvaviveka. When we look more closely at Atiśa's *Introduction to the Two Truths,* we see that his praise of Bhāvaviveka was misplaced. He wrote "The Master scholar Bhavya stated that [the ultimate] is not realized by either conceptual nor nonconceptual consciousness."[53] Lindtner adeptly identifies a very similar statement, to which Atiśa likely referred, in the *Jewel Lamp of the Middle,* a text attributed to Bhāvaviveka.[54] The Bhāvaviveka who wrote the *Jewel Lamp of the Middle,* and who claims to be the author of *Heart of the Middle* and *Blaze of Reasoning* as well,[55] refers favorably to Candrakīrti's *Entrance to the Middle,* and so must post-date him.[56] The Bhāvaviveka who wrote *Heart of the Middle* and *Lamp for Wisdom*—a section of which Candrakīrti critiqued in detail—preceded Candrakīrti, making a common attribution impossible. The statement that Atiśa endorses from the *Jewel Lamp of the Middle* shows much more affinity for Candrakīrti's views—at least as presented by Atiśa—than those expressed in *Heart of the Middle.*

More tellingly, Atiśa criticizes another of Bhāvaviveka's views (without mentioning Bhāvaviveka by name). He writes, "Ultimate truth is only one; others assert that it is two."[57] As we have seen, Candrakīrti and Prajñākaramati rejected the applicability of valid cognition to ultimate truth. Anticipating such criticism, Bhāvaviveka wrote of two kinds of ultimate consciousnesses, which realize two kinds of objects:

> The ultimate is of two types: one engages thoroughly effortlessly, passes beyond the world, is undefiled, and lacks proliferation; the second engages with thorough effort, accords with the collection of merit and wisdom, is called "pure worldly wisdom," and possesses proliferations.[58]

Bhāvaviveka explains that the second kind of ultimate consciousness realizes ultimate truth inferentially; he explains how inference is utilized in knowing ultimate truth. In rejecting that ultimate truth is two, Atiśa rejects Bhāvaviveka's solution to inference's utility. Atiśa further states that, "The deluded whose vision is narrow say that the two [kinds of valid cognition, direct perception and inference] realize emptiness."[59] Atiśa's critique of Bhāvaviveka's use of valid cognition in general and inference in particular, seemingly inspired by Candrakīrti's views, is perhaps the first implicit hierarchical ranking of Candrakīrti over Bhāvaviveka. The validity of human cognition in knowing emptiness is the litmus test in Atiśa's ranking.

Apart from Atiśa's attributions, the later Bhāvaviveka's work itself reveals the impact of Candrakīrti's views and represents a further mark of his growing influence. It may well be that the passage from *Blaze of Reasoning* (*Tarkajvāla*) cited just above does not anticipate Candrakīrti's criticism but, in fact, responds to it. Ruegg utilizes the work of Ejima, who distinguishes an "Ur-*Tarkajvāla*" from a revised version, to suggest that many parts of *Blaze of Reasoning* were not written by the Bhāvaviveka who wrote *Heart of the Middle* (the stanzas upon which *Blaze of Reasoning* comments) but by the later Bhāvaviveka who wrote the *Jewel Lamp of the Middle.*[60] Furthermore, the commonalities between the *Jewel Lamp of the Middle,* the *Compendium of Meanings of the Middle* (*Madhyamakārthasaṃgraha*), and certain parts of *Blaze of Reasoning* suggest that the same hand (Bhāvaviveka II) composed them.[61] The passage I have cited from *Blaze of Reasoning* can likely be considered a later accretion as the *Compendium of Meanings of the Middle* likewise posits a two-fold ultimate truth, a figurative ultimate (*paryāyaparamārtha*) that can be expressed in language and grasped by conceptual thought and a non-figurative ultimate that is beyond expression and thought.[62] This closely mirrors the two-fold ultimate explained in the *Blaze of Reasoning* passage. Bhāvaviveka II in these two texts may have been the earliest Middle Way author to respond to Candrakīrti's critique of utilizing valid cognition in the pursuit of emptiness, showing how a certain kind of ultimate truth can fall within the range of formal reasoning.[63]

Bhāvaviveka II clearly identifies with his namesake's epistemological convictions, as is evident in both the *Jewel Lamp of the Middle* and the *Compendium of Meanings of the Middle.* In these two texts, he evinces views similar to Jñānagarbha's Madhyamaka adoption of Dharmakīrti's "causal efficacy"—which Dharmakīrti took as the mark of ultimate existence—as the mark of conventional existence.[64] Both texts further adopt Jñānagarbha's characterization of conventional existence as "existing as it appears," with the *Jewel Lamp* repeating Jñānagarbha's corollary that the conventional world "exists when not analyzed."[65] Bhāvaviveka II's commitment to the Madhyamaka epistemological project of his namesake extends the earlier figure's ideas with those of the eighth-century confluence of Madhyamaka and Dharmakīrti's philosophy.

However, the *Jewel Lamp of the Middle* evinces several points conceded to Candrakīrti's critique of valid cognition. The *Jewel Lamp* denies that those who use inference can know reality through their analyses, states that ordinary sense perception does not constitute valid cognition, and opines that valid cognition of obscurational truth only functions within worldly conventions, for those whose vision is narrow.[66] This combination of delimiting the scope of valid cognition while yet advancing criteria for the validity of certain kinds of conventional objects and conventional consciousnesses may represent the earliest attempt to reconcile Candrakīrti's critique of the Buddhist epistemological tradition with the philosophy he opposed. This reconciliation would come to characterize Tibetan exegesis of Candrakīrti's works by the late twelfth century.

The themes that we see Prajñākaramati and Atiśa drawing from Candrakīrti's texts are amplified further in Jayānanda's extensive commentary to Candrakīrti's *Entrance to the Middle,* written in the mid-twelfth century (far from India, in the Tangut kingdom) and the only full-fledged commentary on Candrakīrti's writings written by an Indic author.[67] This text offers a fully developed presentation of the conflict Candrakīrti's views engendered on the issue of the ultimate and the value of human intellect. In chapter 3, I examine Jayānanda's understanding of pervasive ignorance that, as it does in Prajñākaramati's presentation, characterizes all human consciousness. Jayānanda directly addresses the characteristic that Buddhist epistemologists employed to define valid cognition, "non-deceptive" (*avisaṃvadin*) or "unmistaken" (*abhrānta*),[68] and declares that no human cognition meets this criterion. In chapters 4 and 5, I show that Jayānanda's views on human ignorance led him to deny human consciousness any direct access to the ultimate. "Knowing" the ultimate becomes metaphorical; in reality, in the ultimate state consciousness ceases—"knowledge" of the ultimate cannot be understood as a cognitive event. These views become Jayānanda's basis for denying the Mādhyamika's use of formal inferences and the broad Epistemological project.

Another clear reference to Candrakīrti's views on the inapplicability of valid cognition to ultimate truth was voiced by an eleventh-century figure also named Candrakīrti.[69] He wrote *Entrance to Middle Way Wisdom*[70] and translated it into Tibetan with Gö Kugpa Lhetse,[71] a student of Atiśa. While brief—only eighteen stanzas in length—this text expresses several of the themes that we have seen Candrakīrti's revivers singling out. He writes that, in the context of ultimate truth, "there is no thesis or reason,"[72] thereby denying that inference has utility in knowing the ultimate. Having argued for the non-existence of mind and mental factors, thereby supporting one of the primary features of Candrakīrti's views that generated controversy in the eleventh and twelfth centuries, Candrakīrti III considers the objection that such a denial contradicts perception; he responds that he does not refute the non-analytical view.[73] Candrakīrti III's "non-analytical" mirrored the first Candrakīrti's injunction that "worldly, conventional truths are not to be analyzed."[74] Despite the brevity of Candrakīrti III's only known text, his framing of the non-analytical view was important to Chapa who adopted this terminology in his portrayal of Candrakīrti's system, which he argued against at length.[75]

Rather than preserved in an unbroken lineage established by Candrakīrti himself, we see Candrakīrti's main texts—however they may have survived up to this point—receiving broader attention beginning around the year 1000. Śāntideva may have been aware of Candrakīrti's ideas but did not develop them. Instead, important eleventh- and twelfth-century Indian scholars suddenly took interest in these forgotten texts and saw in them a basis from which to criticize the widespread importance of valid cognition scholarship among Buddhist philosophers. The consistency with which Candrakīrti's revivalists cited his critiques of valid cognition and his understanding of ultimate truth make clear the philosophical reasons for championing his interpretation of Madhyamaka. The following section explores some possible explanations for the sudden interest in Candrakīrti's critique in the eleventh century, following hundreds of years of Mādhyamikas wrestling with the epistemological foundations and implications of Nāgārjuna's views.

Candrakīrti and Tantra

Atiśa's literary output testifies to his interest in tantric Buddhist theory and practice. We might assume, given the widespread enthusiasm for tantra among

Buddhists of this period, that Prajñākaramati and Jayānanda also maintained interest in tantra. However, neither of these three scholars' writings make any indication that their interest in Candrakīrti's texts was at all tied to late Indian tantric Buddhism. This section explores the ideas of several authors who make just such an explicit connection and who suggest to us that Candrakīrti's views enjoyed their first broad popularity due to the consonances between his ideas on ultimate truth, as well as the inapplicability of valid cognition to its pursuit, and tantric concerns.

Juxtaposing Candrakīrti and Tantras

An important reference to Candrakīrti from a tantric text of this time period is found in Sahajavajra's commentary to Maitrīpāda's *Ten Stanzas on Reality*.[76] Here, what is said may not be as illuminating as the context in which Candrakīrti's views are brought to bear. In discussing the second stanza, Sahajavajra endorses Nāgārjuna's, Āryadeva's, and Candrakīrti's explanation of dependent arising (*pratītyasamutpada*).[77] He further notes that Candrakīrti's *Entrance to the Middle* presents the Indian Buddhist "Mind Only"[78] teaching as requiring interpretation.[79] While these two references do not allow a clear sense of why Sahajavajra singled out Candrakīrti's interpretations, the fact that a late Indian tantric author cites him as an authority is illuminating. Maitrīpāda is often linked to Atiśa, either as Atiśa's teacher or as a student whom Atiśa, in his role as abbot, had to expel from Vikramaśīla Monastery for Maitrīpāda's illicit tantric practices.[80] He is also an important source of writings on the tantric practice, Mahāmudrā; in fact, all of his writings, including *Ten Stanzas on Reality,* are included in the "Tantra Commentaries" (*rgyud 'grel*) section of the Tibetan canon. Tibetan Kagyu sources claim Maitrīpāda, along with Patsab Nyimadrak, as the two sources of their Prāsaṅgika lineage.[81]

Kagyu tradition and Sahajavajra's citation suggest that Maitrīpāda held Candrakīrti's interpretation of Madhyamaka. While Sahajavajra's comment does not allow insight into just what about Candrakīrti's views he found favorable, it establishes a link between Candrakīrti's interpretation and the kinds of antinomian tantras that were created and disseminated across the Himalayas in the tenth and eleventh centuries. One can well imagine that Candrakīrti's rejection of the established practices of valid cognition that so dominated scholastic Buddhism throughout the second part of the first millennium would appeal to the creators and practitioners of these tantras. Furthermore, Candrakīrti's understanding of an ultimate beyond the scope of human cognition fits well with tantric portrayals of a pure, pristine ultimate state in which human consciousness—invariably intertwined with subject-object duality—can play no role.

Another connection between Candrakīrti's idea of the ultimate and late Indian Buddhist tantric concerns appears in the *Compendium of Good Sayings,*[82] an anthology of citations from Buddhist texts that is dominated by extracts from "Highest Yoga Tantras" (*anuttarayogatantra*) but also contains nearly thirty stanzas from Candrakīrti's *Entrance to the Middle.*[83] The *Compendium* cites Candrakīrti's statement on the relationship between obscurational truth and ultimate truth, linking it—as did Prajñākaramati and Jayānanda—with Śāntideva's presentation of obscurational and ultimate truths.[84] The *Compendium* also cites several of Candrakīrti's stanzas that address the disparity between various conceptions of causality and the ultimate perspective, from which there is no causality at all.[85] These stanzas are cited following Nāgārjuna's famous denial of production from "four alternatives," which, in Candrakīrti's *Clear Words,* provided the occasion for Candrakīrti's lengthy criticisms of formal inference's usefulness in inducing knowledge of the ultimate.[86] While the *Compendium of Good Sayings* cites only Candrakīrti's verses from *Entrance to the Middle,* the import of his *Clear Words* is entailed: the *Compendium* endorses Candrakīrti's interpretation of the ultimate, for which formal inference is useless but with which tantra is well in consonance.

Candrakīrti's stanzas denying production from the "four alternatives" are preceded in the *Compendium of Good Sayings* by a similar statement there attributed to the noted tantric author, Saraha (but likely authored by the tantric Āryadeva), stating that reality is devoid of existence, non-existence, both existence and non-existence, and neither.[87] These stanzas of the tantric Āryadeva were adopted into at least four other texts composed by tantric authors in the early part of the eleventh century,[88] including the *Stainless Light* commentary to the *Kālacakra Tantra.*[89] The *Compendium of Good Sayings*'s juxtaposition of these stanzas with Candrakīrti's refutation of production links Candrakīrti's and tantric understandings of the ultimate, suggesting that Candrakīrti's views were valued by proponents of late Indian Buddhist tantra for their utter rejection of the dualities of cause and effect (producer and produced), existence and non-existence. The consonances between Candrakīrti's and late tantric views suggest that Candrakīrti's rise in popularity was due, at least in part, to the rise of "Highest Yoga Tantras" in turn-of-the-millennium India.

Candrakīrti and the "Noble" Lineage

The *Compendium of Good Sayings* links Saraha, Nāgārjuna, and Candrakīrti, a connection well-attested in the "Noble" (Ārya) lineage of the *Guhyasamāja Tantra* transmission. This lineage places three Middle Way luminaries—Nāgārjuna, Āryadeva, and Candrakīrti—as among the earliest to transmit the *Guhyasamāja* in India.[90] The identity of these three tantric authors, all of whom wrote commentarial materials on the *Guhyasamāja,*[91] with the Middle Way authors, all of whom flourished hundreds of years prior to the composition of the *Guhyasamāja* materials, seems to have been widely accepted among Indian and Tibetan Buddhists in the early years of the second millennium.[92] As Wedemeyer points out, the assumed identity—likely on the part of the tantric authors themselves—was no coincidence: the tantric authors appropriated the names of Middle Way authors due to a sense of shared philosophy and as a means of utilizing the earlier authors' authority.[93] While a precise mapping of the philosophical consonances between the tantric authors and their Middle Way namesakes remains a desideratum, Isaacson has identified an excellent starting point, noting the strong correlation and textual parallelism between a statement of the "two stages" of Guhyasamāja yoga and Nāgārjuna's classic pronouncement of the two truths.[94]

Wedemeyer's notion that tantric authors—or their students—sought to invoke the authority of earlier Middle Way personalities, a strongly credible thesis, only works if the Middle Way authors were in fact regarded as authorities. We have good reason to think that Nāgārjuna and Āryadeva had long been well respected as Mahāyāna luminaries. The "Noble" lineage accords Candrakīrti status equal to Āryadeva, as a "son" of Nāgārjuna, perhaps our earliest indication of his new fame. Wedemeyer shows that Āryadeva's major tantric work can be placed safely between 850 and 1000 of the common era and leans toward a more precise dating of the late ninth to early tenth centuries.[95] We might place the tantric Candrakīrti in the same time frame, using the "brotherhood" model of the "Noble" lineage. This would evince perhaps the earliest use of Candrakīrti's authority, pre-dating Prajñākaramati and Atiśa by some decades. If the dating of the tantric Candrakīrti requires a shift forward roughly fifty years,[96] his flourit would barely precede the time frame of Prajñākaramati's and Atiśa's citations of the Middle Way Candrakīrti. In any case, that the identity of the tantric and Middle Way Candrakīrtis was widely accepted in the eleventh century gives us good reason to connect the sudden interest in the Middle Way author with the rise of the "Noble" lineage of the Guhyasamāja.

We have good evidence suggesting that nearly every champion of the Middle Way Candrakīrti identified him with the "Noble" lineage author of the same name. As noted above, the *Compendium of Good Sayings*'s author seems to understand a strong connection between Saraha, Nāgārjuna, and the Middle Way Candrakīrti, making it likely that he saw the tantric and Middle Way Candrakīrtis as the same person. Atiśa, in the passage cited above in which he declares that "Candrakīrti is the disciple of Nāgārjuna" and proceeds to praise the non-tantric Candrakīrti's view, seems to make just such an identification, as the author of *Entrance to the Middle* was not a disciple of any Nāgārjuna but the author of the *Guhyasamāja* commentary seems to have been. The principal Tibetan translator and exponent of the Middle Way Candrakīrti's texts, Patsab Nyimadrak,[97] also translated the tantric Candrakīrti's *Guhyasamāja* commentary with his Indian teacher, Tilakakalaśa;[98] both Patsab and Tilakakalaśa may thus have understood the authors of these texts to have been the same Candrakīrti. Certainly, later Tibetan authors viewed praise of the tantric Candrakīrti's writings by the likes of Naropāda to entail praise of the Middle Way Candrakīrti's viewpoints (there being, in such a view, no difference between the tantric and Middle Way authors).[99] We can say with some certainty that the success of the "Noble" lineage lead to important changes in how late Indian Buddhists perceived the Middle Way Candrakīrti. The "Noble" lineage makes Candrakīrti a direct disciple of Nāgārjuna, rather than a centuries-later commentator (as the *Clear Words* author would have been known), placing him on par with Āryadeva as "sons" of the venerable master. The "Noble" lineage also places Candrakīrti just one step removed from the renowned tantric figure, Saraha, boosting his prestige further.[100] The fame of the *Guhyasamāja* commentator may have been a primary factor in the belated success of Candrakīrti's *Entrance to the Middle* and *Clear Words.* Indian Buddhists who esteemed the *Guhyasamāja* commentary felt compelled to take seriously *Entrance to the Middle* and *Clear Words.*

While serious consideration of the Middle Way Candrakīrti stemmed, at least in part, from the tantric Candrakīrti's importance, the case of the tantric Bhāvaviveka requires further reflection on the Middle Way Candrakīrti's impact. A Bhavyakīrti wrote sub-commentaries on both Nāgārjuna's and Candrakīrti's *Guhyasamāja* works.[101] As discussed above, we see two Middle Way authors taking the name Bhāvaviveka, the first authoring *Lamp for Wisdom* and *Heart of the Middle,* the second authoring *Jewel Lamp of the Middle, Compendium of Meanings of the Middle,* and at least parts of *Blaze of Reasoning* as well. The latter Bhāvaviveka refers favorably to both Candrakīrti's

Entrance to the Middle and (a) Candrakīrti's *Seventy Stanzas on the Three Refuges* apparently seeing no difference between those two authors.[102] Ruegg suggests that this latter Bhāvaviveka, author of the *Jewel Lamp of the Middle,* may be the tantric Bhavyakīrti.[103] If we accept this identity, we could date Bhāvaviveka II to the period immediately after the tantric Candrakīrti's lifetime and immediately preceding Atiśa, who refers to *Jewel Lamp of the Middle:* right about the year 1000. This would place Bhāvaviveka II's Middle Way views in a critical spot. As noted above, the *Jewel Lamp, Compendium of Meanings,* and parts of *Blaze of Reasoning* develop the Middle Way Epistemology blending of their namesake, suggest points of concession to the Middle Way Candrakīrti's critique of that blend, and offer ways of responding to Candrakīrti's critique. Set around the year 1000, these would be the earliest known attempts to incorporate and respond to Candrakīrti's arguments.

Accepting the identity of Bhāvaviveka II and Bhavyakīrti could help answer a further problem with the late Bhāvaviveka. Why would Bhāvaviveka II, clearly indebted to the Middle Way Epistemology blend of his forbears, concede points to Candrakīrti's critique of valid cognition? If he is the Bhavyakīrti sub-commentator on the *Guhyasamāja,* the explanation would be fairly straightforward: Bhāvaviveka II would be indebted to the tantric Candrakīrti's opus and, like so many others in this period, would not distinguish that work from the Middle Way Candrakīrti's corpus. The identity of the two Candrakīrtis forced him to consider the Middle Way Candrakīrti's attacks on the applicability of valid cognition to knowledge of ultimate truth, to concede some points and offer answers to others. Bhāvaviveka II yet was so compelled by his namesake's writings as to identify with that author, to add to at least one of the earlier figure's texts (*Blaze of Reasoning*), and to compose still others in that author's name. While some might think that this sketch would represent an extraordinarily conflicted individual, this cluster of views—tantra, Epistemology, and Candrakīrti's Middle Way—would become increasingly common in the eleventh and twelfth centuries.[104]

Assembling the Pieces: Tantra, Epistemology, and Candrakīrti

While Bhāvaviveka II's writings may strengthen the notion that the Middle Way Candrakīrti's rise was triggered by interest in the tantric Candrakīrti's corpus, they also show that involvement with tantra need not occlude serious interest in the Buddhist Epistemological tradition. We certainly have ample evidence that tantra, Epistemology, and Middle Way philosophy lived together harmoniously. In eighth- and ninth-century India, when a major current of thought was Śāntarakṣita's and Kamalaśīla's synthesis of Middle Way and Epistemology, we see the tantric author of the *Tattvasiddhi* taking the name Śāntarakṣita.[105] Like the Middle Way author, the *Tattvasiddhi* author relies heavily on the valid cognition tradition in order to prove (*siddhi*) his point, in this case that tantric practice leads one to realization of reality (*tattva*), expressed in tantric terminology as "great bliss."[106] The *Tattvasiddhi* (perhaps "*Proof [that Tantric Practice Yields Knowledge of] Reality*") alerts us to how tantra was in some cases allied with the valid cognition tradition, particularly so prior to the rise of Candrakīrti's fame.[107] The *Tattvasiddhi,* and a good many other texts,[108] suggest that Śāntarakṣita's utilization of elements from the Epistemological tradition, as well as Yogācāra ontology, must have been seen by many to be consonant with mainstream Buddhist tantra.

The trends that we have seen in this chapter show the Middle Way Candrakīrti brought to life in opposition to the Epistemological tradition and in consonance with late Indian Buddhist tantra. Thus, certain strains of Buddhist tantric thought emerging in the late tenth century seem to have been less amenable to both the valid cognition project and, perhaps, Yogācāra. We have already seen some consonances between ideals of the tantric revivers of Candrakīrti's writings and themes in those writings that critique the Epistemological tradition. The tantric Candrakīrti may well have been part of this opposition to the valid cognition tradition and to Yogācāra, which the Middle Way Candrakīrti critiqued at length in his *Entrance to the Middle* and *Clear Words.* Wayman suggests that the tantric Candrakīrti's *Guhyasamāja* commentary evinces a move away from Yogācāra ontology, which was a much easier fit with tantra, toward a "pure" Madhyamaka interpretation of tantra. He notes the "Mādhyamika tone of commentary," with its "avoidance of the typical Yogācāra vocabulary found in many other commentaries, especially in the Pañcakrama tradition."[109] Was Wayman simply projecting the Middle Way Candrakīrti's anti-Yogācāra polemic onto the tantric Candrakīrti's *Guhyasamāja* commentary, imagining something like a Yogācāra-Madhyamaka versus Prāsaṅgika-Madhyamaka divide within tantric exegesis?

While Wayman's impressionistic characterization of the tantric Candrakīrti's commentary does not provide textual support, we have softer evidence for a tantric move away from Yogācāra. Two of the tantric authors discussed above deploy the Middle Way Candrakīrti's Yogācāra critique. We saw already that Sahajavajra's commentary on Maitrīpāda's *Ten Stanzas on Reality* praises Candrakīrti's declaration in his *Entrance to the Middle* that Yogācāra is "interpretable." Additionally, the *Compendium of Good*

Sayings cites Candrakīrti's refutation of Yogācāra in *Entrance to the Middle,* amid its collection of tantric extracts.[110] These references alert us to the possibility that certain tantric exegetes attempted to move tantra away from its more comfortable home in Yogācāra ontology toward a "pure" Madhyamaka interpretation. In this attempt, the Middle Way Candrakīrti's Yogācāra critique would prove useful. While Śāntarakṣita argued against Yogācāra as ultimately true, his adaptation of Yogācāra on the level of conventional truth and his widespread utilization of elements of Dharmakīrti's valid cognition theory—which are often tied to Yogācāra—would have made his synthesis look less appealing to those wishing to distance tantra from Yogācāra.

While Candrakīrti's rise coincided with strains of tantric thought that opposed the Buddhist Epistemological tradition, and perhaps Yogācāra as well, at least two Indian Buddhists found ways to harmonize the final developments of tantra and Epistemology, while either taking into account Candrakīrti's views or adducing credible reasons to ignore them. Interestingly, these two scholars, Abhayākaragupta (c. 1025–1125) and Ratnākaraśānti (a contemporary of Prajñākaramati),[111] both adopted a more critical approach to the identity of the Middle Way and tantric Candrakīrtis. Abhayākaragupta, an important scholar of both Nālandā and Vikramaśīla monasteries, wrote and translated numerous works on tantra and tantric practice and the Perfection of Wisdom literature in addition to translating Candrakīrti's commentary on Nāgārjuna's *Seventy Stanzas on Emptiness* with Nur Darmadrak.[112] His *Ornament for the Sage's Thought* refers to "the Master Candrakīrti" when citing *Entrance to the Middle* and to "Ārya Candra" when citing the tantric author.[113] While Abhayākaragupta does not discuss the relationship between these two appellations, by distinguishing the two he seems to acknowledge some discrepancy between their views, if not their personages. Further, when he cites Candrakīrti's *Seventy Stanzas on the Three Refuges,* he does not repeat Atiśa's comment that Candrakīrti was the disciple of Nāgārjuna but instead notes that Candrakīrti "follows Nāgārjuna's thought,"[114] suggesting again that he distinguishes between the Middle Way Candrakīrti who was not Nāgārjuna's disciple and the tantric Candrakīrti who was the tantric Nāgārjuna's disciple.

Ratnākaraśānti explicitly distinguished between the views (but not the personages) of the Middle Way and tantric Candrakīrtis. While he believed that the same Candrakīrti wrote *Entrance to the Middle* and the *Guhyasamāja* commentary, he saw the former text espousing nihilism while only Candrakīrti's tantric writings reflected true insight.[115] Candrakīrti's Middle Way corpus could be safely disregarded, representing merely his immature views.

The critical stances adopted by these two Indian polymaths, who both wrote extensively in the tantric and valid cognition traditions as well as on Madhyamaka, toward Candrakīrti's corpus is matched by their either apologetical or critical approach to the Middle Way Candrakīrti's views. Ratnākaraśānti was openly critical of what he portrayed as Candrakīrti's "nihilism." Abhayākaragupta's citations of Candrakīrti's *Entrance to the Middle* and its autocommentary are less openly critical, choosing to explain what Candrakīrti was "thinking" (*saṃdhi, dgongs pa*) when he made certain problematic declarations, including Candrakīrti's proclamations that mind and mental factors cease upon buddhahood and that enlightenment consists in utter non-perception.[116] Other citations are utilized as supports for a point Abhayākaragupta makes, with no further discussion of the passage;[117] these points suggest his endorsement of certain of Candrakīrti's views that proved useful in advancing his own.

Both authors take the tantric Candrakīrti as an authority but either openly or apologetically criticize the Middle Way Candrakīrti. While the rise of the tantric Candrakīrti contributed to reviving the Middle Way Candrakīrti, these two authors show that enthusiasm for one Candrakīrti need not entail support of the other. Ratnākaraśānti's disavowal of the Middle Way Candrakīrti's work and Abhayākaragupta's apology show that not all tantric authors of this period found Candrakīrti's ideas literally acceptable, particularly when those authors had strong ties to the valid cognition tradition. However, unlike in Śāntarakṣita's day, neither author could simply ignore *Entrance to the Middle.* An eleventh- or twelfth-century tantric author who wished to criticize Candrakīrti's Middle Way views needed to suggest some method for differentiating those views from the position of the esteemed tantric Candrakīrti. We might even hypothesize that Ratnākaraśānti's and Abhayākaragupta's varying strategies suggest the growing authority of Candrakīrti's Middle Way views in the perhaps century separating the two. In Ratnākaraśānti's time (c. 1000), one could differentiate the Middle Way and tantric corpi and criticize the former. By the time Abhayākaragupta wrote *Ornament for the Sage's Thought* in 1113, a distinction could still be drawn, but now problematic Middle Way assertions had to be explained away. Abhayākaragupta clearly disagreed with Candrakīrti's views on buddhahood and ultimate truth but now felt compelled to explain Candrakīrti's "thinking" on these issues.

Situating Candrakīrti's rise within the broader currents of late Indian Buddhist thought allows us to appreciate both the complexity of the period that first gave his corpus serious consideration and the allegiances that his revivers made between his views and the tantric writing of the period. Whether or not Indian Buddhists uniformly confused the tantric Candrakīrti with his Middle Way namesake, eleventh- and twelfth-century tantric authors consistently referred to Candrakīrti's views on ultimate truth and the inapplicability of valid cognition to realizing ultimate truth as well as his arguments against Yogācāra. Candrakīrti's position in late Indian Buddhists' appraisal of why Madhyamaka was superior to Yogācāra, how tantra fit in with either system, and how or if valid cognition could be utilized within a Madhyamaka framework brought his texts their first widespread consideration. As we will see in the following chapter, this nexus of concerns fostered the development of a Prāsaṅgika school in twelfth-century Tibet, the success of which gave Candrakīrti's texts the pre-eminent place in Tibetan Buddhist thought that they retain today.

Resurrecting Candrakīrti, Creating Prāsaṅgika

From the preceding, we can see that Candrakīrti's views, while marginal in his own day, enjoyed a sudden popularity among important Indian Buddhists—but by no means among all Indian Buddhists nor to the exclusion of disparate interpretations of Madhyamaka—beginning in the early part of the eleventh century.[118] We can also see that the central issue upon which Candrakīrti's supporters elevated his once unpopular views revolved around the relationship between valid cognition and knowledge of the ultimate, which in turn led his supporters and detractors to portray the ultimate in disparate ways. To speak of a "Prāsaṅgika" movement—a championing of Candrakīrti's texts—in the eleventh century, then, does not refer only to supporters of a mode of argumentation; it is not just a question of denying the validity of formal inference (or "inferences [accepted] in one's own continuum," *svatantra-anumāna*) in favor of apagogic (*prasaṅga*) reasoning. Crucial also to this movement were the ontological implications of reasoning. When Jayānanda, for the first time in the history of Indian Madhyamaka, writes of "Svātantrika,"[119] he does not only refer (disparagingly) to Mādhyamikas who employ formal inferences but to an interpretation of the ultimate at odds with his own.

We see a great deal of debate among fourteenth-century and later Tibetan scholars, as well as among contemporary scholars, as to whether "Prāsaṅgika" and "Svātantrika" represent competing ontological visions or, instead, merely competing logical methods. Some recent scholarship focusing on "the Svātantrika-Prāsaṅgika distinction" has examined the early Indian evidence—the writings of Bhāvaviveka and Candrakīrti—to determine if ontological concerns entered into Bhāvaviveka's procedural critique of Buddhapālita and Candrakīrti's subsequent defense of Buddhapālita and counter-critique of Bhāvaviveka.[120] Additionally, recent scholarship jumps forward some eight hundred years to examine the distinction that fourteenth- and fifteenth-century Tibetan writers made between these two "schools" of Madhyamaka thought, particularly Tsongkhapa's claim that the two schools hold divergent ontologies and several Sakya scholars' claim, in rebuttal, that the distinction is purely procedural.[121] This scholarship heightens our awareness that the Svātantrika-Prāsaṅgika distinction, as portrayed by Tibetan doxographies, is a distinction made by Tibetan scholars in order to categorize, harmonize, and explicate a wealth of Indian literature, the authors of which very likely never conceived of themselves as members of competing subschools of Madhyamaka. Scholarship has begun to highlight differences between Tibetan doxography and Indian historical reality.

However, scholarship has largely failed to examine the criteria that eleventh- and twelfth-century scholars employed to elevate Candrakīrti's Madhyamaka exegesis out of obscurity to a position where it came, at least in Tibet, to eclipse that of Śāntarakṣita (whose Madhyamaka had already eclipsed that of Bhāvaviveka three hundred years earlier).[122] In sum, we have bypassed those who were the first to make a Prāsaṅgika-Svātantrika distinction. While the distinctions that these eleventh- and twelfth-century scholars drew between Candrakīrti's Madhyamaka—called "Prāsaṅgika" by twelfth-century Tibetans—and what Jayānanda and others called "Svātantrika" differ sharply from the distinction drawn by Tsongkhapa, clearly the issues in the eleventh and twelfth centuries are ontological and not only procedural. Our awareness of the important differences adduced by both Indian and Tibetan scholars in this period prevents us from downplaying the significance of this divide, which amounted to a lively debate over Candrakīrti's importance, particularly concerning the status of ultimate truth.[123]

This chapter has attempted to recover aspects of the historical rise of Candrakīrti, long after his death, and some of the philosophical and doctrinal trends that brought his rise to pass. In so doing, I have attempted to present a more historically plausible picture of Candrakīrti's resurrection than the traditional view, which places his pre-eminence in his own lifetime. I have also tried to draw attention to those figures historically responsible for the rise of what came to be known as Prāsaṅgika. Candrakīrti surely saw himself as arguing against, even "refuting," some of Bhāvaviveka's views. However, the impact of his Bhāvaviveka critique upon the development of the Middle Way was not felt until centuries later. Jñānagarbha, Śāntarakṣita, and

Kamalaśīla were far more concerned with arguing for Madhyamaka's superiority over Yogācāra viewpoints than they were with establishing and defending Madhyamaka subschools. Any interest Śāntarakṣita had in defining a Madhyamaka subschool targeted Bhāvaviveka, not Candrakīrti. Candrakīrti was simply not an influential player in the Madhyamaka debates of the first millennium.[124]

I have suggested that the appellation "Prāsaṅgika" can be applied to Candrakīrti's revivalists, Prajñākaramati, Atiśa, and Jayānanda, particularly when we see that Jayānanda used its companion term, "Svātantrika," to label his—and those whom he saw as Candrakīrti's—opponents. However, regarding eleventh- and twelfth-century Indian Madhyamaka, "Prāsaṅgika" does not refer to a distinct subschool but to an intellectual movement; we see important Middle Way figures supporting Candrakīrti's long-silent philosophical positions.[125] We do not see Indian authors conceiving of Candrakīrti's views as excluding all else—of the authors investigated here, only Jayānanda may have eschewed all but Candrakīrti's Madhyamaka. Nor do we see a polarization of Indian exegesis: Abhayākaragupta shows us how one may take Candrakīrti's ideas seriously (how one may explain his thinking) while yet holding to something like "Svātantrika" viewpoints. While eleventh- and twelfth-century India saw a popularization of Candrakīrti's views, the evidence supports the notion of a "common commentarial project"[126] among Indian Mādhyamikas, more than a sharp division into camps.

A doxographic approach to Madhyamaka yields certain pictures, certain divides, certain sets of issues. From the doxographic view, we have evidence supporting a thematic connection between Bhāvaviveka and Śāntarakṣita and a thematic dissociation of these two from Buddhapālita and Candrakīrti that would support our use of "Svātantrika" for the former two and "Prāsaṅgika" for the latter two. Or, we may show thematic similarities between Bhāvaviveka and Candrakīrti that would support their classification as "pure Mādhyamikas" in contradistinction to Śāntarakṣita's syncretic "Yogācāra-Madhyamaka." Or, to revive earlier Tibetan distinctions, Jñānagarbha could be thematically dissociated from Śāntarakṣita and joined with Candrakīrti in supporting "what is renowned in the world" conventionally, in opposition to those, like Bhāvaviveka and Śāntarakṣita, who sought stronger philosophical grounding for the conventional world. All of these classifications possess exegetical merit and offer greater philosophical clarity.

In drawing these thematic connections, we cannot lose sight of historical patterns. When Bhāvaviveka in the sixth century criticized the logical procedures Buddhapālita utilized in commenting upon Nāgārjuna's foundational Madhyamaka treatise and Candrakīrti in the seventh century rejected Bhāvaviveka's logical methods (largely to deaf ears), we see competing interpretations of the Middle Way. However, only one of these interpretations gained influence over the next three hundred years. When Prajñākaramati, Atiśa, and Jayānanda revived Candrakīrti's writings, these writings—at a great temporal and spatial distance from their creator—engendered expansive eleventh- and twelfth-century Indian and Tibetan controversies. One focus of the controversy centered round the issue of whether a Mādhyamika may employ formal inferences in the manner developed by the great Buddhist logicians, Dignāga and Dharmakīrti, when arguing for Madhyamaka emptiness. Eleventh- and twelfth-century Indian and Tibetan discussions of this logical, procedural issue expanded into wide-ranging areas of Buddhist ontology and gnoseology: the ways in which a Mādhyamika argued said a great deal about what that Mādhyamika held to exist, both from the mundane perspective and from the lofty vision of a Buddha. Finally, Candrakīrti gained a lively following that we might call a Prāsaṅgika movement.

Eleventh-century Tibetans who made the arduous journey to Kashmir or northeastern India found an Indian Buddhist world wrestling with the complex interplay of a ritual theory and praxis seemingly at odds with its metaphysical basis and well-established epistemological practices seemingly at odds with both ritual and metaphysics. We now turn to the activities of several of these Tibetan translators and the debates they touched off when casting this complex of issues in the fractured socio-political landscape of late eleventh- and early twelfth-century Tibet. The open textual horizons of eleventh-century India would coalesce quite quickly into Prāsaṅgika and Svātantrika "schools" of the Tibetan Middle Way.

2. The Birth of Prāsaṅgika

Around the close of the first millennium, Indian interest in issues engendered by Candrakīrti's writings enabled Jayānanda to label and criticize the "Svāṭantrika" interpretation of Madhyamaka, to which he saw himself, and Candrakīrti before him, in opposition.[1] Although the term "Prāsaṅgika" had yet to be used by Indian authors, we may justifiably speak of a burgeoning "Prāsaṅgika movement" as a convenient label for Candrakīrti's newfound supporters.[2] We see Prajñākaramati, Atiśa, and Jayānanda favoring Candrakīrti's interpretation of the Middle Way (or rather their interpretation of Candrakīrti's Middle Way) over what Jayānanda labels "Svātantrika" on the strength of "Prāsaṅgika's" rejection of valid cognition in pursuit of the ultimate. What began in India as a preference for Candrakīrti's interpretation would become in Tibet a well-worn doxographic hierarchy, one in which Prāsaṅgika clearly dominates over Svātantrika as the "correct" Middle Way view.

In between the growing Indian movement toward Prāsaṅgika and the Tibetan doxographical hierarchy, twelfth-century Tibet saw a growing diversity of Prāsaṅgika and Svātantrika interpretations of the Middle Way. Candrakīrti gained new Tibetan partisans who joined Jayānanda in open criticism of Svātantrika, while proponents of an Epistemology–Middle Way union (particularly one articulated by Śāntarakṣita and Kamalaśīla) subjected Candrakīrti's writings to sustained critique, rejecting their authority. This was a time of Buddhist regeneration in Tibet, as the beginning of the second millennium brought the translations of hundreds of Sanskrit Buddhist texts—many for the first time—into Tibetan. While the physical landscape was re-centered around networks of Buddhist monasteries and temples, competing Middle Way allegiances became intertwined with rival socio-political institutions. Institutional competition pushed this Middle Way dispute to take the shape of rival "schools," a categorization which would later become the doxographic categories Prāsaṅgika and Svātantrika. Throughout the eleventh and twelfth centuries, the development of these schools amplified the philosophical concerns that led to Candrakīrti's rebirth in India, creating what would become the dominant philosophical position of Tibetan Buddhism.

Territory and Translations in Tibet's Later Diffusion

The great importance of translating the Buddhist canon into Tibetan is suggested by the language (in Tibetan sources) of two "diffusions" (*dar*) of Buddhism in Tibet that coincide with two periods of translations (*'gyur*). The "early diffusion" (*snga dar*) or "early translation" (*snga 'gyur*) in Central Tibet was controlled primarily by the state, as a newly expanding Tibetan empire's widening conquests created contact between Tibetans and Buddhists of India, Central Asia, and China. The Tibetan emperor Trisong Detsen's (*khri srong lde btsan,* 742–97) proclamation of Buddhism as the official state religion led (directly or indirectly) to the establishment of Tibetan monasticism and the translation of a massive amount of Buddhist scripture. Tradition holds that Trisong Detsen built Samyé (*bsam yas*) Monastery, where the first Tibetan Buddhist monks ordained, and invited the important Indian teachers Śāntarakṣita and Kamalaśīla—the latter reportedly defeating a Chinese Chan monk in the Great Debate at Samyé and establishing the "gradual path" of Buddhist practice in Tibet.[3] Having sponsored the creation of a written version of the Tibetan language, Trisong Detsen and his successors later formulated translation bureaus to render Buddhist scripture into Tibetan.

Official sponsorship of Buddhism during the period of Tibetan empire seems to have focused on sūtra literature and a variety of philosophical materials, while for the most part downplaying tantra. We can get a sense of imperial interests by examining catalogs composed, by royal decree, just prior to the collapse of the Tibetan empire. The catalog of the Den karma collection reveals a great wealth of Indian Buddhist philosophical treatises, including discourses from the Madhyamaka, Yogācāra, Abhidharma, and Epistemological schools.[4] These early state-sponsored translations speak to what Matthew Kapstein called "the charisma of reason"—the appeal that Buddhist treatises and their carefully constructed logic had to rulers wishing to portray themselves as legitimate centers of a well-ordered world, specifically one in which their rule was reasonable and functioned according to universal principles.[5] While their finely nuanced philosophy would not have been the primary concern of royal patrons, the treatises instead provided a model of reason and organization. However, Tibetan emperors were able to recognize the thinly-veiled martial and royal imagery of tantric ritual—a model of divine kingship—in which one identifies with a central deity in an elaborate palace at the center of a fortress-like circle (*maṇḍala*), with lesser deities (or neighboring rulers) in smaller fortresses serving as vassals.[6] Samyé Monastery, Tibet's first state-sponsored monastery, was constructed on the pattern of the Vairocana maṇḍala, a deity often associated with imperial patronage and service.

The early translation period ended with the collapse of the Tibetan empire around 842. Buddhist practice undoubtedly continued outside of state patronage; however, the survival of scholarship is less certain.[7] In what was known in Tibetan histories as a "Dark Period," formal contacts with neighboring Buddhist lands were broken, as were the monastic ordination lineage and state-supported translation efforts. As a measure of prosperity returned to Central Tibet approximately 150 years later, Tibetans sought to renew ordination. We have reliable accounts of Indian and Kashmiri monks sojourning in the borderlands of the newly formed Tangut kingdom (northeast of Tibet) in this period, some remaining while others traveled onward to the Song capitol.[8] It seems many monastic refugees from Central Tibet relocated to the Tibetan-Tangut borderlands around the same time.[9] We can further note the confluence of accounts in Tibetan historical writing of the "purple-robed monks" who took part in the ordination of Central Tibetan pilgrims with the accounts of monks in Tangut lands and neighboring territories receiving honorary purple robes from the Song emperor.[10] As the region maintained a comparatively flourishing Buddhist tradition during Tibet's collapse and proved crucial to Tibet's Buddhist revival, Tangut royal patronage of Buddhism additionally would prove significant in Tibet's Middle Way disputes later in the twelfth century.

Tibetan histories—from the earliest datable into modern times—speak of a small group of pilgrims who set out from Central Tibet seeking ordination such that they in turn could revive monastic Buddhism in their homeland.[11] Following their ordinations in the northeast, these pilgrims returned to Central Tibet, sometimes becoming heirs to imperial temples, sometimes founding new temples and monasteries.[12] Stories found in several Tibetan sources suggest the magnitude and contested nature of the return of monasticism. In the most poignant, survivors of the old royal family welcome the pilgrims back and offer the keys to Samyé Monastery to one of the most important of the new monks, Lumé (*kLu mes*). This act of literally handing over authority from the old dynasty to the new monks, however, is incomplete; upon inspecting the dilapidated monastery, Lumé hands the keys back, only later to repair Samyé's central temple.[13] While difficult to decipher, Lumé's actions hint at a shift in power from old politics to new religion, with monastic lineage trumping royal pedigree. The story takes a further twist when roughly one hundred years later, Lumé's followers fight the followers of his companions-cum-competitors, Ba (*rBa*) and Rakshi (*Rag shi*), leading to the destruction of much of Samyé.[14] These stories suggest a multi-faceted conflict involving surviving royalty, old aristocratic clans, groups newly wealthy, and the new monks competing for patronage for both their travels as well as their reconstruction efforts.

The degree to which the new monks usurped authority from aristocratic clans and the measure of clan authority taking the name of new monasticism are difficult to measure. We can be more certain that, wherever the real power lay, monasteries came to represent small-scale political agency in Central Tibet. Tibetan histories tell of the new monks building, renovating, teaching, and gaining disciples, who in turn built new temples and monasteries aligned with those of their masters. These groups (*sde pa* or *tsho;* "districts") of temples and monasteries linked to a common seat functioned as small-scale political entities or, as van der Kuijp termed them, "administrative-cum-vinaya districts."[15] The re-emergence of hierarchical rule over extended regions of Central Tibet following the "Dark Period" can be attributed to the building and administrative efforts of the new monks. Competition and violence between districts began as groups carved out their territories in Central Tibet. Rather than a strong central authority that funded and controlled monastic Buddhism as in Tibet's imperial period, the renewal of Tibetan monasticism created a number of politically important figures who invoked the prestige of the old emperor in renovating ancient temples and building many more.

From this fractured and competitive socio-political landscape the "later translation" (*phyi 'gyur,* or "new translation" *gsar 'gyur*) effort was spawned. Tibetan translators played a major role in summoning the lost imperial esteem for their monasteries, renewing the state-sponsored project but on a smaller scale. Given present studies, we cannot precisely map each important Tibetan translator with a corresponding district, temple, or clan. We may safely say, however, that the newly formed networks of temples and monasteries sought the same kind of prestige and power that the Tibetan emperor gained in his royal patronage of translation, the poetic legitimization that Sanskrit, even in its translated form, offered.[16] Rather than a central ruler overseeing a unified, large translation project, the later translations were made by heroic individuals who took possession of particular textual canons and formed their intellectual property into the cornerstones of monastic centers. The prestige of Sanskrit radiated from these Tibetan translators, who spent large parts of their lives studying in India. The monastic networks also gained benefit, becoming the forerunners to the great religious orders that would come to dominate Tibetan cultural and political life.

Some of the new monasteries revived translation projects begun in the imperial era; along with monasticism, philosophical literature—Abhidharma, Yogācāra, and Madhyamaka—returned from the northeast.[17] Gradually, Central Tibetans turned their attention west and south, to Kashmir and the Gangetic Plains, and discovered Indian Buddhist literature that had yet to traverse the Himalayas. Texts that had either not yet been written or had yet to gain an Indian following during the early diffusion of Buddhism in Tibet were translated for the first time (and sometimes retranslated) in this later diffusion, and these translations became the cornerstones of competing proto-sectarian schools. While many translators took possession of particular "Highest Yoga Tantras" (*anuttarayogatantra*),[18] several others focused on newly available philosophical materials. Ngok Loden Sherab[19] (1059–1109) made his monastic academy synonymous with the study of Dharmakīrti's philosophy and Yogācāra-Madhyamaka, utilizing new interpretations of the Epistemological tradition previously unknown in Tibet. Patsab Nyimadrak[20] (b. 1055) discovered the new Indian enthusiasm for Candrakīrti's writings and became the first Tibetan to translate his two major works, *Clear Words* and the autocommentary to *Entrance to the Middle.* Utilizing Candrakīrti's interpretation, Patsab also became a principal teacher of Nāgārjuna's treatises in Central Tibet. Though Sanskrit philosophical treatises may have lived in relative harmony in India, their Tibetan translations became the foci for widespread disputes that produced separate schools of the Middle Way.

Ngok and Patsab: Textual Ownership and Competing Communities

Much remains unknown concerning the relationships between clan and royal power, the new monasticism, and the budding generation of translators in eleventh-century Tibet. While some pursued translation as an avocation from their aristocratic backgrounds, others undoubtedly found in the role of translator an entryway to socio-political power. The relationship between eleventh-century translators and the new monasticism varied as well, providing a further level of complexity to the allegiances forming in this period. The Ngok clan affords us one of the more complete pictures of the development of a new translation monastic institute out of the newly re-established ordination lineage. It was a clan that maintained its aristocratic status from imperial times through the latter diffusion; that split between two competing monastic districts in the early years of the latter diffusion; and that built an extremely successful monastic academy, Sangpu (*gsang phu*), supported by one such district and centered around the translations and teachings of its most illustrious member. Sangpu, like many centers for philosophical study, was aligned with the Kadampa (*bKa' gdams pa*) order at the same time that it held a place in one of the competing networks of new monasticism. We know that Sangpu had a competitive relationship with other Kadampa monasteries that held divergent views and were associated with competing networks, suggesting that the Kadampa umbrella sheltered a variety of teachings while district loyalties remained the primary identity marker for monks. These loyalties may well have fueled the creation of Prāsaṅgika and Svātantrika lines of Madhyamaka.

Ngok was an aristocratic clan during the imperial era, and one member was reportedly a minister to the emperor Trisong Detsen.[21] Their fate during the Dark Period, like much else, remains unknown, yet we see them fairing well at the close of the first millennium. Following the return of the pilgrims with the monastic ordination lineage to Central Tibet, divisions appear in the clan's religious allegiances. In 1010, Ngok Jangchub Chungnay[22] became a disciple of Lumé, one of the most influential pilgrims who later undertook renovation and building activity in the Central Tibetan region of U.[23] Ngok Jangchub Chungnay took part in the renovation and expansion of the imperial Yerpa Temple between 1011 and 1020 and built several affiliate temples, coming to be known as one of the "four pillars"[24] that supported the "roof beams" of Lumé and Sumpa Yeshe Lodro,[25] a mark of his significance in expanding the influence of Lumé.[26]

In this same time, Ngok Dorje Zhonu[27] maintained ties with the strains of Buddhism surviving from the early diffusion, suggesting that clan ties were loose enough to allow for a variety of religious affiliations.[28] Further, his son, Ngok Lekpay Sherab,[29] took ordination with Dring Yeshe Lodro,[30] one of Lumé's companions-turned-competitors in returning the ordination lineage to Central Tibet.[31] Ngok Lekpay Sherab made the journey east to study with Jowo Setsun,[32] and to the Western Tibetan kingdom where he worked with the famed translator Rinchen Zangpo (958–1055).[33] From his travel and study, he seems to have built his own reputation, independently from

Ngok Jangchub Chungnay, and built at least three more centers in the Lhasa area, including Sangpu Neutog, to the south of Lhasa, in 1073.[34] When Atiśa arrived in Central Tibet in 1045, Ngok Jangchub Chungnay hosted him at Yerpa, requesting Atiśa to translate Maitreya's *Sublime Continuum*.[35] Ngok Lekpay Sherab studied with Atiśa at Nyetang[36] and requested that Atiśa translate Bhāvaviveka's *Heart of the Middle* and *Blaze of Reasoning*. It is interesting to see that these two members of the Ngok clan were both students of Atiśa and yet were key actors in competing districts.[37] Looking more broadly, we see that three of Atiśa's main students founded monasteries that were respectively supported by the four competing "administrative-cum-vinaya districts" into which the U region of Central Tibet was divided.[38] In these instances, we see the new territorial divisions introduced with the return of the ordination lineage superceding clan loyalties and utilizing the prestige of the very same Indian teacher to advance competing agendas.[39] In these cases, the Kadampa label masks a variety of intellectual and political interests that an awareness of district loyalties illuminates.

In the next generation, Ngok Loden Sherab, having been ordained by his uncle, Ngok Lekpay Sherab,[40] was part of an entourage of Tibetan translators that the king of Western Tibet convened in 1076 and that subsequently traveled to Kashmir, where Ngok studied for seventeen years.[41] Ngok's most important translations were Prajñākaragupta's *Ornament for (Dharmakīrti's) Valid Cognition*,[42] a commentary that emphasizes the confluence of Dharmakīrti's logic and Nāgārjuna's Madhyamaka; Dharmakīrti's second main work, the *Compendium of Valid Cognition*,[43] along with Dharmottara's commentary to it; and Maitreya's *Sublime Continuum*, one of five texts attributed to the future Buddha Maitreya primarily concerned with the "Buddha nature" present in all sentient beings. Furthermore, Ngok is credited with establishing the Tibetan study of "The Three Mādhyamikas from the East," the main Madhyamaka writings of Jñānagarbha, Śāntarakṣita, and Kamalaśīla.[44]

Upon his return to Central Tibet, Ngok became the abbot of Sangpu Monastery where his mastery of Dharmakīrti's writings increased his fame to the point where he was reported to have 23,000 students.[45] Nearly every important figure in Central Tibet was reported to have studied Dharmakīrti's tradition at Sangpu. In addition to establishing Sangpu as the premier institute for Buddhist epistemology, Ngok reportedly wrote summaries (*bsdus don*) of "The Three Mādhyamikas from the East," texts that emphasized the compatibility of Madhyamaka philosophy and Dharmakīrti's epistemology, and on many other Middle Way texts from Nāgārjuna, Bhāvaviveka, and Śāntideva.[46]

Ngok did not translate these texts anew but instead relied on imperial-era translations, suggesting that these materials had already returned to Central Tibet with the return of monasticism and that Ngok found the early translations sufficient. None of his summaries on these texts are presently available, thus greatly limiting our knowledge of his Middle Way views.[47] His reported support of what would later be called Svātantrika accords well with his translation and authorial efforts. Further, Ngok's commitments to the epistemological tradition would place him squarely in opposition to those champions of Candrakīrti who argued against the applicability of valid cognition to the ultimate.[48]

In contradistinction to Ngok Loden Sherab, Patsab Nyimadrak's interests centered on Candrakīrti's writings.[49] Patsab's ties with aristocracy are less clear than Ngok's. While the Patsab clan figures in clan lists from the imperial period, Patsab Nyimadrak was seemingly not esteemed enough to take part in the "dharma council" (*chos 'khor*) of translators commissioned by the king of Western Tibet. He studied in Kashmir for twenty-three years, mainly at Ratnaguptavihāra in Śrīnagar,[50] where he translated into Tibetan Candrakīrti's two most important works, *Entrance to the Middle* and *Clear Words.*[51] He went on to translate Āryadeva's *Four Hundred Stanzas,* one of the foundational Madhyamaka treatises, and Candrakīrti's commentary on it. Additionally, he retranslated and revised several of Nāgārjuna's most important texts including the *Fundamental Treatise on the Middle.*

The disparities between Ngok's and Patsab's translation activities in Kashmir must have been due to personal inclinations and differing senses of mission. Considering the timeframe—Ngok's stay in Kashmir is reported as 1076–93; Patsab's stay was likely 1077–1100[52]—and places of their travels, we can imagine that they would have come into contact with the same Sanskrit Buddhist texts, and that only what they chose to translate differed. This becomes particularly clear when we consider that these two chief Tibetan protagonists in the development of competing schools of Madhyamaka studied with some of the same Indian and Kashmiri teachers. While Patsab translated Candrakīrti's *Entrance to the Middle* with Tilakakalaśa, Ngok translated Dignāga's commentary on the *Eight Thousand Stanza Perfection of Wisdom Sūtra* and Śāntideva's *Compendium of Training* with him. Parahitabhadra taught Ngok Dharmakīrti's *Compendium of Valid Cognition* and *Drop of Reasoning*[53] along with Dharmottara's commentary on the former but is also said to have taught Candrakīrti's *Clear Words* to Mahāsumati, with whom Patsab translated it. Further, Patsab translated Āryadeva's *Four Hundred Stanzas* and Candrakīrti's commentary to it with Sūkṣmajana whose father, Sañjana, taught Ngok Maitreya's *Sublime Continuum*. Sūkṣmajana's grandfather, Mahājana, taught Ngok Maitreya's *Differentiating Phenomena and Noumena,* while his great-grandfather, Ratnavajra, is said to have taught Candrakīrti's *Clear Words* to Parahitabhadra.[54] Bhavyarāja collaborated with Ngok in translating Prajñākaragupta's commentary on Dharmakīrti's *Commentary on [Dignāga's] Valid Cognition,* as well as revising Dharmakīrti's text; he worked with Patsab on the translation of Dharmottara's *Proof of Future Lives.*[55]

Some of these examples, where Kashmiri is seen teaching a text to Kashmiri, may only represent Tibetan attempts to fill in Indian lineages with the names of famed scholars. However, the colophons to the translations mentioned above allow us greater certainty that Ngok and Patsab indeed studied in the same circles. We see many Kashmiri teachers renowned as experts in quite disparate Buddhist literature and that at least some Kashmiris were well familiar with Candrakīrti's writings in the late eleventh century, but not to the exclusion of other studies. Candrakīrti's views, while known in learned, ecumenical Buddhist circles of eleventh-century Kashmir, only became the focus for competing schools of Buddhist thought when Patsab arrived in Central Tibet, with Kanakavarman and Tilakakalaśa in tow, shortly after the year 1100.

There are numerous accounts that Atiśa established Prāsaṅgika in Tibet and that, as discussed in the previous chapter, Atiśa clearly favored Candrakīrti's interpretation of the ultimate. While it might be possible to assume the Kadampas likewise would commit to this preference, there are instead a great variety of doctrinal positions taking the Kadampa name. Naktso, a student of Atiśa, made the first Tibetan translation of Candrakīrti's *Entrance to the Middle* (the stanzas, without autocommentary).[56] However, it is not known to what extent the *Entrance to the Middle* stanzas were taught; without an active teaching tradition and lacking Candrakīrti's autocommentary (as well as Candrakīrti's lengthier companion text, *Clear Words*) Tibetans would have had little hope of appreciating the subtleties in Candrakīrti's writings that led Atiśa to proclaim them as the superior interpretation of Madhyamaka. In the nearly fifty years between Atiśa's death and Patsab's return to Central Tibet, Ngok Lekpay Sherab—also a student of Atiśa's—built Sangpu and his nephew, Ngok Loden Sherab, established it as the pre-eminent center of scholastic Buddhism (witness an account of Loden Sherab's 23,000 students). Thus, rather than a Tibet converted to Prāsaṅgika by Atiśa, Patsab returned to find the study of Buddhist philosophy flourishing in the absence of translations of Candrakīrti's most important texts.

Patsab was not immediately successful in establishing his teaching of Candrakīrti's texts. With Kanakavarman and Tilakakalaśa, he worked at two of Lhasa's most ancient temples, Ramoche and Lhasa Trulnang,[57] revising his translations of Candrakīrti's *Entrance to the Middle* and *Clear Words*—on the basis of manuscripts different from those he had used in Kashmir[58]—as well as revising again Nāgārjuna's *Fundamental Treatise on the Middle.* We have no certainty as to when he moved to Gyel Lhakang,[59] built by another of Lumé's "Four Pillars," near Patsab's birthplace north of Lhasa. There, the Kadampa teacher Sharwapa sent his own students to study Madhyamaka with Patsab;[60] one wonders if Atiśa's Prāsaṅgika preference survived in some Kadampa circles, where the appearance of Candrakīrti's writings in Tibetan was eagerly awaited. In any case, at some time prior to Patsab's death shortly after 1140,[61] Gyel Lhakang became the Tibetan center for Prāsaṅgika and for the study of Nāgārjuna's treatises, based mainly on Patsab's translation and teaching activities.[62] Both Patsab's and Ngok's monasteries were affiliated with the Kadampa order but were supported by competing districts: Gyel Lhakang by the Lumé district, Sangpu by the Dring district. It could well be that these competing districts helped foster unique monastic curricula and doctrinal interpretations, under the aegis of Kadampa's prestige.

What was it about Ngok's and Patsab's translation and teaching activities that led to successful and competing centers of philosophical study? We might first suggest that the quality of their respective translations led to their successes. Saito has shown that Patsab's translation of Nāgārjuna's *Fundamental Treatise on the Middle,* embedded within his translation of Candrakīrti's *Clear Words,* follows the much older translation of Lui Gyeltsen[63] in places where the older translation is clearly incorrect.[64] The accuracy of Patsab's translation, then, could not be a reason for his popularity as a teacher of Nāgārjuna's opus. Additionally, Patsab's re-translation of the stanzas of Candrakīrti's *Entrance to the Middle* and his editing of the earlier translation reveal his selective interest in what he must have considered the "most important" parts of Candrakīrti's text.[65] More generally, we can note that translation, the accuracy of which most Tibetans would not have been in a position to judge, was not a simple matter of substituting Tibetan correspondences for Sanskrit originals but varied both depending on the commentarial tradition that a translator followed and the semantic connotations the translator wished to evoke. Nor can we point to readability as a reason for the translations' success, as translation produces a Tibetan that would have been incomprehensible to literate Tibetans who did not know Sanskrit.

This brings up an interesting point. The Sanskritized Tibetan of translations points to a pressing need for exegesis: translations would require the translator's explanation in order to become meaningful to Tibetans.[66] While translations bore the prestige of Indian textual authenticity, the translators themselves carried an interpretive power with which to teach and form monastic curricula, born of their long years of study with Indian paṇḍitas.[67] While there is limited evidence of Patsab's authorial activities, his status as a teacher of Nāgārjuna and Candrakīrti is unquestionable. Ngok was known to have authored many summaries and commentaries on Epistemological texts, Madhyamaka, and all five of the Maitreya texts. Ngok's compositions can be seen as a direct extension of his teaching role; both his translations and the texts that he inherited from the imperial era required elucidation, which would fuel formal commentary.[68] Though evidence is limited, Ngok and his immediate followers seem to have made primary use of commentarial techniques that restructure an Indian text according to the text's perceived meaning, rather than following the text's own order in a word-by-word fashion.[69] This technique pushes the translated text to the background, retaining the prestige of Sanskrit while foregrounding the commentator's interpretation.[70] Ngok's extensive use of this genre reflects the curriculum he established at Sangpu, encompassing a broader Indian literature than simply the texts he translated.[71] Further, commentary and summary may have additionally operated as a way for new translators to stake a claim to the old texts remaining from the early translation period.[72] While Ngok did not re-translate "The Three Mādhyamikas from the East," these texts became part of Sangpu's Madhyamaka position based on Ngok's commentary and summaries.

Translations, teaching, and commentary weave further threads through the already complex relationships between clans and monastic networks. When translations consisted of certain Perfection of Wisdom sūtras, or especially tantras, the texts contributed directly to the ritual life of the community, in addition to its curriculum. The fact that Patsab translated the lengthy *Guhyasamāja Tantra* suggests that tantric ritual and contemplation figured prominently in his thinking.[73] Ngok's translations and known compositions stick to non-tantric, philosophical materials, yet there are references in his biography to his tantric practice;[74] indeed, it would be a rare exception were tantra not a part of the broader Sangpu community. While community ritual extends to a wider circle of monastics than a textual curriculum would, and so represents a more pervasive communal bond, we cannot underestimate the importance of learning in forming monastic identity and worldview. Thus, the value of Ngok's and Patsab's translation, teaching, and composition efforts must be measured in the successes of their communities, in addition to the lasting intellectual value their work had for future generations of Tibetan scholars. These Tibetan communities centered at least in part on Ngok's and Patsab's translations and compositions, texts that came to form competing practical canons for these communities.

Ngok's and Patsab's roles changed dramatically upon their respective returns to Central Tibet, from student and translator to teacher, author, and (for Ngok) monastic abbot. Their translations stood as the basis for teaching and commentary, giving shape to a curriculum while at the same time serving to authenticate it. The legitimacy the two gained through their lengthy sojourns in Kashmir added to their translations' authority, in turn contributing to their teaching popularity. Built as they were on divergent visions of Buddhist scripture, their institutes' successes would bring conflict over a nexus of issues that centered on the validity of human cognition in the attainment of buddhahood. Although these visions were known during eleventh-century India, it was only when they became the textual bases of competing Tibetan monastic institutes that they became codified into separate Buddhist schools.

Texts in Conflict and the Scholastic Solution

The proximity of Sangpu and Gyel Lhakang to Lhasa—to the south and north, respectively—made conflict between their competing visions of Buddhist doctrine certain to arise. It is feasible that Ngok was familiar with Candrakīrti's writings, given his connections in Kashmir with the same teachers with whom Patsab studied; one can also assume on the same grounds that he was familiar with Patsab. However, the current lack of Ngok's Madhyamaka writings coupled with uncertainty as to exactly when Patsab's fame began to grow prevent us from knowing whether this debate began in the roughly ten years between Patsab's return to Central Tibet just after 1100 and prior to Ngok's death in 1109, or only later.

The recently available texts from Kadampa authors in the generation following Ngok Loden Sherab may, when fully explored, attest to the growing impact of Prāsaṅgika. Presently, it is clear that Drolungpa, one of Ngok's main students and Chapa's teacher of the Perfection of Wisdom literature, does not mention Candrakīrti in his list of Indian commentators to Nāgārjuna, suggesting that Candrakīrti's fame had yet to grow at this time.[75] Drolungpa does engage an opponent who states that only consequential reasoning (*thal 'gyur, prasaṅga*) is valid when arguing about imputed phenomena (*brtags pa'i chos can*), while "real valid cognition in one's own continuum" (*tshad ma dngos rang rgyud pa*) is not valid.[76] While discussions of consequential reasoning abound in Indian Epistemological literature, this particular framing recalls Candrakīrti's critique of inferential reasoning in the first chapter of his *Clear Words.* As Cabezón discusses, Drolungpa's discussion of how inferential reasoning is utilized in coming to realize the ultimate, which he understands to be ineffable, is a creative synthesis of Madhyamaka and Epistemological ideals inherited from his teacher, Ngok.[77] As will be discussed at length herein, an utterly ineffable ultimate became one of the defining features of the twelfth-century Prāsaṅgika movement, while upholding the utility of inference in knowing the ultimate became a signature of Candrakīrti's detractors. That Drolungpa was able to hold both positions—an ineffable ultimate that is still within the purview of inference—in defense of his teacher, Ngok, suggests that Tibetan Madhyamaka had yet to be polarized by this debate.[78]

At present, it is certain only that Candrakīrti's ideas gained sufficient prominence to provoke a lengthy critique by the sixth Sangpu abbot, Chapa Chokyi Sengé (*Phya pa Chos kyi seng ge,* 1109–69). Despite the fairly close proximity of Sangpu and Gyel Lhakang, it may have been Jayānanda's travels in Central Tibet that engendered the clash between their readings of Buddhist literature. Jayānanda worked closely with Khu Dodebar on translating several of Nāgārjuna's writings, including a revision of Nāgārjuna's *Refutation of Objections,*[79] and translating his own *Hammer of Logic,* a text that begins with a direct criticism of "logicians following Dharmakīrti."[80] That he promoted Candrakīrti's interpretation of Nāgārjuna's Madhyamaka is certain from his lengthy commentary to Candrakīrti's *Entrance to the Middle,* which was, however, composed after his stay in Central Tibet. He also worked at least once with Patsab Nyimadrak, in addition to Khu Dodebar, on the translation of Atiśa's *Compendium of Sūtras,* at the request of Patsab's supporter, Sharwapa.[81] We see reports that Jayānanda met Chapa Chokyi Sengé at Sangpu in order to debate the merits of Candrakīrti's interpretation of Madhyamaka; Chapa is said to have prevailed.[82] Following his stay in Central Tibet, Jayānanda traveled to the Tangut kingdom, Xi-xia, where he took part in the massive translation project from Chinese, Tibetan, and Sanskrit sources into the Tangut language.[83] There, he also wrote his commentary to Candrakīrti's *Entrance to the Middle.*

While the particulars of Jayānanda's travels, translations, and writings are not found, I propose this tentative chronology. Jayānanda worked with Khu Dodebar prior to leaving Central Tibet for Xi-xia. The ability to date Khu

Dodebar would aid us in placing a likely year on Jayānanda's arrival in Central Tibet. We know that Khu was also a student of Patsab Nyimadrak, and that Khu and Jayānanda worked with Patsab. Jayānanda also worked with another of Patsab Nyimadrak's students, Patsab Gomnag, who went to Xi-xia with Jayānanda and the Tibetan Kungadrak.[84] Jayānanda was thus active in Central Tibet with Patsab Nyimadrak's junior contemporaries, suggesting that Patsab's reputation as a teacher had already been made; this was likely between 1120 and 1140. Stressing further Jayānanda's relations with Patsab's students and not Patsab himself, we should note that Jayānanda's commentary on Candrakīrti's *Entrance to the Middle* contains many citations of this text and one lengthy citation of Candrakīrti's *Clear Words* that differ markedly from Patsab's translations of the same texts.[85] Jayānanda certainly did not make use of Patsab's translations of Candrakīrti when translating his own composition into Tibetan.

During the reign of the Tangut emperor Renzong (or Renxiao; r. 1139–93) Jayānanda worked in Xi-xia, holding the position of National Preceptor (*guoshi*), with Kungadrak, who served as Dharma Preceptor (*fashi*).[86] Jayānanda wrote his commentary on Candrakīrti's *Entrance to the Middle* in this time and worked on its translation with Kungadrak. While Indian Buddhists were known in Tangut lands from at least 980, and ethnic Tibetans from the neighboring Kokonor region were a constant presence among the Tanguts, Tangut relations with Song China were much more vital, if antagonistic, than relations with its western neighbors until the Jurchen conquest of North China in 1126.[87] Renzong initiated the office of Imperial Preceptor and staffed it with Tibetan monks after 1149.[88] This date is a likely terminus for Jayānanda's sojourn in Central Tibet.

Jayānanda was active in Central Tibet during Chapa Chokyi Sengé's maturity, thus lending some credibility to the report that the two met at Sangpu. Jayānanda's commentary on Candrakīrti's *Entrance to the Middle* had yet to be written during this period; only his *Hammer of Logic* would have been known to Chapa and his contemporaries. Chapa's lengthy critique of Candrakīrti's views in his *Compilation of the Three Mādhyamikas from the East*[89] was clearly written in knowledge of a contemporary portrayal of Prāsaṅgika and not only in response to Candrakīrti's texts. Indeed, it was written in knowledge of Jayānanda's "smashing" the conventions of valid cognition with his *Hammer of Logic* and Jayānanda's presentation, yet unwritten, of Candrakīrti's views.[90] Jayānanda's commentary, in turn, was written in knowledge of and at least partially in response to Chapa's critique of Candrakīrti's understanding of buddhahood.[91] The cross-pollination between Candrakīrti's critique of valid cognition, as portrayed by several important Indian scholars of this period, and the Sangpu tradition that actively propagated Dharmakīrti's epistemology stemmed from the contact, either personally or literarily, between Jayānanda and Chapa.

Chapa's critique of Prāsaṅgika clearly identifies the philosophical concerns at stake in these interpretations of the Middle Way. As discussed in detail in subsequent chapters, the debate focused on a nexus of issues: whether or not human consciousness, prior to the direct realization of emptiness, could be considered valid cognition; whether or not formal inference could be utilized in knowing emptiness; and whether or not a Buddha has cognitive events of any kind—indeed, whether or not the state of buddhahood bears any recognizable relationship to our own mundane state. Chapa's affirmative stance on these issues, and the close relationship he saw between the conventions of valid cognition and knowledge of emptiness, set a course that most Tibetan scholarship would later follow. However, during his lifetime, some of Chapa's best students left him in order to study Prāsaṅgika with Jayānanda and Patsab.[92] This loss signals a shift in Central Tibet away from the Sangpu position—which in this period bore the label "Svātantrika"[93]—toward Prāsaṅgika. Just as the contact between Jayānanda and Chapa began the active debate between these conflicting positions, Chapa's "loss" engendered a new type of Prāsaṅgika, one which had to account for Chapa's many and pertinent criticisms. Accommodating the conventions of valid cognition within a Prāsaṅgika view—which to Chapa and Jayānanda would seem ludicrous—would become a hallmark of Tibetan Prāsaṅgika exegesis, the implications of which are still elaborated upon in present-day Tibetan monasteries.

Three of Chapa's students eventually departed from their teacher in order to study Prāsaṅgika: Tsang Nakpa Tsondru Senge[94] studied with Patsab Nyimadrak; Mabja Jangchub Tsondru[95] studied with Jayānanda, Khu Dodebar, and Patsab; and Tsur Zhonu Senge[96] studied Prāsaṅgika with Tsang Nakpa and Mabja. Mabja's study with Jayānanda and Khu Dodebar suggests that his interest in Prāsaṅgika sprang from Jayānanda's physical or literary presence at Sangpu. Mabja wrote a commentary, not presently available, on Jayānanda's *Hammer of Logic*,[97] a text translated into Tibetan (and perhaps even composed) during Jayānanda's stay in Central Tibet and so very likely known at Sangpu. Mabja also taught *Hammer of Logic* to Tsur Zhonu Senge.[98] Mabja's commentary on *Hammer of Logic* seems to have been the locus for his extensive discussion of a Mādhyamika's use of the conventions of valid cognition, on which Mabja maintained a decidedly Prāsaṅgika stance.[99] It could well be that *Hammer of Logic* swayed Mabja away from Chapa's positions and led to his "conversion" to the Prāsaṅgika view, which he then studied in full with Jayānanda and, following Jayānanda's departure to Tangut lands, with Patsab. This would explain how Mabja is credited with uniting the two Tibetan transmissions of Candrakīrti's writings—that stemming from Patsab and that stemming from Jayānanda.[100]

Given Chapa's interests, his students would have been well-versed in the Buddhist Epistemological tradition that Jayānanda so heatedly criticized. At least one of his students wrote in the Epistemological tradition: Tsang Nakpa's commentary on Dharmakīrti's *Compendium of Valid Cognition* survives into the present.[101] The dispersion of his students should not be seen as a rejection of Chapa's epistemological project. Rather, their adoption of Prāsaṅgika began the process of conjoining Candrakīrti's writings with epistemological pursuits, a process that Jayānanda certainly, and Candrakīrti likely, would have found distasteful. While Mabja certainly did break away from Chapa, he did not fully abandon Sangpu's epistemological tradition but rather applied his early experience and training in defending Prāsaṅgika against Chapa's epistemological critique. As will be discussed at length, the most significant of Mabja's presently-known texts, a commentary on Nāgārjuna's *Fundamental Treatise on the Middle* called the *Ornament of Disputation,*[102] evinces several developments in a Prāsaṅgika position that are not known to have been held by Patsab and were not advocated by Jayānanda.

Specifically, referring to the debate over whether a Mādhyamika may employ formal inference, Mabja allowed that a Mādhyamika may hold a positive thesis (a thesis maintaining the establishment of something) conventionally.[103] Mabja states this immediately after citing two positions that later authors attribute to Patsab and Khu Dodebar, respectively, the former holding that a Mādhyamika may only hold a negative thesis (a thesis maintaining the refutation of something) and the latter holding that a Mādhyamika can hold no thesis at all.[104] Following Jayānanda's and possibly Patsab's idea, Mabja maintains that "objectively gained valid cognition" does not exist, an idea anathema to Chapa.[105] Mabja also writes that a Mādhyamika's use of logical consequences does not imply the statement of a formal inference,[106] directly answering Chapa's claim that any effective logical consequence operates on the same grounds as, and comes to be identical to, formal inference (see the Materials section). Mabja's views evince a split from Chapa's standpoints and also a development from his Prāsaṅgika teachers that incorporates certain epistemological perspectives and argues against others.

Not all of Chapa's students abandoned his anti-Prāsaṅgika polemic. The second Sakya hierarch, Sonam Tsemo (1142–82),[107] studied with Chapa and wrote a commentary on Śāntideva's *Engaging in the Bodhisattva's Practices* that, according to its colophon, was written according to Chapa's teachings.[108] In fact, it is within his commentary to Śāntideva's famed text that is found the earliest known use of "Prāsaṅgika" and "Svātantrika" to distinguish interpretations of the Middle Way. Sonam Tsemo first uses these terms to distinguish two arguments concerning a Buddha's ability to perceive the things that appear to our ordinary consciousnesses (*snang bcas kyi blo*): Prāsaṅgikas hold that Buddhas do not have this ability because perceiving ordinary appearances entails one's entrapment in saṃsāra; Svātantrikas maintain that Buddhas have "conventional wisdom" (*ye shes kun rdzob*) that allows them to perceive ordinary appearances without these perceptions acting as a cause for saṃsāra.[109] Following his report of the Prāsaṅgika view, Sonam Tsemo states "That is not correct," then proceeds to state and endorse the Svātantrika position.[110] On this issue, among others, Sonam Tsemo clearly maintains a Svātantrika position, in keeping with Chapa's views.

Sonam Tsemo further employs the terms "Svātantrika" and "Prāsaṅgika" in listing arguments concerning the possibility of worldly valid cognition. Svātantrikas maintain its necessity, noting that if there were no worldly valid cognition, meditation on emptiness would be pointless. Two varying Prāsaṅgika viewpoints refute worldly valid cognition, one maintaining that all minds are erroneous (*mṛṣā, rdzun pa*) and thereby not valid (the extension of this view is that Buddhas do not have minds) and the other holding that "mere yogic conventional [minds]" (*rnal 'byor gyi kun rdzob tsam*), while still erroneous, can be utilized to refute an opponent's wrong conceptions.[111] Unfortunately, Sonam Tsemo does not authoritatively comment here on the validity of one side or the other. However, both passages in which he uses "Svātantrika" and "Prāsaṅgika" offer more information on the issues that separated these developing schools of exegesis in the latter part of the twelfth-century. Prāsaṅgikas hold a stark divide between saṃsāra and nirvāṇa, disallowing that a Buddha has any mental state concordant with saṃsāra and negating any possibility that worldly consciousness can validly know the ultimate. Svātantrikas soften this divide, offering solutions for how a Buddha still perceives what we perceive and how our states of mind can eliminate false views and develop insight into the ultimate.

The third Sakya hierarch and Sonam Tsemo's younger brother, Drakpa Gyeltsen (1147–1216), offers further insight into the manifold interpretations of Madhyamaka, and the early arguments dividing the Prāsaṅgika and Svātantrika interpretations.[112] His *Clearly Realizing Tantra: A Precious Tree* includes a doxographical section that, when dividing types of Madhyamaka, does not use the terms "Prāsaṅgika" and "Svātantrika" but instead employs a five-fold division of Madhyamaka according to assertions on conventional truth. One of these divisions, "Mādhyamikas of Worldly Renown" (*'jig rten grags sde pa*), is understood by later commentators to encompass followers of Candrakīrti's thought.[113] Later in his text, when discussing whether Buddhas have conventional states of mind or only ultimate states, Drakpa Gyeltsen recounts four separate views, calling the last two "Prāsaṅgika" and "Svātantrika."[114] This presentation allows us to see that the issues that the new Prāsaṅgika interpretation engendered did not, in Drakpa Gyeltsen's estimation, concern issues of conventional truth but centered around the relationship between a Buddha's rarefied consciousness (although some in this debate would not accept the label "consciousness") and the objects perceived by our ordinary consciousness.

Drakpa Gyeltsen devotes no small effort discussing the various views on the relationships between a Buddha's consciousness and ordinary states of mind, and further between our ordinary states of mind and emptiness. He considers Yogācāra-Madhyamaka views on nirvāṇa, followed by two unattributed views, one of which appears to be a Prāsaṅgika answer to Chapa's criticisms (discussed in chapter 5) that the Prāsaṅgika presentation of nirvāṇa amounts to nihilism.[115] In order to distinguish Prāsaṅgika from Svātantrika, Drakpa Gyeltsen looks at Madhyamaka debates that clearly center on various interpretations of how realization of emptiness is made, what transformations that realization entails, and how one so transformed relates to the ordinary world—and not on how various Mādhyamikas posit conventional establishment.

Drakpa Gyeltsen's text is extraordinarily valuable for the many interpretations it presents as well as the insights it offers into the progress of Candrakīrti's views. One might expect Drakpa Gyeltsen to express a strong Yogācāra-Madhyamaka view, following his older brother. And this is, in fact, evidenced in certain passages. When discussing the views on what state of mind a Buddha has, Drakpa favors the Svātantrika position on the grounds that it allows an explanation of non-abiding nirvāṇa.[116] However, when presenting the two truths, he approvingly cites Candrakīrti's authority, quoting *Entrance to the Middle* five times and Candrakīrti's commentary to Nāgārjuna's *Sixty Stanzas of Reasoning* twice.[117] One of these citations is given to criticize contemporary Tibetan Madhyamaka viewpoints (*da lta bod kyi dbu ma pa*) while another shows contemporary Prāsaṅgikas' variance from Candrakīrti's own writings.[118] Drakpa is clearly interested in Candrakīrti's views and aware of Chapa's critique of them. His writings, like Mabja Jangchub Tsondru's, evince criticism of the first generation of Tibetans who presented Candrakīrti's teachings—identified as "contemporary Tibetans" or "Prāsaṅgikas"—and, perhaps, are an attempt to form a Prāsaṅgika that would accommodate the epistemological concerns of Chapa and others.

One final point on Drakpa Gyeltsen's allegiances concerns how to practice the Buddhist path according to a Madhyamaka view. In considering how one realizes emptiness and becomes a Buddha, Drakpa explores the relationships between ordinary consciousness and emptiness, and between a Buddha's consciousness and human consciousnesses. Again, Drakpa Gyeltsen does not clearly express his allegiance to Prāsaṅgika or Svātantrika. He enjoins "those who have faith in Madhyamaka" to train in accordance with Nāgārjuna's *Precious Garland,* Śāntideva's *Engaging in the Bodhisattva's Practices,* and Candrakīrti's *Entrance to the Middle.*[119] This somewhat laconic statement leaves us to wonder why Drakpa Gyeltsen advocates Candrakīrti's text: for its unique presentation of emptiness or for its presentation of the stages of the bodhisattva's path. Later in his text, addressing the issue of how one practices within the doctrine of "emptiness free from extremes," Drakpa Gyeltsen enjoins "practice in the mode of union."[120] As noted above, he equates "Union Thoroughly Non-Abiding [Mādhyamikas]" with Svātantrika-Mādhyamikas. He may then be suggesting that a Svātantrika view is in better line with the practical realization of the Madhyamaka view. However, the texts that he cites in explaining this mode of practice are not Madhyamaka sources, but mostly include tantras,[121] suggesting that he may be advocating tantric practice at this point in his explanation.

The famed nephew of Sonam Tsemo and Drakpa Gyeltsen and the fourth Sakya hierarch, Sakya Paṇḍita Kunga Gyeltsen (1182–1251), may have ended this period of contested Madhyamaka exegesis when he adopted the Prāsaṅgika view.[122] Sapaṇ studied Candrakīrti's *Clear Words* and Jayānanda's *Hammer of Logic* with one of Chapa's lost students, Tsur Zhonu Senge, and Candrakīrti's *Entrance to the Middle* with Drakpa Gyeltsen.[123] Sapaṇ's well-known association with Śākya Śrībhadra and his entourage, including Vibhūticandra who—following Prajñākaramati—linked Candrakīrti's and Śāntideva's views, likely was also a critical influence on his Madhyamaka views. Through his study with Śākya Śrībhadra, Sapaṇ broke the Sangpu monopoly over Dharmakīrti's corpus, making Sakya a center for Buddhist epistemology. His development of a philosophical curriculum at Sakya marks a new turn in Tibetan attempts, begun by Mabja, to work out Buddhist epistemological issues within a Prāsaṅgika view. The broad acceptance of his epistemological views, consistent with—rather than antagonistic to—Candrakīrti's writings, may mark the beginning of Prāsaṅgika's ultimate authority in Central Tibet in the early thirteenth century.

Conclusion: Prāsaṅgika and Svātantrika Schools

The Tibetan evidence of Candrakīrti's impact in the twelfth century shows that although his writings evoked controversy in India, it was the magnification and crystallization of these disputes in Tibet that produced two competing movements of Madhyamaka exegesis. The Prāsaṅgika movement, whether faithful to Candrakīrti or not, championed his writings for their denial of the validity of human intellect in realizing buddhahood, and their concomitant radical separation between ordinary consciousnesses and a Buddha's refined (non-)mental state. The Svātantrika movement, formed in reaction to Prāsaṅgika, maintained the necessity of formal inference to see through the illusions of sensory data and to gain a reasoned knowledge of emptiness. In this view, human intellect can validly know the ultimate and, once transformed, can still validly know the ordinary world. Whatever the value and accuracy of later doxographies, adherence to these two positions is the meaning of "Prāsaṅgika" and "Svātantrika," respectively, in the initial branding of these terms.

While the intellectual issues at stake come into greater focus, two sets of problems remain. The first concerns the relationships between monastic institutions, the socio-political districts that came to define Central Tibet in the eleventh century, and the broader political powers of the region. I have suggested that the communal nature of doctrinal texts would intertwine the fortunes of philosophical positions and their monastic homes. When we are better able to gauge the roles monasteries played in the political life of districts, we may find that the kinds of doctrinal and curricular competition that I have traced here went hand-in-hand with a more basic competition over territorial control. We may find that the relative successes of these districts played an important role in the fortunes of the philosophical positions of Prāsaṅgika and Svātantrika. At the very least, we will be in a position to understand better the processes through which competing networks of monasteries took the shape of enduring religious orders, with their characteristic doctrines and practices.

Sakya Paṇḍita's ties with the Mongol kingdom are well known and put him and his successors in a position to influence a broad swath of Tibetan monasticism. His adoption of Prāsaṅgika, then, may have had repercussions beyond Sakya. However, Central Tibetan political relationships with its neighbors in the twelfth century are more poorly understood. As research into the Tangut kingdom and its adoption of Buddhism develops, we may find that the courting of foreign patronage played a significant role in the successes of Central Tibet's districts and, in turn, in the fortunes of fledgling religious orders. We know, for instance, that the first Karmapa, Dusum Kyenpa,[124] and the founder of the Drikung Kagyu order, Jigten Gonpo,[125] had strong connections with the Tangut court. It is likely that when the Mongols overran the Tangut kingdom in 1227, they inherited a long-established system of patronage of Tibetan orders.[126] The connections we have already seen between Jayānanda (and his Tibetan collaborators) and Tangut royalty make it plausible that his Prāsaṅgika view took greater weight due to this association. While Jayānanda is remembered in Tibetan histories as something of a failure following his defeat in debate to Chapa, his influence from afar on Central Tibet's intellectual life may well have given him the last laugh.

The second set of issues left unresolved here concerns the historical realignment of the Svātantrika-Prāsaṅgika debate. The disputes of this period did not simply vanish with Prāsaṅgika's ascendancy, but continued to inform Middle Way thinking, surfacing in the writings of many Tibetans over the ensuing centuries. As we develop a more complete picture of Tibetan intellectual history, we will be able to trace shifting constellations of viewpoints, with positions that in the twelfth century were argued for under the "Svātantrika" banner being adopted by later "Prāsaṅgika" authors. The process that Mabja Jangchub Tsondru began—the development of Prāsaṅgika answers to Chapa's epistemological critique—would continue for centuries. The zenith of this trajectory (or the nadir, depending on one's perspective) undoubtedly is found in the refined Gelukpa synthesis of Candrakīrti's Middle Way and Dharmakīrti's logic. In the Gelukpa treatment, Prāsaṅgika came to stand for several positions that Chapa argued for, against the twelfth-century proponents of Candrakīrti. However, other Tibetan scholars would reject this synthesis,[127] adopting arguments against the Gelukpa not unlike Jayānanda's critique of Chapa. These developments are complex and fall well beyond the scope of this present work. Here, instead, we turn to a detailed analysis of the twelfth-century philosophical disputes that animate the Svātantrika-Prāsaṅgika divide, beginning with the two sides' conflicting views on the value of human intellect.

3. Taxonomies of Ignorance, Debates on Validity

Buddhist thinkers are committed to the doctrine that ignorance is the fundamental fault that binds human beings to suffering. This truism has created a long-standing tension for those Buddhists who uphold the value of human intellect and yet harbor a radical suspicion of its ultimate utility. On one hand, cultivating the intellect allows us to move beyond the duplicitous appearances given to our senses. On the other hand, the Madhyamaka claim that ultimate truth, emptiness, is ineffable and unknowable implies a circumscription of mind and language. Indeed, "emptiness" suggests an erosion of both the objects of our senses and the very foundations of knowledge. If we portray the Buddhist Epistemological tradition, stemming from the seminal works of Dignāga and Dharmakīrti, as defenders of the intellect's utility and (at least some) Mādhyamikas as supporters of a transcendent ultimate,[1] we can begin to appreciate the difficulties facing those who would endorse the intellect's salvific importance in a world that, in the end, is empty. Candrakīrti's ascension in Tibet brought this long-standing tension to a head, engendering Madhyamaka disputes concerning the very possibility of human valid cognition and both of its instances, perception and inference.

A brief consideration of some of the basic features of the Buddhist Epistemological tradition will help us to appreciate the contours of the debates that played out in twelfth-century Madhyamaka circles. Taking the guise of a commentator on Dignāga's (c. 480–540) work, Dharmakīrti (c. 540–600)[2] was the first to characterize valid cognition, defining it as "non-deceptive" (*avisaṃvādin, bslu med can*) and "the revealing of a yet unknown thing,"[3] two definitions that might seem to run counter to the Buddhist maxim that sentient beings are fundamentally ignorant. Both Dignāga and Dharmakīrti explain that valid cognition (*pramāṇa, tshad ma*) has two types, perception (*pratyakṣa, mngon sum*) and inference (*anumāna, rjes dpag*), and yet both indicate that inference is in some sense a lesser valid cognition than perception.[4] Dignāga defined perception as "free from conceptuality," a characteristic that inference does not share; his initial discussion of inference lists it along with "mistaken cognition" and "cognition of the conventional" as types of pseudo-perceptions.[5] Devendrabuddhi, Dharmakīrti's earliest commentator, makes explicit that Dharmakīrti's first definition of valid cognition extends to both forms, perception and inference.[6] However, Devendrabuddhi understands Dharmakīrti to exclude inference from his second definition of valid cognition, stating that "consciousnesses of universals are not valid cognitions according to this particular definition."[7] Devendrabuddhi explains that only the unmistaken (*abhrānta, 'khrul pa med pa*) consciousness of particulars—that is, valid perception—meets the criterion of the second definition. Elsewhere, Dharmakīrti himself declares that inference is mistaken but is still valid cognition due to being non-deceptive.[8]

What does it mean for inference to be non-deceptive, and so meet Dharmakīrti's first definition of valid cognition, but mistaken, and so—in Devendrabuddhi's estimation—fall short of Dharmakīrti's second definition? Two lines of commentary attempted to sort out this conundrum. Dharmottara (750–810) explains that while perception is unmistaken, "inference is mistaken because it engages its appearing object by way of conceiving what is not a real object to be a real object."[9] In this explanation, "mistaken" hinges on inference's conceptual nature, on inference operating not upon the real particulars of objects but on a conceptual image, which it mistakenly holds as the real object. Dharmottara's explanation would seem to account for the second-class validity that both Dignāga and Dharmakīrti ascribe to inference.[10]

A second line of commentary tended to erase the distinction between perception and inference. Vinītadeva (630–700) sees "unmistaken" and "non-deceptive" as equivalent terms, qualities that both perception and inference share.[11] Dharmottara's interpretation is predicated on two levels of valid cognition such that *some* status ascribed to perception cannot be true of inference. Vinītadeva will allow perception and inference to share in the same non-deceptive, unmistaken status, the two being non-conceptual and conceptual varieties of this status. We must be clear that we are not dealing with a simple matter of semantics but a debate on whether perception and inference are equally valid, the two already being set apart from all other types of human consciousness, which must be considered invalid.

One further distinction made in the Epistemological tradition requires our attention prior to examining Madhyamaka disputes over the validity of the very enterprise. Dharmakīrti speaks of "twofold inference,"[12] a statement that is explained by Karṇakagomin (fl. 800)[13] as referring to the separate categories, "inferences per force of fact" and "inferences dependent on scripture."[14] Inferences dependent on scripture allow one to know matters otherwise completely imperceptible (*atyantaparokṣa*) to the human mind through reliance on Buddhist scriptures; the workings of karma and rebirth belong to this class of phenomena. All other inferences fall into the former category, "inferences per force of fact" or "objectively gained inferences."[15] The Epistemological tradition here acknowledges that some things can be known through reliance on the Buddha's word alone. However, most things are in the sphere of logic, and can be known "objectively." As we will see, this robust characterization of the human intellect would draw the ire of early Prāsaṅgikas, who used this status to characterize and reject the Epistemological enterprise as a whole.[16]

Debates among Buddhist Epistemologists over the status of inference (is it non-deceptive? unmistaken? both?)—indeed, over how some types of human consciousness may be considered valid—form one important context for the eleventh- and twelfth-century debates that Candrakīrti's texts touched off in Tibet. One can immediately see how the Epistemologists' accounts would not be easily squared with the Madhyamaka assessment of fundamental delusion. The marriage of these two philosophical traditions, though, had a long history prior to the rise of Prāsaṅgika in the eleventh and twelfth centuries. Arguably, it reached its zenith in the work of Śāntarakṣita and Kamalaśīla, who so fully integrated Buddhist Epistemology with their interpretation of Nāgārjuna's Madhyamaka that they are viewed as important developers of both traditions.

Śāntarakṣita and Kamalaśīla nuance the Epistemologists' discussion of perception's "unmistaken" validity in order to account for Nāgārjuna's denial of nature. Sara McClintock notes the "sliding-scale" of analysis present in Śāntarakṣita's and Kamalaśīla's philosophy that allows them to consider Dharmakīrti's epistemology from a realist perspective, to adopt it on the level of conventional truth from an idealist perspective, and to move beyond it on the level of ultimate truth from their own Madhyamaka perspective.[17] On a purely realist level, the two can easily adopt Dharmakīrti's definition of perception as "free from conceptuality and unmistaken"; however, from the "idealist" Yogācāra perspective—which they adopt on the level of conventional truth and hold to be superior to the realist view—the appearance of objects external to a perceiving consciousness is said to be generated from mistaken consciousness: realism is mistaken in this interpretation.[18] Kamalaśīla further reconsiders the term "unmistaken" when analyzing perception from a Madhyamaka perspective. He states that because all objects are empty of either a unitary or multiple nature, they have the status of appearances to mistaken consciousness.[19] True unmistaken consciousness is the direct, non-conceptual, meditative realization of selflessness, the (only) real entity, which is established by valid cognition.[20] "Unmistaken" has shifted from the faithful correspondence between a perception and its external object to realization of the Madhyamaka view of the final nature of reality. Kamalaśīla has nuanced the notion of mistake, showing how ordinary perception can be considered valid while, in the end, only realization of emptiness is ultimately true.

Kamalaśīla's refined discussion of levels of "mistake" offers one highly successful way that Madhyamaka could be joined with Epistemology, suggestive of the Epistemological tradition's own debates on the levels of validity that might separate perception and inference. Candrakīrti's revivers argued vehemently against this marriage of philosophies, much as Candrakīrti had argued (to deaf ears) against Bhāvaviveka's adoption of elements of Dignāga's thought. Mādhyamikas with epistemological leanings were again forced to account for their adaptation of Dharmakīrti, to show how his philosophy was compatible within Madhyamaka without making its proponents "realists." The tensions endemic to a wedding of Nāgārjuna and Dharmakīrti were suddenly inescapable. The body of this chapter focuses on how these issues of perception and ignorance were argued among twelfth-century Mādhyamikas and how these arguments contributed toward forming the separate subschools, "Prāsaṅgika" and "Svātantrika." The two sides of this debate shaped a great deal of Tibetan Madhyamaka exegesis in the following centuries that managed to combine Candrakīrti's and Jayānanda's criticisms of valid cognition with the very edifices they argued against. Interweaving these two sides' texts gives us a taxonomy of human ignorance, ranging from the delusion that binds us in suffering to a useful sort of mistake that provides us conceptual understanding of extrasensory reality.

Mistaken Mind, Deceptive Mind

Perhaps counterintuitively, the point of entry into the eleventh- and twelfth-century Madhyamaka debates on perception and ignorance is Candrakīrti's interpretation of the "two truths," a central topic of Madhyamaka exegesis since Nāgārjuna's *Fundamental Treatise on the Middle*.[21] Tillemans has noted that Candrakīrti's presentation of the two truths, in his *Entrance to the Middle,* bears directly on his denial that perception can correctly access a "given."[22] Candrakīrti's text reads:[23]

> The object [found by][24] correct seeing is suchness;
> That [found by] erroneous seeing is called conventional truth.

While this passage can be construed variously, the most straightforward reading is that Candrakīrti sharply bifurcates consciousness into "correct," that is, a direct perception of emptiness, and "erroneous," which would seem to be all other cognition. Recalling the manner in which Kamalaśīla nuanced levels of perception according to realist, idealist, and Madhyamaka viewpoints, allowing for perception to be unmistaken in a variety of ways other than being the ultimate direct perception of emptiness, Candrakīrti's proclamation could well be taken, around the year 1000, as a return to a simpler method of delineating states of consciousness.

Upon the circulation of Candrakīrti's writings in Central Tibet after Patsab's return around the year 1100, Candrakīrti's two truths became the focus of debates concerning the validity of his views.[25] Chapa Chokyi Sengé's *Compilation of the Three Mādhyamikas from the East,* which contains the lengthiest critique of Candrakīrti's views now extant—a critique structured around Candrakīrti's denial of the use of formal "inferences in one's own continuum"[26]—begins his discussion with "Candrakīrti's and others'" method of bifurcating consciousness into mistaken and unmistaken and their positing of the two truths as the respective objects of these two classes of consciousness.[27] Chapa makes clear that he sees Candrakīrti's position on this topic not as traditionalist but iconoclastic in its rejection of the refinements of the valid cognition enterprise.

In presenting the Prāsaṅgika position, Chapa makes two subtle moves. First, where Candrakīrti speaks of "erroneous" (*mṛṣā, rdzun pa*) and "correct" cognition, Chapa reads him as "mistaken" and "unmistaken." Secondly, Candrakīrti's "seeing" becomes Chapa's "consciousness." By making these subtle shifts, Chapa brings Candrakīrti's proclamation of the two truths to bear directly upon Kamalaśīla's levels of perception—and, consequently, the definition of valid cognition. Where Kamalaśīla worked out ways of designating various sorts of perceptions as unmistaken, thereby showing how some classes of ordinary human consciousness can be considered valid cognition, Chapa has Candrakīrti opposing the idea that any consciousness aside from the meditative equipoise of Buddhas and advanced bodhisattvas who are realizing the final nature (*dharmatā, chos nyid*)[28] could be valid. As

Candrakīrti, in this reading, opposes any ordinary valid cognition, the fact that the only valid cognition he holds is the meditative perception of emptiness directs Chapa's challenges toward his portrayal of perception.

When showing the criteria by which Prāsaṅgikas separate out, within the category of mistaken consciousness, both the perceptual illusions of those with defective sense organs and the wrong philosophies of non-Buddhists from useful (if still not "valid") cognition, Chapa again modifies Candrakīrti's words. Where Candrakīrti's *Entrance to the Middle* reads:

> Erroneous seeing has two aspects: clear faculties and faulty faculties. Consciousnesses from faulty faculties are asserted to be wrong relative to consciousnesses from good faculties.[29]

Chapa glosses the passage as "mistaken awareness of erroneous seeing."[30] He sees Prāsaṅgikas as dividing mistake into two groups: consciousnesses believed in the world to be veridical based upon unimpaired senses and mind; and those that superimpose objects—either due to defective senses, specious reasoning, or false beliefs—that are known not to exist even in the world.[31] The pragmatic line—worldly renown—that Chapa draws is well-attested in Candrakīrti's text (if not in the stanza Chapa here cites), as will be discussed below. Of note is that Chapa equates Candrakīrti's "erroneous" and "mistaken" and then bases his division in terms of the latter; all that the world agrees upon as true is still in the broad category of mistake. While this may seem to be an innocuous linguistic turn, again it pits Candrakīrti squarely against the notion of valid cognition. Chapa depicts Candrakīrti as equating all cognition excepting direct perception of emptiness with invalid cognition, thereby denying much of what Buddhists and non-Buddhists would accept as valid cognition.

Indeed, Chapa fleshes out Candrakīrti's category of mistaken cognitions that are renowned in the world to be true with the four types of valid cognition that were commonly accepted in Indian non-Buddhist philosophy (Buddhists accepted only the first two): direct perception (including both the perception of a person who believes that what appears is true and the perception of developed bodhisattvas, those who have "attained a ground," who do not conceive that the appearances outside of meditative equipoise are true), inference, testimony (from authoritative persons or texts), and analogy.[32] Appearance itself is filed under mistaken consciousness, even when a bodhisattva is able to see through those appearances, knowing that they are not as they appear. Mistake, Chapa has Candrakīrti say, is very broad;

validity is extremely narrow. To seal his case that Prāsaṅgikas deny that any worldly consciousness has the status of validity, Chapa cites Candrakīrti's *Entrance to the Middle,* stanza VI.30:

> If the world were valid cognition, the world would see suchness.
> What need would there be for the others, the Superiors, and what would be the use of the Superior path?
> How could foolishness be valid cognition?[33]

Chapa construes Candrakīrti's statement very literally: those who do not perceive appearances due to their advanced meditative state or (even better) enlightenment have valid cognition; all others experience "foolishness."

Having made his case for Prāsaṅgikas' opposition of ordinary human cognition and valid cognition, clinched with Candrakīrti's seeming equations of, on the one hand, valid cognition and seeing suchness and, on the other hand, the world and foolishness, Chapa turns to the respective referents of Candrakīrti's unmistaken and mistaken consciousnesses: his ultimate and obscurational truths. Appearances—all objects of knowledge (*jñeya, shes bya*)—to "the false perception of mistaken awareness"[34] are Candrakīrti's obscurational truths (in Chapa's wording). Grouping all objects of knowledge as obscurational truths plays on the equation between worldly "knowledge" and mistake: just as Candrakīrti (in Chapa's presentation) equates the categories of valid cognition accepted by Buddhists and non-Buddhists with mistake, so the objects of those cognitions are true only for obscuration. Chapa finds ample justification not just in the stanzas he cites (Candrakīrti's *Entrance to the Middle,* VI.25, 26, and 28) but Candrakīrti's proclamation (discussed at length in the following chapter) that ultimate truth is not an object of knowledge: if ultimate truth—the object of the only valid cognition—is not an object of knowledge, objects of knowledge are altogether the domain of mistaken, invalid cognition.

To explain the term "obscurational truth" (*saṃvṛtisatyaṃ, kun rdzob bden pa*), Chapa cites stanza VI.28 of *Entrance to the Middle,* but with one important variation. Candrakīrti's text reads "Delusion is an obscurer because it veils the nature."[35] This explanation draws on a passage from the *Descent into Laṅkā Sūtra,*[36] which equates "the nature" (*svabhāva, rang bzhin*) with "the final nature," ultimate truth: delusion obscures ultimate truth. Obscuring the "real" truth, delusion takes appearances to be true. Appearances are "true for obscuration"; they are "obscurational truths." While Chapa cites Candrakīrti's passage faithfully, he has the Prāsaṅgika explain that "Since we designate them to be true as referents of obscuring awarenesses, which [have] the nature of delusion that veils the pacification of the operation of awareness, they are obscurational truths."[37] Chapa's equation of obscuration and delusion is certainly true to Candrakīrti's writings; however, he turns around the meaning of this verse, making *svabhāva* mean simply "character"—"the nature/character of darkness"—whereas in Candrakīrti's stanza (expressed more clearly in the Sanskrit than in the Tibetan translation) it means "emptiness."

In reinterpreting "the nature" to mean "the character" of delusion, Chapa changes what is obscured or veiled from ultimate truth to "the pacification of the operation of awareness." Chapa subtly shifts attention from emptiness—which any Mādhyamika (including Chapa, as will be seen below) must admit stands apart from all things "known" by delusion—to a cognitive process with which he takes issue. As will be seen in chapter 5, Chapa argues at length against the notion—mentioned by Candrakīrti and elaborated upon by Jayānanda—that consciousness ceases its operation upon buddhahood. Emptiness is unassailable; it is the Prāsaṅgika's version of how one comes to realize emptiness and the utter disconnect that Chapa understands them to posit between ordinary consciousness and buddhahood that Chapa seeks to refute. For Chapa, Candrakīrti's two truths above all draw a rift between ordinary states of mind and Prāsaṅgika buddhahood, a rift that denies validity to ordinary consciousness and places emptiness entirely out of human scope.

Chapa further explains Candrakīrti's ultimate truth as "seeing nothing at all"[38] and "having no object to be observed at all due to mistake being extinguished in an ārya's meditative equipoise [on emptiness]."[39] "Realization" of ultimate truth is only called "realization"; actually, it is not a cognitive event at all as the operation of consciousness has ceased.[40] Chapa cites Candrakīrti's *Entrance to the Middle* stanza VI.29,[41] which compares emptiness to the absence of cataract-induced visions for someone who does not have cataracts, and stanza XII.4,[42] which compares "realization" of emptiness to the way ordinary perception is explained by many Buddhist realists: just as perception does not actually perceive an object but perceives only a mental representation of an object and yet we still call this "perception of an object", so it is with "realization" of emptiness. This "realization" has no object and, indeed, no subject: mistake is extinguished and, concomitantly, consciousness ceases. Chapa has Candrakīrti say that this cessation is the ultimate state.

In focusing on the Prāsaṅgikas' two truths, Chapa's principal interest is on the subjective correlates of these truths: he bases his presentation of Prāsaṅgika on a radical distinction between ordinary consciousness, invariably intertwined with error, and buddhahood, in which consciousness has ceased. This separation marks the fundamental problem Chapa sees in Prāsaṅgika. While Chapa clearly understands Candrakīrti and his followers to be wrongly denying inference any utility in understanding Madhyamaka emptiness, this broader denial of ordinary valid cognition is Chapa's starting point and primary concern. Chapa has Prāsaṅgika assert that any consciousness having an appearing object cannot be valid, even consciousnesses of advanced bodhisattvas who no longer assent to the veracity of appearances.[43] This portrayal of Candrakīrti interprets several crucial passages from his writings in a less than charitable manner, causing one to ask if this opposition is fair to Candrakīrti or, more importantly for this study, to his eleventh- and twelfth-century revivalists. Those familiar with the sophisticated Gelukpa synthesis of Candrakīrti and Dharmakīrti may be inclined to see Chapa's portrayal of Prāsaṅgika as both crude and inaccurate. Surely Candrakīrti's discussion of the difference between "clear faculties" and "faulty faculties," discussed above, could allow for some measure of valid consciousness in the world, even if we reject the full-blown Gelukpa fusion.[44] Rather than conclude that Chapa was simply wrong about Candrakīrti, we must look for the basis of Chapa's portrayal amid his Prāsaṅgika interlocutors, the twelfth-century exponents of Candrakīrti's views. Candrakīrti's champions, chief among them Jayānanda, provide ample support for Chapa's understanding of the new Prāsaṅgika.

Jayānanda's Two Truths

We have seen how Chapa's critique of Prāsaṅgika is predicated upon pitting Candrakīrti's two truths—more precisely, the worldly consciousnesses that cognize obscurational truths—against valid cognition, as defined (and modified) by followers of Dharmakīrti. Jayānanda's reading of Candrakīrti's two truths offers a similarly stark appraisal of the range of human intellect. He draws a radical separation between human intellect and a Buddha's mental state, causing one to wonder (as did Chapa) how the former could be developed into the latter. Such is the separation that the corresponding objects of these consciousnesses cannot be known by the other: ordinary minds cannot know emptiness while Buddhas cannot perceive the appearances that constitute reality for the rest of us. Jayānanda further draws out implications in Candrakīrti's writings to deduce levels of perception according to levels of ignorance. Jayānanda forms these conclusions around a small number of Candrakīrti's stanzas—which Chapa also draws upon—that do indeed facilitate his interpretation. Clearly, these select stanzas were the foci within Candrakīrti's writings around which Prāsaṅgika was either accepted or rejected in twelfth-century Tibet.

Jayānanda's comments center round his two-fold interpretation of "nature" in the first line of *Entrance to the Middle,* stanza VI.28, "Delusion is an obscurer because it veils the nature." Following Candrakīrti, Jayānanda glosses "delusion" with "ignorance" (*avidyā, ma rig pa*), the first of the twelve links of cyclic existence, and writes of its function in obscuring "the nature," emptiness.[45] Where Candrakīrti writes that delusion "veils the nature" and "The nature does not appear in any respect to the ignorant,"[46] Jayānanda states that delusion prevents suchness from appearing and obstructs perception of emptiness.[47] In this reading, "nature" clearly means "emptiness," which is inaccessible to the ignorant.

Candrakīrti's comments suggest Jayānanda's second reading of "nature", "the obscurer that has a nature of delusion,"[48] which is the same interpretation we saw Chapa give above. Both Candrakīrti and Jayānanda equate "the world" with delusion and with obscuration: Candrakīrti writes of obscurational truth as what is "true for the worldly, false obscurer"[49] while Jayānanda writes that, "the world knows only falsely."[50] This second interpretation of "nature" makes a sweeping correlation between the conventional world and delusion, while the first interpretation sets off emptiness from the conventional world—emptiness is veiled by the ignorance that characterizes ordinary consciousness.

Jayānanda elaborates upon delusion's nature of obscuring, noting its two aspects that respectively produce cyclic existence and ordinary appearances:

> Here, "veil" (*āvaraṇa, sgrib pa*) has two aspects: afflictive ignorance and non-afflictive ignorance. Of those, afflictive ignorance is the cause of one continually engaging cyclic existence. Non-afflictive ignorance is the cause of the appearance of form and so forth. The Conquerors have no capacity for either stain and hence, the absence of the causes [that is, the absence of both afflictive and non-afflictive ignorance] results in the absence of effects [that is, cyclic existence and appearance]. Therefore, there is no cyclic existence and no appearance of form and so forth; how could mere conventionalities appear?[51]

In separating the type of ignorance that causes entrapment in cyclic existence from the ignorance responsible for appearances, Jayānanda must separate obscurational (or conventional) truths from "mere conventionalities"[52] on the basis of whether appearances are conceived, or are not conceived, to be true. If appearances are intertwined with the conceptions "I" and "mine," then one is bound in cyclic existence; appearances, without the conception that these appearances are true, do not produce afflictive emotions and so do not entail entrapment.[53] The criterion, "conceived to be true," functions in two ways: it allows for the realization of "Hearers" (*śravaka*), "Solitary Buddhas" (*pratyekabuddha*), and Bodhisattvas (just what sort of bodhisattva will be discussed below) who do not conceive ordinary appearances to be true; and it separates out the perceptual illusions and false beliefs that are not considered to be true "even in the world." Thus, "mere conventionalities" are of two types: ordinary appearances to realized beings and the hallucinations that the world considers false.[54] In this schema, there are four classes of beings, ranging from lowest to highest:

- those perceiving or believing what is widely regarded in the world as untrue—that is, those suffering from perceptual illusions or non-Buddhist views;
- ordinary beings of good faculties who do not hold non-Buddhist beliefs but who yet assent to the validity of appearances;
- realized Buddhists who know appearances are not true but still have the non-afflictive ignorance that results in their perceiving ordinary appearances;
- and Buddhas who possess none of these forms of ignorance.

Jayānanda makes clear that all appearances—even without the conception that they are true—entail a level of ignorance that Buddhas do not have; Buddhas are not so ignorant and consequently do not see the appearances that ordinary people and even realized beings see. He further makes clear the connection between seeing ordinary appearances and being obstructed from emptiness: he states that even a realized being's perception of illusion-like dependent arisings constitutes having the "mere ignorance" that veils emptiness, that keeps emptiness from appearing.[55] In this interpretation, a Buddha's knowledge of emptiness is separate from all other mental states, making a Buddha's knowledge entail a complete absence of perceptual appearances, on the one hand, and placing any perception of appearances in direct conflict with knowledge of emptiness, on the other. Jayānanda constructs a vast divide between "consciousness having appearances" and "consciousness not having appearances."[56]

Jayānanda's sweeping correlation of ignorance and appearance and his consequent denial that a Buddha can perceive the things that appear to us are troublesome issues, well implied (or even explicitly stated) in Candrakīrti, that later exegetes would attempt to soften. That he does not try to smooth over these points but instead amplifies them indicates his rejection both of the integrity of objects of perception—expressed in these passages as "appearances"—and of the validity of common perception. Jayānanda's taxonomy of ignorance allows three classes of ignorant beings. These three classes of ignorant beings all have non-afflictive ignorance and consequently continue to perceive ordinary appearances. What the ignorant perceive appear familiar to them only due to their mental obscuration.

Thus far, Jayānanda has denied the validity of appearances, eroding the value of perception by positing its object as arising only due to ignorance. While the distance between rejecting ordinary perception and rejecting human valid cognition is not great, it is indeed a distance Jayānanda whole-heartedly travels. In starting down this path, he further elaborates on what distinguishes the two types of mere conventionalities from obscurational truths. Where Candrakīrti states that obscurational truths "deceive fools,"[57] Jayānanda explains that just as "the world" does not conceive a mirror reflection to be true (but "a fool" might think his reflection to be truly a person), so those who have overcome afflictive ignorance no longer conceive ordinary appearances to be true. These appearances deceive the rest of us, however, who "conceive what is not true to be true."[58] Those who take obscurational truths as their referents—those who believe ordinary appearances to be true—are deceived. In elaborating on Candrakīrti's distinction, Jayānanda clearly places the consciousnesses of ordinary people in opposition to Dharmakīrti's understanding of valid cognition: no ordinary consciousness can be non-deceptive.[59]

Drawing out the analogy between realized beings and ordinary humans, on the one hand, and ordinary humans and fools (or, those with defective senses), on the other, Jayānanda later comments that just as the illusory floating hairs of one with a cataract-like condition will still appear to such a person's vision even when that person knows that these floating hairs are not real, just so even those realized beings who no longer conceive appearances to be true still perceive those appearances, "because there is still the mistake (*bhrānta, 'khrul pa*) of appearances of the aggregates and so forth due to non-afflictive ignorance."[60] While those who have cultivated their understanding of Madhyamaka emptiness know that appearances are not true and consequently are not deceived into perceiving appearances *as* obscurational truths, they are still mistaken in perceiving appearances. In this reading, non-afflictive ignorance is mistake, the same quality that Dignāga equated with conceptuality and Dharmakīrti utilized to distinguish non-conceptual perception from conceptual inference. Jayānanda extends the mistaken status to include perception, as it, too, is imbued with the conceptuality of subject and object, falling short of the non-dual realization of emptiness that is the Madhyamaka goal.[61] We may recall Dharmottara's explanation that inference's mistake rests in its engaging appearances by way of conceiving what is not a real object to be a real object. Jayānanda would say that no object short of emptiness can be considered real. Whereas the epistemological tradition distinguishes real, causally efficacious objects from conceptual fictions, Jayānanda blankets all appearances as unreal.

The class of realized beings who yet perceive appearances are exempt from deception and so, if Jayānanda is utilizing Dharmakīrti's definition, might be said to possess valid cognition. However, they are still mistaken and so, if Jayānanda understands valid cognition *à la* Vinītadeva and Kamalaśīla, could not be said to possess valid cognition. So, we may ask, which is it? Instead of answering forthrightly, Jayānanda pulls in two different directions in his comments upon the same Candrakīrti stanza that Chapa utilized to show that Prāsaṅgikas deny any worldly valid cognition:

> If the world were valid cognition, the world would see suchness.

In one direction, Jayānanda adopts a Dharmakīrtian definition, stating (seemingly quite clearly) that "If something is non-deceptive, it is just valid cognition."[62] Candrakīrti introduces this stanza by pointing out the contrast between the world, which is not authoritative, and āryas who are, and thus directs this line of the stanza as referring to types of beings rather than to types of mental states. But by appealing to the Dharmakīrtian definition of valid cognition Jayānanda clearly interprets this stanza as referring to mental states.[63] Likewise, his use of the Dharmakīrtian definition would seem to imply that those who perceive appearances but are not deceived into thinking that appearances are true possess valid cognition. However, to this simple statement, he adds:

> Non-deceptive furthermore means having the quality of thoroughly knowing the entity [that is, emptiness] just as it is. This thorough knowledge is also thorough knowledge of the entity free from existence and non-existence. Therefore, if the world was to see suchness, because of that, it would have dispelled ignorance.[64]

These further qualifications of "non-deceptive" seem to restrict the scope of validity. Perceiving appearances but not assenting to their veracity would not qualify in this presentation; only knowing emptiness, seeing suchness, is valid. Where previously he had distinguished afflictive and non-afflictive ignorance, here Jayānanda draws a blanket opposition between seeing emptiness and being ignorant such that both the afflictive and non-afflictive kinds of ignorance seem to oppose valid cognition. Emphasizing this point, Jayānanda explicates the final line of the stanza ("It is not reasonable for foolishness also to be valid cognition") writing, "'Foolishness' lacks thorough knowledge of the entity [emptiness] just as it is and exaggerates falsified (*phyin ci log, viparīta*) entities of existence, non-existence, and so forth."[65] In this account, all cognition but realization of emptiness would be foolishness.

Jayānanda states that the āryas, whom Candrakīrti calls "the only authorities (or, the only possessors of valid cognition),"[66] are those on the "path of seeing,"[67] the third of the five paths leading up to buddhahood. This is the first path involving the attainment of a "ground"—upon which one has direct, but not uninterrupted, perception of emptiness. This identification helps clarify the distinction Jayānanda makes between levels of cognitive validity. Those on the path of seeing would have direct perception of emptiness—valid cognition—within meditation but subsequent to meditation would perceive ordinary appearances—foolishness. Not until buddhahood would this alternation cease (what happens upon buddhahood is an additional point of controversy, examined in chapter 5). We can see in Jayānanda's portrayal a two-tier model of validity, analagous to Dharmakīrti's own: at the highest level is the direct perception of emptiness but at a lesser level is the perception of ordinary appearances within the knowledge that those appearances are not true. The lower level of validity, like Dharmakīrti's inference, is clearly held to be non-deceptive; these developed āryas are not deceived into perceiving appearances as true. However, akin to Dharmakīrti's perception, only the direct perception of emptiness is unmistaken; āryas short of buddhahood still possess mistaken consciousnesses that perceive appearances.

Jayānanda clearly rejects Dharmakīrti's own two-tier model, calling ordinary perception of the conventional world "deceptive" and placing a much more stringent requirement on validity. Validity consists only of the perceptions of realized beings who no longer assent to the truth of appearances. The Dharmakīrti model of valid cognition, adopted and modified by Śāntarakṣita, Kamalaśīla, and Chapa, among others, implies too strong a level of existence for the referents of ordinary perception and inference. In his *Hammer of*

Logic, Jayānanda criticizes "Logicians following Dharmakīrti who propound that reality is realized by way of an objectively gained valid cognition."[68] We can recall that Karṇakagomin posited a two-fold division of inference in order to separate "objectively gained inferences" from inferences derived from scripture, the latter category referring to our only method for knowing "entirely imperceptible phenomena." Karṇakagomin implies that ordinary inferences make known facts on the strength of those facts themselves, indeed embodying the kind of "deference" to an objective world with which Tillemans characterizes realism.[69] Jayānanda's rejection of Dharmakīrtian valid cognition clearly intends to dispense with any purported factual state of the objective world, rejecting the truthfulness of what is given to common perception and allowing only a second-tier validity to the post-meditative perceptions of those āryas short of buddhahood.

However, in rejecting Dharmakīrtian valid cognition, Jayānanda elides what Karṇakagomin posited as a category of inference to characterize the project as a whole.[70] Jayānanda might here be guilty of drawing a caricature of his Mādhyamika opponents, whom he labeled "Svātantrika" and sees as adhering to a realism at odds with Nāgārjuna's writings.[71] After stating a quite accurate summary of both of Dharmakīrti's valid cognition definitions (as elaborated by his followers),[72] Jayānanda argues—by way of examining the distinction between "substance" (*dravya*) and "isolate" (*vyāvṛtti*)—against these definitions, rejecting the possibility that perception could reach a particular or a universal. After noting the tension in the epistemologists' depiction of perception "reaching an identified object" but also being perception of a momentary, constantly changing object, Jayānanda notes that if one (in response to this tension) dispenses with "substance" (as he would have us), valid cognition would no longer be consciousness of an entity (*vastu*).[73] This would nullify the Dharmakīrtian notion of ordinary perception. Note that Jayānanda equates "substance" and "entity," which is the same term that Jayānanda borrows from Karṇakagomin in labeling Dharmakīrtian epistemology "objectively gained" (*vastubalapravṛtta*). Where Karṇakagomin referred to a type of "objective" inference, Jayānanda sees perception likewise to have a purported "objectivity," to cognize faithfully an object that factually exists. Jayānanda rejects Dharmakīrtian perception because he understands it as the claimed perception of a real entity, the existence of which Nāgārjuna rejected.

Note also how the critique moves from subject to object: valid cognition is denied because of the overly strong status such validity would necessitate for the existence of its object. Jayānanda rejects the possibility that valid cognition could be defined as "cognizing a true object" since "truthfulness" is the very quality lacking in appearances; such a definition of valid cognition would make invalid cognition valid,[74] as a cognition conceiving of the truthfulness of its object is the principal form of invalidity for Jayānanda. Since the objects of ordinary perception are fundamentally false, any cognition of them cannot be considered valid. Indeed, he notes that if one posits a true object, one would posit that wrong consciousness—perception of a true object—is valid cognition.[75] The perception of true objects counters Jayānanda's most basic Madhyamaka principles.

Levels of Validity

Candrakīrti and Jayānanda (and, as will be seen, Mabja) discuss valid cognition within a broader discussion of Nāgārjuna's two truths; Jayānanda clearly pits his interpretation of the two truths against the possibility of worldly valid cognition.[76] Chapa's view of the necessity of ordinary valid cognition to religious development does not allow him to oppose cognition of obscurational truths with valid cognition. However, he still must posit a sharp distinction between the two truths, between the objects of ordinary cognition and ultimate reality. He accomplishes this by dividing validity broadly into "valid cognition of final analysis" and "valid cognition of non-final analysis."[77] This allows Chapa to hold that cognitions of all "truths" are valid—and that everything knowable is one kind or the other of the two truths[78]—but that cognitions of ultimate and obscurational truths are valid in different ways.

Chapa provides his own etymology of the word "obscurational," similar to that given by Candrakīrti and Jayānanda (based on the *Descent to Laṅkā Sūtra*), that plays on a correlation between ordinary consciousness and a veiling of the final nature of reality[79] and explains "truth" in "obscurational truth" as meaning that "The referents of that [veiling consciousness], all established appearances that do not bear analysis, are true in the perspective of mistaken thought."[80] However, he softens the distinction between the "veil" and the realization of emptiness by allowing for "non-analytical" validity. He states that obscurational truths are true when not analyzed,[81] while ultimate truth is able to bear analysis and so is true for the "valid cognition comprehending finality."[82] Only the kind of Madhyamaka analysis that investigates a phenomenon's ultimate existence results in obscurational truths being seen as untrue. Chapa further divides obscurational truth into "real" and "unreal," with the former being characterized as "that which is a referent of [an awareness] that does not comprehend finality but is not an object apprehended by mistake,"[83] while unreal obscurational truths are apprehended by mistake. Real obscurational truths, while not being finally true when subjected to analysis, are unmistakenly known by the valid cognition that does not perform such analysis. For Chapa, unmistaken validity comes in ordinary and ultimate varieties.

What of Jayānanda's strong correlation between mistaken consciousness and appearances? We have seen Chapa state that obscurational truths are true for mistaken thought, but then subdivide this class of truths into real and unreal on the basis of being apprehended by unmistaken and mistaken consciousnesses, respectively. So are appearances indicative of mistaken consciousness? Chapa replies that appearances do entail mistake but that mistake itself is of two kinds, one that implies and another that does not imply that its bearer possesses defilements:

> The mistake that conceives what does not exist among objects of knowledge to exist—for instance, the conception of a permanent entity—and the mistake that takes what is empty of performing functions as its apprehended referent—for instance, the appearances of two moons, concepts (*don spyi*), and so forth—entail obstructions. However, if you state the fault that it follows that Buddhas have obstructions because of not having that capacity [for mistake], your reason is not established [that is, Buddhas have the capacity for mistake]. If you say that Buddhas have obstructions because of having the capacity for the mistake that is a referent-taker [that is, a consciousness] that does not bear analysis, your entailment is not established [that is, having the capacity for this kind of mistake does not entail having obstructions].[84]

Chapa is willing to concede that appearances indicate a level of mistake but holds that not all mistakes are problematic. On one level, cognitions of real obscurational truths can be called unmistaken even though such cognitions entail appearances; on another level, Buddhas can perceive appearances without this perception—though mistaken—necessitating defilement.

In these passages, one sees Chapa wrestling with the same conundrum that Jayānanda was drawn into: All Mādhyamikas must interpret Nāgārjuna's two truths such that emptiness remains the only ultimately true phenomenon. At the same time, many objects of worldly perception bear some level of validity, earning them the label, "obscurational truth." They are in some sense "true" but in a way that is overturned by ultimate analysis. Jayānanda's commitment to what he understands to be Candrakīrti's rejection of the Epistemological tradition leads him to interpret the "truth" in "obscurational truths" in quite weak terms, rejecting conventional valid cognition. Chapa sides with the Dharmakīrti tradition, continuing a line of Middle Way exegesis stretching back to Śāntarakṣita and Kamalaśīla and placing great importance on the valid establishment of the conventional world. Chapa's obscurational truths are truer than Jayānanda understands them to be.

As discussed in chapter 2, Chapa's way of addressing the need for epistemological grounding within Madhyamaka quickly lost favor with many of his students. However, his concerns left their mark on Tibetan Madhyamaka, beginning with the work of his student, Mabja Jangchub Tsondru,[85] who left Chapa to study with Jayānanda. A brief analysis of Mabja's understanding of the role of valid cognition within Madhyamaka reveals that while he renounced Chapa's views, he incorporated Chapa's method of distinguishing levels of validity into his Prāsaṅgika view. Mabja may represent the earliest Prāsaṅgika to attempt to harmonize the Epistemological tradition with Candrakīrti's philosophy, a harmony that continues to take various shapes among Tibetan exegetes.

Mabja voices the very same opposition between the Madhyamaka view and "objectively gained valid cognition" that Jayānanda discussed in his *Hammer of Logic.*[86] Jayānanda would seem to be the source of Mabja's discussion and, as suggested in chapter 2, was likely influential in swaying Mabja to the Prāsaṅgika view. Mabja's most significant known text, a commentary on Nāgārjuna's *Fundamental Treatise on the Middle* called the *Ornament of Disputation,* criticizes "Svātantrikas" for positing knowledge by way of "objectively gained valid cognition that is renowned to both proponent and opponent [in a debate] or by valid cognition having an unmistaken mode of apprehension."[87] Where Jayānanda kept closely to the Dharmakīrtian explanation of valid cognition (although characterizing it as "objectively gained"), Mabja sees "unmistaken" as a defining feature of valid cognition, quite possibly as a result of his study with Chapa. Mabja rejects such valid cognition even on the conventional level, positing instead a "mere valid cognition that is renowned to one's opponent or in the world."[88]

In distinguishing his own "mere valid cognition" from his opponents' "objectively gained valid cognition," Mabja quickly points out that his usage neither becomes a cognition "in one's own continuum (*rang rgyud, svatantra*) nor a consequence that implies a proof because there is not even conventionally an ascertainment of a tenet objectively known nor an implication [asserting] the opposite [of what one disproves]."[89] He equates *svatantra* with "objectively gained," eliding the term that Candrakīrti had used to pejoratively label Bhāvaviveka's form of inference in order to criticize not just the use of formal inference but the Madhyamaka adaptation of the valid cognition enterprise. Mabja further distinguishes his opponents' understanding of "valid cognition having an unmistaken mode of apprehension" from his own position, following Jayānanda, that "the referents of consciousness having appearance" are true only for a mistaken mind.[90] Perceiving appearances indicates mistaken perception; almost all of what the Epistemological tradition calls unmistaken is, in Mabja's portrayal, mistake.[91]

Despite this strong correlation between appearance and mistake, Mabja nuances levels of mistake in a way that opens the path toward ordinary valid cognition and that is reminiscent of Chapa's portrayal. Although he divides obscurational truth from ultimate truth on the basis of what is true for a mistaken consciousness and an unmistaken consciousness,[92] respectively, he allows that "real obscurational truths" are perceived by worldly unmistaken consciousnesses.[93] This "worldly unmistaken consciousness" seems to be identical to Chapa's "non-analytical unmistaken consciousness" that cognizes real obscurational truths. Chapa takes the additional step of calling such a consciousness "valid cognition." Mabja instead writes of "mere" or "worldly renowned valid cognition." Mabja has redefined Svātantrika valid cognition as "objectively gained" and as having "an unmistaken mode of apprehension." In so doing, he has pushed his opponents (including Chapa) into a quasi-realist extreme, allowing him to admit a worldly level of unmistaken validity into his own Middle Way. In essence Mabja has recast Chapa's position on ordinary valid cognition in a Prāsaṅgika mold.

Additionally Mabja is willing to include, within an ārya's unmistaken consciousness, inferential knowledge of emptiness: ultimate truth is "true as a referent of unmistaken consciousness, that is, true in the perspective of either the non-conceptual wisdom of an ārya's meditative absorption or a reasoning consciousness that analyzes finality—suchness—by way of a triple-moded reason."[94] Mabja's "reasoning consciousness" is very close (if not identical) to Chapa's "valid cognition comprehending finality," the analysis-driven knowledge of emptiness. The "triple-moded reason" refers to Dharmakīrtian inference. Chapa regards the inferential knowledge of emptiness to be essential to religious development, to the passage from believing the truth of appearances to understanding their empty reality. Mabja, like Jayānanda, attempts to displace his Svātantrika opponents from the middle, arguing that their epistemological adaptations align them with "realism." Influenced by his study with Chapa, Mabja takes the additional step of adopting epistemological concerns—the provisional unmistaken status of ordinary consciousness and the necessity of inference in understanding ultimate truth—within a Prāsaṅgika view.

Mabja's "mere valid cognition that is renowned to one's opponent or in the world" opens the way to his accepting—along with Candrakīrti and Jayānanda[95]—four valid cognitions, an ironic twist after rejecting the Dharmakīrtian two-fold model of valid cognition. Mabja introduces his discussion of the four types—perception, inference, testimony, and analogy—by calling them "the four valid cognitions renowned in the world."[96] Mabja combines the non-Buddhist Nyāya conception of a four-fold model of valid cognition with the Candrakīrtian notion of what is "renowned in the world." One would expect the four-fold model to represent what is "renowned to one's [non-Buddhist] opponent." However, Mabja—a Tibetan who likely never met a Naiyāyika—places the four-fold system in the hands of "the world," a move that points to a new distinction, not between Buddhist and non-Buddhist systems of validity (which was an important distinction in India) but between a two-fold system wrongly adopted by logic-addicted Mādhyamikas (the only tenet system held in Tibet) and a "worldly" understanding.

Mabja, like Candrakīrti and Jayānanda before him, does not hold to the Naiyāyika model but instead adopts a looser standard of validity that allows him to claim, on the worldly level, four valid cognitions, all of which still fall within the category of mistake. Accepting a four-fold model does not show Prāsaṅgika allegiance to the valid cognition enterprise but indicates just how far they place themselves outside of the Dharmakīrtian tradition, a distance that allows them nominally to adopt a non-Buddhist model. Mabja offers a hedge toward ordinary valid cognition with his notion of worldly unmistaken consciousness and a four-fold "worldly renown" valid cognition. However, he presents the correlation between human consciousness and mistake as a basic maxim, held by any (good) Mādhyamika: "Mādhyamikas assert—just as they assert suchness in entities—that all referents of mind having appearance are erroneous and all mind is mistaken."[97]

Conclusion: Competing Schools of Philosophy, Unified Religious Vision

Like Candrakīrti and Jayānanda, Mabja's arguments against valid cognition occur within a larger presentation of the two truths.[98] Jayānanda and

Mabja read Candrakīrti's interpretation of Nāgārjuna's two truths as staking out a stark divide between human consciousness and the āryas' perspective, a divide that negates the possibility of Dharmakīrtian valid cognition (as they construe it). Any follower of Nāgārjuna must posit a fundamental distinction between ordinary "truths" and emptiness, as well as between the classes of consciousnesses that cognize them. Chapa, too, presents a distinction between the two truths and between ordinary consciousnesses and cognition of emptiness. The Prāsaṅgika distinction lies in pitting human consciousness, characterized by mistake, in blatant opposition with validity as Dharmakīrti and his followers define it. Both sides of this Madhyamaka debate take up the basic terms of the Indian Buddhist Epistemologists' discussion of what characterizes valid cognition, either working out ways to incorporate the notion of validity within the Madhyamaka view of human ignorance or rejecting the possibility of human unmistaken consciousness because of that ignorance. Clearly, the Epistemologists' notion of mistake (*bhrānta*) displaced concern with delusion (*moha*) in the twelfth-century Madhyamaka debates that saw the school divided into Prāsaṅgika and Svātantrika interpretations.

Mabja's bold statement of what Mādhyamikas assert can be read as an attempt to define a tradition. Mādhyamikas, Mabja would have us believe, reject Dharmakīrti, adopt a worldly notion of valid cognition (although whose world one must wonder), interpret Nāgārjuna's two truths as opposing unmistaken human cognition, and rely on Candrakīrti and Śāntideva in reaching these conclusions. Chapa's positions, with which Mabja was well familiar, are labeled Svātantrika Madhyamaka,[99] in opposition to what "Mādhyamikas assert." If Mabja goes further than Jayānanda toward accomodating human valid cognition, he does so only by first stigmatizing a Madhyamaka position that openly welcomes Dharmakīrti's epistemology. In the caricature they draw of Svātantrika, Jayānanda and Mabja stake out variant canons: their own Candrakīrti-Śāntideva line of interpreting Nāgārjuna and, in opposition to this, Mādhyamikas who adopt the Dharmakīrti tradition and so, in their eyes, reject Nāgārjuna's most fundamental tenets. In one sense, the creation of two subschools of Madhyamaka consists in this construction of competing canons, the invention of two traditions of exegesis that share little overlap.

In another sense, as I have tried to detail throughout this chapter, the creation of these two subschools of Madhyamaka entailed significant philosophical differences, leading the respective schools to reach opposing answers to their common Madhyamaka problems. The competing allegiances separating Prāsaṅgikas and Svātantrikas in twelfth-century Tibet brings into focus a tension between the Madhyamaka rejection of "nature" and epistemological foundationalism, and between the sweeping ignorance with which Madhyamaka would seem to characterize the human condition, and the need to posit distinctions between valid and deceptive human consciousnesses. If Prāsaṅgikas more clearly recognized this tension and brought their interpretation of Madhyamaka into open conflict with Buddhist Epistemology, can we say that their characterization of Svātantrika as "realists" is accurate? Does twelfth-century Svātantrika amount to realism? Do Svātantrikas hold that phenomena are (to use the much later Gelukpa criticism) conventionally established by way of their own character (*rang gi mtshan nyid kyis grub pa*)? Chapa, like Śāntarakṣita and Kamalaśīla, would not admit to adopting the extreme of realism.

Moving beyond the issue of Chapa's self-identity, the levels of validity that he posits (both to preserve the distinction between the two truths and to allow for the grounded use of human cognition as a tool for religious development) suggest that "realism" is an unfit label. The type of sturdy existence he is accused of granting to conventional reality—in which things exist "out there" in such a way that they impinge upon one's consciousness "in here"—is undermined by the Madhyamaka analysis Chapa enjoins, concluding with the realization that things do not exist as either unitary or multiple phenomena. Moreover, Prāsaṅgikas themselves—beginning with Mabja and extending to later Tibetan developers of the tradition—saw that their eventual triumph over the Svātantrika position necessitated that they ameliorate the conflict between Madhyamaka and Buddhist Epistemology not by rejecting Dharmakīrti—as Jayānanda was wont to do—but by making the epistemological project palatable within a Prāsaṅgika world. The triumph of valid cognition within Tibetan Madhyamaka is Chapa's greatest defense.

The survival of some of Chapa's most central views within a system that he vehemently argued against points to the need to move from asking "Are Svātantrikas guilty of realism?" to appreciating the totality—the functioning Buddhist universe in which enlightenment is possible—that these figures wished to construct. In this vein, it is helpful to see that the most serious charges each side threw at the other were nearly identical: Chapa accuses Prāsaṅgika of making buddhahood no different from nihilism.[100] Jayānanda, following Candrakīrti, claims that Epistemologists who adhere to the possibility of worldly valid cognition must think that the world has dispelled ignorance, thereby making the Buddhist path pointless.[101] For Chapa, a continuum of validity is essential to the progress from ignorance to enlightenment. For twelfth-century Prāsaṅgikas, the epistemological turn is too strong, giving unwarranted credence to ordinary cognition without motivating us to seek the āryas' path to buddhahood. Despite strongly held convictions of their opponent's flaws, the two sides share a common motivation: the construction of a cogent and coherent path to enlightenment. Their differing means for constructing this religious path compelled the Prāsaṅgika-Svātantrika division in twelfth-century Tibet, giving rise to two related debates over the status of ultimate truth and those who are transformed by it, to which we will turn in the remaining two chapters.

4. What Can Be Said About the Ineffable?

BUDDHIST PHILOSOPHY has long held that what is salvifically essential cannot be expressed directly, but only pointed to with descriptive, metaphoric, or sometimes expository language.[1] In the Madhyamaka context, ultimate truth—the object of salvific knowledge—has frequently been described as ineffable (*anabhilāpya*) and beyond conceptual thought (*vikalpa*). In a well-known passage of *Entrance to the Middle*, Candrakīrti extends this line of thinking, declaring that the ultimate "is ineffable and just not an object of consciousness."[2] This extension singles out the soteriological importance of the ultimate for Madhyamaka, and raises the crucial salvific problem of whether or not ordinary consciousness can be developed to know the ultimate. His formulation raises a fundamental issue in Buddhist thinking: if human consciousness is fundamentally flawed, how can it gain transformative knowledge? In Candrakīrti's Madhyamaka treatment, the issue becomes more pointed, as the object of liberating knowledge would seem to be entirely outside of our mental capabilities. Surely Candrakīrti, like all Buddhists, holds strongly to the possibility of enlightenment. However, his provocative statement begs the question, *how* do sentient beings realize the ultimate if it cannot be an object of our consciousnesses?

In the present chapter, I intend to consider some responses to Candrakīrti's proclamation of ultimate truth. Candrakīrti may have understood his interpretation of Nāgārjuna's two truths (and much else in his philosophy, particularly his opposition to the dominant Epistemological turn in Buddhist thinking) to be a traditionalist return to the roots of Madhyamaka. Certainly his use of copious sūtra citations to back up his contentions on ultimate truth supports an interpretation of his conservative views. However, the radical manner in which eleventh- and twelfth-century popularizers utilized his views to construct the ultimate must have been received by Buddhists of the day as nothing short of iconoclastic. The rise of Candrakīrti's corpus was fueled in large part by this portrayal of ultimate truth. The iconoclastic interpretation of Candrakīrti's ultimate was advanced mainly by Jayānanda and, to a milder extent, by Prajñākaramati (c. 950–1030). In response, several Tibetan authors, most notably Chapa Chokyi Sengé and Drakpa Gyeltsen (*Grags pa rgyal mtshan,* 1147–1216), voiced heated criticism of this iconoclastic ultimate, directing their denunciation toward both contemporary Prāsaṅgikas and Candrakīrti. When Candrakīrti's corpus gained wide exposure in the early years of the second millennium, Mādhyamikas were forced to account for and recast his unique view of ultimate truth. Consequently, interpretation of the ultimate became a central focus of this period.

The Prāsaṅgika Ultimate

Commenting on Candrakīrti's proclamation that the ultimate is "just not an object of consciousness," Jayānanda writes that the ultimate "is not in the sphere of conceptual consciousness because those [consciousnesses] engage an object (*yul*) that exists, does not exist, and so forth."[3] Jayānanda, one of the chief figures responsible for bringing Candrakīrti's writings to a wide audience, states that it is "conceptual knowledge" that cannot know the ultimate, suggesting that this passage simply restates the older Buddhist maxim that the ultimate is beyond conceptuality. However, he also suggests in this same passage that consciousness carries with it conceptions of existence and nonexistence, which Nāgārjuna declared to be ultimately untenable. In this sense, Jayānanda may well be implicating all forms of consciousness and declaring them to be useless in realizing the ultimate. This interpretation is borne out by Jayānanda's position that consciousness does not know the ultimate and ceases upon buddhahood, a position we will consider more fully in the next chapter. That the ultimate is not an object of any kind of consciousness became, at least for Jayānanda, a hallmark of a fledgling Prāsaṅgika interpretation of Madhyamaka.

A very similar idea is voiced in Śāntideva's *Engaging in the Bodhisattva's Practices,* in his discussion of the two truths:

> It is asserted that there are two truths—obscurational and ultimate.
> The ultimate is not a referent of awareness; awareness is said to be obscurational.[4]

As previously noted, this brief poetic statement leaves open many possible translations; to suggest just one, Śāntideva could simply mean that "awareness" signifies "conceptual awareness," such that knowing the ultimate requires one to surpass conceptuality. Also, whether or not Śāntideva intended to echo Candrakīrti in this statement is debatable. But most significant to our investigation of the rise of Candrakīrti's views, Śāntideva's commentator, Prajñākaramati, explicitly links Candrakīrti's and Śāntideva's ideas by quoting Candrakīrti four times in his commentary on this Śāntideva stanza.[5] He additionally offers his understanding of the thrust of Śāntideva's statement, noting "the ultimate, in reality, is just not a referent of obscurational consciousness."[6] Explaining Śāntideva's meaning behind "not a referent of awareness," he writes that "awareness" means "all consciousness," that the ultimate is "not a referent because of surpassing the sphere of all consciousness," and elaborates that it is "impossible to bring [the ultimate] within the sphere of all awareness in any way."[7] Taken in aggregate, Prajñākaramati's restatement of Śāntideva's stanza makes a broad correlation between all consciousnesses and obscuration. However, his qualification "in reality" (*vastutaḥ*) allows for the possibility that the ultimate surpasses consciousness, imbued with ignorance, only at a rarefied level of religious practice. Prajñākaramati valued the role of "obscurational consciousness" in coming to a reasoned understanding of the ultimate. His broad correlation between consciousness and obscuration suggests that at the rarefied level, consciousness itself is eliminated, at which point the ultimate can no longer be said to be an object of consciousness. This leaves the burning question for Prajñākaramati and for Jayānanda (as will be seen): if not consciousness, what is it that realizes the ultimate?

Both Prajñākaramati and Candrakīrti support the contention that the ultimate is in some essential way unknowable by ordinary cognition by citing a passage from the *Introduction to the Two Truths Sūtra*. The passage reads:

> Devaputra, if ultimate truth were ultimately a referent of body, of speech, or of mind, it would not be reckoned as "ultimate truth"; it would be just an obscurational truth. However, Devaputra, ultimate truth is passed beyond all conventions and it is not particularized. It is not produced and does not cease; it is devoid of object of speech and speech itself, as well as object of knowledge and consciousness. Ultimate truth is passed beyond entities ranging right through the referents of omniscient wisdoms endowed with the supreme of all aspects. It is not as expressed in the phrase "ultimate truth."

> All phenomena are erroneous and thus are deceptive phenomena. Devaputra, ultimate truth cannot be taught. If you ask "Why?" All phenomena—whoever teaches, whatever is taught, whomever is taught—are ultimately utterly unproduced. Utterly unproduced phenomena cannot be explained because they are utterly unproduced.[8]

This shows a lengthy pedigree to the notion that the ultimate cannot be known by human intellect; the sūtra declares it to be not a referent of mind, devoid of object of knowledge and consciousness. These latter terms are paired with the sūtra's rejection of speech and its object, referencing the ineffability of the ultimate. Taken together, the sūtra sounds a common Buddhist rejection of duality, here the dualities of speech and of knowledge. While the sūtra suggests that human knowledge is inherently dualistic, like Prajñākaramati it offers an important qualification, stating that ultimate truth "ultimately" is not a referent of speech or mind. The attributes that the sūtra ascribes to ultimate truth and human consciousness at minimum imply a disconnect between the two, in which human consciousness is unable to know ultimate truth, "ultimately."

Prajñākaramati additionally cites the *Meeting of Father and Son Sūtra,* which speaks of the ultimate similarly, declaring that, "the ultimate is ineffable, incomprehensible, unknowable, inconceivable."[9] These sūtra passages illustrate a deep concern among Indian Mādhyamikas for the singular importance of the ultimate, and additionally to the growing problem in Madhyamaka thinking of how to uphold the unique character of ultimate truth while yet maintaining a practitioner's ability to realize it. With Prajñākaramati and Jayānanda in the eleventh and twelfth centuries, these concerns came to the forefront, heightening the debate within Madhyamaka over the ultimate, how it can be realized, and the status of the resulting state, buddhahood.

Prajñākaramati gives us further insight into just what it is about human intellect that renders it insufficient in ultimate concerns. He introduces his citation of the *Introduction to the Two Truths Sūtra* by stating that "all awareness has a nature of conceptuality . . . [and] all conceptuality has a nature of ignorance."[10] He then follows the sūtra passage by stating that the ultimate is "not a referent of conceptual construction."[11] Prajñākaramati's framing indicates that, in his interpretation, conceptuality is what invalidates ordinary consciousness. It may well be that conceptuality invalidates only certain kinds of ordinary consciousnesses but not others—that is, Prajñākaramati could well be ascribing to the broad Buddhist division of non-conceptual and conceptual consciousnesses and, within that division, rejecting only the latter. Non-conceptual consciousness could still be a valid means of knowing the ultimate. In this interpretation, one would surmise that Prajñākaramati rejects the possibility of inferential knowledge of the ultimate, but accepts a rarefied consciousness that directly perceives the ultimate. However, his comments cited above, that the ultimate surpasses all consciousness, suggest that the kind of conceptuality he objects to is found in all consciousness—all consciousnesses operate in the duality of subject and object.

In commenting on Candrakīrti's citation of the *Introduction to the Two Truths Sūtra,* Jayānanda states that the sūtra's rejection of the dualities of speech and knowledge means that the ultimate "is not a sphere for the activities of words and conceptuality."[12] He reads the rejection of knowledge as a rejection of conceptuality. The remainder of his comments on this sūtra passage have a similar tenor, as he notes that ultimate truth "is not an object of the word or concept 'suchness.'"[13] However, again, just how deep Jayānanda sees conceptuality running in human consciousness requires investigation: in rejecting conceptuality, does he reject a class of consciousness? Or are conceptuality and consciousness equated? Conceptuality in his treatment seems to be any consciousness taking an object. In addition to his denial that the ultimate can be an object of conceptuality, he explains why the ultimate surpasses even the sphere of omniscience: "It is not reasonable for [ultimate truth], which is free from the four extremes, to be an entity that is a referent (*yul gyi dngos po*); we impute it to be an entity that is a referent when we say, for [the sake of] trainees, 'omniscience knows suchness.'"[14] Convention leads us to speak as though the realization of the ultimate entails subject-object duality, but it does not. Knowing, for Jayānanda, involves subject-object duality and so can have no place in realizing the ultimate. Coupled with his amplification of Candrakīrti's rejection of mind and mental factors upon reaching buddhahood (treated at length in the following chapter), this deep-seated equation of duality and conceptuality gives the impression that all forms of consciousness have no place in ultimate truth. For Jayānanda the ultimate is unknowable. He acknowledges that we do *say* that "omniscience knows suchness"; he does not deny that something happens vis-à-vis the ultimate and that this "something" in turn yields enlightenment. However, calling that "something" "knowledge" is only done for the sake of trainees; in reality, consciousness and knowledge play no role.

Certainly Candrakīrti, Prajñākaramati, and Jayānanda all saw realization of the ultimate as of fundamental soteriological importance and as the goal of Buddhist practice. While we may well tease out a variety of interpretations in these three authors' respective writings, in declaring that the ultimate is not a referent of consciousness they forge a basic disjunction between the functioning of consciousness and ordinary knowledge, on the one hand, and salvific realization on the other. Rather than posit a type of consciousness purified of conceptuality that knows the ultimate, they choose to disavow consciousness "ultimately" and, as we will see in the following chapter, reject that Buddhas have consciousness. This basic disjunction struck some Mādhyamikas of the day as untenable, as it would seem to leave no way of cultivating ordinary mental states into a Buddha's wisdom, making the ultimate entirely inaccessible. These Mādhyamikas sought ways of emphasizing the singularly efficacious status of the ultimate while yet allowing for a continuity of consciousness such that one could gradually come to know the ultimate.

Chapa's Ultimate

Chapa Chokyi Sengé, one of the chief opponents of Candrakīrti's revivalists, argued directly against the budding Prāsaṅgika notion that the ultimate surpasses the sphere of consciousness. I set aside Chapa's understanding of how consciousness comes to know the ultimate until the following chapter where it will be investigated alongside the Prāsaṅgika notion that "knowing" the ultimate is merely metaphoric. Here, I examine his rejoinders to the Prāsaṅgika take on the nature of the ultimate and explore his own unique interpretation of ultimate truth. Chapa declared—in the highly formal language of scholastic discourse—that the basis of division into two truths must be the broad category of objects of knowledge (*jñeya, shes bya*).[15] In other words, ultimate truth, just like conventional truths, is a phenomenon knowable by consciousness.

Chapa begins his critique by drawing a portrait of Candrakīrti's views that relies a great deal on twelfth-century developments. He characterized the Prāsaṅgika position as follows:

> A certain proponent of reasoning says: "The character of ultimate truth passes beyond the mark of objects of knowledge. No matter how one knows ultimate truth—as existent, non-existent, both [existent and non-existent] or neither [existent nor non-existent]—those are proliferations; but ultimate truth, due to being devoid of all proliferations, passes beyond the mark of

> objects of knowledge. Furthermore, since it is not in any way to be taken as a convention, it is uncharacterizable even by any means of positing; hence, it has no character either. Since it is not the conceived object (*zhen yul*) of words or conceptuality, it is also without proliferations. Since it is not established as not empty, it is also emptiness. Since it is not a compounded entity (*'dus byas kyi dngos po*), it is also a non-entity. Since it is not established as produced, ceasing, and so forth, it is also non-dual (*gnyis su myed pa*)."[16]

Chapa's characterization follows Jayānanda's above-cited comments closely, stating that any way of knowing the ultimate would involve conceptions of existence or non-existence, and so ultimate truth cannot be an object of knowledge. One also hears overtones of the *Introduction to the Two Truths Sūtra* passage that Candrakīrti and Prajñākaramati cited, as Chapa has his opponent speak of the ultimate as beyond conventions and without character. Much as we saw with Prajñākaramati and Jayānanda, Chapa's Prāsaṅgika opponent equates knowledge with conceptuality and with proliferations (*prapañca*)—the verbal and conceptual overlay that blinds us to the ultimate and ensnares us in further suffering, which ultimate truth per force lacks. Ultimate truth, then, cannot come within the domain of consciousness in any way without losing its status as ultimate truth; it cannot be an object or referent of knowledge.

Chapa's rejoinders to the Prāsaṅgika understanding of an unknowable ultimate, as well as his own explication of ultimate truth, center on a close association of valid knowledge and the referents of valid knowledge. For Chapa, knowledge of any real object—and we will see below how he nuances "real"—must be valid knowledge. If the Prāsaṅgika wants to say that the ultimate, the very absence of proliferations, is not an object of knowledge, then it would not be an object of valid cognition (*gzhal bya, prameya*);[17] valid cognition itself would be useless in knowing the ultimate and ceasing proliferations. I suspect that the Prāsaṅgikas we have examined here would not object. However, to clarify his own position, Chapa has his opponent object that "Proliferations are ceased [by valid cognition] but there is no cognition (*gzhal ba*) of voidness of proliferations"; Chapa responds: "The very dispelling of the superimposition of proliferations is the meaning of cognizing voidness of proliferations."[18] The opponent argues for a valid negation of proliferations that merely negates without inducing cognition of emptiness. Rather than knowing emptiness, the negation of proliferations would negate any object of consciousness and negate consciousness as well. Chapa's answer makes clear that in his view emptiness is known in the very act of negating proliferations—the mental processes that overcome obstructions realize the ultimate. For Chapa, consciousness validly knows the ultimate.

As noted in the previous chapter, one of the ways Chapa stakes out the singular importance of ultimate truth from all other objects of valid knowledge is by creating a hierarchy among the types of valid cognition and the objects of these cognitions. While consciousnesses of both kinds of "truths" are valid cognitions, they are valid on different levels: "that which is delineated by the valid cognition of final analysis is ultimate truth; that which is delineated by the valid cognition of non-final analysis is an obscurational truth."[19] "Final analysis" consists of the cognitive processes that investigate the ultimate mode of phenomena's subsistence; this analysis will find phenomena to be without establishment, empty. Chapa tells us "this very non-establishment is ultimate truth since it abides as the object cognized by final analysis."[20] Ultimate truth is the object known by this "final" form of valid cognition. Ordinary phenomena are validly established, but only by valid cognition that does not perform this final analysis. Chapa holds two levels of validity such that all truths are validly known, yet only ultimate truth is valid finally.

Speaking to what "final analysis" entails, Chapa describes how phenomena that are validly established conventionally (positive phenomena or affirming negatives)[21] are invalidated ultimately:

> Mādhyamikas [assert that] the conceptions that temporal continua and spatial wholes are true are to be reversed through differentiating them into moments and particles [respectively]. Moreover, the conceptions that subtle particles and moments are true are to be reversed through differentiating those into [a particle's] ten directions and [a moment's] beginning, middle, and end. Similarly, the conception of truth with regard to parts is to be reversed through differentiating into parts within parts, since parts are endless. Thus, it is impossible for affirming negatives to be true as objects cognized by cognitions of finality.[22]

Only emptiness, the ultimate lack of establishment, holds up to this analysis; the conception that ordinary phenomena are true is overturned when one analyzes by division.

Clearly, for Chapa, ultimate truth is an object of knowledge and is found by final analysis. Additionally, ultimate truth is the sole phenomenon that is, in the end, "true" and that "bears analysis" (*dpyad bzod pa*). Mādhyamikas beginning with Nāgārjuna hold that the ultimate alone is true.[23] One suspects that this common assertion led Jayānanda and other early Prāsaṅgikas to reject the possibility of conventional valid cognition (as discussed in chapter 3)—if only the ultimate is true, conventionalities are false and "knowledge" of them must not be valid. However, Chapa has a unique take on what qualifies the ultimate to be true, namely, that it bears the analysis of division. He writes, "Since emptiness of a true nature is not established as any entity at all, it is empty of all distinctions. Therefore, since [emptiness] is indivisible into distinctions, there is no reversing the conception of truth by dividing distinctions; hence, it bears analysis. . . . Emptiness of a true nature is also true as an object of final cognition."[24] For Chapa, the ultimate is an object of a special type of refined cognition, is true in final analysis, and—rather than just standing as the result of analysis—is able to bear that analysis: we believe that it is true and, upon analysis, our belief is not overturned.[25]

In the passage above, we see that Chapa holds an ultimate that lacks any distinctions (*khyad par, viśeṣa*)—there are no characteristics that would allow one to divide the ultimate and overturn the sense of its veracity. He additionally makes clear that this ultimate without distinctions is a non-affirming negative: "Since a non-affirming negative that negates a mere positive phenomenon as a referent of reasoning has no mere distinctions to be examined, the conception of truth cannot be reversed through analyzing its distinctions."[26] If, instead of a "mere" phenomenon, a phenomenon with particular qualities (or distinctions)—such as permanence—is analyzed, finding its emptiness will not be *final*, as further qualities will still require analysis: one will find the emptiness of a permanent phenomenon but the possibility of an impermanent phenomenon remains. Finding the emptiness of permanence would suggest an affirming negation that would itself have to be negated.[27] Only non-affirming negatives will require no further negation; only non-affirming negatives are final.

Chapa seems to have developed his unique interpretation of an ultimate that exists without any distinctions in response to what he saw as the Prāsaṅgika denial that the ultimate exists at all. Whether or not Chapa's understanding of his Prāsaṅgika opponents is accurate, one can see that Candrakīrti's, Prajñākaramati's, and Jayānanda's denial of the ultimate as an object of knowledge easily allows Chapa to conclude that, for them, the ultimate does not exist. Chapa sees the Prāsaṅgika as rejecting any thesis regarding the ultimate whatsoever, and he portrays them as denying that the ultimate either exists or does not exist. Chapa views this interpretation as logically impossible and develops an ultimate that exists without any distinctions, or qualities that can be predicated of it, in response. He makes clear that his ultimate without distinctions opposes what he understands to be the Prāsaṅgika notion of an ultimate that neither exists nor does not exist in a particularly tricky passage:[28]

> How can proponents of thesislessness refute those who propound the existence of the [following] thesis: "A clear awareness that is singularly established by experience only exists ultimately"?
>
> [A Prāsaṅgika might say] We perform the analysis, "Is that awareness unitary or manifold; produced or not produced; permanent or impermanent?"
>
> [We respond:] That action [of analysis] itself also should be analyzed: is it a true entity or empty of being such?
>
> [A Prāsaṅgika] might say, "We have no assertions whatsoever."
>
> [We respond:] We, also, do not assert any distinction regarding the ultimate, [which the hypothetical opponent we began with holds to be] clear [awareness].
>
> [A Prāsaṅgika] might say, "Not asserting any distinctions regarding an entity [claimed by you to be] existent is not feasible."
>
> [We respond:] Casting out both of two explicit contradictories [that is, unitary or manifold, produced or not produced, permanent or impermanent, existing or not existing] is not feasible.
>
> [A Prāsaṅgika] might say, "Although [two things] are established for the world as explicit contradictories, that is not established for us."
>
> [We respond:] Regarding an existent entity, not passing beyond permanent and impermanent or one and many, and so forth, is established in the world. However, this is not established for us.

Chapa has the Prāsaṅgika state that his own claim of an ultimate that exists without distinctions is illogical only to show that the Prāsaṅgika notion of an ultimate that is neither of two explicit contradictories (*dngos 'gal, sākṣād virodha*),[29] likewise, is illogical. He clearly sees the Prāsaṅgika notion that the ultimate neither exists nor does not exist to stem from their utter rejection of any thesis. Throughout these pages of his text, Chapa is intent on showing that if Prāsaṅgikas deny one thing, they must hold the contradictory of that thing—they must at least have a thesis that states the non-existence of the thing they negate.[30] Quite typical of his arguments against Prāsaṅgika, Chapa concludes by showing that Prāsaṅgikas have the same faults that they accuse him of having. Both sides need to step outside of "worldly" logic in their presentations of the ultimate: Chapa would seem to acknowledge that his own ultimate without distinctions does not conform to worldly logic.

Throughout the back-and-forth style he adopts in his "debate," Chapa adduces hypothetical positions that he does not hold simply because they cause problems for the Prāsaṅgika.[31] These positions bring out weaknesses in the Prāsaṅgika position but do not reflect his own view. While the passage cited above could be understood as Chapa holding that the mind, or "clear awareness," is the ultimate that lacks any distinctions, interpreting this ultimately existing awareness as a hypothetical position better fits the evidence. That Chapa could hold the mind itself to be the ultimate does not square with the many other clear statements he makes regarding the ultimate as a non-affirming negative and utter non-establishment. Even if one suggests that he holds the mind's ultimate non-establishment to be the ultimate, an emptiness of establishment would still be his ultimate, not the mind.

Further evidence that mind is not Chapa's ultimate occurs in his explanation of Nāgārjuna's famous claim that "If I had a thesis, I would have a fault. Since I have no thesis, I am only faultless."[32] Having argued at length against the Prāsaṅgika's over-literal interpretation of thesislessness, Chapa states:

> It is not the case that emptiness does not exist as the basic disposition (*gshis*) of objects of knowledge because if emptiness does not abide, it would [absurdly] follow that a true entity (*bden pa'i dngos po*) is established. The intention of [Nāgārjuna's] declaration of no thesis is that although the emptiness of true entities is ultimate truth, the thesis holder's awareness (*dam 'cha' ba bo'i blo*) is not established when analyzed through reasoning and, hence, this is not established as a thesis.[33]

Chapa clearly holds that emptiness is ultimate truth and leads to a positive statement regarding the nature of phenomena: all phenomena are empty. Whether or not he portrays Nāgārjuna's "intention" more faithfully than Prāsaṅgikas do, his interpretation makes clear that, in his view, the awareness that realizes the thesis "all phenomena are empty" itself does not hold up to analysis. Awareness is not the ultimate.

We have seen that for Chapa the non-affirming negative, emptiness, is true in final analysis because it is not overturned by that analysis; it "bears analysis." Additionally, we have seen that it is "true as an object of final cognition." But does Chapa hold that the ultimate is "truly established"? Emptiness exists as the ultimate; but does it ultimately exist? In this text, I have not found Chapa using the term "truly established" (*bden par grub pa*), nor does he seem to distinguish between existing as the ultimate and ultimately existing (*don dam du yod pa/don dam par yod pa*).[34] Very likely, these are distinctions made by later Tibetan scholars and were not part of twelfth-century discussions. However, we can pose these questions to Chapa's work in order to highlight the differences between his understanding of the ultimate and the views of later and better-known Tibetan scholars. As discussed above, he states clearly that the ultimate is utter non-establishment. It would therefore seem that the ultimate would not be truly established, as nothing is. Additionally, for Chapa, the non-affirming negative, emptiness, exists without distinctions and is the ultimate; it would then "exist as the ultimate." That emptiness is found by final analysis suggests that Chapa may view it as ultimately existing, if by "ultimately" we mean "in final analysis." However, in a passage that continues from his interpretation of Nāgārjuna's "thesislessness," Chapa writes:

> Regarding suchness, or utter non-establishment, the phenomenon that is an object of valid cognition, and so forth, does not exist ultimately (*don dam par*). However, the phenomenon [suchness] that is a manifest object of valid cognition relative to yogic direct perception and is a hidden object of valid cognition relative to the inference that cuts proliferations abides conventionally (*tha snyad du*).[35]

For Chapa, the emptiness that is the object of a yogi's meditation or of a valid inference proving that phenomena are empty conventionally exists. He may only be saying that the meditative and logical practices leading to awakening and the realization of emptiness exist conventionally. However, the most straightforward way of reading this passage is that the ultimate does not ultimately exist.[36]

The ultimate that Chapa argues for is unique in the history of Madhyamaka thought. He and his contemporaries grappled with the question of how to maintain the ultimate's singularly important status but yet allow it to come under the same principles of valid cognition that bear on the conventional world. The solutions he adduces were not always adopted by others, yet we see elements of his explanation and responses to his answers surviving into the present. In certain regards, Chapa's ultimate comes dangerously close to a "positive emptiness," consistently eschewed by Mādhyamikas. His language suggests that the ultimate is more than a simple absence, that emptiness—the final nature—holds up to analysis, that something stands out of nothing. However, this nature is a negation that does not affirm or imply the presence of something else but is utter non-establishment. As such, Chapa's ultimate is even more strongly aligned with a "negative" interpretation of emptiness. In sum, Chapa holds that the ultimate

- is ultimately true,
- bears final analysis,
- exists without characteristic,
- conventionally exists,
- is a non-affirming negative, and
- is utterly non-established.

This combination of characteristics allows for the ultimate to be found by inferential reasoning and exist as the fundamental nature of all phenomena while yet being the negation of all conceptual proliferation. Chapa's emphasis on a knowable ultimate ran directly counter to his Prāsaṅgika contemporaries yet foreshadowed the direction that Tibetan Madhyamaka exegesis would take in the ensuing centuries.

Almost the Ultimate

We have seen Chapa's insistence that ultimate truth is a non-affirming negative and is the final nature of phenomena. This combination of traits poses certain problems, one of which is how positive phenomena (or affirming negatives) can have a final nature that is a non-affirming negative. Chapa's exploration of this problem adduces certain phenomena that are *almost* the ultimate, phenomena that he calls "concordant ultimates" (*mthun pa'i don dam*).[37] The notion of concordant ultimates was utilized by Chapa and other early Tibetan Svātantrikas to explain how the ultimate can be realized by human cognition and to explain how enlightened beings can still perceive appearances; concordant ultimates soften the divide between conventional and ultimate that all Mādhyamikas uphold. The early Prāsaṅgika rejection of concordant ultimates marks another key distinction between Prāsaṅgika and Svātantrika Madhyamaka in twelfth-century Tibet.

In the course of explicating how the two truths are of one entity (*ngo bo gcig pa*), Chapa addresses the criticism that since appearances do not bear analysis, an emptiness that is of the same nature as appearances would likewise not bear analysis and would, therefore, not be ultimate truth (assuming Chapa's correlation of ultimate truth and bearing analysis). The opponent argues that some other emptiness that is not of the same nature as appearances (an emptiness that is not an object of knowledge?) must be the "real [literally, 'non-figurative'] ultimate truth" (*rnam grangs ma yin pa'i don dam*) while the emptiness that shares a nature with appearances is only a "concordant ultimate, included among the obscurational."[38] Chapa replies that if "real" ultimate truth was not of the same nature as appearances, realizing emptiness would not overturn the false belief in ultimately existing phenomena.[39] Without explaining the tension between an ultimate that bears analysis and appearances that do not, he upholds the dictum that an emptiness that is a non-affirming negative is the "real ultimate truth," of one nature with appearances.

Chapa counts certain affirming negatives among concordant ultimates. Given his own insistence that the ultimate bears analysis due to existing without any distinctions and given his inclusion of positive phenomena within affirming negatives, Chapa has an opponent ask whether the non-affirming negation of positive phenomena could be ultimate truth. If so, "it would be contradictory to explain it as a concordant ultimate,"[40] for it would be the actual ultimate. On one hand, the emptiness of positive phenomena would also establish the emptiness of affirming negatives; only the emptiness of non-affirming negatives would remain to be established. On the other hand, establishing the emptiness of positive phenomena would establish the emptiness of the "distinction,"[41] positive, and Chapa's ultimate has no distinctions. Chapa adjures that it cannot be a real ultimate; although one realizing the emptiness of positive phenomena "realizes a factor of ultimate truth," such a practitioner "does not dispel all obstructions"[42] and so has not realized ultimate truth. Additionally, he states that while a non-affirming negative is not a concordant ultimate, the negation of the distinction, which itself is a positive, comes to have an affirming negative that is a concordant ultimate:

> The negatives that are connected with that basis [positive phenomena] or that appear to the conceptuality that eliminates the object of negation are affirming negatives and are conventional entities. By the factor of being empty of the object of negation, they are similar to a non-affirming negative; hence, they are

> explained to be concordant ultimates. The non-affirming negative is not explained to be a concordant ultimate.[43]

Affirming negatives that are deeply connected with an emptiness, such as the negation of a positive phenomenon that could be the first step toward a non-affirming negation of positive and negative phenomena, are here considered concordant ultimates.

Chapa's discussion of some things that are *not* the ultimate bears on the present discussion of how he understands concordant ultimates, even though he does not utilize the term in his discussion. Immediately following the above passage on the emptiness of positive phenomena, Chapa addresses the possibility that the illusion-like (*sgyu ma lta bu*) nature of appearances could be considered ultimate truth. The illusion-like nature of phenomena is seen by a practitioner who realizes the naturelessness of phenomena and, retaining that realization, subsequently perceives appearances. Thus, as Chapa tells us, "illusion-like" is a composite of naturelessness and appearance.[44] If this composite were ultimate truth, the parts of the composite, naturelessness and appearance, could not be analytically separated nor overturned by analysis; they would be final. Then, appearances, as one inseparable part of ultimate truth, could not be nullified by analysis and would have to exist ultimately.[45] However, appearances are not found (*rnyed pa*) by final analysis and so a composite of appearance and naturelessness cannot be found by final analysis; the composite—and therefore, illusion-like nature—cannot be ultimate truth.[46]

Elsewhere, Chapa tells us that the inference that proves phenomena to have an illusion-like nature is an affirming negative and a conventional consciousness.[47] He does not label it a concordant ultimate but contrasts it with the non-affirming negative, emptiness, found by a reasoning consciousness (*rigs shes*).[48] Over two hundred years later, the Tibetan polymath, Tsongkhapa,[49] called illusion-like nature a concordant ultimate and argued against the notion that an illusion-like nature is established by a reasoning consciousness (*sgyu ma rigs grub pa*). In arguing against this, Tsongkhapa additionally shows that Śāntarakṣita, Kamalaśīla, and Haribhadra also do not hold the illusion-like nature to be the ultimate.[50] Chapa's and Tsongkhapa's rejections that an illusion-like nature is found by a reasoning consciousness would seem to be very much in line with each other and with their Indian forebears. We see the category of Mādhyamikas who hold that the illusion-like nature is established by a reasoning consciousness (*rgyu ma rigs grub pa*) in Tibetan Madhyamaka literature, along with speculations by some scholars that this category can be equated with Svātantrika Mādhyamikas.[51] In relation to eighth-century

Indian authors and twelfth-century Tibetan authors who would be labeled Svātantrikas, we can see that this equation is without veracity. Chapa, the chief proponent of early Svātantrika, and the Indian authors whom he relies upon in no way accept that the illusion-like nature is ultimate truth.[52]

Further developing the idea that a reasoning consciousness does not establish the illusion-like nature, Chapa emphasizes the distinction between the non-affirming negative, emptiness, that is realized by a reasoning consciousness and the affirming negative, the composite of appearance and emptiness (the illusion-like nature), that is comprehended by inference. The inference that proves "entities are empty of a true nature" must realize an affirming negative because it associates the inferential subject, "entity," with the predicate, "emptiness." However, a reasoning consciousness realizes only the non-affirming negative, "empty of a true nature," based on this inference. Since emptiness is of the same substance (*rdzas gcig*) as "entity," a reasoning consciousness realizes the substance of "entity"; it realizes the emptiness of a true entity, not an emptiness unrelated with entity.[53] Again, Chapa is concerned to have the realization of emptiness be the realization of a non-affirming negative that operates along with affirming negatives, here the illusion-like nature. While he does not label illusion-like nature as a concordant ultimate, he may well regard it so.

In his discussion of concordant and actual (*dngos*) ultimates, Tsongkhapa argues similarly to Chapa that the actual ultimate is intimately tied with conventional appearances but, as we have seen, the composite of appearance and emptiness is a concordant ultimate. He cites Kamalaśīla's *Illumination of the Middle,* which states that the absence of production "accords with the ultimate,"[54] and Śāntarakṣita's *Ornament for the Middle,* which contains a similar statement,[55] before noting:

> Many earlier [scholars] treated these as the two ultimate truths: figurative and non-figurative. [They identified] the emptiness that is a negative of ultimate production, and so forth, of phenomena such as forms as the figurative ultimate, asserting that this is imputed to be ultimate truth but has the character of obscurational truth. They asserted that the non-figurative ultimate truth cannot be taken as an object of any mind and therefore is not an object of knowledge.[56]

Tsongkhapa argues against these earlier scholars who interpreted Kamalaśīla's statement—and others like it in the writings of Śāntarakṣita and Jñānagarbha—to mean that these Mādhyamikas held the emptiness of ultimate production, realized by inference, to be only a concordant ultimate while the actual ultimate is beyond consciousness. He explains that "in the perspective of a conceptual reasoning consciousness," emptiness is not the actual ultimate, but emptiness "in the perspective of a non-conceptual reasoning consciousness" is.[57] The distinction that Tsongkhapa sees Kamalaśīla making is between the conceptual and non-conceptual realization of the ultimate. While a conceptually realized emptiness can then be termed a concordant ultimate, since the object of conceptual reasoning consciousnesses is actually the same emptiness as the emptiness realized by non-conceptual wisdom it is only differentiated by the conceptual manner in which it is realized.[58] Both Chapa and Tsongkhapa argue that an emptiness intimately tied with ordinary appearances, knowledge of which is inferentially induced, is the actual ultimate truth. It could be that Chapa, like Tsongkhapa many years later (possibly under Chapa's influence), attempted to rectify what he understood to be a misinterpretation of Jñānagarbha's, Śāntarakṣita's, and Kamalaśīla's understanding of concordant ultimates.[59]

Another point of interest in Tsongkhapa's account of concordant ultimates, bearing on the understanding of the concept by early Prāsaṅgikas and Svātantrikas, is his discussion of subjective concordant ultimates. In Chapa's account, only objects are considered concordant ultimates.[60] Tsongkhapa explains that Bhāvaviveka, Jñānagarbha, Śāntarakṣita, and Kamalaśīla held both subjective and objective concordant ultimates: all four Indian scholars understood the reasoning consciousness that realizes emptiness to have a conceptual and a non-conceptual variety. Conceptual reasoning consciousnesses and their objects are designated as concordant ultimates, giving us a subjective and an objective concordant ultimate. While only emptiness is truly the ultimate, the non-conceptual wisdom realizing emptiness comes to be called the ultimate, not a concordant ultimate.[61] Unfortunately, Chapa does not explicate this topic in the detail that Tsongkhapa does, leaving us uncertain as to whether concordant ultimates include, for him, consciousnesses or only their objects.

Tsongkhapa's discussion of the division of ultimate truths into real (or "non-figurative") and concordant (or "figurative") ultimates cites the writings of Bhāvaviveka, Śāntarakṣita, Kamalaśīla, and Jñānagarbha—all of whom Tsongkhapa regards as Svātantrikas. He notes that the ultimate is divided differently in the writings of Candrakīrti, the Prāsaṅgika *par excellence*.[62] It would seem that Tsongkhapa recognized that "concordant ultimate" was a topic developed by Indian Mādhyamikas whom he regarded as Svātantrika.[63] Furthermore, he recognized that some exegetes incorrectly saw the importance of concordant ultimates as separating actual ultimate truth from the purview of the mind: while a concordant ultimate could be talked and thought about, the actual ultimate could not. While he does not tell us who those Tibetans were, the notion that the ultimate is not an object of knowledge is clearly a view of early Prāsaṅgikas. No surviving evidence shows early Prāsaṅgikas adopting a distinction between real and concordant ultimates, but one can well imagine this distinction—made by such eminent Indian Mādhyamikas—being recast by Tibetan Prāsaṅgikas to highlight the difference between an ultimate that is a topic of ordinary parlance and the "real" ultimate that cannot be known.

The third Sakya hierarch, Drakpa Gyeltsen, saw a greater division between Prāsaṅgika and Svātantrika on the issue of concordant ultimates. In his *Clearly Realizing Tantra: A Precious Tree,*[64] he discusses concordant ultimates mainly in terms of mental states but also secondarily in terms of objects of mental states that accord with ultimate truth. His position both develops Chapa's ideas and prefigures the views of Tsongkhapa. He saw Svātantrikas developing the notion of concordant ultimates as an answer for how ordinary consciousness can ascertain the ultimate and how Buddhas can continue to perceive and interact with the conventional world. Prāsaṅgikas, in his depiction, reject concordant ultimates with their views of an ultimate unreachable by ordinary consciousness and a buddhahood that cannot perceive ordinary appearances.

Setting up his discussion of concordant ultimates, Drakpa Gyeltsen lists four positions on the issues of what classes of beings have ultimate states of awareness and whether a Buddha has conventional states of mind or only ultimate states—this latter question amounting to whether a Buddha can or cannot perceive ordinary appearances.[65] He then writes:

> Prāsaṅgikas hold, "All ordinary beings' awarenesses are only conventional. The meditative absorptions of the three classes of āryas are ultimate; their subsequent practices are conventional awarenesses. Since buddhas are always in meditative absorption, they only have ultimate [awareness]." This, too, is not correct for [this view] has the fault that it would follow that buddhas would not enter non-abiding nirvāṇa. Also, [this view] has the fault of contradicting the master Candrakīrti's assertion, in his *Commentary on [Nāgārjuna's] Sixty Stanzas on Reasoning,* "Truths are posited as two from the perspective of worldly awareness."[66]

In Drakpa Gyeltsen's characterization, Prāsaṅgikas hold a stark divide between ordinary and enlightened, where ordinary beings are incapable of knowing the ultimate and Buddhas are always absorbed in emptiness and therefore unable to perceive ordinary appearances. He criticizes this view on the grounds that it would not allow for a presentation of non-abiding nirvāṇa (*apratiṣṭhitanirvāṇa, mi gnas pa'i mya ngan las 'das pa*), in which Buddhas are able to remain in meditation on emptiness and simultaneously aid ordinary beings. Additionally, Drakpa Gyeltsen directly addresses the view that "Ultimate truth is not the referent of any awareness," writing, "Saying that would be senseless."[67] He rejects a clean divide between ordinary and ultimate awarenesses as well as the idea that ultimate truth passes beyond all awareness.

Drakpa Gyeltsen understands Candrakīrti's comment, "Truths are posited as two from the perspective of worldly awareness," to mean that the two truths are explicated in accordance with worldly awareness: in technical terms, he writes, "worldly awareness is the basis for division [into the two truths]."[68] Drawing heavily on the *Hevajra Tantra,* in addition to Candrakīrti, he explains that the two truths themselves are not awarenesses but that the same substratum is perceived as obscurational truth from the perspective of ordinary awareness and is perceived as ultimate truth from the perspective of ultimate awareness; the referents of the two types of awareness come to be posited as the two truths.[69] While the referent of ordinary, obscured awareness is obscurational truth, "being true as the referent of unmistaken awareness is purified cyclic existence; this is nirvāṇa."[70] Worldly awareness, then, is the basis of division for the two truths because it "establishes the conventional and blocks (*'gegs pa*) the ultimate."[71] Worldly awareness demarcates obscurational truth; its presence "blocks" ultimate truth while its purification marks the realization of nirvāṇa.

Drakpa Gyeltsen's explication of how Candrakīrti's comment should be understood to mean that worldly awareness is the basis of division for the two truths may not be immediately distinguishable from the Prāsaṅgika view that he criticizes. However, he goes on to explain how the Svātantrika view allows for concordant ultimates and, consequently, non-abiding nirvāṇa. In contrast to the hard and fast distinction between ordinary and ultimate awareness found in the Prāsaṅgika view,

> Svātantrikas hold that for an ordinary being, all subjects—that is, mental awarenesses—are conventional awarenesses. It is indeed the case that a consciousness of the nature (*chos nyid*) is also conventional. However, since the reasoning that knows that the nature is

> unproduced is partially concordant with a Buddha's mind (*thugs*) that knows that the nature is unproduced, it is called a concordant ultimate.
>
> As for the three classes of āryas' consciousnesses, meditative absorptions are ultimate; subsequent practices are conventional.
>
> Buddhas' non-conceptual minds are ultimate; [their] pure worldly wisdom (*dag pa 'jig rten pa'i ye shes*), being supported by [non-conceptual] wisdom, is a figurative conventional. Therefore, this is also non-abiding nirvāṇa.
>
> Wisdom, alternately, is unsurpassed; thus it is ultimate. It is also continuous meditative equipoise. Regarding this also, it should not be disputed that this concordant ultimate is just the ultimate.[72]

While all ordinary awarenesses must be categorized as conventional, certain realizations accord with non-conceptual wisdom, the ultimate awareness. Ordinary awareness can be developed to have an understanding of the unproduced nature of phenomena, which, while falling short of full realization of emptiness, is a stepping stone to that realization. Later, in consideration of the same passage from the *Introduction to the Two Truths Sūtra* that Candrakīrti and Prajñākaramati cited in support of their claim that ultimate truth is not a referent of consciousness ("Ultimate truth is passed beyond entities ranging right through the referents of omniscient wisdoms"), Drakpa Gyeltsen writes, "The emptiness conceived by ordinary beings' awareness, the absence of production, and so forth are not ultimate truth. . . . Those, also, however, are causes producing the ultimate and thus are figurative ultimates."[73] Rather than interpret the sūtra passage to mean that the ultimate is entirely out of the scope of ordinary consciousness, he understands that ordinary awareness can gain an image of emptiness that acts as a "cause" bringing about non-conceptual realization of emptiness.

Drakpa Gyeltsen seems to hold non-conceptual wisdom itself as a special kind of concordant ultimate. As we saw with Chapa and Tsongkhapa, Drakpa Gyeltsen speaks of ultimate truth as emptiness, the object of non-conceptual, ultimate consciousness. At the end of the passage quoted above, he calls wisdom "the ultimate" and "continuous meditative absorption" before noting that "this concordant ultimate is just the ultimate." Drakpa Gyeltsen categorizes wisdom as a concordant ultimate—a notion suggested in the passages from Chapa and Tsongkhapa—but then singles out non-conceptual wisdom from ordinary awareness's conceptual understanding of emptiness, which he also categorizes as a concordant ultimate. He understands the concordant ultimate, non-conceptual wisdom, to be "just the ultimate." This would seem to single out the importance of this mental state, rather than leading him to the unlikely conclusion that a kind of consciousness is ultimate truth.

We additionally see Drakpa Gyeltsen introducing a previously unseen notion into this discussion: "figurative conventionals." As hinted at previously and discussed in full in the following chapter, the Prāsaṅgika notion of buddhahood moves toward denying ordinary perception to Buddhas. Drakpa Gyeltsen characterizes Prāsaṅgika as holding that Buddhas only have ultimate awareness, non-conceptual meditative absorption on emptiness. The Svātantrika position, in contrast, affords Buddhas "pure worldly wisdom" that adheres to the non-conceptual realization of emptiness—the "purified" view of cyclic existence—but allows perception of worldly appearances. Pure worldly wisdom accords with conventional awarenesses, allowing perception of conventional truths. Whereas Drakpa Gyeltsen faulted the Prāsaṅgika view for not allowing non-abiding nirvāṇa, the Svātantrika view of a Buddha having both non-conceptual wisdom and a pure worldly wisdom enables an explanation of non-abiding nirvāṇa, in which Buddhas are both fully realized and fully able to aid sentient beings.

The notion of "pure worldly wisdom" goes back at least as far as Bhāvaviveka's *Blaze of Reasoning*, in which we read of two kinds of ultimate consciousnesses:

> The ultimate has two aspects: one engages non-conceptually, passes beyond the world, is undefiled, and lacks proliferation; the second engages conceptually, accords with the collection of merit and wisdom, is called "pure worldly wisdom," and possesses proliferations.[74]

Bhāvaviveka understands pure worldly wisdom to be a form of conceptual consciousness and, consequently, to be embroiled with "proliferations." However, unlike non-conceptual wisdom, it allows for perception of worldly conventionalities. Drakpa Gyeltsen draws upon Bhāvaviveka's idea to solve the problem of how Buddhas can both abide in non-conceptual realization and still perceive and aid ordinary beings.

A presentation of figurative ultimates, both subjective and objective, that forms the likely basis for Drakpa Gyeltsen's discussion is found in Bhāvaviveka's *Compendium of Meanings of the Middle*.[75] Declaring that the ultimate has two varieties, Bhāvaviveka explains that the real ultimate is the "emptiness of all proliferations."[76] Figurative ultimates include both consciousnesses: the "reasoning figurative ultimate," the consciousness that utilizes the four reasons to refute the four alternatives (*catuṣkoti,* here listed as "production, cessation, and so forth"); and objects: "the ultimate of the negation of production," and "all appearing entities."[77] The first type of figurative ultimate, the likely basis for Drakpa Gyeltsen's understanding of reasoning consciousnesses as concordant ultimates, conceptually realizes the emptiness of production and cessation. One suspects that this conceptual realization induces non-conceptual wisdom and could be considered a "cause" of ultimate consciousness, as we saw with Drakpa Gyeltsen. Bhāvaviveka does not write of non-conceptual wisdom in this short text, but may include it with reasoning consciousnesses as a type of concordant ultimate. As noted above, Bhāvaviveka holds that the non-figurative ultimate is only the emptiness of all proliferations, and, thus, does not understand wisdom to be an actual ultimate.

The objective figurative ultimate found in the *Compendium of Meanings* refers to the first of the four steps in the reasoning process, the negation of production. Chapa and Drakpa Gyeltsen similarly spoke of the negation of a positive phenomenon and the absence of production, respectively, as concordant ultimates. As we saw, Chapa understood the negation of a positive phenomenon to be an affirming negative, a negation that would require the further negation of negative phenomena. Bhāvaviveka may consider the negation of production to be a concordant ultimate for the same reason: the negation of production would still require the negation of cessation (and the negation of both production and cessation and the negation of neither production nor cessation). The negation of production accords with and leads to the negation of all four alternatives, which itself is the actual ultimate, the emptiness of all proliferations. Bhāvaviveka may understand "all appearing entities" to be concordant ultimates in the same way that Chapa and Tsongkhapa discussed the union of appearance and emptiness as, respectively, *not* the ultimate and a concordant ultimate. All appearing entities are, indeed, empty and their emptiness is ultimate truth. However, the appearance of entities can only accord with their ultimate emptiness.

While not wishing to elide the differences between these thinkers' projects, we can trace a common thread on the issue of concordant, or figurative, ultimates in the writings of Bhāvaviveka, Chapa, Drakpa Gyeltsen, and Tsongkhapa (while I have only touched upon their works above, we can also include Śāntarakṣita, Kamalaśīla, and Jñānagarbha). All of these Buddhist scholars placed a high premium on explicating an ultimate truth that could be accessed by ordinary consciousness. Tsongkhapa utilized concordant ultimates to explain how emptiness can be known conceptually. While not developing the notion as clearly, Chapa, in passages that run parallel to (and perhaps prefiguring) Tsongkhapa's, explains how conceptual inference knows the composite of appearance, or entity, and naturelessness, or emptiness. Bhāvaviveka and Drakpa Gyeltsen utilize the notion of subjective concordant ultimates to show how ordinary mind can conceptually know the ultimate. These two and Chapa (and quite likely Jñānagarbha, Śāntarakṣita, and Kamalaśīla) write of objective concordant ultimates to explain how realization of emptiness develops in stages: one can realize the emptiness of production, a concordant ultimate, which leads to realizing the emptiness of all proliferations. Authors whom, with the exception of Tsongkhapa, we can thematically regard as Svātantrikas developed concordant ultimates as solutions to making the ultimate accessible to ordinary cognition.[78]

Drakpa Gyeltsen makes clear that the acceptance or rejection of concordant ultimates was a dividing line in the formation of Svātantrika and Prāsaṅgika schools in twelfth-century Tibet. Tsongkhapa's mention of earlier scholars who distinguished concordant ultimates, which could be talked and thought about, from the actual ultimate, which they posited as not an object of knowledge, suggests that certain Prāsaṅgikas reinterpreted the idea of concordant ultimates as a way to continue to separate real ultimate truth from the scope of ordinary mind. This reinterpretation runs counter to the thrust of the Svātantrika development of concordant ultimates, which included a softening of the distinction between the conventional and the ultimate, and amounts to a rejection of concordant ultimates as understood by Svātantrika authors.

In addition to the lack of discussion of concordant ultimates in any of the Prāsaṅgika-leaning authors examined here, we find evidence that some of Candrakīrti's revivalists directly rejected the possibility of concordant ultimates. Whereas the author of the *Compendium of Meanings of the Middle* writes that the ultimate has two varieties, figurative and non-figurative, other authors specifically denied that the ultimate could be twofold. In his *Introduction to the Two Truths,* Atiśa writes, "The ultimate is only one; others assert that it is two."[79] Atiśa's comment takes a very literal reading of the common Madhyamaka dictum that ultimate truth is singular and unique, a dictum that is emblemized in Nāgārjuna's famous statement, "Only nirvāṇa is true." The interpretation of this dictum formed a significant part of the Madhyamaka controversy of this period. Drakpa Gyeltsen understood his development of concordant ultimates as countering what he saw as a too-literal understanding of Nāgārjuna's statement.[80] Those with Prāsaṅgika leanings, like Atiśa, who upheld a strict interpretation of Nāgārjuna's dictum, rejected the presentations of a manifold ultimate as exemplified in the writings of Bhāvaviveka.

Conclusion: The Importance of the Ultimate

Chapter 1 demonstrated the importance of the ultimate to the rise of Candrakīrti in eleventh-century India, while chapter 2 pointed to the role of the ultimate in the formation of Prāsaṅgika and Svātantrika schools in twelfth-century Tibet. Our present discussion of the competing conceptions of the ultimate, while supporting Gelukpa doxographical claims that Prāsaṅgika and Svātantrika hold differing views on emptiness, does not defend those claims, but instead shows that the twelfth-century debate centered on the ultimate in a very different way than understood in Geluk circles. In place of Gelukpa concerns over phenomena being or not being "established by way of their own character" (*rang gi mtshan nyid kyis grub pa*), in the twelfth century we see debates over ultimate truth being a knowable phenomenon and over the existence of states of consciousness and referents of consciousness that accord with the ultimate. Just what the ultimate *is* formed an important nexus of issues in this period.

Additionally, arguments from both sides point out the soteriological importance of the ultimate for Madhyamaka. For Prāsaṅgikas, the salvifically essential role of the ultimate required that it be kept out of the category of knowable phenomena altogether. All other phenomena invoke dualistic knowledge and entrapment in cyclic existence; ultimate truth induces release and so must be beyond all dualistic conceptions. The ultimate's importance led Svātantrikas down a different route. Instead of emphasizing the unique ontological status of ultimate truth, they sought explanations that allowed the ultimate to come into the sphere of consciousness. In their view, consciousness could be successively developed to know the ultimate. The status of the ultimate in these two schools of thought led quickly to divergent views on transformation and buddhahood. We now move to explore debates between these two sides on how one knows the ultimate and transforms the ordinary mind and body into buddhahood, and how, once transformed, a Buddha continues to know the conventional world.

5. Prāsaṅgika vs. Svātantrika on Non-Abiding Nirvāṇa

As we saw in the previous chapter, those who reject concordant ultimates discard both an ultimate that is realized in stages and an ordinary consciousness that can gain conceptual insight into emptiness. The Prāsaṅgika rejection of the latter, subjective concordant ultimates, ties closely to their assertion that the ultimate is not knowable by ordinary consciousness. If concordant ultimates were developed to bring the ultimate into the scope of ordinary awareness, the rejection of concordant ultimates clearly reinforces the interpretation that ultimate truth is singularly set off from human cognition.

This chapter focuses upon the views on transformation and buddhahood among eleventh- and twelfth-century Mādhyamikas who argued for a transcendent ultimate truth, one that is both beyond the scope of ordinary mind and against states of mind that accord with the realization of ultimate truth. Foundational to their emerging Prāsaṅgika interpretation was a metaphoric view of "knowing" the ultimate; in reality, mind has no relationship to the ultimate and in fact ceases altogether upon realization. Prāsaṅgikas attempted to account for a practitioner's transformation to buddhahood in the absence of mind and understood a Buddha to "perceive" ordinary appearances without the mental instrument of perception. Early Prāsaṅgikas were forced to reconcile their unique interpretation of buddhahood with the wider Mahāyāna Buddhist understanding of non-abiding nirvāṇa (*apratiṣṭhitanirvāṇa, mi gnas pa'i mya ngan las 'das pa*), in which a Buddha is both constantly in meditation on emptiness and working for the welfare of sentient beings.[1] How a Buddha could do both, particularly the latter, in the absence of consciousness proved to be a major stumbling block for this new school of Madhyamaka. The final section of this chapter moves to examine critics of the early Prāsaṅgika solutions, Chapa Chokyi Sengé, his student Sonam Tsemo, and

Drakpa Gyeltsen, who developed views of transformation and enlightenment consistent with concordant ultimates, allowing for a more coherent model of buddhahood.

"Knowing" the Ultimate: Transformation in the Absence of Mind

We have already examined the Prāsaṅgika claim that the ultimate is entirely outside the scope of ordinary consciousness. As a corollary of this claim, we see early Prāsaṅgikas rejecting the legitimacy of valid cognition (*pramāṇa, tshad ma*) in knowing the ultimate and rejecting that the ultimate is "known" at all. In his *Introduction to the Two Truths,* the same text in which he declared, "The ultimate is only one," Atiśa argued against the possibility that any kind of ordinary valid cognition can know the ultimate.[2] He examines the two types of valid cognition, perception and inference, rejects the ability of either to know the ultimate, and writes, "The deluded whose vision is narrow say that the two [kinds of valid cognition, direct perception and inference] realize emptiness."[3] Having dispensed with the ordinary ways in which we may go about knowing the ultimate, Atiśa cryptically states that while emptiness is utterly undifferentiated, "We realize it through not realizing; hence, we impute the convention, 'seeing emptiness.'"[4] Seeing emptiness can be spoken of conventionally, but in truth there is no act of perception, only a mysterious way of "realizing through not realizing." One suspects, much as we saw in Jayānanda's writings, that Atiśa understands consciousness to be inextricably imbued with subject-object duality; consequently, "realizing" must mean the process of a subject realizing an object.[5] Only by rejecting the dualistic model of knowledge can Atiśa speak of "realizing emptiness." However, "realizing" is stripped of its usual cognitive force and "seeing emptiness" becomes only a conventional designation.

Jayānanda details his understanding of a practitioner's realization of the ultimate through explicating Candrakīrti's famous proclamation that "realizing the ultimate" can only be said metaphorically.[6] Candrakīrti draws upon a Sautrāntika[7] model of ordinary perception in which an external object causes a perceiving consciousness to be produced in the aspect (*ākāra, rnam pa*) of the object; one perceives the aspect of the external object, not the object itself, but yet this is still called "perceiving the object." Just so, Candrakīrti tells us, an awareness takes on the aspect of the ultimate but never really perceives the ultimate; merely taking on the aspect of the ultimate is conveniently called "realizing suchness." He writes,

> Since the final nature is without production and the mind also is devoid of production,
> Due to that [object] in the basis [that is, the mind] that has the aspect of that [birthless final nature, this is said to be] like "knowing reality."
> Hence, "knowing" [reality] is in dependence upon conventions,
> Just as [in Sautrāntika] a mind knows well its object due to arising in the aspect of that object.[8]

Jayānanda explains that "knowing" is simply a convention applied to the process of stopping all perception:

> Awareness also has the aspect of birthlessness. Hence, it is as though that awareness realizes suchness, which has the nature of birthlessness.... In that, there is no [duality of] illuminator and illuminated.... Just as one knows blue, knowing in dependence on convention in that way, we say that one knows (*adhigama, thugs su chud pa*) suchness in dependence on convention, not ultimately.... Thus, the very lack of observing (*anupalambha, mi dmigs pa*)[9] any suitable entity at all is knowing suchness.[10]

An awareness that approaches "perceiving" the ultimate takes on the aspect of its birthless nature. However, as we saw Jayānanda explain above, subject-object duality can play no part in "knowing" the ultimate. Awareness is intimately tied with duality and so cannot actually perceive or know the ultimate. Jayānanda's metaphor of "illuminator and illuminated" is a common means of referring to cognitive acts, in which the "light" of consciousness casts itself upon an object. Jettisoning this understanding of cognition, Jayānanda writes that not observing any entity is to realize the ultimate. Similar to Atiśa's portrayal, "knowing the ultimate" is simply a convention applied to the cessation of perception.

Not only does perception cease in Jayānanda's process of becoming Buddha, but ordinary mind itself stops. He offers a very literal interpretation of Candrakīrti's claim that at buddhahood, mind and mental factors (*citta-caitta*) cease.[11] Rather than a true transformation of ordinary consciousness, as is found in the Yogācāra model of "transformation of the basis",[12] Jayānanda understands ordinary mind simply to cease along with all dualistic cognitive activity. He writes,

> Since enlightenment is by way of not knowing (*anadhigama*) at all, we assert that the activities of mind and mental factors—feeling

> and so forth—having the character of experiencing, have ceased their engagement. There is no engagement of mind and mental factors. Therefore, there is no appearance at all, because all conceptuality has been blocked.[13]

Just as he has described "realizing the ultimate" to be a lack of perceiving, Jayānanda here explains that enlightenment is a process of "not knowing" and is characterized by the elimination of the knowing instrument, the mind. In this view, knowing is imbued with dualistic notions of subject and object and so, too, is ordinary mind itself.

As we have seen in the previous chapters, Jayānanda seems to understand the subject-object model of perception to operate conceptually. With conceptuality "blocked," he tells us here, perceptual referents do not appear. This point is amplified elsewhere, as Jayānanda distinguishes between obscurational (or conventional) truths and "mere conventionalities": Those who have contemplatively realized the emptiness of phenomena but have yet to attain buddhahood continue to perceive appearances outside of meditation but, unlike ordinary people, no longer believe in the truth of those appearances; appearances for these beings are "mere conventionalities" rather than conventional truths.[14] However, Buddhas lack ordinary consciousnesses and so do not even perceive appearances: "Mere conventionalities do not appear to Supramundane Victor Buddhas who do not have the capacity to experience consciousnesses that have the aspect of blue and so forth."[15] Jayānanda here denies Buddhas both subjects and objects. In his schema, there seems to be no overlap between the objects of ordinary, ignorant consciousness and the object (if we may call it that) of a Buddha's wisdom. Jayānanda's examination of the transformative process presents fundamental disjunctions between ordinary mind and enlightenment and between the appearances to ordinary consciousness and the utter lack of appearances to a Buddha.

In Atiśa's and Jayānanda's views, subjective concordant ultimates—which would allow for ordinary consciousness developing toward a conceptual and then non-conceptual understanding of the ultimate—are missing. In their place, we see explanations of a metaphoric realization of emptiness that present a disjunction between ordinary consciousness and realization of the ultimate, rather than the model of progression implicit in concordant ultimates (most strongly exemplified by Drakpa Gyeltsen's statement that concordant ultimates are the "cause" producing realization of the ultimate). The question remains in these early Prāsaṅgika viewpoints of the process of transformation from ordinary awareness to "realization": what induces the cessation of dualistic knowing and how can buddhahood arise from it?

Atiśa's brief poetic text provides no answer. However, Jayānanda, well aware of the pitfalls of his model, is very concerned with demonstrating how his Prāsaṅgika interpretation allows for transformation from an advanced Buddhist practitioner into a Buddha. Particularly, he wants to demonstrate how the cessation of a practitioner's mind can engender the three bodies (*kāya*) of a Buddha and how, without mind and appearances, Buddhas can still aid sentient beings. He imagines a lengthy objection:

> [Objector:] "If you assert that Supramundane Victors' minds and mental factors have ceased, positing the three bodies and the welfare of sentient beings is not feasible. If in this way [that you describe] the movement of the Supramundane Victors' minds and mental factors cease in all aspects, since thereby nothing at all remains, the Dharma Body (*dharmakāya*) is not feasible. Regarding that, 'dharma' is the qualities, such as the [ten] powers and the [four] fearlessnesses. 'Body' is the nature (*svabhāva*). Due to [your explanation of] emptiness, dharmas do not exist and hence, [their] nature does not exist. Therefore, the Dharma Body does not exist. Similarly, since mind and mental factors have ceased, there can be no uninterrupted enjoyment of the ambrosia of dharma, and hence the Complete Enjoyment Body (*sāmbhogikakāya*) is also unreasonable. Similarly, since there is no emanation, due to the cessation of mind and mental factors, how also are the Emanation Bodies (*nairmāṇikakāya*) reasonable? Similarly, because there is no wisdom, which is the cause of Dharma teaching, there is no positing of the welfare of sentient beings. Hence, how can you assert that the movement of Supramundane Victors' minds and mental factors has ceased?"
>
> We answer: "This very master [Candrakīrti] explained [this], on the occasion of praising the Supramundane Victors of the three bodies, [in his stanzas] on the Buddha ground; hence, he did not say [the same thing] here [in this discussion of the two truths]."[16]

The objector sees that without a continuity of mind into buddhahood, the qualities that make up the Buddha bodies would be impossible: the characteristics that mark the state of buddhahood—the ten powers and four fearlessnesses—

could not arise, as these characteristics would be entirely void; enjoyment of the state of buddhahood could not arise without mind; and a Buddha's wisdoms, being purified states of mind, would not exist, thus making it impossible for a Buddha to teach others and so work for their benefit.

Jayānanda's intriguing answer would seem to indicate that Candrakīrti has worked out these difficulties already. However, one familiar with Candrakīrti's presentation of the "ground of buddhahood" (*buddhabhūmi*) will know that Jayānanda's response is only literally true: Candrakīrti does, indeed, state that buddhahood consists of ten powers and three bodies and that one class of these bodies, the emanation bodies, works for the welfare of sentient beings.[17] However, Candrakīrti makes no attempt to answer the kinds of criticisms stemming from the denial of mind to a Buddha that Jayānanda admits. After some 180 folios in Jayānanda's commentary,[18] we find that his answer does not rely directly on Candrakīrti's text but seeks a solution elsewhere: Jayānanda attempts to resolve a decidedly Prāsaṅgika understanding of buddhahood—a Buddha without mind and appearances—utilizing resources from the Yogācāra tradition.

Jayānanda's solution borrows heavily, and rather oddly given his commitments, on well-worked Yogācāra models of transformation. In particular, he cites Candragomin's model of "The five wisdoms encapsulated in the three bodies [of a Buddha]."[19] With very little modification, Jayānanda explains Candragomin's system in which the eight types of ordinary consciousness in the Yogācāra model are transformed into the five wisdoms of buddhahood. The five wisdoms—wisdom of the pristine sphere of reality, mirror-like wisdom, wisdom of equality, wisdom of individual attention, and all-accomplishing wisdom—account for a Buddha's extraordinary realization and abilities. Jayānanda explains how two in particular allow for a Buddha's meditation on emptiness and simultaneous compassionate activity. The "wisdom of the pristine sphere of reality" (*dharmadhātuviśuddhijñāna*),[20] also called non-conceptual wisdom (*nirvikalpajñāna*) of the ultimate nature of reality, "brings to finality contemplation on suchness, dominion over the collections to be dispelled and realized, compassion and non-dual wisdom devoid of the two obstructions along with their predispositions."[21] The "wisdom of individual attention" (*pratyavekṣājñāna*) allows them to "attend individually to the deeds of sentient beings through the previous prayer-wishes [of the now-enlightened being] and the merit of sentient beings, even though Supramundane Victors already only have non-conceptual [wisdom] due to their meditative absorption."[22] Together, these two of the five wisdoms go far toward covering the ground traversed by concordant ultimates (and Drakpa

Gyeltsen's idea of concordant conventionals). They allow a Buddha to be in constant meditative absorption and to aid sentient beings, even if only by way of their previous aspirations and sentient beings' continued merit. In sum, the wisdoms explain non-abiding nirvāṇa.

In adopting a Yogācāra model of transformation, Jayānanda presents a conservative view of slow progress throughout a bodhisattva's career, the acquisition of limitless merit and the purification of even the most subtle taints, the overcoming of obstructions to both liberation and omniscience that culminates finally in perfect meditative absorption. His explanation of the five wisdoms espouses a standard Mahāyāna Buddhist vision of transformation: ordinary consciousnesses yield Buddhas' wisdoms through the completion of meditative processses. His descriptions also evince a strong sense of the continuities between Buddhist practice and the goal of buddhahood, with collections of merit and aspirations yielding buddhahood and contemplative practices being developed and brought to fruition in realization of the ultimate. Jayānanda does little more than recast the Yogācāra model in his own Prāsaṅgika system. This strategy ties his unique views to a well-established vision of Mahāyāna Buddhist practice. The root text that Jayānanda follows, Candrakīrti's *Entrance to the Middle,* similarly embeds a unique and perhaps radical philosophy within a widely accepted path-structure model.[23] While Candrakīrti was consigned to arguing (to largely deaf ears) against a vibrant Yogācāra movement, Jayānanda could more freely adopt features from Yogācāra into a Prāsaṅgika context.

However, Jayānanda's views evince problems that the Yogācāra model cannot solve. We have seen that early Prāsaṅgikas rejected concordant ultimates that would allow for a progressive model of cognitive transformation. While Jayānanda attempts to smooth over the problem of transformation with his account of the five wisdoms, he overlooks the process of *how* ordinary consciousnesses transform. His adaptation of the classical Yogācāra notion of "non-perception" loses its essence when transplanted to his Prāsaṅgika viewpoint. As explained by the important Yogācāra commentator, Sthiramati (fourth century), "non-perception" is a meditative process that is the "means for entering into buddhahood."[24] Sthiramati explains that upon attaining the first bodhisattva ground (*bhūmi*), a practitioner no longer perceives the imaginary nature (*parikalpitasvabhāva*), the false conception of subject-object duality, and that this non-perception is the supreme perception, the perception of the perfected nature (*pariniṣpannasvabhāva*).[25] Sthiramati's Yogācāra model entails that an unreal nature is through contemplation not perceived, reality is thereby contemplatively perceived, and this yogic process is the means for entry into buddhahood.

In contrast, for Jayānanda, non-perception entails the cessation of mind itself; nothing is thereupon perceived. Candrakīrti, aware of the difficulties involved with holding that mind ceases at buddhahood, enigmatically writes, "Through burning all the dry kindling of objects of knowledge, peace; . . . Through stopping the mind, it is made manifest by the body"[26] and "Since mind and mental factors do not engage, we conventionally posit that [suchness] is made manifest by only the body."[27] Jayānanda comes to read the cessation of mind as something approximating a method for enlightenment. He writes that one experiences "'peace' because of being devoid of mind and mental factors"[28] and that one "finds the nature of suchness, which has the quality of peace, by stopping mind and mental factors."[29] He explains Candrakīrti's enigmatic statements:

> If one asks, "Well then, if one stops mind and mental factors, how is the Dharma Body made manifest?" [Candrakīrti's] answer to this is "Through stopping the mind, it is made manifest by the body." By stopping the mind, which has a nature of proliferations, the Complete Enjoyment Body finds [the Dharma Body] by way of making it manifest, through the method of not seeing. Therefore, we posit that [the Dharma Body] is made manifest by the body.[30]

Jayānanda tells us that one Buddha body, the Dharma Body, is realized by another, the Complete Enjoyment Body. When a bodhisattva ceases both perception and the mind, the nature of reality is "made manifest."[31]

Jayānanda fails to discuss how the Complete Enjoyment Body first arises in order to "manifest" the Dharma Body. Turning back to his citation of Candragomin, we find that he summarizes Candragomin's stanza, "Afflicted intellect (*kliṣṭamanas*) when transformed is called 'wisdom of equality' (*samatājñāna*); Mental consciousness (*manovijñāna*) is the wisdom of individual attention (*pratyavekṣājñāna*)" by writing that these two wisdoms are the Complete Enjoyment Body.[32] He glosses Candragomin's "transformed" with "due to having dispelled the afflictive obstructions and the obstructions to omniscience, along with their predispositions, [afflicted intellect] comes to be the wisdom of equality of self and other, devoid of the view of self and so forth."[33] This very general account of dispelling the two classes of obstructions does little to answer the question of how transformation occurs. Instead, we are left with the tension between conflicting models of transformation. Following Candragomin, Jayānanda wants the three bodies to encompass the five wisdoms, which themselves are transformations of ordinary consciousness. Following Candrakīrti, one body realizes another upon the utter cessation of consciousness. Whereas his explanation of a Buddha's five wisdoms emphasizes a continuity between practitioner, practice, and buddhahood, his discussion of the details of transformation yields a fundamental discontinuity between practitioner and Buddha.

Jayānanda's denial of appearances to Buddhas highlights another difference between his views and the Yogācāra model of buddhahood that he adopts. In discussing "What else remains" in the Yogācāra understanding of buddhahood, Urban and Griffiths show that a mainstream current of Yogācāra presents a phenomenological explanation of what remains: upon negating the false constructs of subject-object dualism, a Buddha experiences a pure stream of consciousness that is not negated by emptiness.[34] While Griffiths and Urban critique this very notion, it is clear that, at least in the *Differentiation of the Middle and Extremes* literature, a Buddha has experience without conceptual construction; emptiness does not negate appearances. However, in the Prāsaṅgika thinking of Jayānanda, the possibility of non-conceptual perception seems to be denied. Holding the perception of any appearance to be inherently imbued with dualist conceptuality, his emptiness negates appearances along with conceptuality; no "pure stream" of experience is posited.[35]

The common Mahāyāna doctrine of non-abiding nirvāṇa poses definite problems of how we might conceive a Buddha engaged in constant meditative absorption on emptiness while at the same time able to constantly aid sentient beings. Yogācāra scholars developed a conception that allows a Buddha a pure stream of experience, in addition to a compatible means of transforming ordinary consciousnesses into the five wisdoms that individually account for the various aspects of non-abiding nirvāṇa. As I have shown in the previous chapter, some Indian and early Tibetan Mādhyamikas developed the idea of concordant ultimates (and, in at least one case, concordant conventionals) to explain how the Madhyamaka presentation of two truths can still allow for both constant realization of ultimate truth and perception of the conventional. Candrakīrti, also, saw the need to bring these disparate impulses into a coherent whole, writing that Buddhas "are intent on establishing the welfare of sentient beings and do not waver even for a moment from the sphere of reality (*dharmadhātu*)."[36] Unfortunately, Candrakīrti did not square these already difficult poles of buddhahood with his conception of a "mindless" Buddha. This left Jayānanda with the tasks of making mental cessation compatible with transformation and of reconciling a Buddha's mindless wisdom with compassionate worldly activity, both much more difficult endeavors than Yogācāra philosophers faced. The problems left unsolved in his attempt to adopt the Yogācāra model of Candragomin point to a gulf between the systematic conception of the Mahāyāna path resulting in buddhahood and the Prāsaṅgika understanding of an emptiness that negates ordinary mind as well as appearances, a gulf that would be left for generations of Tibetan Prāsaṅgika exegetes to bridge.[37]

Making a Blind Buddha See

Jayānanda was certainly aware that Candragomin's explanation of five wisdoms encompassed within the three Buddha bodies does not answer all the problems of his unique conception of a Buddha arisen upon the negation of mind and lacking the ability to perceive appearances. If we allow that Jayānanda's three Buddha bodies do in fact arise even though mind has ceased, that the Complete Enjoyment Body somehow arises and makes manifest the Dharma Body and that Emanation Bodies arise from this process, we can adjure that he has offered an account of transformation from advanced bodhisattva to Buddha. However, he has a further problem, that of how his Buddha's Emanation Bodies perceive and aid sentient beings. If buddhahood entails compassionately aiding transmigrating beings, Buddhas would surely need to perceive those beings and the difficulties in which they find themselves. Jayānanda is forced to work out a way for Buddhas to see and aid others, consistent with his views that Buddhas do not possess consciousness.[38]

Rather than fall back on the Yogācāra model, in which three of the five wisdoms offer an explanation of how a Buddha can know ordinary objects and compassionately aid beings,[39] Jayānanda resorts to metaphor to explain how Buddhas can perceive appearances. Having already correlated appearances with non-afflictive ignorance,[40] Jayānanda addresses the question whether the dawning of wisdom to a Buddha entails a Buddha's ignorance. He answers,

> [In explaining the twelve links of cyclic existence, the Buddha][41] said that consciousnesses of afflicted cyclic existence are caused by ignorance; it is not the case that all consciousnesses are caused by it. Supramundane Victors' wisdom has as its cause compassion because, through the force of compassion, Supramundane Victors abide as long as cyclic existence abides. For instance, although a single lamp is already [burning] caused by its oil, upon the extinguishing of the oil if one pours oil in, it does not die. Similarly,

> here also although consciousness is already caused by ignorance, upon ceasing ignorance wisdom dawns through the force of compassion; hence, it does not follow that Supramundane Victors possess ignorance [due to wisdom dawning].[42]

Jayānanda hints here that a Buddha's wisdom is a type of consciousness—this after denying that Buddhas have minds—but a special kind of consciousness, one brought about entirely by compassion. His lamp metaphor does not really address how a Buddha perceives appearances but offers something of an explanation for the continuity from Buddhist practitioner to Buddha. Mind ceases upon the extinguishing of its fuel, ignorance. Wisdom arises due to the "pouring in" of compassion. Jayānanda may have in mind Candrakīrti's statement at the opening of his *Entrance to the Middle:* "The causes of conqueror's children are the compassionate mind, non-dual awareness, and the mind of enlightenment."[43] In explicating his lamp metaphor, Jayānanda might contend that while non-dual wisdom extinguishes ignorance, the "cause" of ordinary appearances, compassion "causes" a renewed perception of the world. Jayānanda unfortunately does not explain his metaphor; certainly, though, he (like Candrakīrti) adopts the common Mahāyāna conception that buddhahood comprises wisdom and compassion. While the details of transformation remain fuzzy, Jayānanda clearly considers some kind of "flame" to continue unwaveringly into buddhahood: wisdom dawns when ordinary consciousness ceases.

Jayānanda's metaphor leads into a lengthy discussion of variant views on how a Buddha's wisdom dawns and how a Buddha remains compassionately active in this world.[44] Several of these trade on the Mahāyāna truisms of Buddha bodies and a Buddha's previous aspirations to aid sentient beings. The most interesting of these positions, none of which Jayānanda definitively favors, would seem to be attempts at solving Candrakīrti's dilemma, addressing how a Prāsaṅgika can evade the fault that a Buddha is "cut off" from the everyday world. Jayānanda entertains the view that a Buddha is able to perceive sentient beings and their needs due to retaining a certain level of ignorance, suggesting that Buddhas "have the capacity to dispel ignorance, [but] through the force of their compassion they do not dispel ignorance, for otherwise they would be cut off."[45] This view retains the close connection between appearances and ignorance; in order to maintain the false sense of subject-object duality that marks our perceptual states, Buddhas would share in some level of our ignorance, enabling them to continue to perceive and aid us. A related possibility is that because Buddhas know the ignorance that is responsible for perceiving appearances to be just ignorance, we can say that Buddhas are not really ignorant.[46] Both of these positions attempt to render "ignorance" harmless, either due to a Buddha's great power ("the capacity to dispel ignorance") or wisdom (knowing ignorance to be ignorance). Neither position quite aligns with Jayānanda's metaphoric suggestion that a Buddha's sight returns due to compassion.

We can appreciate Jayānanda's reluctance to stand whole-heartedly behind any of these solutions to Candrakīrti's "mindless" Buddha. That Buddhas' compassionate activity necessitates that they operate within some level of ignorance raises many exegetical and soteriological quandaries. As noted already, we must presume that Buddhas are ignorant in some unproblematic way, much in the same way that Chapa portrayed Buddhas as having an unproblematic version of "mistake," allowing them to perceive appearances. A pressing concern for those (whoever they may be) claiming a Buddha possesses unproblematic ignorance is to distinguish Buddhas from bodhisattvas who have seen through the truth of appearances but have yet to complete the bodhisattva path. Recall that Jayānanda's discussion of "mere conventionalities" addresses these bodhisattvas, stating that "non-afflictive ignorance" causes them to perceive appearances even though they do not assent to the truth of those appearances. Jayānanda was comfortable with labeling the cause of those appearances "ignorance" yet shrinks away from concluding the same for a Buddha's appearances. Somehow, Buddhas' perceptions are different.

Jayānanda's lamp metaphor did not prove a lasting solution to Candrakīrti's mindless Buddha. Tibetan Prāsaṅgikas would continue to reinterpret Candrakīrti's problematic claim in order to better integrate his views with Mahāyāna buddhahood. However, as Candrakīrti's philosophy grew in importance in India and, especially, in Tibet, Jayānanda's efforts represent an early Prāsaṅgika attempt to work out aspects of his views that had been left undeveloped and difficult to accept. Where earlier Buddhists could safely disregard Candrakīrti's unpalatable notions, the growing success of his views helped his champions to smooth over the rough edges of his buddhahood in order to make it more appetizing to Buddhists concerned with the continuities between a practitioner and a Buddha and between a Buddha and sentient beings.

Svātantrika Solutions to Buddha Vision

Those Mādhyamikas who developed concordant ultimates did so in part to evade the kinds of difficulties inherent in positing the transformation from bodhisattva to Buddha, without falling back on something like the Yogācāra doctrine of "transformation of the basis." As seen in the previous chapter, concordant ultimates were the purview of Svātantrika-leaning Mādhyamikas. In contrast to those who took seriously Candrakīrti's claims that mind ceases upon enlightenment and that Buddhas do not perceive ordinary appearances, several twelfth-century Tibetan authors, among the earliest to be called Svātantrika, developed alternative answers to Madhyamaka buddhahood. Chapa Chokyi Sengé, Sonam Tsemo, and Drakpa Gyeltsen argued against the Prāsaṅgika interpretation of buddhahood, taking to task each of the unique features of this interpretation: the metaphoric nature of realization, the cessation of mind upon realization, and the inability of Buddhas to perceive ordinary appearances. While critiquing these Prāsaṅgika views of buddhahood, they offer their own solution to how a cognitively pure Buddha can perceive an ultimately unreal world.

Chapa's presentation of Prāsaṅgika buddhahood mirrors closely Jayānanda's writings on the topic, while filling in connections that are suggested but not made explicit by Jayānanda. Chapa, presenting the Prāsaṅgika view, writes,

> During the meditative absorption of [a bodhisattva] who has attained a ground and upon the ground of buddhahood, since no referent (*yul*)—that is, object of knowledge (*shes bya*)—is established, the engagement of a referent-taker [that is, a consciousness] is pacified. Thus, just the cutting off of the engagement of the mind and mental factors is designated the non-mistaken mind of reality through realizing the final nature. Just as Sautrāntikas call an awareness that is like blue "the realization of blue," so an awareness that is devoid of birth is similar to the birthless final nature and, hence, is to be called "the realization of the final nature."[47]

In Chapa's presentation, Prāsaṅgika buddhahood is much like advanced bodhisattvas' meditation but is continuous: where bodhisattvas attain a dissolution of object and subject in meditative absorption but perceive appearances when outside of the meditative state, Buddhas have a continual absence of mind and appearances. Jayānanda writes that complete "non-perception" is conventionally labelled "knowing the ultimate" and that "knowing the ultimate" is actually not knowing at all since it entails the cessation of mind and mental factors. Chapa alters this subtly, stating that the very cessation of mind and mental factors is called "realizing the ultimate." In Chapa's rendition, just as in Jayānanda's and Candrakīrti's, realization is only metaphoric for

Prāsaṅgika. Instead of true realization and transformation, Chapa's Prāsaṅgika sets forth only a mind-blowing meditative experience of blankness that they call "buddhahood." When we recall the difficulties Jayānanda faced in discussing how the five wisdoms of a Buddha arise, we appreciate what Chapa is driving at; without creatively recasting the Yogācāra presentation of transformation Prāsaṅgikas are left with "non-perception" and a simple cessation of mind and mental factors out of which, somehow, a Buddha arises.

In drawing out just how the Prāsaṅgika understands mental cessation-cum-realization, Chapa suggests that Prāsaṅgikas utilize valid cognition to eliminate proliferations (*prapañca, spros pa*)—otherwise, how could they eliminate them?—but upon the elimination of proliferations, no object of valid cognition remains.[48] Upon eliminating proliferations, a meditative consciousness—"yogic direct perception" (*yogipratyakṣa, rnal 'byor mngon sum*)—should cognize (*gzhal ba*) emptiness; but in the Prāsaṅgika view, there is nothing left to cognize nor any cognizing agent. Chapa avers that if yogic direct perception is left without an object to cognize, it would be mistaken (*bhrānta, 'khrul ba*) and so not valid.[49] If realizing the ultimate is only metaphoric, as Prāsaṅgikas say, without a real object, it cannot be valid. Consistent with his contention that the ultimate is a knowable phenomenon (discussed in chapter 4), Chapa argues that the ultimate is truly (and not just metaphorically) known and is known by valid cognition. His attempt to tease out what the Prāsaṅgika could mean by metaphoric realization highlights the differences between his and Jayānanda's approaches. Where Jayānanda emphasizes mental cessation as the defining moment of transformation, Chapa stresses the continuity of mind: a reasoning consciousness inferentially knows emptiness whereupon this valid inferential consciousness is contemplatively developed into nonconceptual realization of emptiness.

Essential to Chapa's portrayal of mental cultivation is the basic notion that the mental continuum cannot be cut. The continuity of some form of mental stream forms the ground of a great deal of Indian and Tibetan religious thought. The standard Buddhist explanation is that one moment of awareness produces the next; awareness is separate from body, is not produced from the body, and cannot be stopped. One dissenting current in India were the Cārvākas, who maintained that mind and body alike end at death. Chapa's first attack on the Prāsaṅgika notion that mind ceases upon realization is to ask how Prāsaṅgika buddhahood is different from the Cārvāka understanding of death: both claim that a certain moment of awareness, unlike all moments of awareness up to that point, lacks the ability to produce a further moment of awareness.

The Prāsaṅgika must understand the meditative absorption that engenders metaphoric realization to be unlike every previous moment of awareness. Chapa offers that, unlike other moments, this meditative awareness lacks "craving" (*tṛṣṇā, sred pa*) and so does not produce further awareness.[50] He rejects this possibility, holding to the common Buddhist line that every awareness produces further awareness. If an awareness lacks craving, along with the other chief non-virtues, hatred and delusion, it produces a pure awareness instead of an impure one: "A pure consciousness is produced from the immediately preceding [consciousness], which is the virtuous mind of non-attachment, non-hatred, and non-delusion."[51] For Chapa, mind continues upon buddhahood just as it does through death: both the mind prior to buddhahood and the mind of buddhahood share in the basic status of being mind.

In Chapa's view, practice of the Buddhist path negates the non-virtues, not ordinary mind. While a Buddha's wisdom is a highly developed and unique state of mind, it develops out of a practitioner's ordinary consciousness. Reminiscent of the lengthy objection Jayānanda entertains, Chapa tells us that if awareness itself is cut, a Buddha's wisdom—which in his view is a special kind of awareness—cannot arise and so cannot give rise to the form bodies that enact sentient beings' welfare.[52] In an interesting turn, Chapa offers that a Prāsaṅgika might argue that a Buddha's form bodies arise out of emptiness itself. This possibility is one way of making sense out of Candrakīrti's claim that the Complete Enjoyment Body makes manifest the Dharma Body, which is the nature of reality, and that form bodies are somehow produced in this mix. However, Chapa points out that if the Prāsaṅgika would claim that emptiness produces form bodies, emptiness—the ultimate—would be an "ultimate entity," an ultimate capable of causal efficacy.[53] An ultimate entity is impossible in Madhyamaka logic and, for Chapa and other Mādhyamikas, constitutes the chief object to be negated by Madhyamaka reasoning.[54]

Finally, Chapa considers the possibility that, while mind has ceased, a Buddha's form bodies and the consequent activity for the welfare of sentient beings could arise from the bodhisattva's collections of merit and wisdom and from the bodhisattva's aspirations to attain enlightenment for the sake of aiding others. Chapa adjures that this solution, which resembles one of Jayānanda's answers to the problem, is impossible as without a mental continuum there is nothing to carry those collections into buddhahood and, consequently, the welfare of sentient beings "would arise upon being cut off" (recall Jayānanda's consideration of various possibilities of how a Buddha is not "cut off" from the ordinary world).[55] Having found all these possibilities unsatisfactory, Chapa concludes that a Prāsaṅgika Buddha would utterly lack the abilities to generate form bodies and to work for the welfare of sentient beings and so would be no different from one attaining a "Hearer's nirvāṇa without remainder, which is the mere pacification of afflictions and suffering, like extinguishing a butter lamp."[56] In Chapa's estimation, denying Buddhas mind and mental factors would disallow the fundamental predicates of Mahāyāna Buddhology, rendering it no different from non-Mahāyāna conceptions of the religious goal.

Having considered Chapa's arguments against Prāsaṅgika views on metaphoric realization and the cessation of mind and mental factors, we can examine his case against denying Buddhas ordinary appearances. Chapa's arguments for the continuity of mind from bodhisattva to Buddha tie closely to his arguments for the continuity of ordinary appearances into buddhahood. He begins by considering the "illusion-like" nature, the union of emptiness and appearances, asking whether "an awareness having appearance and realizing [appearances] to be like illusions"[57] is an afflictive obstruction or an obstruction to the object of knowledge, emptiness.[58] We can recall that Jayānanda understood appearances to be caused by "mere ignorance," not afflictive ignorance, and that a Buddha overcoming obstructions to the object of knowledge no longer perceives ordinary appearances (unless, somehow, compassion regenerates a form of perception). Chapa, in contradistinction, will argue that a consciousness perceiving appearances is not negated by practice of the Buddhist path: realizing emptiness dispels the conception that appearances are true, not the perception of appearances themselves.

Chapa quickly dispenses with the possibility that a Buddha's consciousness perceiving appearances would entail afflictive obstructions (which no one has claimed to be the case). He explains that an awareness perceiving appearances but knowing them to be like illusions has necessarily overcome the conception of a "self of persons" through realizing that the five psycho-physical aggregates that make up the person are not permanent, unitary, or self-powered.[59] This level of realization is enough to overcome afflictive obstructions, including afflictive ignorance. Even in the Prāsaṅgika presentation, one with this realization would continue to perceive appearances outside of the meditative state but would not conceive that those appearances are real.

Coming to address the Prāsaṅgika claim that perception of appearances is caused by the ignorance that is an obstruction to the object of knowledge, emptiness, Chapa conjectures that the Prāsaṅgika could claim that conventional appearances and their ultimate emptiness are contradictory (*'gal ba, virodha*), such that emptiness would per force negate appearances.

A consciousness perceiving appearances would then be contradictory with the realization of emptiness—no consciousness of the illusion-like nature would be possible. Yet no contradiction between emptiness and appearances can be claimed because emptiness, as all Mādhyamikas know, must be the final nature of appearances.[60] Chapa sees the need to preserve the relationship between emptiness and appearances and so must reject their mutual contradiction.[61] Additionally, Chapa reasons, in the Prāsaṅgika view, emptiness would negate the entire world of appearances, leaving no feasible way to explain cause and effect; all notions of religious development—especially over the course of many lifetimes—would be ruined.[62]

Having pointed out difficulties with conceiving emptiness to negate conventional appearances, Chapa explains how he understands appearances and emptiness to co-exist on different levels. He writes:

> The establishment of appearances from a non-analytic point of view dispels non-appearance from a non-analytic point of view; however, it does not dispel [their] utter non-establishment when analyzed. Hence, how would [the establishment of appearances from a non-analytic point of view] block the realization of [their] utter non-establishment when analyzed?[63]

The world of appearances, of causes that produce effects, is established when not analyzed. When the causal process is analyzed, according to whether effects are produced from causes that are either the same as, different from, both the same as and different from, or neither the same as nor different from themselves, one finds the emptiness of production. Appearances cannot "bear analysis" (*dpyad bzod*); their emptiness is found by that analysis. However, when this sort of analysis is not performed, "from a non-analytical point of view," appearances are established; the ultimate emptiness of phenomena when analyzed does not negate the appearance of phenomena when not analyzed. Madhyamaka analysis forms Chapa's mechanism for moving from conventional to ultimate. Lack of analysis is his explanation for how phenomena validly appear.

Non-analytic appearances perhaps solve the issue of how even advanced bodhisattvas continue to perceive appearances outside of their meditative states. Jayānanda presumably would not object to this explanation, as we have seen him explain that bodhisattvas perceive "mere appearances" outside of meditative absorption: appearances would disappear during contemplation but "reappear" afterward. However, it is difficult to believe that

Chapa intends non-analysis to explain how Buddhas perceive ordinary appearances: Buddhas would presumably not need to analyze in order to see the emptiness of appearances. Chapa's explanation of consciousnesses perceiving the illusion-like nature does not rely on an alternation—brought on by analysis—between perceiving emptiness and perceiving appearances. Rather, he speaks of perceiving the "composite" (*tshogs*) of emptiness and appearances.

We saw in chapter 4 that one of Chapa's arguments against holding the illusion-like nature as ultimate truth is that the illusion-like nature is a composite of emptiness and appearance and if this composite were ultimate truth, each part of the composite would have to bear analysis. This would establish that appearances bear analysis. Additionally, Chapa has argued that appearances are not an obstruction to perceiving emptiness and that Buddhist practice does not eliminate appearances.[64] Putting these pieces together, we can conclude that while bodhisattvas alternate between meditative realization of emptiness and post-meditative perception of appearances, part of the transformation to buddhahood involves the ability to perceive appearances and their emptiness of bearing analysis at the same time, constantly. Where Jayānanda understood overcoming obstructions to the object of knowledge, emptiness, to negate appearances when emptiness is realized (appearances and emptiness being incompatible), Chapa views overcoming obstructions to the object of knowledge to involve both realizing emptiness and knowing all objects of knowledge—both emptiness and appearances are known simultaneously.[65]

An outflow of Chapa's position is that he, unlike Jayānanda, does not consider ignorance to be the cause of perceiving ordinary appearances, since this perception is neither kind of obstruction. Perhaps the duality that would seem to be inherent in a consciousness perceiving ordinary appearances is separable from this perception, allowing Buddhas to see non-dualistically. Chapa only hints at his solution to *how* Buddhas continue to perceive ordinary appearances, having overcome their false duality. He tells us that while the referents of Buddhas' perceptions are called "mistaken appearance," the term loses its connotations in this context:

> Since [an awareness] having appearance and realizing [appearances] to be like illusions is a referent-taker of what is unable to bear analysis, we apply the convention, "mistaken appearance" (*'khrul snang,* "appearance to mistake"). However, it is neither of the two kinds of obstructions. Hence, it is not feasible for that [consciousness having appearance] to be dispelled by a Buddha.[66]

A Buddha's consciousness perceiving ordinary appearances cognizes objects that, like all objects except emptiness, do not bear analysis. That these appearances do not hold up to analysis forces the conclusion that they do not exist in the way they appear. Thus, we can call the consciousnesses perceiving appearances "mistaken" even though a Buddha knows the emptiness of appearances along with the appearances themselves. For Chapa, appearances are not tied to either type of obstruction in the way that Jayānanda conceives and, consequently, are not cast off by Buddhas.

We can note in the above passage that Chapa moves quickly from "mistaken appearance" to "obstructions": we label a Buddha's consciousness perceiving appearances "mistaken" but it is neither kind of obstruction. He does not stop to answer the more basic question: is it mistaken? In a lengthy passage noted in chapter 3, Chapa writes of levels of mistake that, not unlike Jayānanda's solution, leaves even a Buddha's appearances tied closely to (mostly harmless) mistake:

> [Objection:] If Buddhas' [consciousnesses] having appearances are also mistaken and their referents are also true in mistaken perspective, then since Buddhas have the capacity for mistake, Buddhas have obstructions.
>
> [We reply:] The mistake that conceives what does not exist among objects of knowledge to exist—for instance, the conception of a permanent entity—and the mistake that takes what is empty of performing functions as its apprehended referent—for instance, the appearances of two moons, concepts (*don spyi*), and so forth—entail obstructions. However, if you state the fault that it follows that Buddhas have obstructions because of not having that capacity [for mistake], your reason is not established [that is, Buddhas have the capacity for mistake]. If you say that Buddhas have obstructions because of having the capacity for the mistake that is a referent-taker [that is, a consciousness] of that which does not bear analysis, your entailment is not established [that is, having the capacity for this kind of mistake does not entail having obstructions].[67]

Chapa identifies at least three types of mistake: the truly problematic mistake that conceives of entirely unreal phenomena, binding us in cyclic existence; a useful kind of mistake that allows us conceptual mental functioning;[68] and the mistake that allows Buddhas to perceive appearances. It may be possible to correlate the first two types of mistake with afflictive obstructions and obstructions to the object of knowledge, respectively. The third type of mistake does not entail either class of obstruction so is not discarded by a Buddha. Chapa has argued that Buddhas without the ability to perceive ordinary appearances would not be Buddhas. We can conclude that Buddhas need this third type of mistake, that their ability to perceive appearances depends on it. Chapa notes that this mistaken consciousness perceives objects that do not bear analysis. It seems reasonable to extend his correlation, noted just above, between perceiving what does not bear analysis and mistake: that Buddhas perceive appearances that do not bear analysis is what makes the perceptions mistaken. In contrast to these Buddha perceptions, the cognition of emptiness (the one phenomenon that bears analysis), Chapa tells us, "is non-deceptive regarding what bears analysis."[69] Only this cognition has no kind of mistake.

In sum, Chapa's argument against mind and mental factors—and with them the ability to perceive ordinary appearances—being cut off at buddhahood is three-fold: appearances involve neither kind of obstruction to enlightenment, are not negated by practice of the path, and are a requirement of Mahāyāna buddhahood. Chapa's arguments amount to the notions that Buddhas *must* have appearances and there is no reason for them not to. When pushed to account for how Buddhas perceive appearances, his answer—like Jayānanda's—softens, falling back on the role of some kind of unproblematic mistake. Buddhas perceive both appearances that do not bear analysis and the emptiness that is appearances' lack of bearing analysis. The incongruity between these two referents perhaps warrants Chapa's label, "mistake."

In addition to the very different conclusions they reach—Jayānanda that Buddhas have no mind and Chapa that mind must continue into buddhahood—an important difference between these two routes to explaining non-abiding nirvāṇa is the status each ascribes to perception itself. Jayānanda equates perception of appearances with ignorance and seems to regard the subject-object duality of perception to entail a kind of conceptuality. Full realization of emptiness negates the perception of ordinary appearances. Chapa clearly places conceptual mistake and a Buddha's mistake that allows perception of appearances into different categories: the former is an obstruction that is overcome by Buddhas while the latter is not. Realizing emptiness does not negate perception of appearances. Put in the terms of later Tibetan Madhyamaka scholarship, early Prāsaṅgika puts forth a broader "object of negation" (*dgag bya*), negating perception itself, than the Svātantrika conception.[70]

In the following generation of scholarship, the positions that Jayānanda and Chapa created in their explorations of non-abiding nirvāṇa became identified with competing schools of Madhyamaka exegesis. While many of Chapa's viewpoints quickly fell into disfavor, the route he took toward working out a Madhyamaka conception of buddhahood was championed by early Sakya scholars. Chapa's student, Sonam Tsemo, saw the issue of a Buddha's ability to perceive ordinary appearances as a key dividing line between Prāsaṅgika and Svātantrika. He neatly summarizes the two sides: Prāsaṅgikas hold that Buddhas do not perceive ordinary appearances because the ignorance responsible for perception would entail entrapment in cyclic existence; Svātantrikas maintain that Buddhas have "conventional wisdom" (*ye shes kun rdzob*) that allows them to perceive ordinary appearances without these perceptions acting as a cause for cyclic existence.[71] Sonam Tsemo criticizes the Prāsaṅgika answer for its failure to allow for non-abiding nirvāṇa and endorses the Svātantrika solution.[72]

Sonam Tsemo's younger brother and successor as abbot of Sakya Monastery, Drakpa Gyeltsen, enables us to see that the issue of buddhahood, engendered by the circulation of Candrakīrti's texts, was crucial to the Madhyamaka debates of his day. We saw in chapter 4 that Drakpa Gyeltsen favors the Svātantrika view that offers concordant ultimates and concordant conventionals to explain transformation to buddhahood and a Buddha's ability to perceive ordinary appearances, respectively.[73] His explanation of concordant conventionals as "pure worldly wisdom"[74] echoes his brother's notion of a Buddha's "conventional wisdom." Having detailed his solution to the problem of non-abiding nirvāṇa, Drakpa Gyeltsen casts scorn on what he characterizes as the common Tibetan interpretation of buddhahood, an interpretation centered on Candrakīrti's claim that "realizing the ultimate" is only said metaphorically:

> Some assert that it is established that āryas' minds (*thugs*) are ultimate. Those [minds'] referent—without production or cessation, free from elaborations—is ultimate truth. [To the objection:] Well then, [what about the *Introduction to the Two Truths Sūtra*] saying 'Ultimate truth is passed beyond the referents of omniscient wisdom'? [They respond:] That is indeed true; [ultimate truth] is not known in the manner of referent and referent taker. As Candrakīrti says,

> Since the final nature is without production and the mind also is devoid of production,
> Due to that [object] in the basis [that is, the mind] that has the aspect of that [birthless final nature, this is said to be] like 'knowing reality.'
> Hence, "knowing" [reality] is in dependence upon conventions,
> Just as [in Sautrāntika] a mind knows well its object due to arising in the aspect of that object.
>
> That is called "realizing utterly unestablished suchness." In that way, suchness is called "nirvāṇa" and "the unconstructed reality" (*dharmatā*). Suchness is called the ārya Hearers' nirvāṇa.
>
> Most contemporary Tibetan Mādhyamikas also assert similarly. This is not correct; I debunked this already.[75]

Drakpa Gyeltsen tells us that many Tibetans have been led astray by Candrakīrti's notion of metaphorical realization and by the sūtra passage that Candrakīrti and Prajñākaramati cite to support their contention that the ultimate is beyond the scope of human intellect (examined in chapter 4). Through their misunderstanding of Candrakīrti,[76] "most" held the ultimate to be beyond all notions of dualistic knowing. Drakpa Gyeltsen's comments show that Jayānanda's and Chapa's attempts to work out a Madhyamaka notion of nirvāṇa were not isolated arguments but instead indicate a wider problem, instigated by Candrakīrti, in the formation of doctrinal schools in twelfth-century Tibet.

Conclusion: Madhyamaka Nirvāṇa

In these varied conceptions of transformation and enlightenment, we can see that arguments over buddhahood were central to the formation of Prāsaṅgika and Svātantrika schools and that constructing a workable path to enlightenment was one of the crucial issues of twelfth-century Madhyamaka, engendered by the rise of Candrakīrti. Prāsaṅgika buddhahood prioritized the cutting of a clear division between the ordinary and the ultimate, with ordinary mind ceasing upon enlightenment and a Buddha, in full realization, unable to perceive the ordinary world. The distance between ordinary being and Buddha matches well with the features of early Prāsaṅgika examined in the previous chapters. In their rejection of the validity of ordinary consciousness, their espousal of an ultimate truth entirely out of the scope of human intellect, and their presentation of Buddhas without minds, we see Prāsaṅgikas drawing a blanket correlation between ordinary consciousness and the conventional world: as long as ordinary consciousness operates, the ultimate is not realized and as long as ordinary objects are perceived a Buddha's state is not attained. In contrast, we see early Svātantrikas emphasizing the continuities between ordinary mind and a Buddha's wisdom and between ordinary appearances and their ultimate emptiness. These continuities are crucial to a coherent picture of transformation and enlightenment and explain the success of the twelfth-century Svātantrika understanding of buddhahood, such that we can detect it in much later Tibetan presentations of enlightenment.

Through focusing on Jayānanda's and Chapa's solutions, we see the difficulties entailed in constructing a Madhyamaka conception of non-abiding nirvāṇa. Chapa's lengthy criticisms of Prāsaṅgika buddhahood show how tricky non-abiding nirvāṇa is to posit for Mādhyamikas who take seriously Candrakīrti's claims. Chapa's views, too, ran into difficulties and had to admit some level of "mistake" into a Buddha's mental state. While their routes diverge in significant ways, each side in this debate is forced to come back to a position that embraces both of the conflicting poles of non-abiding nirvāṇa: pure realization of emptiness and constant compassionate activity. In their construction of a workable model for practice, transformation, and enlightenment, Madhyamaka authors faced problems that Yogācāra theorists did not. Without a notion of a "pure stream" of experience that can easily elide the passage from ordinary to enlightened, Mādhyamikas had to develop their own explanations of nirvāṇa that could fit the common Mahāyāna model and at the same time allow for their unique understandings of emptiness. Candrakīrti's *Entrance to the Middle* took strides toward a uniquely Madhyamaka enlightenment. However, his iconoclastic claims left many holes where a coherent model was needed. While the requirement for a coherent model of nirvāṇa was not novel to their time, eleventh- and twelfth-century Mādhyamikas devoted unprecedented energy toward creating solutions to the twin problems of transformation and buddhahood, forging answers that would chart the directions for later Tibetan exegesis.

Conclusion: The Prāsaṅgika Victory

My aim in the previous chapters has been to uncover aspects of the early Prāsaṅgika and Svātantrika movements, to trace the rise of Candrakīrti through his champions and detractors. In focusing on the historical rise of Prāsaṅgika, it becomes clear that Indian interest in Candrakīrti's texts centered in large part on his understanding of ultimate truth. Likewise, the formation in Tibet of a Prāsaṅgika school championing his texts was based on unique interpretations of ultimate truth and buddhahood, as well as issues of the validity of human consciousness in reaching liberative knowledge. When examined through a twelfth-century lens, Candrakīrti appears vastly different from the Candrakīrti who is presented within eighteenth-century Tibetan doxography, or a good deal of twentieth-century European-language scholarship.

Most literature on Candrakīrti, his Prāsaṅgika School, and its Svātantrika competitor concerns the logical considerations from which these two schools derived their names.[1] Tibetan scholarship either takes a similar tack or, in Gelukpa circles, examines their differing conceptions of emptiness, with the Prāsaṅgika understanding of emptiness alone negating that phenomena are "established by their own character" (*rang gi mtshan nyid kyis grub pa*). This Gelukpa strategy for dividing Prāsaṅgika and Svātantrika additionally allows them to claim that Candrakīrti and his followers did not reject the Buddhist Epistemological tradition nor the more specific use of inference as a tool for knowing ultimate truth. In contrast to the elaborate Gelukpa distinction, eleventh- and twelfth-century Mādhyamikas opposed each other in sharp terms: Prāsaṅgikas rebuffed Buddhist Epistemology and presented a pristine, "mindless" Buddha; Svātantrikas defended a marriage of Epistemology and the Middle Way and softened the distinction between ignorance and cognitive purity. The early debate certainly took on ontological, in addition to logical, concerns; however, we are left with a portrait looking very little like that which Gelukpa scholars paint.[2]

My identification of the issues dividing the early Prāsaṅgika and Svātantrika schools—the issues of the validity of human consciousness, the interpretation of ultimate truth, and the development of Madhyamaka buddhahood—has not touched on issues of logical procedure. Even my examination in chapter 3 of the debates on valid cognition focuses either on the valid cognition project as a whole or upon perception, rather than on inference alone. Logical concerns were certainly important to the formation of these schools, as their names suggest. Jayānanda wrote disparagingly of Svātantrikas' insistence on formal inference yet defended his own method of dispensing with inference.[3] Chapa wrote at length concerning the inability of logical "consequences" (*prasaṅga*) to negate the "object of negation" and to establish emptiness and of the necessity of inferences "of one's own" to establish emptiness.[4] Several of Chapa's arguments on logical procedure have been investigated in Tauscher's two articles;[5] much of his discussion of logical procedure can be read in the following Materials section. Debates over the logical procedures befitting a Mādhyamika were one basis for the division into Prāsaṅgika and Svātantrika schools in this period.

As can be seen in the Materials section, even the debates on logical procedure had wider implications concerning competing views of what emptiness negates, how the world of appearance is validly established, and how one develops the mind to realize the ultimate. Chapa's exploration of "commonly appearing [inferential] subjects" (*chos can mthun snang*)—a requirement of the Dignāga and Dharmakīrti approach to inference in which the subject of an inference must appear in common to both parties of a debate—makes clear that he sees the Prāsaṅgika rejection of common appearance to hinge upon their close association of appearances and ignorance, as does his endeavor to show that emptiness does not negate appearance.[6]

Two major factors contributed to the less-refined Prāsaṅgika-Svātantrika distinction in this period. The first may be obvious: in the eleventh and twelfth centuries Candrakīrti's major texts received their first sustained exposure. While contemporary scholarship may debate many issues, all can agree that Candrakīrti is not easy.[7] Indian and Tibetan exegetes alike wrestled with complex issues in his now-popular corpus. Those accustomed to the Gelukpa presentation of Candrakīrti, a presentation first synthesized over the course of a lifetime by one of Tibet's greatest thinkers, hundreds of years after Candrakīrti's works first made their mark, and further refined for hundreds of years further, may judge Jayānanda's interpretation of some of these issues to be off the mark, crude, or simply wrong. In many cases, Jayānanda's interpretations are straightforward, offering little to temper some of Candrakīrti's more problematic views. Candrakīrti's detractors, noting the ways his philosophy countered some dominant Mahāyāna trends, pushed his views even further from the center: in a manner that Candrakīrti might well have appreciated, Chapa was wont to deduce the absurd consequences of an overly-literal (and none too charitable) reading of Candrakīrti.

The second factor contributing to a wide Prāsaṅgika-Svātantrika divide was that, unlike later doxographies, the twelfth-century distinction lacked a fixed outcome. The doxographic impulses driving Tibetan scholarship on the Prāsaṅgika-Svātantrika distinction of the fourteenth century and onward demanded an ordered and ranked harmony among the wealth of Indian Buddhist literature. Categories were constructed based on typologies abstracted from hundreds of Indian texts, and were then populated according to thematic similarities with the founders, who themselves were chosen for their doctrinal importance. While the names for these categories had historical referents and perhaps were employed with belief in their historical validity, conceptual construction was clearly a goal held more deeply than historical representation. When we shift from thematically important figures to figures historically important to the formation of Prāsaṅgika and Svātantrika schools, we see that in the absence of hierarchical rankings, Prāsaṅgika and Svātantrika traditions were first constructed and argued for as equally viable options. We deal with competing models for religious pursuits that spill over into issues of authority and legitimacy for the participants and their communities. Rather than the fixed ends of doxography, we see a multitude of potential directions and open outcomes.

Appreciating the myriad possibilities of twelfth-century Tibet leads us to consider why Prāsaṅgika triumphed over Svātantrika to become the exegetical system favored by nearly every Tibetan scholar from the thirteenth century into the present. Accepting that Candrakīrti did not establish Prāsaṅgika's superiority, nor was he even taken seriously until the close of the first millennium, the questions become more pointed: why Candrakīrti? why the twelfth century? why in Tibet? As I have shown in chapter 1, interest in Candrakīrti did not arise only in Tibet; rather we see several important Indian Buddhists taking interest in Candrakīrti's views on ultimate truth in the eleventh century. Some of this interest was tied to concerns with the later developments of Indian Buddhist tantra. The affinities between tantric views and Candrakīrti's portrayal (or his supporter's portrayal) of a radical disjunction between conventional and ultimate, between ordinary awareness and a

Buddha's state would seem to tie Candrakīrti's revival to the popularity of tantra. A wider circulation of Candrakīrti's texts could not fail to bring to attention the clear differences between his presentation of Madhyamaka and that of Bhāvaviveka or of Śāntarakṣita and Kamalaśīla.

The sense of differing Madhyamaka currents attested by eleventh-century Indian sources proliferated in the fractious socio-political landscape of twelfth-century Tibet to form competing subschools. As detailed in chapter 2, Tibetan translators took possession of particular strains of Indian Buddhist literature that became the hallmark of their monastic academy's curriculum. The broader competition between the administrative units that monasteries comprised undoubtedly influenced and amplified doctrinal divergences. The fine philosophical nuances of an exegete's interpretation of doctrine would not alone yield the triumph of one school of thought over another. The success of the monastic academies, in which these doctrines were developed and for which they shaped the intellectual and religious environment, in gaining broader influence surely would contribute to these Madhyamaka schools' relative fortunes.

When we examine Candrakīrti's much belated triumph, it becomes clear that his victory was decisive but yet in many ways nominal. Virtually every important Tibetan exegete from the thirteenth century to the present ranks Candrakīrti's Prāsaṅgika as the highest interpretation of Buddhist doctrine and delineates the ways in which it is superior to Svātantrika. Svātantrika, identified with the philosophies of Bhāvaviveka, in a realist vein, and Śāntarakṣita and Kamalaśīla, in an idealist vein, is studied seriously in monastic curricula, but always within the knowledge that it is somehow deficient. More than Svātantrika's survival in monastic study, the many vestiges of Chapa's, Sonam Tsemo's, and Drakpa Gyeltsen's views in later Tibetans' presentation of Prāsaṅgika constitute Svātantrika's primary subversion of Candrakīrti's triumph. Indeed, recurrent themes throughout this present work are the ways in which Chapa's students abandoned his postion, adopted Candrakīrti's philosophy, and then worked out Prāsaṅgika defenses to Chapa's critiques that came to strongly resemble Chapa's own views. Tibetans almost uniformly became champions of Candrakīrti but developed a Prāsaṅgika that combined some of his most important insights with viewpoints he would have vehemently criticized. In seeking to understand how Candrakīrti rose from obscurity to become the paragon of Tibetan Buddhist philosophy, we see some of the creative transformations cast by Tibetans in their mammoth project of reconfiguring the world in a Buddhist mold.

Materials: The Arguments against *Prasaṅgas* and for *Svatantra* Inference in Chapa Chokyi Sengé's *Compilation of the Three Mādhyamikas from the East*

As one of the very few texts that present a sustained argument against Prāsaṅgika, Chapa's *Compilation of the Three Mādhyamikas from the East*[1] is extremely important to our understanding of the issues engendered by Candrakīrti's texts upon their dissemination in twelfth-century Tibet. The following is a translation, based on Helmut Tauscher's edition,[2] of a portion of this text.[3] The translation draws from Chapa's long excursus on the proper way for a Mādhyamika to "Refute a real entity," which is the primary purpose of Madhyamaka reasoning. Chapa begins by presenting the Prāsaṅgika method for refuting a real entity by way of "consequential" (*prasaṅga*) reasoning, then takes that method to task for its inability to do so. He then discusses the correct way to refute a real entity, through the use of formal inference "in one's own continuum" or "of one's own" (*svatantra*). Along the way, he critiques several important Prāsaṅgika positions, discussed in chapters 3 through 5, on the impossibility of human valid cognition (*pramāṇa, tshad ma*), the unknowable ultimate, and the mindless Buddha. As Chapa presents his own positions on these issues, in addition to his critique of Prāsaṅgika, this portion of his text is perhaps our most important document for understanding the formation of Prāsaṅgika and Svātantrika schools of Tibetan Madhyamaka.

Throughout, numbers in curly brackets refer to the page and line numbers in Tauscher's edition. Square brackets give translator additions intended to improve the readability of the translation. Parentheses provide the original Tibetan terms, along with the Sanskrit equivalents when appropriate. The outline apparatus is drawn from the text's internal topical outline (*sa bcad*). Endnotes provide explanatory information intended to improve the translation's clarity. Tauscher's edition notes the variance in Chapa's citations of Candrakīrti's *Entrance to the Middle* from La Vallée Poussin's edition of that text.[4] As it is in most cases important to Chapa's interpretation of Prāsaṅgika, I follow Chapa's "misquotations" except where noted. Tauscher has translated several passages utilized herein; [5] where important, I note my divergence from his translation.

The ascertainment that affirming negatives—illustrations of ultimate truths—are empty of being established by reasoning {58.3}.

This section has two parts: refuting a real entity and refuting some other affirming negative that is related to that.[6]

Refuting a Real Entity {58.5}

This section has two parts: debunking [Candrakīrti's position] that consequences negate the object of negation and [our own] mode of negating the object of negation through inference.

1. Debunking that Consequences Negate the Object of Negation {58.7}

This topic is to be ascertained in four parts: setting up the opponents' system, debunking that, positing our system, and dispelling objections to that.

a. Setting up the opponents' system {58.9}

This section is to be posited in four parts: the master Candrakīrti's and others'

- division of mistaken awareness and non-mistaken awareness,
- mode of division [of phenomena] into the two truths in dependence upon that,
- debunking that proliferations are negated by [inferences] of one's own, and
- mode of negating proliferations through consequences.

i. The division of non-mistaken awareness and mistaken awareness by the master Candrakīrti and others. {58.12}

[Non-mistaken awareness]

During the meditative equipoise of one who has attained a ground and upon the ground of buddhahood, since no referent (*yul, viṣaya*)—that is, object of knowledge (*shes bya, jñeya*)—is established, the engagement of a referent-taker [that is, a consciousness] is pacified. Thus, just the cutting off of the engagement of the mind and mental factors is designated the non-mistaken mind of reality through realizing the final nature (*chos nyid, dharmatā*). Just as Sautrāntikas call an awareness that is like blue "the realization of blue," so an awareness that is devoid of birth is similar to the birthless final nature and, hence, is to be called "the realization of the final nature." As it says [in Candrakīrti's *Entrance to the Middle, Madhyamakāvatāra* XII.4]:

> Since the final nature is birthless and the mind [realizing it] is devoid of birth,
> Due to that [object] in the basis [that is, the mind] that has the aspect of that [birthless final nature, this is said to be] like "knowing reality."
> Hence, "knowing" [reality] is in dependence upon conventions,
> Just as [in Sautrāntika] a mind knows well its object due to arising in the aspect of that object.

[Mistaken awareness]

Mistaken awarenesses of false vision are:

(1) Cognitions that are renowned in the world to be true; that is, worldly awarenesses that rely on the unimpaired six sense faculties, such as:

- The direct perception of (i.) a common being, who has the conception that appearances are true and of (ii.) one who has attained a ground, who perceives forms and so forth, without having the conception that these appearances are true, subsequent [to meditative equipoise];
- The inference that conceives of fire and so forth;
- The ascertainment of future lives and so forth, which depends upon sound (that is, scripture);
- Inference by analogy, and so forth.

(2) Sense consciousnesses to which appear two moons, floating hairs, and so forth, that is, superimpositions of objects that are renowned to be non-

existent even as a worldly referent—[consciousnesses] that depend on the impaired six sense faculties—*and* polluted mental consciousnesses that superimpose self and so forth in dependence upon specious inferences and bad tenets.

As it says [in *Entrance to the Middle* VI.24]:

> Erroneous perception has two aspects: clear faculties and faulty faculties.
> Consciousnesses from faulty faculties are asserted to be wrong relative to consciousnesses from good faculties.

ii. [Candrakīrti's] Mode of Division into Two Truths in Dependence Upon That {59.11}

This section has three parts: the division into two truths; positing the nature of conventionalities; and positing the nature of the ultimate.

(a.) The Division into Two Truths {59.13}

Appearances—as various objects of knowledge—in the perspective of the false perception of mistaken (*'khrul ba, bhrānta*) awareness are obscurational truths. Since there is nothing that correct perception sees, that is ultimate truth. As it says [in *Entrance to the Middle* VI.23]:[7]

> All entities bear two natures—
> Entities found by correct perception and by erroneous perception.
> Whatever object is [found by] correct perception is suchness;
> That [found by] erroneous perception is said to be an obscurational truth.

(b.) Positing the nature of conventionalities {60.1}

Objects of the six unimpaired sense consciousnesses—form, and so forth—that are true in the face of worldly minds (*'jig rten pa'i bsam*) are real conventionalities. Objects of the six impaired sense consciousnesses—two moons, dreams, and so forth—are non-existent even in the face of worldly minds. Since these are [only] imputed, they are unreal conventionalities. Both [real and unreal conventionalities] are imputed to be true as referents of the obscuring awareness (*kun rdzob kyi blo*) having the nature of delusion that veils the pacification of the operation of awareness. Thus, they are obscurational truths. As it is said [in *Entrance to the Middle* VI.25–26, 28]:

Anything that the world holds to be
Apprehended by the six unimpaired faculties
Is true only within the world.
The remainder are considered wrong (*mithyā, log pa*) even in the world.[8]

Whatever entities are imputed
By Non-Buddhists who are agitated by the sleep of ignorance
As well as imputations of illusions and mirages
Are seen to be non-existent even in the world.

Since it has a nature of delusion, which obscures, it is a concealer (*saṃvṛti*).[9]
Whatever entities that are imputed to be true by that [concealer][10]
The Sage called concealing-truths (*saṃvṛtisatya*).
Fabricated truths are conventionalities.[11]

(c.) Positing the nature of the ultimate {60.14}

Just as good eyes do not see at all those falling hairs that appear to a mistaken awareness, so a superior's meditative equipoise, when directed toward the very objects of observation that appear variously to mistaken awarenesses, has no object to be observed at all, due to having extinguished mistake. [This absence] is ultimate truth. It is said [in *Entrance to the Middle* VI.29]:

Know suchness to be like the nature
With which one with good eyes sees
Those unreal (*vitatha, log pa*) things—floating hairs, and so forth—
Imputed through the power of ophthalmia.[12]

iii. [Candrakīrti's] Debunking that proliferations are negated by [inferences] of one's own {61.4}

[Proponents of inferences of one's own say:] Regarding what is said in a [proof] statement of one's own, since the reason must fulfill the three modes (*tshul gsum, trairūpya*), a basis that appears in common (*gzhi mthun snang*) [to the two parties in a debate] entails that one's own inquiry is supported by a reason that proves it.

[Candrakīrti and others respond:] A basis does not appear in common.

- Since this appearance is an object of a mistaken mind, a worldly mind, and is not an object of a middle way mind, a basis does not appear to me.
- Even if it were allowed that [a basis] appears, if one says that an appearance that is like an illusion is the basis, it would not be established for a proponent of entities, and if one says that a true appearance is the basis, then this is not established for us.

[Some might say,] "Just as it is the case that, in the proof that sound is impermanent, a permanent sound is not established for Buddhists and an impermanent sound is not established for outsiders, but [both sides] have an appearance of mere sound in common, so, true appearances are not established for me and false appearances are not established for an outsider, but [we both] have a common mere appearance." This cannot be said because when a mistaken appearance is proved to be impermanent, an unanalyzed appearance that is common [to both parties] as mere sound is sufficient [to be the basis]. However, in this case, when ultimate truth is delineated, it is not suitable to take appearances that are common to mistaken minds as the basis; two moons appearing in common to two ophthalmics do not become suitable to be a basis for proving [that such an appearance is] true.

Even if we allow that a basis appears [in common], the probandum that one desires to know is not to be proved[13] and, hence, a reason proving that [probandum] and a [proof] statement of one's own that demonstrates this reason are not feasible. This is because a Mādhyamika does not make any assertions at all, as whatever one asserts—existence, non-existence, both existence and non-existence, and neither existence nor non-existence—is an extreme.

Even a reason that validly[14] fulfills the three modes is undemonstrable

- because all of these reasons, pervasions, and so forth, are objects of worldly awarenesses and worldly awareness is not at all valid cognition, as it says [in *Entrance to the Middle* VI.30]:

> If the world were authoritative,
> The world would see suchness.
> What need would there be for the others, the Superiors, and what
> would be the use of the Superior path?
> How could foolishness be valid cognition?[15]

- and because a Mādhyamika who does not assert anything has no appearances at all and, hence, has no ascertainment of a sign, pervasion, and so forth.[16]

Furthermore, through assertions being internally contradictory, [the opponent] is debunked, as in the following:

- If a thing already exists, this contradicts production being sensible, and
- If production is sensible, this contradicts the already existent, and so forth.

Therefore, a reason of one's own that is proved by valid cognition is not necessary. Furthermore, if [an opponent] denies [that these are] contradictory, that [opponent] would also deny [a reason of one's own that is proved by] valid cognition. Hence, proofs of one's own have no power. As it says [in Nāgārjuna's *Refutation of Objections* (*Vigrahavyāvartanī*), stanza 29]:[17]

> If I had a thesis,
> I would have a fault.
> Since I have no thesis,
> I am only faultless.

Or, as it says [in Āryadeva's *400 Stanzas* (*Catuḥśataka*) XVI.25]:

> Whoever does not assert existence, non-existence, [both] existence and non-existence
> Cannot be criticized, even for a long time.

In that way, a Mādhyamika has no theses whatsoever. Hence, a reason proving that [thesis] and an [inference] of one's own demonstrating it are not feasible. Therefore, [inferences] of one's own do not cut off proliferations.

iv. [Candrakīrti's] Mode of Negating Proliferations through Consequences {63.1}

Therefore, proliferations are cut off only by consequences that contradict the assertion [as in the refutation of production, discussed at length here].

[Refutation of Production from Self]
Sāṃkhya asserts:

- Production is necessarily senseless for the manifest, and so forth, which already exist.

- The entity of an effect already exists even at the time of its causal entity.

[The Prāsaṅgika replies:] It says [in *Entrance to the Middle* VI.8cd]:

> There is no value [to say] that a thing is produced from itself, and
> It is just not reasonable that a produced thing is produced again.

If one asserts that the unmanifest—an internal sense sphere, and so forth—already exists even at the time of its cause and asserts that production is still necessary, then we assert a contradictory consequence,[18] "It follows that the production of an internal sense sphere is senseless because it already exists at the time of its cause."

If one considers that entailment to be unestablished, then [we prove the entailment through] drawing parallels:[19]

- In as much as even that which already exists when it is unmanifest is produced, so, that which already exists when manifest also would require production.
- In as much as that [which already exists when it is manifest] does not require production, so, already existing even when unmanifest entails that production is unnecessary.

One might differentiate as follows: manifest existence entails that production is unnecessary, however unmanifest existence does not entail that production is unnecessary. [We respond:] That distinction is the same as what is to be proved. Just as an effect existing in the cause is not established for us, that distinction [between manifest and unmanifest existence] also is not established. Hence, production from self is negated.

[Refutation of Production from Other]

Followers of the One Gone to Bliss [that is, Buddhists] assert that:

- Others are producers, since they assert that smoke is produced from fire—which is other than itself.
- Darkness is not produced from a tongue of fire.

To this, we state the contradictory consequence: It follows that a tongue of flame produces darkness because of being other than darkness. As it says [in *Entrance to the Middle* VI.14ab]:

If one thing arose in dependence upon another,
Then thick darkness would arise even from a tongue of flame.

If one considers that entailment to be unestablished, then we establish the entailment through drawing parallels:

- In as much as darkness is not produced from a tongue of flame, which is other than darkness, so it is not suitable that smoke would be produced from fire, which is other than smoke.
- In as much as smoke is produced from fire, which is other than smoke, so darkness also must be produced from a tongue of flame, which is other than darkness.

One might say, "In that case, fire that is other than smoke has the power to produce smoke, whereby there is production [of smoke from fire]. However, a tongue of fire that is other than darkness does not have the power to produce darkness, whereby there is no production [of darkness from a tongue of fire]." [We respond:] That distinction is the same as what is to be proved; just as production from another is not established for us, it is not established that "Fire has the power to produce smoke but a tongue of fire does not have the power to produce darkness." [Hence] production from other is refuted.

[Refutation of Production from Both Self and Other]

Similarly, since it has both faults, production from both [self and other] is refuted.

[Refutation of Causeless Production]

It says [in *Entrance to the Middle* VI.100]:[20]

If the world were without cause,
Just like the scent and color of a lotus in the sky, it would not be apprehended.
Since the world in its exceedingly great variety is apprehended,
It should be known that, just like one's own awareness, the world arises from causes.

In this way, if one asserts causeless production, we state a contradictory consequence: It follows that there is no apprehension [of worldly] variety by direct perception because the world has no cause. If one considers that entailment to be unestablished, the entailment is established through drawing a parallel:

- In as much as there are variegated appearances of the world even though the world has no cause, so too the scent and color of a lotus in the sky must appear to direct perception even though it has no cause.

One might assert, "While they are similar in being causeless, the world is an existent entity and, hence, appears. However, the scent and color of a lotus in the sky are non-existent entities and, hence, do not appear." [We respond:] That distinction is the same as what is to be proved. Just as causeless production is not established for us, so it is not established that "The world is an existent entity but the scent and color of a lotus in the sky are non-existent entities." Hence, causeless production is refuted.

In this way, proponents of entities are refuted.

b. Debunking the opponents' system {65.1}

This section has three parts: the unfeasibility of not asserting inferences of one's own, the unfeasibility of refuting proponents of entities by way of consequences, and the unfeasibility that minds and mental factors are cut off in buddhahood.

i. The unfeasibility of not asserting inferences of one's own {65.4}

This section has three parts: the absence of a commonly appearing inferential subject is not a suitable reason [for not asserting inferences of one's own]; the absence of theses is not a suitable reason [for not asserting inferences of one's own]; and the absence of ascertainment by valid cognition that the reason is a property of the inferential subject[21] and of the reason's [forward and reverse] pervasions is not a suitable reason [for not asserting inferences of one's own].

(a.) The absence of a commonly appearing inferential subject is not a suitable reason [for not asserting inferences of one's own] {65.7}

[A follower of Candrakīrti] might say, "Illusion-like appearances are not established for proponents of entities and appearances that can bear analysis are not established for Mādhyamikas; thus, there are no commonly appearing inferential subjects. Hence, it is not feasible to give an [inferential] reason for that [subject]."

[We respond:] An illusion-like person is not established for proponents of entities and a person that can bear analysis is not established for Mādhyamikas; hence, there is no common appearance of the person who is debunked. Hence, it is not feasible to state a consequence to that [person].

[A follower of Candrakīrti] might say, "We state a consequence to that person who propounds entities and who is established to both of us, no matter if that person bears analysis or not."

[We respond:] We affix a reason to an [inferential] subject (*gzhi*) that is established to both of us as a mere appearance, a mere entity, or a mere object of knowledge, no matter if it bears analysis or not.

[A follower of Candrakīrti] might say, "An appearance in common to mistaken awarenesses, just like an appearance of floating hairs in common to two ophthalmics, is not suitable to be an inferential subject that is proved to have the property of [either] emptiness or bearing analysis."

[We respond:] An appearance as a person to a mistaken awareness, just like an appearance as an illusory person in common to two persons whose eyes are affected [by a mantra], is not a referent (*yul*) to whom one could state a consequence that would clear away the wrong conceptions of proponents of true entities.

[A follower of Candrakīrti] might say, "Although I am refuting the object of negation—the wrong conception of true entities—since I refute the wrong conception of existence for a person whom I do not analyze,[22] the appearance as a person to [my own] mistaken awareness is the person to whom a consequence is stated."

[We respond:] Although I prove the property, [either] voidness of proliferations or bearing analysis, it is proved in regard to an unanalyzed inferential subject; hence, it is feasible to affix a reason to an inferential subject that appears in common to mistaken minds.

[A follower of Candrakīrti] might say, "Although an inferential subject (*chos can*) appears, it [appears to] a worldly awareness. However, it is not feasible for a Mādhyamika, who makes no assertion at all, to state a reason, due to not perceiving [that appearance] as a subject (*gzhi*)."

[We respond:] Although a person who propounds entities appears, [that appearance] is an object of a worldly mind; however, it is not feasible for a Mādhyamika, who makes no assertions at all, to state a consequence to that [person], due to not perceiving a person. If you state a consequence even while not perceiving the person yourself, I could state a reason although an [inferential] subject (*gzhi*) does not appear to me.

[A follower of Candrakīrti] might say, "Well then, one could also affix a reason to the horns of a rabbit or the vase of a flesh eater."

[We respond:] In that case, you also could state a consequence to the son of a barren woman or to a flesh eater.[23]

(b.) The absence of theses is not suitable to be a reason [for not asserting inferences of one's own] {66.7}

This section has three parts: [In the absence of theses] it would not be feasible to refute wrong conceptions; it is not feasible to cast out both explicit contradictories; and [in the absence of theses] one would be unable to refute a mere consciousness that bears analysis.

(i.) [In the absence of theses] it would not be feasible to refute wrong conceptions {66.10}

[A follower of Candrakīrti] might say, "It is not reasonable to state a reason because nothing is established for a Mādhyamika."

[We respond: According to you who holds no thesis whatsoever] the opponent does not have a wrong conception that is discordant with the basic disposition (*gshis*) of objects of knowledge [since you make no claim regarding this basic disposition]. Hence, it is not reasonable to state a consequence that refutes that.

[A follower of Candrakīrti] might say, "Asserting ultimate entities is a wrong conception that does not accord with the basic disposition of objects of knowledge."

[We respond:] Well then, [your claim] of thesislessness deteriorates [because] you assert the emptiness of ultimate entities as the basic disposition of objects of knowledge.

(ii.) It is not feasible to cast out both explicit contradictories {66.15}

If one asserts neither entities nor the emptiness of entities as the ultimate, how would one refute the assertion of both?

[A follower of Candrakīrti] might say, "[Your] very establishment of one casts out the other; hence, asserting both is contradictory."

[We respond:] Just refuting one establishes the other; hence, asserting neither is contradictory.

[A follower of Candrakīrti] might say, "This very thing is not established."

[We respond:] The former, also, is not established.

[A follower of Candrakīrti] might say, "Regarding contradictories in the sense of mutual exclusion,[24] just the establishment of one is the refutation of the counterpart."

[We respond:] Regarding explicit contradictories,[25] just the refutation of one is the establishment of the other.

[A follower of Candrakīrti] might say, "The very ascertainment [of two things] as explicit contradictories is a worldly awareness."

[We respond:] The ascertainment of contradictories [in the sense of mutual exclusion] is a worldly awareness.

[A follower of Candrakīrti] might say, "While it is a worldly awareness, it is not harmed conventionally and is established through experience and [therefore] cannot be cast out."

[We respond:] Also, the limitation [of two things] as explicit contradictories is similar to that [in being unharmed conventionally and established through experience].

(iii.) [In the absence of theses] one would be unable to refute a mere consciousness that bears analysis[26] *{67.4}*

How can proponents of thesislessness refute proponents of existence [who hold] the thesis that a clear awareness that is singularly established by experience only exists ultimately?

[A follower of Candrakīrti might say] We perform the analysis, "Is that awareness unitary or manifold; produced or not produced; permanent or impermanent?"

[We respond:] That action [of analysis] itself also should be analyzed: is it a true entity or empty of being such?

[A follower of Candrakīrti] might say, "We have no theses whatsoever."

[We respond:] We, also, do not assert any distinction regarding the ultimate, [which the hypothetical "proponent of existence" we began with holds to be] clear [awareness].

[A follower of Candrakīrti] might say, "Not asserting any particulars regarding an entity [claimed by you to be] existent is not feasible."

[We respond:] Casting out both of two explicit contradictories [that is, unitary or manifold, produced or not produced, permanent or impermanent] is not feasible.

[A follower of Candrakīrti] might say, "Although [two things] are established for the worldly as explicit contradictories, that is not established for us."

[We respond:] Regarding an existent entity, not passing beyond permanent and impermanent or one and many, and so forth, is established in the world. However, this is not established for us.

[A follower of Candrakīrti] might say, "Due to non-invalidated experience, you cannot cast out the limitation as entailer and entailed [in this case, existence and particulars]."

[We respond:] Due to non-invalidated[27] experience, you cannot cast out the establishment [of two things] as explicit contradictories.

(c.) The absence of ascertainment by valid cognition that the reason is a property of the inferential subject[28] and of the reason's [forward and reverse] entailments is not suitable to be a reason [for not asserting inferences of one's own] {68.1}

[A follower of Candrakīrti] might say, "A reason that establishes the voidness of proliferations is impossible."

[We respond:] A consequence that refutes proliferations is also impossible.

[A follower of Candrakīrti] might say, "[Consequences stated] to those who propound that the effect exists in the cause, such as 'It follows that production is pointless because the effect exists in the cause,' are consequences that refute proliferations."

[We respond:] Regarding [the inferential subject] entities, the [reason] emptiness of real unity or multiplicity establishes the [probandum] emptiness of a real nature, and so forth, and is a reason that refutes proliferations.

[A follower of Candrakīrti] might say, "There is no ascertainment that the reason is a property of the inferential subject nor of the [forward and reverse] entailments regarding that [reason]."

[We respond:] A person who propounds that the effect exists in the cause and that person's holding wrong conceptions are not established. Hence, it is not feasible to state a consequence.

[A follower of Candrakīrti] might say, "The person is manifestly established. [That person's holding wrong conceptions] is established from the very inference that infers by way of the verbal communication [that is, the speech of the opponent] that [indicates that the opponent holds] a superimposition that the effect exists within the cause."

[We respond: Your defense of the use of consequences by establishing, through direct perception and inference, the person to whom a consequence is stated and the wrong conceptions of that person that are refuted by consequences] is similar to the following [defense of the use of inferences by establishing, through direct perception and inference, the reason's entailments and that the reason is a property of the inferential subject]: It is established by direct perception that the existence [of anything] entails that [the thing] is either unitary or manifold. By reason of being associated with manifold time, a unitary continuum is refuted. By reason of the impossibility of not being connected with earlier and later [moments], the possibility of a unit existing within a continuum is refuted. [These two refutations of the unitary] are established by inference. Due to the non-existence of units, the manifold [being a collection of units] does not exist, by reason of which multiplicity is refuted. Thus, the reason [absence of real unity and multiplicity] being a property of the inferential subject [entities] is established by inference.

[A follower of Candrakīrti] might say, "Direct perception and inference themselves are worldly awarenesses and are not valid cognition. Hence, they are not feasible to be ascertainers that the reason is a property of the inferential subject or of the reason's [forward and reverse] entailments."

[We respond: The statement] "It follows that production is pointless because of the effect existing in the cause" is not even a proper consequence for one who propounds that the effect exists in the cause. Hence, it is not feasible to refute the wrong conceptions of others by means of that [consequence].

[A follower of Candrakīrti] might say, "That [consequence] has the ability to establish an undesired thesis [against the opponent] because of the general definition of mere consequence: the reason and the pervasion are established for the opponent. Hence, it is not established that it is not a proper consequence."

[We respond:] Direct perception and inference also possess the general definition of mere valid cognition: being contradictory with superimpositions upon a previously unrealized object by an awareness that is non-mistaken regarding that object. Hence, it is not suitable that they are not valid cognition.

[A follower of Candrakīrti] might say, "As it says [in *Entrance to the Middle* VI.30]:

> If the world were authoritative, the world would see suchness.
> What need would there be for the others, the Superiors, and what
> would be the use of the Superior path?
> How could foolishness be valid cognition?

If [worldly awarenesses, such as direct perception and inference] were valid cognition, it follows that a [worldly] awareness sees the truth."

[We reply:] If your consequence is proper, there also would be a reason that is asserted [by the opponent, namely, "the effect exists in the cause"], an entailment [namely, "if an effect exists in its cause, production is pointless"] that is ascertained by valid cognition, and [in a way similar to an inference] the dispelling of the [opponent's] thesis.

[A follower of Candrakīrti] might say, "There is no entailment because there are also consequences in which the entailment is asserted [by the opponent] and the thesis is dispelled by their own words."

[We reply:] Then also there is no entailment [in your statement] that it follows that a [worldly] awareness would see the truth. This is because it is not contradictory for there to be direct perception and inference that comprehend the conventional and for there also to be inference that comprehends ultimate truth without perceiving [ultimate] truth.[29]

[A follower of Candrakīrti] might say, "A short-sighted[30] awareness [that is, an awareness not directed at emptiness] involves mistake. Hence, such an awareness cannot establish that the reason is a property of the inferential subject or the reason's entailments."

[We reply:] Your short-sighted awareness involves mistake, and hence you cannot refute the [opponent's] denial, "I did not assert that reason," and the [opponent's] denial of contradiction.

[A follower of Candrakīrti] might say, "If one denies an object that is renowned in the world, [such a denial] is harmed by a worldly awareness itself."

[We reply:] If one denies that the reason is a property of the inferential subject and the reason's pervasions that are renowned in the world, these [denials] also are harmed by the world.

[A follower of Candrakīrti] might say, "A worldly awareness perceives the reason and entailments; however, nothing is established for a Mādhyamika who holds no theses whatsoever. Hence, a Mādhyamika does not state reasons."

[We reply:] The world also perceives the reason and entailment as asserted [by opponents who would be refuted by consequences employing their own words]. However, a Mādhyamika does not perceive [the reason and entailment]. Hence, it is not reasonable for a Mādhyamika to state a consequence.

[A follower of Candrakīrti] might say, "A worldly awareness that comprehends conventions is also included within the continuum[31] of the very Mādhyamika who accepts nothing at all as the ultimate. Hence, reasons and entailments are established as asserted [by the opponent] for this very person who propounds the middle.

[We reply:] Due to that very [point] the reason being a property of the inferential subject and the reason's entailments are also established for the very person who propounds the middle.

ii. Consequences are unable to refute proponents of entities {70.1}

This section has three parts: [consequences] are unable to refute completely[32] the object of negation; even if they were able [to refute the object of negation, consequences] are unable to refute all proliferations; and [consequences] are unable to dispel the qualm that proliferations exist.

(a.) [Consequences] are unable to refute completely the object of negation {70.4}

Proper consequences, such as "It follows that production is pointless, due to [a thing] existing already" and "It follows that [things] do not appear to direct perception, due to their being causeless," are to be examined as follows. Is one contradictory object refuted upon stating its contradictory counterpart as a reason, by way of the opponent's mere assertion that the already existent is contradictory with meaningful production; or, is one contradictory object refuted upon stating its contradictory counterpart as a reason, by way of ascertaining that, in the basic disposition of objects of knowledge, [the already existent] is contradictory [with meaningful production]?

In the first case, I would be able to prove the entity of the ultimate upon [stating] the reason of dependent arising, by way of [simply] asserting that the appearance of dependent arising to a worldly awareness is related to the entity of the ultimate.[33]

[A follower of Candrakīrti] might say, "If [the opponent] ascertains, by valid cognition, [two things] to be related, upon [the opponent] perceiving one, I am able to establish the related object. However, the mere assertion that [two things] are related cannot establish the related object."

[We reply:] If one ascertains, by valid cognition, [two things] to be contradictory, the perception of one contradictory object refutes its contradictory counterpart. However, the mere assertion that [two things] are contradictory does not refute the contradictory counterpart.

Also [in the second case] if one ascertains that [the already existent] is contradictory with [meaningful production] in the actual disposition of objects of knowledge:

- Is further production refuted, having established "already existing" as the basic disposition of objects of knowledge, or
- Is the already existent refuted, having established "further production" as the basic disposition of objects of knowledge, or
- Is merely the collection of these two [that is, the already existent and

further production] refuted by ascertaining that the two are contradictory, or

- Although neither [pre-existence or further production] is established as the basic disposition of objects of knowledge, is one object refuted when its contradictory is asserted?

In the first case,

- The property of the inferential subject is "'already existing' established as the basic disposition of objects of knowledge";
- There is an entailment due to the delimitation that "'already existing' established as the basic disposition of objects of knowledge" is contradictory with "further production";
- The probandum is "the emptiness of further production."

Therefore, just that explicit statement [of a consequence] comes to be a reason in one's own continuum *(rang rgyud kyi rtags)*.[34]

In the second case,

- The property of the inferential subject is "further production being definite as the basic disposition of objects of knowledge";
- The entailment is the delimitation that "[further] production and 'already existing' are contradictory";
- The probandum is "the emptiness of pre-existence."

Therefore, hurling consequences comes to be a reason in one's own continuum.

In the third case, the valid cognition itself that ascertains [the two] to be contradictory [has already] per force blocked the collection [of the two]. Hence, stating a consequence is pointless. Also, even though the collection [of the two] is blocked, mere "already existing" and mere further production are not blocked. Hence, one set of proliferations would not be blocked.

In the fourth case, if [the opponent] has a wrong conception asserting one contradictory object, then the contradictory counterpart is per force blocked; if there is no such wrong conception, the contradictory counterpart is not blocked. Hence, the refutation of the object of negation would depend on a wrong conception. [If this were the case] it would [absurdly] follow that the [wrong] assertion that the entity of the ultimate must be ultimately one or many would prove that [the entity of the ultimate] is ultimately one or many.

Also, it would [absurdly] follow that the [wrong] assertion that, conventionally, the five aggregates have a mere existence that contradicts being causeless and [at the same time] that the five aggregates have a permanence that contradicts having a cause would block being conventionally both causeless and with cause. Also, the assertion that there is fire on a mass of snow would block the touch of cold.[35]

Therefore, internally contradictory assertions incur terminological faults but not faults of meaning. Hence, assertions such as [a woman] being a mother and a barren woman come to be [terminological] contrarieties.[36] However, they do not block the possibility of contradictory objects.[37]

Furthermore, [a follower of Candrakīrti] might state [the consequence] "It follows that a tongue of flame produces darkness because it is other than darkness" to one who propounds production from other.

[We respond:] Well then, if a consequence refutes production from other, then since [the statement] "It follows that production is pointless because of already existing" is a consequence also, it would refute production from other.

[A follower of Candrakīrti] might say, "That is not entailed."

[We respond:] Your previous consequence [that darkness would arise from flame] also is not entailed.

[A follower of Candrakīrti] might say, "The assertion that 'other' produces deteriorates."

[We respond:] The assertion that a consequence refutes production from other deteriorates.

[A follower of Candrakīrti] might say, "We propound that the means of refuting production from other is necessarily a consequence. However, we do not propound that [every] consequence necessarily refutes production from other."

[We respond:] We propound that producers are necessarily other. However, we do not propound that others are necessarily producers.

[A follower of Candrakīrti] might say, "Among what are merely other, producing and not producing are contradictory."

[We respond:] Also, among mere consequences, refuting production from other and not refuting production from other are contradictory.

[A follower of Candrakīrti] might say, "Since [mere consequences] are the same concept but different substances,[38] there is no contradiction."

[We reply:] Mere difference, also, is similar to that.

(b.) Consequences do not block all proliferations {72.4}

In the event that these consequences refute production from self, causeless production, production from other, and production from both [self and other]: is it ascertained that all four types of production are impossible or is there the qualm that some might be possible? In the latter case, the possibility of proliferations is not blocked. In the former case, we must ask: is it definite that all proliferations are covered by the four types of production or is it not definite?

In the first case, through ascertaining the absence of the entailed [that is, the four types of production], the ascertainment of the absence of the entailer [that is, all proliferations] comes to be a reason in one's own continuum *(rang rgyud kyi rtags)*.[39] In the second case, proliferations that are not covered by the four [types of production] would not be blocked.

Furthermore, [returning to the first case, one must ask:] do consequences block what proliferations entail [that is, the four types of production] or do consequences not block what proliferations entail? In the first case, the entailed [that is, the four types of production] would not be observed [since consequences have blocked them].[40] In the second case, the qualm that proliferations are possible would not be cut off.

(c.) Consequences are unable to clear away the qualm that proliferations exist {72.12}

If you state to those who think that the effect exists in the cause, "It follows that production is pointless," how is the qualm that the effect exists in the cause refuted? Such a qualm is not refuted by a consequence because a reason for that [consequence] is not asserted.[41] If that [qualm] is not blocked, since there is still the qualm that proliferations are possible, you are not able to bring [the opponent] to the mode of not asserting anything whatsoever.

iii. It is not feasible that minds and mental factors are cut off in buddhahood {72.16}

Even if we allow that since the features of objects of knowledge are not established ultimately, an awareness that observes them is not feasible, it is not feasible for conventionalities that appear like illusions to be non-existent [upon buddhahood] because

- It is not feasible that there be no power to impel later [moments] of consciousness
- It is not feasible that [consciousness] having appearance be dispelled by antidotes
- If [a Buddha's consciousness] did not have appearances, [buddhahood] would be no different from a Hearer's nirvāṇa without remainder.

(a.) **It is not feasible that there be no power to impel later [moments] of consciousness {73.1}**

If you assert that an awareness during the adamantine meditative equipoise[42] [which is the awareness immediately preceding buddhahood] does not have the power to impel later [moments] of awareness, how do you refute those Hedonists[43] who do not assert future [re]births due to [their claim] that an awareness at the moment of death does not have the power to impel later [moments] of awareness?

[A follower of Candrakīrti] might say, "Just as a mere butter lamp entails the unobstructed power to produce light, it is established through experience that mere awareness also entails the unobstructed power to produce later awareness. Hence, one can infer that since an awareness at the moment of death is also a mere awareness, it has the power to produce later [awareness]."

[We reply:] An awareness during the adamantine meditative equipoise is also a mere awareness. Hence, how can you not infer that it has the power definitely to produce later [awareness]?

[A follower of Candrakīrti] might say, "Mere awareness does not entail the power to produce later [awareness]. Awareness that is conjoined with craving entails the power to produce later [awareness]. Since there is no craving during the adamantine meditative equipoise, further awareness is not impelled."

[We reply: If a Hedonist said] "Awareness that is conjoined with craving does not entail the power to produce later [awareness]. Awareness that is connected with a body entails the power to produce later [awareness]. At death, since there is no awareness that is connected with the body, later [awareness] is not impelled," what would you answer?

[A follower of Candrakīrti] might say, "A sense awareness depends on the body in this very lifetime. However, it is experienced (*myong*) that a mental awareness is produced from merely an immediately preceding [awareness]."

[We reply:] An impure consciousness depends upon craving, and so forth, in this very lifetime. However, it is experienced that a pure consciousness is produced from the immediately preceding [consciousness], which is the virtuous mind of non-attachment, non-hatred, and non-delusion.

(b.) It is not feasible that [consciousness] having appearance is dispelled by antidotes {73.15}

[This section has two parts: consciousness] having appearance is not an obstruction and, hence, is not to be dispelled; and there is no antidote to that [consciousness having appearance].

(i.) [A consciousness] having appearance is not an obstruction and, hence, is not to be dispelled {73.17}

If an awareness having appearance and realizing [appearances] to be like illusions is an obstruction, is it an afflictive obstruction [that is, an obstruction to liberation] or an obstruction to the object of knowledge?

The first case is not feasible because, whereas afflictions entail connection with the conception of a self of persons, [an awareness] having appearance [and realizing appearances to be like illusions]

- dispels the conception of the five aggregates as being permanent and unitary through knowing that they are momentary and multiple; and
- dispels the conception of the five aggregates as being self-powered through knowing that they arise from earlier [causes]; and thus

is not connected with the conception [of the five aggregates] as a self of persons.

If [you say that an awareness having appearance and realizing appearances to be like illusions] is an obstruction to the object of knowledge, does it obstruct knowledge of the mode of being[44]—the realization that, ultimately, [things] are devoid of proliferations—or does it obstruct knowledge of the varieties[45]—the realization of all objects of knowledge, conventionally?

In the first case, does [an awareness having appearance and realizing appearances to be like illusions] obstruct [knowledge of the mode of being] within the context that appearances of conventionalities and ultimate utter non-establishment are contradictory or is it an obstruction even without these two being contradictory?

In the first case:

- Voidness of proliferations would not be the reality of appearances[46]
- Appearances that are established by experience, having per force blocked the voidness of proliferations, would come to have proliferations

- Ultimate utter non-establishment, having per force blocked appearances, would completely cut off [the existence of] conventionalities
- Illusion-like appearances would not entail ultimate utter non-establishment.

Hence, the Realist *(dngos por smra ba)* position would be established.

[In the second case] if [an awareness having appearance and realizing appearances to be like illusions] obstructs [knowledge of the mode of being] even without [appearances of conventionalities and ultimate non-establishment] being contradictory, the realization of blue would block the realization of impermanence.

[A follower of Candrakīrti] might say, "Just as the ascertainment of blue dispels not-blue but does not dispel impermanence, how would it block the realization of impermanence?"

[We reply:] The establishment of appearances from a non-analytic point of view dispels non-appearance from a non-analytic point of view; however, it does not dispel [their] utter non-establishment when analyzed. Hence, how would [the establishment of appearances from a non-analytic point of view] block the realization of [their] utter non-establishment when analyzed?[47]

Also, [an awareness having appearance and realizing appearances to be like illusions] does not obstruct the realization of the varieties of objects of knowledge because it is contradictory for something to obstruct itself, realization of the varieties being the very [awareness] having appearance [and realizing appearances to be like illusions]. Therefore, since [an awareness] having appearance and realizing [appearances] to be like illusions is a referent-taker of what is unable to bear analysis, we apply the convention, "mistaken appearance"; however, it is not either of the two kinds of obstructions. Hence, it is not feasible for that [consciousness having appearance] to be dispelled by a Buddha.

(ii.) There is no antidote to consciousness having appearance[48] *{74.17}*

The collection of merit focuses on affirming negations[49] and, hence, it is certain that appearances exist conventionally. However, it is not an awareness that negates and so is not an antidote to [consciousness] having appearance. If some awarenesses that perform negations were antidotes, are [such awarenesses] antidotes to appearance due to negating proliferations ultimately, or are they antidotes to [consciousness] having appearance [due to] ascertaining that the very appearances of conventionalities do not exist?

In the first case, is the negation of proliferations an antidote to appearances due to the ultimate emptiness of proliferations being contradictory with these appearances or is it an antidote even though [emptiness and appearances] are not contradictory?

In the first case, if one states a consequence that blocks proliferations, due to being contradictory with the absence of proliferations all appearances would be blocked. If you assert this, in thoroughly blocking all afflicted and pure [phenomena] and all cause and effect, the system of the Hedonists flourishes. Also, the faults expressed earlier would be difficult to dispel.[50]

In the second case [in which the negation of proliferations serves as an antidote to appearances even though emptiness and appearances are not contradictory], the ascertainment of impermanence would also dispel appearances.

[A follower of Candrakīrti] might say, "The awareness of impermanence is able to dispel the superimposition of permanence, which is contradictory with that. However, [the awareness of impermanence] does not dispel the observation of conventionalities, which are not contradictory with it."

[We reply:] The ascertainment of the voidness of proliferations dispels the conception of proliferations, yet, how could it dispel conventional appearances, which are not contradictory with the voidness of proliferations?[51]

Secondly, [if a follower of Candrakīrti holds that an awareness that performs a negation is an antidote to a consciousness having appearance, that person might say:] "The ascertainment that the very appearance of conventionalities does not exist dispels conventional appearances."

[We reply:] Is the ascertainment that conventionalities do not exist a wrong awareness or a correct awareness? In the first case, it is not feasible for a wrong awareness to dispel an object to be dispelled. It is also not feasible to cultivate a wrong awareness as a path. In the second case, since conventionalities would be utterly non-existent, cause and effect would be annihilated and you would spread the system of nihilism.[52]

(c.) If [a Buddha] did not have [consciousness] having appearance, [buddhahood] would be no different from nirvāṇa without remainder {75.14}

If the continuum of mind and mental factors is cut off at buddhahood, how is this different from the assertion that the Hearer's nirvāṇa without remainder is the mere pacification of afflictions and suffering, like extinguishing a butter lamp?

In the case that [a follower of Candrakīrti] says, "The appearance of a form body and Buddha activities for others do not arise from one who attains a Hearer's fruit. However, the appearance of a form body for trainees does arise from a Buddha, and that [appearance] accomplishes the task of setting [trainees] upon the three uncontaminated paths [of Hearers, Solitary Buddhas, and Bodhisattvas]."

[We reply:] In what does the capacity to give rise to the accomplishment of Buddha activities and appearances exist? It is not feasible that [the capacity] exists in wisdom because [for you] the continuum of awareness is cut. It is not feasible that it exists in suchness because [suchness] is ultimate truth alone and if [suchness] is able to perform the function of accomplishing Buddha activities, it would follow that it is established as an ultimate entity.[53]

In the case that [a follower of Candrakīrti] says, "The capacity to accomplish Buddha activities exists in the previous accomplishment of the collections and the performance of prayer-wishes for others' welfare."

[We reply:] The collections and wishes having ceased, the time for aiding transmigrating beings arises later, after a long time has passed. Hence, [aiding migrating beings] would arise upon being cut off [from the collections and prayer-wishes]. Since accumulating the collections and making prayer-wishes are included within the continuums of bodhisattvas only, these would be only bodhisattva activities; Buddha activities would be utterly unfeasible.

c. Positing our own system {76.6}

Either by a reason that refutes what is entailed by a real entity—[being] a real singular or plural, and so forth—or by reason of dependent arising, and so forth, which contradicts what is entailed by a real entity, a real entity is explicitly refuted. A real affirming negative, object of knowledge and so forth, qualified by that [real entity] is implicitly refuted.[54] Thus, when mere proliferations are refuted, all particularities of proliferations are implicitly refuted. When the possibility of proliferations is explicitly refuted in an [inferential] base—mere object of knowledge—they are implicitly refuted [in] particular objects of knowledge.[55] Thus, the possibility of proliferations is refuted through inference. The basis of that [inference]—object of knowledge, entity, and so forth—is established in common appearance by conventional valid cognition that is not qualified by either truth or falsity.

d. Dispelling [objections of] unfeasibility toward our system {76.13}

[A follower of Candrakīrti] might say, "Since proliferations are refuted by a consequence that is an assemblage of contradictions,[56] there is no need for [an inference] of one's own."

[We reply:] If contradiction with the object of negation is established to be true [such a consequence] does not pass beyond [an inference] of one's own, as was expressed above.[57] If the contradictory object is refuted by a mere assertion even though it is not established to be true, then the *assertion* of an ultimate entity [by a proponent of entities] would establish [an object to be] a real singular or multiple. Also, this [assertion that an object is refuted by an assertion] would harm your position of not asserting anything at all.

[A follower of Candrakīrti] might say, "If the real entity itself [that you seek to refute] is not established to be true, how could you [inferentially] refute the establishment of what is entailed by that [real entity, such as being a real singular or plural] or refute [by reason of] what is contradictory with that [real entity, such as dependent arising]?"[58]

[We reply:] If the very thing that is contradictory with the object of negation is also not established to be true, how could you refute [through consequences the object of negation] that is contradictory with it? Moreover, conventionally, by asserting that [a woman] is a mother, her inability to produce a child is blocked; by asserting that [the same] woman is barren, her ability to produce a child is blocked. Hence, that base—the [same] woman—would [absurdly] neither be unable nor able to produce a child [because of these assertions].

[A follower of Candrakīrti] might say, "By asserting that a woman is barren, the statement asserting that she is a mother becomes faulty. However, there is no certainty [from that assertion] that it is impossible for that base [that is, that woman] to have the ability to produce a child.

[We reply:] Although a statement asserting the object of negation becomes faulty by an assertion that contradicts the object of negation, it is not established that the object of negation does not exist in a basis. Hence, the nonexistence of the object of negation is proved by way of a correct reason; it is not the case that an [inference] of one's own is not necessary. A probandum that is proved by a reason that is established in common appearance cannot be denied [by the opponent]. Hence, it is not the case that an [inference] of one's own has no power. If you say that an [inference] of one's own is not feasible due to [a Mādhyamika's] thesislessness, I have already stated that consequences would similarly be unfeasible due to wrong conceptions not being refutations.[59]

Even though [Nāgārjuna, in his *Refutation of Objections*] said, "I have no thesis," it is not the case that emptiness does not exist as the basic disposition of objects of knowledge because if emptiness does not abide, it would [absurdly] follow that a true entity is established. The intention [of Nāgārjuna's statement] is that although the emptiness of true entities is ultimate truth, the thesis holder's awareness[60] is not established when analyzed through reason and, hence, this is not established as a thesis. Furthermore, that is clearly said in [Nāgārjuna's] *Treatise called "The Finely Woven."*[61]

The awareness of a proponent who wishes to establish [a thesis] and the awareness of an opponent in whom establishment and dispellation do not arise are only obscurational truths; hence, these do not establish nor dispel emptiness. [The proponent's awareness] has the phenomenon [emptiness] that is taken as an object due to wanting to prove it; but this is so conventionally, not ultimately. Therefore, as an answer to an opponent [who said] "It follows that inference is pointless because the reason, and so forth, are not established as ultimate entities," the master Kamalaśīla said,[62]

> I accept the consequence that inference does not exist ultimately, for the conventions of inference and what is inferred are conventional. They are not in reality (*de kho nar*).

Therefore, it being the case that suchness is utter non-establishment, the phenomenon [emptiness] that is an object of valid cognition, and so forth, does not exist ultimately. However, the phenomenon [emptiness] that is a manifest object of valid cognition relative to yogic direct perception and is a hidden object of valid cognition relative to the inference that cuts proliferations abides conventionally. Hence, for ordinary beings, only inference refutes proliferations.

2. The Way of Refuting Proliferations Through Inference

This section has two parts: (a.) positing a general division between reasons that prove pervasive emptiness and reasons that do not and (b.) positing particular reasons that prove pervasive emptiness.

a. Positing a general division between reasons that prove pervasive emptiness and reasons that do not {78.4}

An ultimate entity does not exist among objects of knowledge. Hence, all specificities (*ldog pa*) that exist among objects of knowledge entail the emptiness of an ultimate entity. Due to that, there is no specificity that does not serve as a reason that proves that some inferential subject is empty of a true entity. The inference that proves an inferential subject that is a particular (*bye *brag*) object of knowledge or entity to be empty of a true entity comprehends only a trifling emptiness. Hence, the Madhyamaka system is not delineated through that. The Madhyamaka system is delineated through only that inference that proves all objects of knowledge entail emptiness.[63]

Regarding that, all specificities exist as one of the two: (1.) those that are not entailed by a mere entity and (2.) those that are.

(1.) Specificities that are not entailed by a mere entity are "arisen from exertion" or "having form," and so forth. When those [specificities] are stated as a reason, it is certain that such a reason entails [the probandum] emptiness. However, that very reason is not entailed by [the inferential subject, "mere] entity." Hence, that [reason] is not able to establish that all mere entities are empty. Thus, it only establishes a trifling emptiness.

(2.) [Specificities] that are entailed by [mere] entity are dependent arising, voidness of one and many, and so forth. Such [specificities] are of two types: (a.) those that must be ascertained as entailed by [mere] entity by way of direct perception [and so do not prove pervasive emptiness] and (b.) those that must be ascertained as entailed by [mere] entity by way of inference.

(a.) Specificities that must be ascertained as entailed by a [mere] entity by way of direct perception are mere appearance, object of knowledge, object of valid cognition, and so forth. These, too, are not reasons that prove that all mere entities are empty. If they were, it would be established that all sounds are impermanent because all sounds are "objects of hearing."

Someone might say, "In that case, if one ascertains experientially that sound and object of hearing are indivisible, the same valid cognition that ascertains that all objects of hearing are impermanent would ascertain that all sounds, also, are impermanent. Hence, that all sounds are impermanent would not be inferable."

[We reply:] It is ascertained by way of direct perception that [mere] entity is indivisible from [mere] appearance, object of knowledge, object of valid cognition, and so forth. Hence, the same valid cognition that ascertains that all [mere] appearances, objects of knowledge, objects of comprehension, and so forth, are empty ascertains that all [mere] entities also are empty. Hence, that all [mere] entities are empty [absurdly] would not be inferable.

[Opponent:] "If object of hearing is not suitable to delineate the entailment with respect to something other than the basis of debate [that is, the inferential subject, sound], is it not the case that since object of knowledge, and so forth, applies to non-entity—that which is other than [mere] entity—once one has ascertained the pervasion in relation to [the example] non-entity, [the pervasion] would be then inferable in relation to [the inferential subject] entity [thereby making such inference meaningful]? Otherwise, is it not the case that since "all sounds exist" is ascertained by way of direct perception, if it is ascertained that all existents are momentary, it is ascertained that all sounds, also, are momentary, whereby there would be no inference [that sound is momentary]?

[We reply:] Well then, when it is ascertained that all objects of knowledge are empty in relation to non-entity, why does one not ascertain that the reason [being an object of knowledge] is a property of the inferential subject [entities], that is, that all entities are objects of knowledge, and the probandum, that is, all entities are empty?

[Opponent:] Well then, when one ascertains that all existents are momentary in relation to [the example] pot, and so forth, why does one not ascertain that the reason [existing] is a property of the inferential subject [sound], that is, that all sounds exist, and the probandum, that is, all sounds are momentary?

[We reply:] It is so because when ascertaining the entailment [that all existing things are momentary, in relation to pot], one does not ascertain sound at all.

[Opponent:] Well then, when ascertaining that all objects of knowledge are empty [in relation to non-entity], that the reason [being an object of knowledge] is a property of the inferential subject [entities] and the probandum [all entities are empty] are not ascertained in relation to existent[64] because existent is not taken as an object at all.

[We reply:] Well then, it follows that the self-cognition (*rang rig, svasaṃvedana*) that exists with the valid cognition that ascertains the entailment [that all objects of knowledge are empty] is not a valid cognition because if [that self-cognition] does not ascertain the mere existence [of the valid cognition], then it would not be suitable for it to ascertain [that the valid cognition is] consciousness either.

(b.) Specificities that must be ascertained as entailed by [mere] entity by way of inference are dependent arising, voidness of one and many, and so forth. As for those, if it is ascertained that dependent arising entails emptiness in relation to the example of pot, it is seen also that dependent arising relates to [mere] entity. However, since one still must infer that the reason [dependent arising] is a property of the subject [entity],[65] it must be inferred also that all [mere] entities are empty. Hence, [dependent arising] proves pervasive emptiness. When it is ascertained that lack of a real one or many entails emptiness in relation to the example of a non-entity, if "all entities or objects of knowledge are void of one or many" still requires inference, then "all entities or objects of knowledge are empty" also still requires inference. Hence, [lack of a real one or many] proves pervasive emptiness.

One might say: Since object of knowledge entails lack of a real one or many, if it is true that "all mere objects of knowledge are empty" can be inferred due to that [lack of a real one or many], how can pervasive emptiness be inferred by reason of dependent arising, which is not entailed by object of knowledge?[66]

[We reply:] Although [dependent arising] is not entailed by object of knowledge, it is entailed by entity. Hence, when one ascertains that entity entails emptiness [because of] that [reason, dependent arising], then whatever is an entity, due to the reason [of dependent arising] is ascertained to be empty. Whatever is a non-entity is not isolated from a real collection with entity,[67] due to being isolated [only] from mere entity; the [opponent's] qualm is not generated. Hence, pervasive emptiness is ascertained.

b. Delineating the specific reason that proves pervasive emptiness {80.9}

[The reason is a case of] non-observation of the entailed:[68] "Anything that entails emptiness of a real one or many entails emptiness of real nature,[69] like the appearance of the meaning generalities,[70] non-entity and void of one or many, to a conceptual consciousness. Object of knowledge, object of valid cognition, appearance, and mere entity also entail emptiness of a real one or many."[71]

Notes

Notes to the Introduction

1 For a philosophically informed discussion of the "foundationalist" nature of the Dignāga-Dharmakīrti tradition and an examination of how Madhyamaka—in some Indian presentations—conflicts with that foundationalism, see Dan Arnold, *Buddhists, Brahmins, and Belief: Epistemology in South Asian Philosophy of Religion* (New York: Columbia University Press, 2005).

2 *dbu tshad seng ge mjing snol gyi snyan ming;* see Jeffrey Hopkins, *Maps of the Profound* (Ithaca, NY: Snow Lion Publications, 2003), 527ff (particularly, 536) for sTag tshang Shes rab rin chen's critique of this approach.

3 Bhāvaviveka's *Tarkajvala* and Śāntarakṣita's *Tattvasaṃgraha,* along with Kamalaśīla's commentary, offer broad surveys of Buddhist and non-Buddhist thought that may have served as Indian models for the earliest Tibetan doxographers, Ye shes sde and sKa ba dpal brtsegs. Closer in tenor to Tibetan doxographies are Āryadeva's *Jñānasārasamuccaya* and Jitāri's *Sugatamatavibhaṅga,* both of which very likely postdate the work of Ye shes sde and sKa ba dpal brtsegs. As will be discussed in chapter 1, early Tibetan doxographies do not divide the Middle Way into subschools centering on Candrakīrti and Bhāvaviveka. Such a subdivision became a standard feature of Tibetan doxographies perhaps by the thirteenth century and is seen in many well-known examples, available in English translation. See Jeffrey Hopkins, *Maps of the Profound,* for a recent and massive example.

4 As I discuss below, the doxographical category "Prāsaṅgika" was a Tibetan invention; no known Indian text uses Prāsaṅgika as a subdivision of Madhyamaka. Further, calling Prāsaṅgika "Candrakīrti's subschool" is an oversimplification, as Tibetan scholars (along with Jayānanda) will point out that Candrakīrti's critique of Bhāvaviveka includes a lengthy defense of Buddhapālita (c. 500), whom Bhāvaviveka criticizes and whom Tibetan scholars acknowledge to be a pre-Candrakīrti Prāsaṅgika.

5 As I will argue throughout this work, the two schools in their earliest Tibetan formations stood for a great deal more than opposing logical techniques. For this reason, among others, I avoid the appellations "Consequentialist" and "Own Continuumist."

6 This very rough sketch of Tibetan presentations of Candrakīrti most closely resembles the Geluk (*dge lugs*) view, forcefully delineated by the Geluk founder, Tsongkhapa (*tsong kha pa blo bzang grags pa*). Many Sakya (*sa skya*) authors hold that Candrakīrti's superiority lies in his method of ascertaining emptiness, not in his presentation of emptiness itself. These issues will be discussed and expanded upon throughout the present work.

7 Many Tibetan scholars acknowledge that the division of the Middle Way into

Prāsaṅgika and Svātantrika was a Tibetan invention, albeit based on Indian precedent and so justifiable.

8 It is well known that many Tibetan monastic libraries were destroyed during the Cultural Revolution. However, many early Tibetan doctrinal texts are known to have been either rare or entirely unavailable to Tibetans well before this time, as witnessed in such "rare books" lists as A khu ching shes rab rgya mtsho's (1803–75) *dpe rgyun dkon pa 'ga' zhig gi tho yig don gnyer yid kyi kunda bzhad pa'i zla 'od 'bum gyi snye ma,* reprinted in Lokesh Chandra's *Materials for a History of Tibetan Literature* (Kyoto: Rinsen, 1981), 503–601.

9 Of great pertinence to the present study are the misrepresentations of the Sangpu (*gSang phu ne'u thog*) abbots and authors, Ngok Loden Sherab (*rNgog lo tsā ba bLo ldan shes rab,* 1059–1109) and Chapa Chokyi Sengé. We see contemporary scholarship presenting these two scholars' views, based on the writings of much later Gelukpa (*dge lugs pa*) and Sakyapa (*sa skya pa*) authors, especially Shākya Chokden's (*Shākya mchog ldan,* 1428–1507) intellectual histories (especially his *dBu ma rnam par nges pa'i mdzod lung dang rigs pa'i rgya mtsho, Collected Works,* vol. 14 [Thimphu, Bhutan: Kunzang Tobgey, 1975]). With the recent publication of several of Ngok's and Chapa's texts (see below), we see great problems with the manner in which these two are represented and see distinctions between the views of these two that would call into question a common "Sangpu position."

10 I choose the word "flourished" as, in Tibetan portrayals, several of these figures are attributed extraordinarily long lives.

11 The absence of texts has surely contributed to scholarly misperceptions of an Indian Prāsaṅgika school that passed from Candrakīrti to fourteenth-century Tibetan scholars. Candrakīrti's major writings have long been widely available in Louis de la Vallée Poussin's editions of *Clear Words* and *Entrance to the Middle:* Louis de la Vallée Poussin, *Mūlamadhyamakakārikās de Nāgārjuna avec la Prasannapadā Commentaire de Candrakīrti,* Bibliotheca Buddhica, 4 (Osnabrück, Germany: Biblio Verlag, 1970 [originally, St. Petersburg, 1903–13]) and Louis de la Vallée Poussin, *Madhyamakāvatāra par Candrakīrti,* Bibliotheca Buddhica, 9 (Osnabrück, Germany: Biblio Verlag, 1970 [originally, St. Petersburg, 1907–12]). The availability of these texts and the Madhyamaka writings of fourteenth-century (and later) Tibetan authors would lend to the illusion of a continuity.

12 Later Tibetan authors themselves did not forget the intervening centuries. In Tibetan scholarship, we see references to predecessors' works, sometimes identified by name but more often acknowledged with the ubiquitous "Some earlier Tibetans said . . .". Such tips in the works of Tsongkhapa marked the starting point for this present investigation.

13 Phya pa chos kyi seṅ ge, *dbu ma śar gsum gyi stoṅ thun,* ed. Helmut Tauscher (Vienna: Arbeitskreis für Tibetische und Buddhistische Studien Universität Wien, 1999). The manuscript Tauscher edited was discovered in Beijing by Prof. Leonard van der Kuijp. Since Tauscher's edition, a second manuscript of Chapa's text has been added to the materials in Gene Smith's Tibetan Buddhist Resource Center.

14 As I point out below, some Tibetan scholars do, indeed, consider the Indian silent response to Candrakīrti evidence for the supremacy of his views: so stunning were his arguments, no one could think up an adequate response.

15 Jayānanda, *Madhyamakāvatāraṭīkā,* Toh. 3870, *sde dge* edition, *dbu ma,* vol. *ra.* The recently discovered, anonymous *Lakṣaṇaṭīkā* may well represent a second Indian commentary on Candrakīrti's works. The brief (18 folios) text comments on four of Candrakīrti's works: the *Prasannapadā, Madhyamakāvatāra, Catuḥśatakaṭīkā,* and (perhaps) *Yuktiṣaṣṭikāvṛtti.* Yonezawa believes that these comments stem from the famed Indian Buddhist scholar Abhayākaragupta, through the pen of his Tibetan disciple sNur Dar ma grags, who is listed as the scribe of this manuscript. See Yoshiyasu Yonezawa, *Introduction to the Facsimile Edition of a Collection of Sanskrit Palm-leaf Manuscripts in Tibetan* dBu med *Script* (Tokyo: The Institute for Comprehensive Studies of Buddhism, Taishō University, 2001), particularly pp. 26–28.

16 In assigning Jayānanda to the twelfth century, I differ from David Seyfort Ruegg's assessment in his *The Literature of the Madhyamaka School of Philosophy in India* (Wiesbaden: Otto Harrassowitz, 1981), 113; I discuss this in full in chapter 2. The inclusion of Jayānanda's commentary in the *bstan 'gyur* ("Translations of Treatises") section of the Tibetan canon cannot be taken as indication of its authoritative status for Tibetans, as it was not frequently utilized by Tibetan scholars and when it was cited, it was often in order to criticize Jayānanda's interpretation.

17 I discuss the multiple Candrakīrtis and their dates in chapter 1.

18 As noted above, Abhayākaragupta may be the author of a collection of notes on several of Candrakīrti's texts, making him the second known Indian to author a text on Candrakīrti. The "muted criticism" to which I here refer is found in his *Muṇimatālaṃkāra* and is discussed in chapter 1.

19 bSod nams rtse mo, *Byang chub sems dpa'i spyod pa la 'jug pa'i 'grel pa,* in *Sa skya pa'i bka' 'bum,* vol. 2 (Tokyo: Toyo Bunko, 1968) and Grags pa rgyal mtshan, *rGyud kyi mngon par rtogs pa rin po che'i ljong shing,* in *Sa skya pa'i bka' 'bum,* vol. 3.

20 rMa bya pa Byang chub brtson 'grus, *dBu ma rtsa ba shes rab kyi 'grel pa 'Thad pa'i rgyan* (Rumtek, Sikkim: Dharma Chakra Center, 1975).

21 *bKa' gdams gsung 'bum phyogs bgrigs* (Lhasa: dPal brtsegs bod yig dpe rnying zhib 'jug khang, 2006).

22 Ronald Davidson, *Tibetan Renaissance: Tantric Buddhism in the Rebirth of Tibetan Culture* (New York: Columbia University Press, 2005).

23 While I agree with Cabezón that Tibetan scholasticism is temporally co-extensive with Tibetan Buddhism—that Tibetans inherited scholastic Buddhism from India and maintain it into the present—here I claim that a particular trajectory of Tibet's scholasticism was formed in the twelfth century and that this trajectory gives Tibetan Buddhist scholasticism a different flavor from any version of Indian Buddhist scholasticism. See José Ignacio Cabezón, *Buddhism and Language* (Albany, NY: State University of New York Press, 1994), especially 194–99.

24 Dreyfus examines the variant educational models found in Gelukpa and Nyingmapa monasticism and finds similarities in the textual bases of the two but varying pedagogical emphases. He also sees a variety of philosophical positions within Nyingmapa monasticism. These findings suggest multiple scholasticisms within Tibetan religion, in terms of both pedagogy and philosophy. See Georges B.J. Dreyfus, *The Sound of Two Hands Clapping: The Education of a Tibetan Buddhist Monk* (Berkeley, CA: University of California Press, 2003) and Georges Dreyfus, "Where Do Commentarial Schools Come From? Reflections on the History of Tibetan Scholasticism," *Journal*

of the International Association of Buddhist Studies 28, no. 2 (2005): 273–97. Dreyfus suggests a pedagogical uniformity at the time of Tsongkhapa's education in the mid-fourteenth century, seeing a "catholic" early tradition that later fractured into sectarian divides ("Where do Commentarial Schools Come From?"). The question remains as to whether Tsongkhapa-era "catholicism" can be extrapolated into the more distant past. At present, we can only hope that historical materials will come to light that will allow a sophisticated analysis of early Tibetan scholastic pedagogy along the lines of Dreyfus's work. As I discuss here, it is clear that early scholastic authors exhibit a variety of philosophical positions, particularly on issues surrounding the marriage of Dharmakīrti and Candrakīrti. This tension is an enduring, if not universal, feature of Tibetan scholasticism.

25 To call the epistemological positions that Candrakīrti rejects "Dharmakīrtian" is surely an anachronism, as the former did not seem to have been aware of the latter. Instead, Candrakīrti critiques Dignāga, upon whose major work Dharmakīrti commented. Also, we certainly do not need the twelfth-century materials to tell us that Candrakīrti rejects, rather than accepts, the Dignāga program, as Dan Arnold makes abundantly clear in his excellent study, *Buddhists, Brahmins, and Belief.*

26 As discussed in chapter 1, I understand the similarity of Candrakīrti and Śāntideva on the issue of ultimate truth's ineffability in this light: while we see an undeniable doctrinal similarity here, I am not convinced that Śāntideva was directly influenced by Candrakīrti.

27 José Ignacio Cabezón, "The Canonization of Philosophy and the Rhetoric of Siddhānta in Tibetan Buddhism," in *Buddha Nature: A Festschrift in Honor of Minoru Kiyota,* eds. Paul J. Griffiths and John P. Keenan, 7–26 (Tokyo: Buddhist Books International, 1990).

28 A well-documented example is the Sa skya pa sTag tshang Shes rab rin chen's critique of Tsong kha pa's portrayal of Prāsaṅgika and 'Jam dbyang bzhad pa'i rdo rje's response in Jeffrey Hopkins, *Maps of the Profound,* 527ff.

29 This is similar to one of the outflows of the "canonization of philosophy" that Cabezón discusses, "the rhetoric of incompatibility"; see "The Canonization of Philosophy," 17.

30 Again, I have in mind sTag tshang Shes rab rin chen's critique of Tsong kha pa seen in Hopkins, *Maps of the Profound,* 527ff.

31 bSod nams rtse mo's *Byang chub sems dpa'i spyod pa la 'jug pa'i 'grel pa* is the earliest text we now possess that uses the paired categories "Svātantrika" and "Prāsaṅgika"; his usage is discussed in chapters 2 and 5.

32 This leads us to ask when a "movement" becomes a standard "category"; is it only when Prāsaṅgika's acceptance becomes dominant in Tibet? This distinction requires the kind of nuance that consideration of later developments of thirteenth- and fourteenth-century Tibet can hopefully provide.

33 Translated in Jeffrey Hopkins, *Maps of the Profound,* 499–500.

34 This is not to suggest that thirteenth- and fourteenth-century Tibetan scholars invented Buddhist doxography, a tradition that has roots in Bhāvaviveka's sixth-century writings. As noted already, the four-fold system of Buddhist thought—Vaibhāṣika, Sautrāntika, Yogācāra, and Madhyamaka—was well known in tenth- to twelfth-century India and in eighth-century Tibet.

35 Hopkins explains how Gelukpa scholars probe for deeper meaning and creatively express their novel insights within the confines of Tsongkhapa's (*Tsong kha pa bLo bzang grags pa*, 1357–1419) *Essence of Eloquence* (*Legs bshad snying po*), a doxographical treatise on the Yogācāra, Svātantrika Madhyamaka, and Prāsaṅgika Madhyamaka systems; see "The Steel Bow and Arrow" in Jeffrey Hopkins, *Emptiness in the Mind-Only School of Buddhism* (Berkeley, CA: University of California Press, 1999), 15–25.

Notes to Chapter 1

1 This date and the dates of Indian Mādhyamikas except where noted are drawn from David Seyfort Ruegg, *The Literature of the Madhyamaka School of Philosophy in India* (Wiesbaden: Otto Harrassowitz, 1981) to which one may refer for a discussion of the complexities preventing more precise dating.

2 Toshihiko Kimura, "A New Chronology of Dharmakīrti," *Dharmakīrti's Thought and Its Impact on Indian and Tibetan Philosophy*, ed. Shoryu Katsura (Vienna: Österreichischen Akademie der Wissenschaften, 1999), 209–14.

3 The Sanskrit of Nāgārjuna's *Mūlamadhyamakakārikāḥ* is found in J.W. de Jong, *Nāgārjuna, Mūlamadhyamakakārikāḥ* (Madras, India: Adyar Library and Research Centre, 1977) while the Tibetan translation is *sde dge* edition, *dbu ma*, vol. *tsa*, 3824. Candrakīrti's attacks on Bhāvaviveka are in his commentary, *Prasannapadā* ("Clear Words"): Sanskrit text in Louis de la Vallée Pousin, *Mūlamadhyamakakārikās de Nāgārjuna avec la Prasannapadā Commentaire de Candrakīrti*, Bibliotheca Buddhica, 4 (Osnabrück, Germany: Biblio Verlag, 1970); Tibetan text *sde dge* 3860, *dbu ma*, vol. *'a*. Bhāvaviveka's views that were the basis for Candrakīrti's critique are found in his commentary upon Nāgārjuna's *Fundamental Treatise*, called *Prajñāpradīpa* ("Lamp for Wisdom"); Tibetan text (*dbu ma rtsa ba'i 'grel pa shes rab sgron ma*) *sde dge* 3863, vol. *dza*.

4 While Tsong kha pa (1357–1419) admitted that the terms "Prāsaṅgika" and "Svātantrika" were coined by earlier Tibetans, he devoted a great deal of effort to showing how the terms applied to Buddhapālita and Candrakīrti, on the one hand, and to Bhāvaviveka, on the other, and concludes that the terms were not Tibetans' "own invention" (*rang bzo*). See his *Legs bshad snying po* (Sarnath, India: Pleasure of Elegant Sayings Press, 1973), 139, and *Lam rim chen mo* (in *The Collected Works [gSuṅ 'bum] of rJe Tsoṅ-kha-pa Blo-bzaṅ-grags-pa*, vol. 19–20 [New Delhi: Ngawang Gelek Demo, 1975]), 343a.

5 My rationale for dating Jayānanda to the twelfth century is discussed in chapter 2.

6 His commentary, *Madhyamakāvatāraṭīkā* (*dbu ma la 'jug pa 'grel pa; sde dge* 3870, *dbu ma*, vol. *ya*) is discussed at length in the following chapters. The details of his life, travels in Central Tibet and Tangut lands, and his writings are treated in chapter 2.

7 *Abhisamayālaṃkāra, mngon rtogs rgyan.*

8 Ruegg notes the presence of one (sometimes two) Vidyākokila (*rigs pa'i khu byug*) in lineages drawn from Candrakīrti to the eleventh-century Indian teacher of Patsab, Kanakavarman; see David Seyfort Ruegg, *Three Studies in the History of Indian and Tibetan Madhyamaka Philosophy, Studies in Indian and Tibetan Madhyamaka*

Thought, Part I (Vienna: Arbeitskreis für Tibetische und Buddhistische Studien Universität Wien, 2000), 9, n. 10.

9 An example of significance to this study is the Eighth Karmapa, Mi bskyod rdo rje's use of rMa bya byang chub brtson 'grus's commentary on Jayānanda's *Tarkamudgara,* a commentary no longer accessible; see Paul Williams, "rMa bya pa Byang chub brtson 'grus on Madhyamaka Method," *Journal of Indian Philosophy* 13 (1985): 207 and 220, nn. 7 and 8. A classic list of "rare books" is A khu ching shes rab rgya mtsho's (1803–75) *dpe rgyun dkon pa 'ga' zhig gi tho yig don gnyer yid kyi kunda bzhad pa'i zla 'od 'bum gyi snye ma,* reprinted in Lokesh Chandra's *Materials for a History of Tibetan Literature* (Kyoto: Rinsen, 1981), 503–601. An Indian example is Avalokitavrata's list of eight commentaries on Nāgārjuna's *Fundamental Treatise on the Middle,* four of which were never translated into Tibetan.

10 I am grateful to Karen Lang and Robert Hueckstedt, who pointed out the necessity of repeated copying to the survival of Candrakīrti's texts through the humidity of Gangetic and Kaśmiri India.

11 The text comments on Candrakīrti's *Prasannapadā, Madhyamakāvatāra,* and *Catuḥśatakaṭīkā,* with an additional two lines that may be notations on his *Yuktiṣaṣṭikāvṛtti.* See Yoshiyasu Yonezawa, *Introduction to the Facsimile Edition of a Collection of Sanskrit Palm-leaf Manuscripts in Tibetan* dBu med *Script* (Tokyo: The Institute for Comprehensive Studies of Buddhism, Taishō University, 2001), 26–28. This exciting discovery has been the subject of several articles that provide critical editions of portions of it: Yoshiyasu Yonezawa, "*Lakṣaṇaṭīkā:* A Sanskrit Manuscript of an Anonymous Commentary on the *Prasannapadā,*" *Journal of Indian and Buddhist Studies* 47, 2 (1999): 1024–1022; Yoshiyasu Yonezawa, "Sanskrit notes on the *Madhyamakāvatārabhāṣya* Chapter 1 in the **Lakṣaṇaṭīkā,*" *Journal of Indian and Buddhist Studies (Indobukkyogaku Kenkyu)* 49, no. 2 (2001): 47–49; Koshin Suzuki, "A Transliteration of the Sanskrit Notes on the *Catuḥśatakaṭīkā* in the **Lakṣaṇaṭīkā,*" in *Gedenkschrift J. W. de Jong,* ed. H.W. Bodewitz and Minoru Hara (Tokyo: The International Institute for Buddhist Studies of The International College for Advanced Buddhist Studies, 2004), 189–206; Yoshiyasu Yonezawa, "**Lakṣaṇaṭīkā.* Sanskrit notes on the *Prasannapadā* (1)", *Journal of the Naritasan Institute for Buddhist Studies* 27 (2004): 115–54; Yoshiyasu Yonezawa, "**Lakṣaṇaṭīkā.* Sanskrit notes on the *Prasannapadā* (2)", *Journal of the Naritasan Institute for Buddhist Studies* 28 (2005): 159–79; and Yoshiyasu Yonezawa, "**Lakṣaṇaṭīkā.* Sanskrit notes on the *Prasannapadā* (3)", *Journal of the Naritasan Institute for Buddhist Studies* 29 (2006): 135–63.

12 Yonezawa, *Introduction,* 27: "It is very likely that the Tibetan scribe, called Dharmakīrti or snur/gnur Dharma grags, wrote down the texts for the sake of his understanding under the supervision of Abhayākaragupta." These two were responsible for the Tibetan translation of Candrakīrti's *Śūnyatāsaptativṛtti.*

13 *Prajñāpradīpaṭīkā* (*shes rab sgron me'i rgya cher 'grel pa*), *sde dge* 3559, Peking 5259, *dbu ma,* vol. *wa,* 85a.8. The others listed are Nāgārjuna, Buddhapālita, Devaśarman, Guṇaśrī, Guṇamati, Sthiramati, and Bhāvaviveka.

14 Jñānagarbha (c. 700–760) is frequently grouped philosophically, doxographically, and sometimes even personally with Śāntarakṣita and Kamalaśīla; see Malcolm David Eckel, *Jñānagarbha's Commentary on the Distinction between the Two Truths* (Albany, NY: State University of New York Press, 1987), 5ff. Eckel suggests that

Jñānagarbha may have responded to Candrakīrti obliquely, introducing a passage in his translation of Jñānagarbha (p. 92) that begins "Some, who are notorious for their bad arguments," with the topic heading "Candrakīrti (?) on the Nature of Relative Truth." Eckel notes (p. 141, n. 120) that neither Jñānagarbha nor his commentator identify these purveyors of "bad arguments" but adduces a passage in Candrakīrti's *Madhyamakāvatāra* (VI.36–38) that might fit the description. Jñānagarbha states these bad argumentators "argue that if things do not arise in a real sense, they also do not arise in a relative sense" (Eckel's translation, p. 92). This position counters Jñānagarbha's own view that the conventional world (Eckel uses "relative truth") exists when it is not analyzed, accords with worldly renown, and accords with appearances (see Eckel, 85ff). The attribution of the "bad argument" to Candrakīrti requires further exploration, as some Tibetan doxographers see Jñānagarbha and Candrakīrti both asserting that the conventional accords with worldly renown and so place them together in the category of "Mādhyamikas whose practice accords with worldly renown" (*'jig rten grags sde spyod pa'i dbu ma pa*); see Katsumi Mimaki, *Blo gsal grub mtha'* (Kyoto: Université de Kyoto, 1982), 27ff.

15 Tillemans (Tom J.F. Tillemans, *Materials for the Study of Āryadeva, Dharmapāla and Candrakīrti* [Vienna: Arbeitskreis für Tibetische und Buddhistische Studien Universität Wien, 1990], 42–43) records several of their rejoinders to Dharmapāla. Rather than argue that the incompatibility of formal inference and the Madhyamaka ultimate requires the abandonment of formal inference "for oneself" (*svārthānumāna*), as Candrakīrti would have it, Dharmapāla argued that the incompatibility requires the abandonment of Madhyamaka ontology.

16 Masamichi Ichigō, "Śāntarakṣita and Bhāviveka as Opponents of the Mādhyamika in the *Madhyamakāloka*," in *Wisdom, Compassion, and the Search for Understanding: The Buddhist Studies Legacy of Gadjin M. Nagao,* ed. Jonathan A. Silk (Honolulu: University of Hawai'i Press, 2000), 147–70.

17 Dreyfus and McClintock ("Introduction" in *The Svātantrika-Prāsaṅgika Distinction: What Difference Does a Difference Make?* eds. Georges B.J. Dreyfus and Sara L. McClintock [Boston: Wisdom Publications, 2002], 33–34, n. 6) note that Kamalaśīla seems to refer to two types of Madhyamaka (*dbu ma'i lam gnyis*), one corresponding to Bhāvaviveka's views on the conventional existence of external objects and the other corresponding to Śāntarakṣita's views on the nonexistence of external objects, in his commentary to Śāntarakṣita's *Madhyamakālaṃkāra* (*Madhyamakālaṃkārapañjikā,* Toh. 3886, *sde dge* edition, *dbu ma,* vol. *sa,* 128a). While this classification leaves room for Candrakīrti as a supporter of conventional external objects, it is further evidence that Kamalaśīla was not concerned with the most substantial of Candrakīrti's Madhyamaka interpretations.

18 *Yuktiṣaṣṭikāvṛtti* (*rigs pa drug cu pa'i 'grel pa*), *sde dge* 3864, *dbu ma,* vol. *ya*; Cristina Anna Scherrer-Schaub, *Yuktiṣaṣṭikāvṛtti. Commentaire à la soixantaine sur le raisonnement ou Du vrai enseignement de la causalité par le Maitre indien Candrakīrti,* Mélanges chinois et bouddhiques, 25 (Bruselles: Institut belge des hautes etudes chinoises, 1991). Scherrer-Schaub (p. xxv) notes that the Tibetan translation of Nāgārjuna's verses preserved within Candrakīrti's commentary (translated by Jinamitra, Dānaśīla, Śīlendrabodhi, and Ye shes sde) bear close relation with the verses preserved in the Dunhuang collection.

19 The Tibetan translation of Candrakīrti's *Śūnyatāsaptativṛtti* that is preserved in the Tibetan *bstan 'gyur* was translated by Abhayākaragupta and sNur D[h]arma grags around the year 1100. We have fragmentary evidence of the early translation of this text from Dunhuang. I thank José Cabezón for alerting me to the fragment's presence on the website of the International Dunhuang Project, where it can be located by the India Office catalog number: IOL Tib J 643.

20 Similarly, the translations of Buddhapālita's commentary on Nāgārjuna's *Fundamental Treatise on the Middle* and of Śāntideva's *Engaging in the Bodhisattva's Practice* do not indicate "Prāsaṅgika's" establishment in the early diffusion. While Ruegg (*Three Studies,* 16) notes "the existence of a *sṅa dar* translation of a major work connected with the Prāsaṅgika tradition, namely Buddhapālita's commentary on the *Madhyamakakārikās,*" we must appreciate when Buddhapālita's text was determined to express a "Prāsaṅgika" view. Until Candrakīrti's views became widespread in Tibet in the twelfth century, Buddhapālita's text was not labeled "Prāsaṅgika," but only "Madhyamaka." Bhāvaviveka's criticisms of Buddhapālita and Candrakīrti's countercritique of Bhāvaviveka presuppose their mutual adherence to Nāgārjuna's writings—to a Madhyamaka school—and not, as fourteenth-century and later Tibetan literature maintains, to separate subschools. Śāntideva's writings are treated below.

21 Tibetan doxographies from the fourteenth century on classify them as Yogācāra-Svātantrika-Mādhyamikas, whereas the earliest Tibetan doxographies, as noted just below, write only of Yogācāra-Mādhyamikas.

22 As recorded in the *lDan dkar ma* catalog edited by Marcelle Lalou, "Les textes Bouddhiques au temps du roi khri-srong-lde-bcan," *Journal Asiatique* 241 (1953): 333, nos. 578–85.

23 Ruegg, *Three Studies,* 23–25 contains the full array of references to these two early doxographies, as well as a listing of other early Tibetan Madhyamaka writing not now available.

24 Ruegg, *Three Studies,* 55–56 discusses the relevant passages of Rong zom's *lTa ba'i brjed byang, Grub mtha'i brjed byang,* and *Man ngag lta ba'i phreng ba zhes bya ba'i 'grel pa.*

25 *pramāṇa, tshad ma.*

26 His poetry is *Engaging in the Bodhisattva's Practice* (*Bodhisattvacaryāvatāra, byang chub sems dpa'i spyod pa la 'jug pa*), found in Louis de la Vallée Poussin, *Prajñākaramati's Commentary to the Bodhicaryāvatāra of Çāntideva,* Bibliotheca Indica (Calcutta: Asiatic Society of Bengal, 1902–14); La Vallée Poussin's edition of Śāntideva's stanzas advances that of I.P. Minaev, "Bodhicaryāvatāra," *Zapiski Vostočnago Otdělenija Imperatorskago Russkago Archeologičeskago Obščestva* 4 (1889), 153–228. Saito's work and the *lDan dkar ma* catalog, referenced below, clarify that the early title of Śāntideva's stanzas was *Bodhisattvacaryāvatāra,* "*Engaging in the Bodhisattva's Practice,*" rather than *Bodhicaryāvatāra,* "*Engaging in the Practice of Enlightenment,*" which the surviving Sanskrit manuscripts attest. Śāntideva's sūtra collection and comments is the *Compendium of Training* (*Śīkṣāsamuccaya, bslab pa kun las btus pa*), found in Cecil Bendall, *Çikshāsamuccaya: A Compendium of Buddhistic Teaching,* Bibliotheca Buddhica I (Osnabrück, Germany: Biblio Verlag, 1970).

27 Stanzas IX.2, IX.35, and IX.24–26; La Vallée Poussin, *Prajñākaramati's Commentary,* (1905): 352, (1907): 417, and (1907): 399–401. These first two topics are discussed at

length herein. Śāntideva's refutation of self-cognizing consciousness (*svasaṃvedana, rang rig*) is discussed fully in Paul Williams, *The Reflexive Nature of Awareness* (London: Curzon Press, 1998), chapters 3 and 4.

28 Akira Saito, "Śāntideva in the History of Mādhyamika Philosophy," in *Buddhism in India and Abroad,* ed. Kalpakam Sankarnarayan, Motohiro Yoritomi, and Shubhada A. Joshi (Mumbai and New Delhi: Somaiya Publications, 1996), 259. Saito notes that these two commentaries are on the version of Śāntideva's text found in the Dunhuang collection and not on the version in the Tibetan canon. This virtually ensures that these two commentaries are from the early diffusion period although neither is mentioned in the catalog of texts collected in the Den Karma (*lDan dkar ma*) palace around the year 800. Mention should further be made of Śāntarakṣita's favorable citations of Śāntideva's stanzas in his *Tattvasiddhi* (38b.6–7). In this regard, however, we should allow for the possibility that the ninth chapter of Śāntideva's text—in which his "Prāsaṅgika"-like statements are found—was not available to Śāntarakṣita. As discussed immediately following, Śāntideva's text grew over the centuries.

29 The whereabouts of Ngok the Translator's (*rNgog lo tsa ba bLo ldan shes rab,* 1059–1109) commenary is presently unknown. Chapa's (*Phya pa Chos kyi seng ge,* 1109–69) "summary" (*spyod 'jug bsdus don*), along with several early bKa' gdams pa commentaries on the *Bodhicaryāvatāra,* has been published in the *bKa' gdams gsung 'bum* collection. These supplement the commentary by Chapa's Sakya student, Sonam Tsemo (*bSod nams rtse mo,* 1142–82), which has long been available and states in its colophon to be based on Chapa's teaching; portions of this text are treated in chapters 4 and 5.

30 See the *ldan dkar ma* catalog, edited by Marcelle Lalou ("Les textes Bouddhiques"), number 659.

31 Saito, "Śāntideva in the History of Mādhyamika," 258. Additionally, Bu ston's (1290–1364) report that several Tibetan scholars ascribe authorship of the entire ninth chapter to Akṣayamati, not Śāntideva (Ruegg, *Literature of the Madhyamaka,* 82, n. 267), cannot be entirely overlooked. While Saito ("Śāntideva in the History of Mādhyamika," 258) shows that in the Dunhuang version the author of the entire text is called Akṣayamati (suggesting that Akṣayamati and Śāntideva are the same author), the possibility that the 168 stanzas of the ninth chapter circulated separately or were a later accretion remains.

32 Prajñākaramati's *Bodhicaryāvatārapañjikā* is thereby a major source of Sanskrit fragments of Candrakīrti's *Madhyamakāvatāra.*

33 He also cites *Madhyamakāvatāra* VI.27 in his comments to *Bodhicaryāvatāra* IX.3.

34 He cites *Entrance to the Middle,* stanzas VI.28 and VI.25, although attributes the latter to Nāgārjuna; *Bodhicaryāvatāratātparyapañjikā Viśeṣadyotanī, byang chub kyi spyod pa la 'jug pa'i dgongs pa'i 'grel pa khyad par gsal byed* (Peking 5282) 285b.5 and 286a.1. This misattribution suggests that Vibhūticandra may not have been well familiar with Candrakīrti's works and perhaps instead drew these citations from Prajñākaramati's earlier commentary.

35 J.W. de Jong, "La légende de Śāntideva," *Indo-Iranian Journal* 16 (1975): 164–65.

36 David Jackson, "Madhyamaka Studies Among the Early Sa-skya-pas," *Tibet Journal* X, no. 2 (1985): 24.

37 Stanza IX.2; La Vallée Poussin, *Prajñākaramati's Commentary* (1905), 352: *saṃvṛtiḥ paramārthaś ca satyadvayam idaṃ matam / buddher agocaras tattvaṃ buddhiḥ saṃvṛtir ucyate //.* The Tibetan of pāda cd (D3871, vol. *ya,* 31a.1) reads: *don dam blo yi spyod yul min / blo ni kun rdzob yin par brjod //.* Saito ("Śāntideva in the History of Mādhyamika," 261, n. 3) reports that the Dunhuang version for pāda d reads: *blo dang sgra ni kun rdzob yin //* (= *buddhiḥ śabdaś ca saṃvṛtiḥ,* "awareness and speech are obscurational").

38 Introducing stanza VI.29; Louis de la Vallée Poussin, *Madhyamakāvatāra par Candrakīrti,* Bibliotheca Buddhica, 9 (Osnabrück, Germany: Biblio Verlag, 1970), 109.2–3: *shes pa'i yul ma yin pa nyid.*

39 La Vallée Poussin, *Prajñākaramati's Commentary* (1905), 363.7: *buddheḥ sarvajñānānāṃ / samatikrāntasarvajñānaviṣayatvādagocaraḥ / aviṣayaḥ / kena cit prakāreṇa tatsarvabuddhiviṣayīkartuṃ na śakyata.*

40 La Vallée Poussin, *Prajñākaramati's Commentary* (1905), 366.2–4: *sarvā hi buddhirālambananirālambanatayā vikalpasvabhāvā / vikalpaśca sarva evāvidyāsvabhāvaḥ /.*

41 Prajñākaramati (La Vallée Poussin, *Prajñākaramati's Commentary* [1905], 364–65) refers to Candrakīrti's *Entrance to the Middle,* stanza VI.29 and autocommentary (La Vallée Poussin, *Madhyamakāvatāra,* 109.6ff), calling Candrakīrti "knower of treatise" (*śāstravid*).

42 The sūtra passage, which Candrakīrti also cited in support of this issue, is discussed in chapter 4.

43 La Vallée Poussin, *Prajñākaramati's Commentary* [1905], 367.12–13: *tadetadāryāṇāmeva svasaṃviditasvabhāvatayā pratyātmavedyaṃ / atastadevātra pramāṇaṃ /.*

44 Introducing stanza VI.30; La Vallée Poussin, *Madhyamakāvatāra,* 111.18–20.

45 Atiśa's *Introduction to the Two Truths* (*satyadvayāvatāra, bden gnyis la 'jug pa*), stanza 19, cites Candrakīrti's *Entrance to the Middle,* stanza VI.80 (La Vallée Poussin, *Madhyamakāvatāra,* 175.3), on the relationship between obscurational truth and ultimate truth—the former being the means to the latter.

46 Stanza 15cd–16ab; Christian Lindtner, "Atiśa's Introduction to the Two Truths," *Journal of Indian Philosophy* 9 (1981): 191: *chos nyid bden pa gzigs pa yi / klu sgrub slob ma zla grags yin // de las brgyud pa'i man ngag gis / chos nyid bden pa rtogs par 'gyur /*). In the *sde dge* edition, this is 3902, *dbu ma,* vol. *a,* 72b.4–72b.5.

47 Stanzas 10–14; Lindtner, "Introduction," 191.

48 In stanza 14; Lindtner, "Introduction," 191: *lung las kyang ni gsal po ru / rtog bcas rtog pa med pa yi / shes pa gnyis kyis mi rtogs shes / slob dpon mkhas pa bha bya gsung //* "The Master scholar Bhavya stated clearly in scripture that [the ultimate] is not realized by either conceptual nor nonconceptual consciousness."

49 *Madhyamakahṛdaya* and *Tarkajvāla, sde dge* edition 3855 and 3856, *dbu ma,* vol. *dza.* Both texts were partially translated in the early diffusion as is evidenced by the Den karma catalog (number 732; Lalou, "Les textes Bouddhiques," 337). Atiśa translated two other texts that he (and many Tibetan Buddhists and at least one contemporary scholar) believed was authored by Bhāvaviveka, *Compendium of Meanings of the Middle* (*Madhyamakārthasaṃgraha, sde dge* 3857) and *Jewel Lamp of the Middle* (*Madhyamakaratnapradīpa, sde dge* 3854). However, like Ruegg (D. Seyfort Ruegg, "On the authorship of some works ascribed to Bhāvaviveka/Bhavya," in *Earliest Buddhism and Madhyamaka,* ed. David Seyfort Ruegg and Lambert Schmithausen

[Leiden: E.J. Brill, 1990], 59–71), I see no way that the ideas expressed in these texts could have been written by the same author who wrote *Heart of the Middle*. More on the multiple Bhāvavivekas follows.

50 *rNgog Legs pa'i shes rab; The Blue Annals,* George N. Roerich, trans. (Delhi: Motilal Banarsidass, 1949 [1996]), 258–59.

51 Atiśa's *Bodhimārgapradīpapañjikā, sde dge* 3948, *dbu ma,* vol. *a,* 280a; also, Richard Sherburne, *The Complete Works of Atīśa* (New Delhi: Aditya Prakashan, 2000), 236–37.

52 Ruegg, *Three Studies,* 17.

53 See note 48.

54 See note 56. Lindtner supports Atiśa in this misattribution.

55 Ruegg, "Some Works Ascribed to Bhāvaviveka," 63.

56 See Lindtner's translation of the "Two Truths" section of the *Madhyamakaratnapradīpa* in his "Atiśa's Introduction," 171 and 173. Lindtner (ibid., 200, n. 14 and 202, n. 34) accepts the attribution of the *Madhyamakaratnapradīpa* and *Madhyamakārthasaṃgraha* to the same Bhāvaviveka who wrote *Heart of the Middle,* seeing no "external evidence" to disprove this. However, these very citations offer ample internal evidence of multiple Bhāvavivekas.

57 Stanza 4ab; Lindtner, "Atiśa's Introduction," 190: *dam pa'i don ni gcig nyid de / gzhan dag rnam pa gnyis su 'dod /.*

58 *Tarkajvāla, sde dge* edition 3856, *dbu ma,* vol. *dza,* 60b.4–5: *don dam pa ni rnam gnyis te / de la gcig ni mngon par 'du byed pa med par 'jug pa 'jig rten las 'das pa zag pa med pa spros pa med pa'o // gnyis pa ni mngon par 'du byed pa dang bcas par 'jug pa bsod nams dang ye shes kyi tshogs kyi rjes su mthun pa dag pa 'jig rten pa'i ye shes zhes bya ba spros pa dang bcas pa ste /.*

59 Stanza 10cd; Lindtner, "Atiśa's Introduction," 191: *gnyis pos stong nyid rtogs so zhes / tshu rol mthong ba'i rmongs pa smra /.* My bracketed addition is drawn from stanza 10ab.

60 Ruegg, "Some Works Ascribed to Bhāvaviveka," 64–65. Even if we regard this passage from the *Blaze of Reasoning* as authored by the later Bhāvaviveka, my point concerning Atiśa remains: Atiśa, who considered these works to have been authored by the same Bhāvaviveka, rejects this solution to inference's applicability to ultimate truth.

61 Ruegg, "Some Works Ascribed to Bhāvaviveka," 64–65.

62 Stanzas four and five; Lindtner, "Atiśa's Introduction," 200, n. 14 and Y. Ejima, *Chūgan-shisō no tenkai—Bhāvaviveka kenkyū* (Tokyo: Shunjūsha, 1980), 18.

63 I give one possibility for Bhāvaviveka II's dates below.

64 In the *Jewel Lamp of the Middle,* he writes (Lindtner, "Atiśa's Introduction," 173) that obscurational, or conventional, truth consists of all things known by their specific and general characters (*svasāmānyalakṣaṇa*), which are the two criteria by which Dharmakīrti divides ultimate and conventional truths, as well as knowledge itself. Real obscurational truth (*tathyasaṃvṛtisatya,* as opposed to false obscurational truth or *mithyāsaṃvṛtisatya,* this distinction itself being an eighth-century invention unknown to the sūtric Bhāvaviveka) is characterized as produced by causes and able to produce effects (ibid., 170). The *Compendium of Meanings of the Middle* also divides obscurational truth into real and false and differentiates the two on the

grounds of causal efficacy (*arthakriyāsamartha*) in stanzas nine and ten (ibid., 200–201, n. 14, and Ejima, *Bhāvaviveka,* 19–20).

65 For Jñānangarbha's development of "causal efficacy" (*arthakriyāsamartha*) and "existing as it is seen/appears" (*yathādarśana* or *yathābhāsa*), see Eckel, *Jñānagarbha on the Two Truths,* 51–58, and the corresponding portions of his translation and text. For the *Jewel Lamp*'s and the *Compendium of Meaning*'s uses of the latter notion, see Lindtner, "Atiśa's Introduction," 170, 172, and 200, n. 14. "Existing when not analyzed" offers interesting parallels to some of Candrakīrti's standpoints.

66 See Lindtner's translation in "Atiśa's Introduction," 169, 170, and 172.

67 Jayānanda was Kashmiri. Prajñākaramati was a scholar at Vikramaśīla monastery in northeastern India, where Atiśa later served as abbot (Ruegg, *Literature of the Madhyamaka,* 116 and 111). Candrakīrti's texts, then, gained currency in both of the major centers of Buddhist study during this final phase of Indian Buddhism.

68 As discussed further in chapter 3, "non-deceptive" was Dharmakīrti's definition of valid cognition (*pramāṇa, tshad ma*)—both direct perception (*pratyakṣa, mngon sum*) and inference (*anumāna, rjes dpag*) meeting this criterion—while only direct perception was "unmistaken." The Mādhyamika Kamalaśīla (c. 740–95) extended "unmistaken" to inference and, hence, "non-deceptive" and "unmistaken" came to be used by Kamalaśīla and several others synonymously. See Toru Funayama, "Kamalaśīla's Interpretation of 'Non-Erroneous' in the Definition of Direct Perception and Related Problems," in *Dharmakīrti's Thought and Its Impact on Indian and Tibetan Philosophy,* ed. Shoryu Katsura (Vienna: Österreichischen Akademie der Wissenschaften, 1999), 74 and 79. Jayānanda's use of "unmistaken" in denying that worldly cognition is valid shows his familiarity with Kamalaśīla's developments.

69 This figure is likely the third Candrakīrti. The second Candrakīrti can be placed in the late tenth to early eleventh centuries and is the author of the *Guhyasamāja Tantra* commentary, *Pradīpoddyotana;* he is discussed below. Given this chronology, it may be possible to identify these "second" and "third" Candrakīrtis as the same figure.

70 *Madhyamakāvatāraprajñā, dbu ma shes rab la 'jug pa;* Tohoku 3863, *sde dge* edition, *dbu ma,* vol. *'a,* 348b–349a. The Sanskrit title suggests an English translation of *Entrance to the Middle [Called] Wisdom.* However, the text begins with this statement of purpose (348b.1–2): "I will explain the meaning of entering into Middle Way wisdom" (*dbu ma shes rab la 'jug pa'i don ni bdag gis bshad par bya*).

71 'Gos khug pa lhas btsas. Gö also revised the Tibetan translation of the tantric Candrakīrti's *Pradīpoddyotana* with "Nag po" (= Kṛṣṇapāda), raising the possibility that he understood some strong connection between the second and third Candrakīrtis.

72 Toh. 3863, *sde dge* edition, *dbu ma,* vol. *'a,* 348b.7 (stanza 9a): *dam bca' gtan tshig nyid ma yin /.*

73 Stanza 8 (348b.6): */ mngon sum la sogs 'gal zhe na / / ma yin ma brtags nyams dga' ba / / de ni bdag gis bkag pa med / / tha snyad tsam zhig bsgrub pa'i phyir /* "If you say this contradicts perception and so forth, it does not because I establish a mere convention, no cessation, [through] a non-analytical perspective." The term, *ma brtags nyams dga' ba,* "a non-analytical perspective," more literally would be "relaxed about not analyzing."

74 *Madhyamakāvatāra,* stanza VI.35; La Vallée Pousin, *Madhyamakāvatāra,* 120.5–8: *gang phyir dngos po 'di dag rnam dpyad na / de nyid bdag can dngos las tshu rol tu / gnas rnyed ma yin de phyir 'jig rten gyi / tha snyad bden la rnam bar dpyad mi bya /.*

75 Candrakīrti III's phrasing, *ma brtags nyams dga' ba* ("relaxed about not analyzing") appears in Chapa's text at Helmut Tauscher, ed., *Phya pa chos kyi seṅ ge: dbu ma śar gsum gyi stoṅ thun* (Vienna: Arbeitskreis für Tibetische und Buddhistische Studien, 1999), 65.19. Chapa's views are discussed at length throughout the remaining chapters of this book.

76 Maitrīpāda's text is *Tattvadaśaka, sde dge* 2236; Sahajavajra's commentary is *Tattvadaśakaṭīkā, sde dge* 2254.

77 Sahajavajra writes: *dbu ma pa 'phags pa klu sgrub dang / 'phags pa lha dang zla ba grags pa la sogs pas bzhed pa rten cing 'brel bar 'byung pa'i mtshan nyid de / de bzhin nyid ni 'dod pa'i don yin par 'gyur ro //* "The nature of dependent arising that the Mādhyamikas Ārya Nāgārjuna, Āryadeva, Candrakīrti and others accept is suchness, the desired object."

78 *cittamātra.*

79 *neyārtha,* literally "leading." Sahajavajra, just prior to referring to *Entrance to the Middle,* quoted the *Samādhirāja Sūtra,* and simply notes that *Entrance to the Middle* espouses a similar view.

80 Mark Tatz, "Maitrī-pa and Atiśa," In *Tibetan Studies: Proceedings of the 4th Seminar of the International Association for Tibetan Studies,* edited by Helga Uebach and Jampa L. Panglung (Munchen: Kommission für Zentralasiatische Studien Bayerische Akademie der Wissenschaften, 1988), 473–82.

81 D.S. Ruegg, "A Kar Ma bKa' brGyud Work on the Lineages and Traditions of the Indo-Tibetan dBu ma (Madhyamaka)," In *Orientalia Iosephi Tucci memoriae dicata,* edited by G. Gnoli and L. Lanciotti (Rome: Istituto italiano per il Medio ed Estremo Oriente, 1985), 1252–79.

82 *Subhāṣitasaṃgraha,* edited by Cecil Bendall, *Muséon* IV (1903): 375–402 and V (1904): 5–46 and 245–74. I have been unable to precisely date this anonymous text. However, the texts that it cites would make around 1000 the earliest possible date for its composition.

83 Along with Prajñākaramati's commentary on Śāntideva's *Engaging in the Bodhisattva's Practice,* the *Subhāṣitasaṃgraha* is one of the most important sources for Sanskrit fragments of Candrakīrti's *Entrance to the Middle.*

84 The *Subhāṣitasaṃgraha* (1903: 396) cites *Entrance to the Middle,* VI.79–80, followed by Śāntideva's *Engaging in the Bodhisattva's Practices,* IX.2, 33–35, 54, and 56–57. Jayānanda cites *Engaging in the Bodhisattva's Practices,* IX.2 and 33–35, when explicating Candrakīrti's two truths.

85 The *Subhāṣitasaṃgraha* (1903: 390–92) cites *Entrance to the Middle,* VI.12, 14–17, and 103–5 in this context, denying production from self, other, and causeless production (no citation is given for the denial of production from both self and other). Candrakīrti held that production from the "four alternatives" (*catuṣkoṭi*) could be denied even from the worldly perspective.

86 Nāgārjuna's famous first stanza of the *Fundamental Treatise on the Middle* reads (de Jong, *Mūlamadhyamakakārikā,* 1): *na svato nāpi parato na dvābhyāṃ nāpy ahetutaḥ / utpannā jātu vidyante bhāvāḥ kva cana ke cana //* ("Nothing is produced anywhere, ever; not from self, also not from other; not from both, also not causelessly").

The *Subhāṣitasaṃgraha* (1903: 389) reads *bhāvā* for *bhāvāḥ*. Candrakīrti first supports Buddhapālita's commentary on this stanza, responding to Bhāvaviveka's critique of Buddhapālita, then criticizes Bhāvaviveka at length for his insistence that inference is necessary to understand emptiness. See Louis de la Vallée Poussin, *Mūlamadhyamakakārikās de Nāgārjuna avec la Prasannapadā Commentaire de Candrakīrti,* Bibliotheca Buddhica, 4 (Osnabrück, Germany: Biblio Verlag, 1970), 14.1–36.2.

87 Bendall, *Subhāṣitasaṃgraha* (1903): 389: *na san nāsan nasadasan na cāpy anubhayātmakaṃ / catuṣkoṭivinirmuktaṃ tattvaṃ mādhyamikā viduḥ //* "Mādhyamikas assert reality devoid of the four extremes: having a nature not existent, nor non-existent, nor both existent and non-existent, and also not neither." The *Subhāṣitasaṃgraha* cites this and the preceding two stanzas, which are stanzas 26–28 of the tantric Āryadeva's *Jñānasārasamuccaya;* see the edition of Katsumi Mimaki, "*Jñānasārasamuccaya* kk. 20–28, *Mise au point* with a Sanskrit Manuscript," in *Wisdom, Compassion, and the Search for Understanding: The Buddhist Studies Legacy of Gadjin M. Nagao,* ed. Jonathan A. Silk (Honolulu: University of Hawai'i Press, 2000), 240–41. As Bendall notes (p. 389, n. 4), the final stanza is also cited by Prajñākaramati in his commentary to *Engaging in the Bodhisattva Practices* (La Vallée Poussin, *Prajñākaramati's Commentary* [1905]: 359.10). See also Ruegg, *Three Studies,* 142–45, where this stanza is shown to be present in the writings of Maitrīpāda and to draw on much older sūtra sources.

88 The *Subhāṣitasaṃgraha's* misattribution of the stanzas may indicate it to be at a greater distance from the original of the *Jñānasārasamuccaya.*

89 John Newman, "Buddhist Siddhānta in the Kālacakra Tantra," *Wiener Zeitschrift für die Kunde Südasiens* 36 (1992): 229–30.

90 The standard listing has Saraha teaching Nāgārjuna, who has four chief disciples: Śākyamitra, Āryadeva, Nāgabodhi, and Candrakīrti; among other sources, see *Blue Annals,* 359–60.

91 The tantric Nāgārjuna wrote the *Pañcakrama* (Peking 2667, vol. 61), an important text on the stages of practicing the *Guhyasamāja Tantra,* and considered the foundational text of the Ārya lineage of Guhyasamāja practice and exegesis. See Katsumi Mimaki and Toru Tomabechi, *Pañcakrama: Sanskrit and Tibetan Texts Critically Edited with Verse Index and Facsimile Edition of the Sanskrit Manuscripts,* Bibliotheca Codicum Asiaticorum 8 (Tokyo: The Centre for East Asian Cultural Studies for Unesco, 1994) and Toru Tomabechi, *Étude du Pañcakrama. Introduction et traduction annotée* (Thèse de doctorat, Faculté des Lettres, Université de Lausanne, 2006). The tantric Āryadeva wrote the *Caryāmelāpakapradīpa* (Peking 2668, vol. 61), an elaboration of the *Pañcakrama,* expounding the "gradualist" method of practicing Guhyasamāja yoga. See the study, edition, and translation in Christian K. Wedemeyer, *Āryadeva's Lamp That Integrates The Practices* (*Caryāmelāpakapradīpa*): *The Gradual Path of Vajrayāna Buddhism according to the Esoteric Communion Noble Tradition* (New York: Columbia University Press, 2007). The tantric Candrakīrti wrote the most important commentary on the *Guhyasamāja Tantra* in the Ārya lineage, the *Pradīpoddyotana* (Peking 2650, vol. 60).

92 A nuanced and well-documented discussion of the widespread Buddhist phenomenon of identifying later literature with earlier authors as a means of authenticity

and authority, centering on the "Noble" Guhyasamāja lineage, is found in the introduction to Wedemeyer's *Āryadeva's Lamp.* Wedemeyer shows this to be a well-worn Buddhist strategy, practiced from a very early point in the tradition's Indian development, and not simply the product of relatively late tantric authors.

93 See the introduction to Wedemeyer's *Āryadeva's Lamp.*

94 The parallel language connecting *Guhyasamājottaratantra* XVIII.84 to Nāgārjuna's prouncement in *Mūlamadhyamakakārikā* XXIV.8 was pointed out in Harunaga Isaacson, "Ratnākaraśānti's *Hevajrasahajasadyoga* (Studies in Ratnākaraśānti's Tantric Works I)," in *Le Parole e i Marmi: studi in onore di Raniero Gnoli nel suo 70° compleanno,* ed. Raffaele Torella (Roma: Istituto Italiano per l'Africa e l'Oriente. Serie Orientale Roma XCII, 2001), 469. I thank Christian Wedemeyer for bringing my attention to this reference.

95 See the introduction to Wedemeyer's *Āryadeva's Lamp.*

96 In personal communication, Christian Wedemeyer related, "I have tentatively placed the revelation of Candrakīrti's *Pradīpoddyotana* to the late tenth or early eleventh century . . . ca. 975–1025." In either scenario, the author of the *Pradīpoddyotana*—writing sometime between 850–1025—is unlikely to have been the author of *Seventy Stanzas on the Three Refuges* (*Triśaraṇasaptati;* Tohoku 3971, *sde dge* edition, *dbu ma,* vol. *gi,* 251a–253b; Per K. Sorensen, *Triśaraṇasaptati: The Septuagint on the Three Refuges* [Vienna: Arbeitskreis für Tibetische und Buddhistische Studien Universität Wien, 1986]), if the latter text is indeed quoted by Haribhadra (late eighth century). Ruegg (*Literature of the Madhyamaka,* 105, n. 334) notes that *Seventy Stanzas on the Three Refuges* is very unlikely authored by the Middle Way Candrakīrti, due to the presence of tantric notions unknown in and developed later than the latter's writings, such as the idea of seven "baskets" (*piṭaka*), one of which is the "knowledge-holder basket" (*vidyādharapiṭaka*). If *Seventy Stanzas on the Three Refuges* is cited by Haribhadra, we may well need to posit four surviving authors by the name of Candrakīrti: the Middle Way author, the author of *Seventy Stanzas,* the author of the *Pradīpoddyotana,* and the author of *Entrance to Middle Way Wisdom* (whom I referred to earlier in this chapter as Candrakīrti III). Even if we push the dates of the *Pradīpoddyotana* author into the early eleventh century, I do not believe we can identify him with the author of *Entrance to Middle Way Wisdom,* as the latter author translated his composition into Tibetan with 'Gos khug pa lhas rtse, who was responsible for revising the Tibetan translation of the *Pradīpoddyotana.* Had 'Gos worked directly with the author of the *Pradīpoddyotana,* it seems extremely likely that he would have announced that connection prominently in his revision of the text. Rather than allowing us to identify these two Candrakīrtis, the 'Gos evidence again suggests a thematic connection between the authors bearing that name. Ruegg noted the problems with identifying the author of *Seventy Stanzas on the Three Refuges* with the Middle Way Candrakīrti, writing (*Literature of the Madhyamaka,* 105, n. 334) that "Verse 33 [of *Seventy Stanzas*] seems to be quoted by Haribhadra, Abhisamayālaṃkārālokā i. 3 (p. 8–9)." Stanza 33 (*sde dge* edition, *dbu ma,* vol. *gi,* 252a.3–4) reads: */sangs rgyas chos dang dge 'dun ni/ /bdud rnams bye ba brgya yis kyang/ /gang phyir dbye bar mi nus pa/ /de phyir dge 'dun zhes bshad do/.* The Sanskrit of Haribhadra's citation reads (Unrai Wogihara, *Abhisamayālaṃkārālokā Prajñāpāramitāvyākhyā* [Tokyo: Toyo Bunko, 1932–35], 8–9): *buddha-dharmau*

tathā saṃgho māra-koṭi-śatair api / bhettuṃ na śakyate yasmāt tasmāt saṃgho 'bhidhīyate //.

97 *Pa tshab nyi ma grags,* b. 1055. Much more on Patsab's translation activity is found in chapter 2.

98 Candrakīrti's commentary, the *Pradīpoddyotana,* had already been translated by Śraddhākaravarman and Rin chen bzang bo; this first translation is preserved in the Tibetan *bstan 'gyur.* The *Blue Annals* (p. 366) reports that Patsab's translation did not flourish.

99 See, for instance, mKhas grub dGe legs dpal bzang's comments in José Ignacio Cabezón's *A Dose of Emptiness* (Albany, NY: State University of New York Press, 1992), 86–87.

100 We also see Saraha and Candrakīrti appearing together, along with Maitrīpāda, in Kagyu lineages of Madhyamaka; see Ruegg, "A Kar Ma bKa' brGyud Work," 1255. Two further links between Maitrīpāda and Saraha are made by the short "Question and Answer" text, *Śrī Saraha Prabhu Maitrīpāda praśnottara,* recording Maitrīpāda's questions on Mahāmudrā and Saraha's answers (P5048, vol. 87, 122.2.6–122.5.6) and Maitrīpāda's commentary to Saraha's *Dohākoṣa* (ed. Prabodh Chandra Bagchi, Calcutta Sanskrit Series, 1938).

101 *Pañcakramapañjikā* (Peking 2696, vol. 62) on Nāgārjuna's *Pañcakrama* and *Abhisaṃdhiprakāśika* (Peking 2658, vols. 60–61) on Candrakīrti's *Pradīpoddyotana.*

102 Abhayākaragupta, who identifies the Candrakīrti who wrote the *Pradīpoddyotana* as "ārya Candrakīrti" and the author of *Entrance to the Middle* as "Master Candrakīrti", also attributes *Seventy Stanzas on the Three Refuges* to "Master Candrakīrti."

103 Ruegg, *Literature of the Madhyamaka,* 106, n. 339.

104 Perhaps even the name, Bhavyakīrti, suggests a blending of the ideas of these two: Bhāvaviveka (frequently referred to as Bhavya) and Candrakīrti.

105 While this text does not seem to date significantly later than the Middle Way works of Śāntarakṣita, Steinkellner casts doubt on the identity of this author with the Yogācāra-Madhyamaka author of the same name. See Ernst Steinkellner, "Yogic Cognition, Tantric Goal, and Other Methodological Applications of Dharmakīrti's *Kāryānumāna* Theorem," in *Dharmakīrti's Thought and Its Impact on Indian and Tibetan Philosophy,* ed. S. Katsura (Vienna: Österreichischen Akademie der Wissenschaften, 1999), 356–57.

106 Steinkellner, "Yogic Cognition, Tantric Goal," 355–56.

107 The complex relationship—sometimes antagonistic but eventually soothed into harmony within Buddhist monastic education—between tantra and valid cognition deserves much more investigation. Ronald Davidson ("Masquerading as *Pramāṇa:* Esoteric Buddhism and Epistemological Nomenclature," in *Dharmakīrti's Thought and Its Impact on Indian and Tibetan Philosophy,* ed. S. Katsura [Vienna: Österreichischen Akademie der Wissenschaften, 1999], 25–35) suggests that tantric authors utilized valid cognition conventions to show the authority of tantras and tantric masters and as a step toward gaining institutional acceptance.

108 Steinkellner points to several other "tantristic texts transmitted under Śāntarakṣita's name" ("Yogic Cognition, Tantric Goal," 356).

109 Wayman, *Yoga of the Guhyasamāja,* 103. Wayman is discussing, at that point, Bu ston's continuation of "the Mādhyamika tone of commentary" found in Candrakīrti's *Pradīpoddyotana.* At p. 93, Wayman discusses the *Pradīpoddyotana*'s penchant for turning away from Yogācāra terminology and notes that Bhavyakīrti's *Prakāśikā* returns to Yogācāra language.

110 The *Compendium* author cites *Entrance to the Middle,* VI.43, 45–51, and 88–89; Bendall, "Subhāṣita-Saṃgraha," (1903): 392–93.

111 Ruegg, *Literature of the Madhyamaka,* 122.

112 On Abhayākaragupta's life and works and sNur Dhar ma grags, see Felix Erb, *Śūnyatāsaptativṛtti* (Stuttgart: Franz Steiner Verlag, 1997), 27–29.

113 In his *Munimatālaṃkāra,* written in 1113 (Erb, *Śūnyatāsaptativṛtti,* 29), Abhayākaragupta four times refers to *slob dpon zla ba grags* ("the Master Candrakīrti"), each time citing *Entrance to the Middle* or its autocommentary. *Munimatālaṃkāra* (Toh. 3903, *sde dge* edition, *dbu ma,* vol. *a*) 175b.5 cites *Entrance to the Middle,* stanza I.8; 180a.5 cites the autocommentary to stanza VIII.3; 208a.4 cites the autocommentary to stanzas XII.8–9; and 218b.1 cites stanza XII.4. At *Munimatālaṃkāra* 222b.2, Abhayākaragupta cites stanza VI.214, attributing it only to *zla ba grags,* without using *slob dpon* or *'phags pa.* Three additional passages [101b.6, 113a.7, and 219a.5] likely refer obliquely to *Entrance to the Middle;* the former and latter attribute the view discussed to *slob dpon zla ba grags,* while 113a.7 uses only *zla ba grags.* At 111b.1–2, Abhayākaragupta refers to what "Ārya Candra said in his *Lamp [Commentary to the Guhyasamāja Tantra]*" (*'phags pa zla ba sgron mar gsungs pa*). Abhayākaragupta's appellations may not carry the intention that the "Master" and "Ārya" Candrakīrtis were different people but instead be used to distinguish between different bodies of literature, sūtric and tantric, much as Ratnākaraśānti distinguished these bodies.

114 The authorship of the *Triśaraṇasaptati* is discussed above. Abhayākaragupta's text reads (82a.6–7): *'phags pa klu sgrub zhabs kyi dgongs pa'i rjes su 'brang ba'i zla ba grags pa.*

115 As pointed out already by Ruegg (*Literature of the Madhyamaka,* 122), Ratnākaraśānti's colophon to his *Madhyamakālaṃkāropadeśa* states that he composed the text to refute "Bhadanta Candrakīrti's" views, but notes that Candrakīrti later "abandoned nihilism" in his *Guhyasamāja* commentary. The text may be the earliest critique of Candrakīrti's views extant and as such presents more evidence that Candrakīrti only became important around the year 1000.

116 The *Munimatālaṃkāra* (Toh. 3903, *sde dge* edition, *dbu ma,* vol. *a,* 180a.5ff) discusses Candrakīrti's "thinking" behind his discussion of non-conceptual wisdom in his autocommentary to *Entrance to the Middle,* stanza VIII.3. At 208a.4–208b.2, Abhayākaragupta spells out Candrakīrti's "thinking" behind his proclamation, in his autocommentary to stanzas XII.8–9, that minds and mental factors cease upon buddhahood.

117 See the list of references above in note 113.

118 A number of Indian scholars, mostly Kashmiris, could be included in this examination of the Indian origins of Prāsaṅgika. However, as these scholars did not write on Prāsaṅgika and their contributions consisted of teaching and working with Tibetan translators, their contributions will be evaluated along with their Tibetan students in the following section.

119 In his *Madhyamakāvatāraṭīkā, sde dge* edition 3870, *dbu ma,* vol. *ra,* 281a.6 and 281b.6. In both cases, Jayānanda glosses a pronoun (*de,* "that") found in Candrakīrti's text that is the butt of Candrakīrti's criticism. Jayānanda's glosses, substituting "Svātantrika" for "that," make it clear that he sees himself and Candrakīrti as opponents to the "Svātantrika" interpretation. He does not, however, refer to himself or Candrakīrti as "Prāsaṅgikas," an appellation that may have been first used by Patsab Nyimadrak, the main Tibetan translator of Candrakīrti's writings. "Prāsaṅgika" (*thal 'gyur pa*) is used by Chapa's student, Sonam Tsemo.

120 William L. Ames, "Bhāvaviveka's Own View of His Differences with Buddhapālita" and C.W. Huntington, Jr., "Was Candrakīrti a Prāsaṅgika?" both in *The Svātantrika-Prāsaṅgika Distinction: What Difference Does a Difference Make?* eds. Georges B.J. Dreyfus and Sara L. McClintock (Boston: Wisdom Publications, 2002), 41–66 and 67–91.

121 Jeffrey Hopkins, "A Tibetan Delineation of Different Views of Emptiness in the Indian Middle Way School: Dzong-ka-ba's Two Interpretations of the *Locus Classicus* in Chandrakīrti's Clear Words Showing Bhāvaviveka's Assertion of Commonly Appearing Subjects and Inherent Existence," *Tibet Journal* 14, no. 1 (1989): 10–43; Tom J.F. Tillemans, "Tsong kha pa *et al.* on the Bhāvaviveka-Candrakīrti Debate," in *Tibetan Studies: Proceedings of the 5th Seminar of the International Association for Tibetan Studies,* Monograph Series of Naritasan Institute for Buddhist Studies: Occasional Papers 2, ed. Ihara Shōren and Yamaguchi Zuihō (Narita: Naritasan Shinshōji, 1992), vol. 1, 315–26; Kodo Yotsuya, *The Critique of Svatantra Reasoning by Candrakīrti and Tsong-kha-pa: A Study of Philosophical Proof According to Two Prāsaṅgika Madhyamaka Traditions of India and Tibet.* Tibetan and Indo-Tibetan Studies, 8 (Stuttgart: Franz Steiner Verlag, 1999); Chizuko Yoshimizu, "Tsong kha pa's Reevaluation of Candrakīrti's Criticism of Autonomous Inference," in *Svātantrika-Prāsaṅgika Distinction,* 257–88; and José Ignacio Cabezón, "Two Views on the Svātantrika-Prāsaṅgika Distinction in Fourteenth-Century Tibet," in *Svātantrika-Prāsaṅgika Distinction,* 289–315.

122 We see brief attempts at surveying the Madhyamaka literature pertaining to the Prāsaṅgika-Svātantrika distinction in this period in Helmut Tauscher, "Phya pa chos kyi seng ge as a Svātantrika," in *Svātantrika-Prāsaṅgika Distinction,* 207–55, particularly 209–12, and Cabezón, "Two Views on the Svātantrika-Prāsaṅgika Distinction," 291–94.

123 Thus, I do not agree with the conclusion found in the "Introduction" to Dreyfus and McClintock, *Svātantrika-Prāsaṅgika Distinction,* 5 and 18, that the distinction proceeds solely out of Tibetan concerns. Eleventh- and twelfth-century Indians were divided over Candrakīrti's corpus. However, as I show in the following chapter, full-fledged subschools of Madhyamaka only formed in twelfth-century Tibet.

124 While Huntington ("Was Candrakīrti a Prāsaṅgika?") argues that Candrakīrti did not *wish* to establish a Madhyamaka subschool but did so only grudgingly, we must acknowledge that Candrakīrti's intention had very little to do with the historical rise of Prāsaṅgika hundreds of years following his death.

125 Cabezón ("Two Views on the Svātantrika-Prāsaṅgika Distinction," 290) writes of the possibility of conceiving of Prāsaṅgika and Svātantrika as having "internal coherence" sufficient to speak of them as "distinct intellectual movement(s)." It is

fair to say that both Prāsaṅgika and Svātantrika were movements in eleventh- and twelfth-century India. However, we have no evidence to support the existence of a Prāsaṅgika movement in India from Candrakīrti's lifetime until around the year 1000, if by "movement" we mean authors explicating, defending, and championing a view. By twelfth-century Tibet, as I argue in the following chapter, the "movement" coalesces into a "school."

126 Dreyfus and McClintock, "Introduction," 18.

Notes to Chapter 2

1 We also see the anonymous twelfth-century author of the Sanskrit *Lakṣaṇaṭīkā* using the term "*svatantrasādhanavādin*"; see Yoshiyasu Yonezawa, "*Lakṣaṇaṭīkā:* A Sanskrit Manuscript of an Anonymous Commentary on the *Prasannapadā*," *Journal of Indian and Buddhist Studies* 47, no. 2 (1999): 1023–22.

2 However, Patsab's recently discovered text uses the term "Prāsaṅgika" and attributes it to his Indian teacher Hasumati (Mahāsumati).

3 On this debate, see Paul Demiéville, *Le concile de Lhasa* (Paris: Imprimerie nationale de France, 1952).

4 The *dbu ma'i bstan bcos* (Madhyamaka treatises) are Lalou (Marcelle Lalou, "Les textes Bouddhiques au temps du roi khri-srong-lde-bcan," *Journal Asiatique* 241 [1953]: 333) numbers 573–605, the *rnam par shes pa'i bstan bcos* (Consciousness-[Only] treatises) are numbers 614–54, the *theg pa chung ngu'i bstan bcos* (*abhidharma* treatises) are numbers 686–94, and the *tarka'i phyogs* (logic section) are numbers 695–722.

5 Matthew Kapstein, *The Tibetan Assimilation of Buddhism* (New York: Oxford University Press, 2000), 54.

6 On the royal and military symbolism of tantra and its uses in India, see Ronald M. Davidson, *Indian Esoteric Buddhism: A Social History of the Tantric Movement* (New York: Columbia University Press, 2002), 118–44. On Tibetan emperors' appropriation of this symbolism, see Kapstein, *Tibetan Assimilation,* 60–62.

7 Kapstein (*Tibetan Assimilation,* 11–15) points to the survival of the Tibetan translation language through the Dark Period as evidence for the continuation of Buddhist scholarship, in addition to Buddhist practice, during this period. Scholarship on the Dark Period is quite limited; see Jacob Dalton, *Uses of the* Dgongs pa 'dus pa'i mdo *In the Development of the* Rnying-ma *School* (Ph.D. dissertation, University of Michigan, 2002) and Ronald M. Davidson, *Tibetan Renaissance: Tantric Buddhism in the Rebirth of Tibetan Culture* (New York: Columbia University Press, 2005), 61–83.

8 See Jan Yün-hua, "Buddhist Relations between India and Sung China," parts 1 and 2, *History of Religions* 6, no. 1 (August 1966): 24–42 and 6, no. 2 (November 1966): 135–68.

9 Davidson, *Tibetan Renaissance,* 88–92.

10 Ruth W. Dunnell, *The Great State of White and High* (Honolulu: University of Hawaii Press, 1996), 30 and 188, n. 11, records such an event as occurring in 980, the period when Tibetan pilgrims sought ordination to the east. Tsutomu Iwasaki

("The Tibetan Tribes of Ho-hsi and Buddhism During the Northern Sung Period," *Acta Asiatica* 64 [1993]: 17–37) discusses the significance of the purple robe in these regions as a marker of political service to the Song court. Davidson notes that by the early eleventh century, Tibetans in these borderlands were recipients of Song purple robes (Davidson, *Tibetan Renaissance,* 91).

11 See Craig Earl Watson, "The Second Propagation of Buddhism from Eastern Tibet According to the 'Short Biography of dGongs-pa rab-gsal' by the Third Thukvan bLo-bzaṅ chos-kyi nyi-ma (1737–1802)," *Central Asiatic Journal* 22, nos. 3–4 (1978): 263–85; Craig Earl Watson, "The Introduction of the Second Propagation of Buddhism in Tibet According to R.A. Stein's Edition of the Sba-bzhed," *Tibet Journal* 5, no. 4 (1980): 20–27; and Davidson, *Tibetan Renaissance,* 84–116.

12 See Roberto Vitali, *Early Temples of Central Tibet* (London: Serindia, 1990), 37ff. Vitali (p. 62, n. 2) provides a complete listing of these figures from a variety of Tibetan accounts that variously list ten, six, or four pilgrims. Davidson (*Tibetan Renaissance,* 92–105) provides an excellent discussion of these new monks' activities in Central Tibet. As the personal names of the new monks vary in Tibetan sources, I use only the simplest versions.

13 Davidson (*Tibetan Renaissance,* 94–95) translates a version of this story.

14 *The Blue Annals,* George N. Roerich, trans. (Delhi: Motilal Banarsidass, 1949), 378.

15 Leonard W.J. van der Kuijp, "The Monastery of Gsang-phu ne'u-thog and its Abbatial Succession from ca. 1073 to 1250," *Berliner Indologische Studien* 3 (1987): 108–9.

16 On the idea of the poetic power of Sanskrit, see Sheldon Pollack, "The Sanskrit Cosmopolis, 300–1300 CE: Transculturation, Vernacularization, and the Question of Ideology," in *Ideology and Status of Sanskrit: Contributions to the History of the Sanskrit Language,* ed. Jan E.M. Houben (Leiden: E.J. Brill, 1996), 197–247.

17 Davidson, *Tibetan Renaissance,* 104–5 discusses some of the curriculum taught in the new monasteries, noting that Sol nag thang bo che became an early center of philosophical studies.

18 For instance, on Drokmi's (*'brog mi*) monopoly of the "Path and Fruit" tantric system, see Davidson, *Tibetan Renaissance,* 161ff.

19 *rNgog lo tsa ba bLo ldan shes rab.* A biography of Ngok Lotsawa, written by his immediate disciple, is now available: Dram Dul, *'Jig rten mig gcig blo ldan śes rab kyi rnam thar, Biography of Blo ldan śes rab, The Unique Eye of the World by Gro luṅ pa Blo gros 'byuṅ gnas, The Xylograph Compared with a Bhutanese Manuscript* (Vienna: Arbeitskreis für Tibetische und Buddhistische Studien Universität Wien, 2004).

20 *sPa tshab Nyi ma grags.* Van der Kuijp ("*Ratnāvali* in Tibet," *Tibet Journal* 10, no. 2 [1985]: 4) casts doubt on the year of Patsab's birth, noting that Patsab could consider a trip across the Himalayas in 1136 and was still able to participate in an ordination in 1140. While it does seem unlikely that an eighty-one-year old could even consider a trans-Himalayan trip, Lang ("Spa-tshab Nyi-ma-grags and the Introduction of Prāsaṅgika Madhyamaka into Tibet," in *Reflections on Tibetan Culture: Essays in memory of Turrell V. Wylie,* eds. Lawrence Epstein and Richard F. Sherbourne [Lewiston, NY: E. Mellon Press, 1990], 134) notes that Patsab very likely returned to Tibet from his twenty-three-year sojourn in Kashmir by 1101. If Patsab arrived in Kashmir in 1077, he could not have been born long after 1055.

21 *Blue Annals,* 324.

22 *rNgog Byang chub 'byung gnas.*
23 *Blue Annals,* 74.
24 *ka ba bzhi.* We frequently see important founders and their disciples referred to as parts of a building. The founder seems to be equated with the roof beams (*gdung*), while his most important disciples are the pillars, lesser disciples are doors, planks, and so on. This "construction" metaphor reflects the role of disciples spreading their teacher's influence not simply through teaching but in staking out territory through temple construction.
25 *Sum pa Ye shes blo gros.* Sumpa was another of the "Ten Men" who returned the ordination lineage to Central Tibet. He was one of five men from the U (*dbus*) region. However, his importance seems to have been joined with or eclipsed by Lumé's, as the division of U into the districts connected with the figures from U, reported by Grags pa rgyal mtshan around 1200 (*rGya bod kyi sde pa'i gyes mdo, Sa skya bka' 'bum,* vol. 4 [Tokyo: Toyo Bunko, 1968], 296.4.2–298.3.3), includes only four names, leaving out Sumpa.
26 *Blue Annals,* 74–75.
27 *rNgog rDo rje gzhon nu.*
28 Leonard W.J. van der Kuijp, *Contributions to the Development of Tibetan Buddhist Epistemology from the Eleventh to the Thirteenth Century* (Wiesbaden: Franz Steiner Verlag, 1983), 30.
29 *rNgog Legs pa'i shes rab.*
30 *'Bring Ye shes blo gros.*
31 Van der Kuijp, *Contributions,* 30.
32 *Jo bo se btsun.*
33 *Rin chen bzang po;* see *Blue Annals,* 93 and 324.
34 Accounts of the history of Sangpu (*gsang phu ne'u thog*) are found in van der Kuijp, "The Monastery of Gsang-phu ne'u-thog," 103–27.
35 *Uttaratantra* or *Ratnagotravibhāga.* See *Blue Annals,* 259.
36 *sNye thang,* built by Atiśa's pre-eminent Tibetan disciple, Dromton (*'Brom ston rGyal ba'i 'byung gnas,* 1004–63) in 1055. See *Blue Annals,* 324.
37 We also see a third division of the Ngok clan, stemming from rNgok Chos kyi rdo rje (1036–1102) who was instrumental in spreading Mar pa's teachings. See *Blue Annals,* 403 and 667.
38 Compare the discussions in Van der Kuijp, "Monastery of Gsang-phu ne'u-thog," 108–9 and Davidson, *Tibetan Renaissance,* 111–12. The four districts were Lumé, Ba (*sBa*), Raksha (*Rag sha*), and Dring. Ba and Raksha (whose districts seem to have joined at an early date) are together listed as supporters of Nyetang, explaining how three monasteries can be supported by four competing districts. This division of U (*dbu*) is also reported by Grags pa rgyal mtshan in his *rGya bod kyi sde pa'i gyes mdo,* 296.4.2–298.3.3.
39 Davidson's suggestion (*Tibetan Renaissance,* 110–12) that Atiśa's teaching activities in Central Tibet were dictated by important members of the new monasticism districts fits the Ngok clan evidence well. The competing monasteries each wanted the prestige of hosting Atiśa yet wanted specific teachings from the Indian master that perhaps were not indicative of Atiśa's own interests.
40 Van der Kuijp, *Contributions,* 31.

41 The "religious council" (*chos 'khor*) was convened by rTse lde, king of mNga' ris 'khor gsum at Tho ling; rTse lde's son, dBang phyug lde, sponsored Ngok's trip to Kashmir. See *Blue Annals*, 71, 325; Lobsang Shastri, "The Fire Dragon *Chos 'khor* (1076 AD)," in *Tibetan Studies: Proceedings of the 7th Seminar of the International Association for Tibetan Studies,* edited by Helmut Krasser, Michael Torsten Much, Ernst Steinkellner, Helmut Tauscher (Vienna: Österreichischen Akademie der Wissenschaften, 1997), vol. 2, 873–82; and Roberto Vitali, *The Kingdoms of Gu.ge Pu.hrang According to mNga'.ris rgyal.rabs by Gu.ge mkhan.chen Ngag.dbang.grags.pa* (Dharamsala, India: Library of Tibetan Works and Archives, 1996).

42 *Pramāṇavārttikālaṃkāra.* Van der Kuijp (*Contributions,* 31–32) notes the confusion that this text was reportedly already translated prior to Ngok Loden Sherab's journey to Kashmir and offers the following solution: The text was indeed translated already by Zangs dkar lo tsa ba 'Phags pa'i shes rab, but this translation was found faulty. Ngok translated it again in Kashmir, whereupon his translation arrived in Western Tibet prior to his return, allowing Zangs dkar to edit the translation. Upon Ngok's return, he edited the translation again. This convoluted explanation accounts for the facts that we know about the text. A very similar explanation is given in Marek Mejor, "On the Date of the Tibetan Translations of the *Pramāṇasamuccaya* and the *Pramāṇavārttika,*" in *Studies in the Buddhist Epistemological Tradition,* ed. Ernst Steinkellner (Vienna: Österreichischen Akademie der Wissenschaften, 1991), 184–85, where it is suggested that bTsan kha bo che—who traveled to Kashmir with Ngok but returned prior to him—brought Ngok's first translation back to Western Tibet.

43 *Pramāṇaviniścaya.*

44 The *dbu ma shar gsum* are Jñānagarbha's *Distinguishing the Two Truths* (*Satyadvayavibhaṅga*), Śāntarakṣita's *Ornament for the Middle Way* (*Madhyamakālaṃkāra*), and Kamalaśīla's *Illumination of the Middle Way* (*Madhyamakāloka*).

45 *Blue Annals,* 73. This tradition needs to be reconciled with the accounts, reported by van der Kuijp ("Monastery of Gsang-phu ne'u-thog," 107), that two of Ngok's students, Tshes spong ba Chos kyi bla ma and Gro lung pa Blo gros 'byung gnas, were responsible for expanding Sangpu's physical size, apparently after Ngok Loden Sherab's death.

46 See Dram Dul, *Biography of Blo ldan śes rab;* Ruegg, *Three Studies,* 29–30; and van der Kuijp, *Contributions,* 57. Kazuo Kano, *rNgog Blo-ldan-shes-rab's Summary of the* Ratnagotravibhāga (Ph.D. dissertation, Hamburg University, 2006), 131–34, contains a table of Ngok's compositions.

47 At present, several of Ngok's writings on the Maitreya texts and his commentary and summary to Dharmakīrti's *Pramāṇaviniścaya* are available. The first chapter of Ngok's summary of Maitreya's *Ratnagotravibhāga* is edited and translated in Kano, *rNgog Blo-ldan-shes-rab's Summary.*

48 Ngok Loden Sherab's summary of the *Ratnagotravibhāga* (*Theg chen rgyud bla ma'i don bsdus pa* [Dharamsala, India: Library of Tibetan Works and Archives, 1993]) echoes Śāntideva's proclamation that the ultimate is not a referent of consciousness, a notion Candrakīrti's revivers expounded upon at length. One hopes for the discovery of more of Ngok's writings in order to illuminate how he understood Śāntideva. As has been noted above, Śāntideva's writings have been interpreted from

a decidedly non-Prāsaṅgika viewpoint. One suspects that Ngok, with his emphasis on Dharmakīrti's epistemology, could not have meant, as Jayānanda from the Prāsaṅgika viewpoint wrote, that human valid cognition can play no role in ascertaining the ultimate.

49 On Patsab, see Karen Lang, "Spa-tshab Nyi-ma-grags," 127–41.

50 Jean Naudou, *Buddhists of Kaśmīr* (Delhi: Agam Kala Prakashan, 1980), 210.

51 The former text consists of stanzas and autocommentary; while the stanzas had been translated prior to Patsab's work, by Kṛṣṇa Paṇḍita and Nag tsho Tshul khrims rgyal ba (b. 1011), his translation of the stanzas and autocommentary was the version that became widely known in Tibet.

52 Lang, "Spa-tshab Nyi-ma-grags," 132 and 134.

53 *Nyāyabindu;* Ngok translated Dharmottara's commentary on this text with Sumatikīrti who also translated Prajñākaramati's commentary on Śāntideva's *Engaging in the Bodhisattva's Practice* with Marpa Chos kyi dbang phyug and gNyan Dar ma grags at lCung ka mkhar in dBu ru. Ngok worked again with Sumatikīrti on the translation of another of Prajñākaramati's texts, his commentary on the *Ornament of Clear Realizations* (*Abhisamayālaṃkāravṛtti-piṇḍārtha, sde dge* edition 3795), showing Ngok's familiarity with at least one of Prajñākaramati's texts. The *Nyāyabinduṭīkā* of Vinītadeva was translated in the early diffusion by Ye shes sde.

54 Naudou, *Buddhists of Kaśmīr,* 230.

55 *Paralokasiddhi.*

56 It is possible that Naktso did translate Candrakīrti's autocommentary but that his translation was lost over time and was never included in any canonical collection. Tsongkhapa, in his own commentary to Candrakīrti's *Entrance to the Middle* (his *dGongs pa rab gsal*), refers several times to what he calls Naktso's translation of Candrakīrti's autocommentary. Another commentary on Candrakīrti's text, written by one of Tsongkhapa's teachers, Rendawa (*Red mda' ba gzhon nu blo gros*), likewise seems to have had access to Naktso's translation of Candrakīrti's autocommentary.

57 *lha sa* (or, *ra sa*) *'phrul snang.*

58 Ruegg (David Seyfort Ruegg, *Three Studies in the History of Indian and Tibetan Madhyamaka Philosophy, Studies in Indian and Tibetan Madhyamaka Thought, Part I* [Vienna: Arbeitskreis für Tibetische und Buddhistische Studien Universität Wien, 2000], 45) translates the phrase *nyi 'og shar phyogs* in the colophons to these translations—describing the provenance of the manuscripts Patsab utilized at Ramoche—as "eastern borderland," and notes the identification of *nyi 'og* with the Sanskrit Aparāntaka.

59 *rgyal lha khang* in *'phan yul* was built in 1012 by the bKa' gdams pa Zhang sna nam rDo rje dbang phyug (976–1060). Ruegg (*Three Studies,* 45, n. 89) points out that its destruction by a Mongol army in 1240 may account for the lack of information we have on Patsab. Patsab does not figure in the listing of rGyal lha khang's abbatial succession given in *Blue Annals,* 88–93. On an inscribed pillar at the temple, see Hugh Richardson, "A Tibetan Inscription from Rgyal Lha-khaṅ; and a Note on Tibetan Chronology from A.D. 841 to A.D. 1042," *Journal of the Royal Asiatic Society* (April 1957): 56–78.

60 *Blue Annals,* 272 and 342; Shar ba pa Yon tan grags's dates are 1070–1141.

61 If more of Ngok Loden Sherab's (died in 1109) writings become available, we may be better able to pin down the rise of Patsab's teaching career according to whether

or not Ngok refers at length to Prāsaṅgika notions. Ngok's denial that the ultimate is an object of knowledge and his followers' opposition to Candrakīrti's views could be rendered more comprehensible if Ngok drew the former notion from Śāntideva's writings, without intimate knowledge of Candrakīrti's positing a similar idea—that is, Ngok may have written before Patsab successfully spread Candrakīrti's writings. Some traditions, discussed below, have Chapa's (1109–69) students leaving Sangpu to study with Patsab. If this were so, Patsab's fame may have come quite late in his life, as Chapa could not have had students to lose to Patsab until roughly 1130.

62 We now have to our avail two significant Patsab texts, a fifty-two folio commentary on Nāgārjuna's *Mūlamadhyamakakārikās* and a sixty-six folio commentary on Candrakīrti's *Prasannapadā.* Patsab is known to have written another brief text, a "Questions and Answers on Madhyamaka" (*dbu ma'i dris lan*), written to Shar ba pa. This text does not survive but is noted in 'Jam dbyangs bzhad pa's *Grub mtha' chen mo* and in A khu Shes rab rgya mtsho's rare books list, *dPe rgyun dkon pa 'ga' zhig gi tho yig.* See Ruegg, *Three Studies,* 45, n. 88 and 47, n. 96.

63 *Cog ro klu'i rgyal mtshan.*

64 Akira Saito, "Problems in Translating the *Mūlamadhyamakakārikā* as Cited in its Commentaries," in *Buddhist Translations: Problems and Perspectives,* ed. Doboom Tulku (New Delhi: Manohar, 1995), 87–96. Saito shows that Lui Gyeltsen translated Nāgārjuna's stanzas in accordance with Avalokitavrata's massive sub-commentary to Bhāvaviveka's *Lamp for Wisdom:* Avalokitavrata's text, in which Bhāvaviveka's and Nāgārjuna's texts are embedded in their entirety, was translated first, then Bhāvaviveka's and Nāgārjuna's texts were rendered according to Avalokitavrata's explanation. Lui Gyeltsen then translated two additional commentaries on Nāgārjuna's stanzas, Buddhapālita's and the *Akutobhayā,* which in places (Saito lists twelve instances) explain the stanzas differently from Avalokitavrata, and yet Lui Gyeltsen still utilized Avalokitavrata's rendering of these stanzas. In such places, Lui Gyeltsen's translation of Nāgārjuna's stanzas embedded in Buddhapālita's commentary and in the *Akutobhayā* is not in keeping with the explanation these commentaries give; a different translation was required. Patsab's translation of Nāgārjuna's stanzas—which was made according to Candrakīrti's explanation of the stanzas in his *Clear Words*—retained Lui Gyelsten's wording in some places (Saito focuses on one instance) where a differing translation should have been given.

65 Tauscher has shown that Patsab edited—in conformity with his re-translation—only the parts of Naktso's translation of Candrakīrti's *Entrance to the Middle* that he found most important (Helmut Tauscher, "Some Problems of Textual History in Connection with the Tibetan Translations of the *Madhyamakāvatāra* and its Commentary," in *Contributions on Tibetan and Buddhist Religion and Philosophy,* ed. Ernst Steinkellner and Helmut Tauscher [Vienna: Arbeitskreis für Tibetische und Buddhistische Studien, 1983], 293–303). Even in those edited portions, we see disparities in the two Tibetan translations including instances, discussed in chapter 3, where Naktso's translation utilized a term crucial to the valid cognition tradition (*'khrul ba*) in places where Patsab chose a varying Tibetan term (*rdzun pa*).

66 Pollack ("The Sanskrit Cosmopolis," 244) writes of the turn across south and southeast Asia in the early years of the second millennium from composing high literature in Sanskrit to composing in vernacular, noting that the vernacular literature composed under the influence of the "Sanskrit Cosmopolis" was intelligible only to

those who knew Sanskrit. Tibetan translations, much moreso than compositions, require a background in Sanskrit. Kellner points to the need for exegesis of the early valid cognition literature, asking "how to conceive of the interrelation between translational activities, exegetical enterprises and individual interpretation in medieval Tibetan monastic culture." See Birgit Kellner, "Types of Incompatibility (*'gal ba*) and Types of Non-Cognition (*ma/mi dmigs*) in Early Tibetan *tshad ma* Literature," *Tibetan Studies: Proceedings of the 7th Seminar of the International Association for Tibetan Studies*, vol. 1, 496.

67 The role of Tibetan translators in this regard bears similarity to their medieval European counterparts. Stock sees European community leaders who were conversant in both the "high" literature and the vernacular serving as readers for the larger community, interpreters who delineated the community's views. See Brian Stock, *Listening for the Text: On the Uses of the Past* (Philadelphia: University of Pennsylvania Press, 1996), 22–23. Anne Blackburn has adopted Stock's ideas in her analysis of eighteenth-century Śri Laṅkan Buddhist communities in Anne M. Blackburn, *Buddhist Learning and Textual Practice in Eighteenth-Century Lankan Monastic Culture* (Princeton: Princeton University Press, 2001).

68 Dagenais's concept, "lecturature," texts born out of reading and responding to received texts, bears on Tibetan activities of this period. See John Dagenais, *The Ethics of Reading in Manuscript Culture: Glossing the 'Libro de buen amor'* (Princeton: Princeton University Press, 1994), 24.

69 On the many kinds of commentary identified in the Indian and Tibetan Buddhist traditions, see Georges B.J. Dreyfus, *The Sound of Two Hands Clapping: The Education of a Tibetan Buddhist Monk* (Berkeley, CA: University of California Press, 2003), 183ff. The varieties amount to a distinction between "word commentaries" (*tshig 'grel*) and "meaning commentaries" (*don 'grel*). Among Ngok's currently available texts, we have both summaries (*bsdus don/don bsdus*) and commentaries (*'grel pa*), including exemplars of both forms on the *Ratnagotravibhāga* and on Dharmakīrti's *Pramāṇaviniścaya.* Ngok seems to favor a synoptic style, overlaying his own topical outline (*sa bcad*) in order to present the subject matter of the text.

70 Stock (*Listening for the Text*, 27) notes that the commentarial reading of a text, rather than the "root" text, is the version of a text that lives in a given community's minds. Irvine sees the "authority of the gloss" both marking a text as canonical and then imperceptibly coming to replace it, as the commentarial meaning becomes the text's meaning. See Martin Irvine, *The Making of Textual Culture* (Cambridge: Cambridge University Press, 1994), 390. Copeland likewise speaks to the primacy of commentary, noting that it can be oriented toward the "changing conditions of understanding" of a community of readers, whereas the text itself must remain stable. See Rita Copeland, *Rhetoric, Hermeneutics, and Translation in the Middle Ages* (Cambridge: Cambridge University Press, 1991), 64.

71 Van der Kuijp ("Monastery of Gsang-phu ne'u-thog," 111) lists four topics of the Sangpu curriculum: Epistemology, the Maitreya texts, abhidharma, and monastic discipline (*vinaya*). We also know that the Madhyamaka interpretation following Śāntarakṣita and Kamalaśīla was taught there. Ngok's commentaries, in turn, fall mainly in three areas: Epistemology, the Maitreya texts, and Madhyamaka; see the handy table in Kano, *rNgog Blo-ldan-shes-rab's Summary*, 125–28.

72 Patsab's re-translations of Nāgārjuna's texts suggest an alternate method of claiming possession of an already translated body of literature.

73 As noted in chapter 1, Patsab's translation of the *Guhyasamāja* did not circulate widely and is not the version canonized in the bKa' 'gyur.

74 Kano, *rNgog Blo-ldan-shes-rab's Summary,* 121–22.

75 Gro lung pa bLo gros 'byung gnas's *bsTan rim chen mo* lists Āryadeva, Nāgabodhi, Buddhapālita, and Bhāvaviveka but not Candrakīrti. See José Ignacio Cabezón, "The Madhyamaka in Gro lung pa's *Bstan Rim chen mo,*" *Proceedings of the 11th Seminar of the International Association of Tibetan Studies 2006* (forthcoming).

76 Cabezón, "The Madhyamaka in Gro lung pa."

77 Cabezón, "The Madhyamaka in Gro lung pa."

78 In deference to the accounts of Drolungpa's long life, which places him still teaching at Sangpu during Chapa's abbacy, we might hypothesize that what we see in Drolungpa's account amounts to an attempt to reconcile the debate between Chapa and Jayānanda, although I believe this to be a less likely accounting.

79 *Vigrahavyāvartanī.*

80 *Tarkamudgara, rtog ge tho ba,* stanza 1; *sde dge* edition 3869, vol. *ya,* 374b.3–4: *yul dngos stobs kyis zhugs pa yi // tshad mas de nyid rtogs so zhes // chos kyi grags pa'i rjes 'brang ba'i // rtog ge ba rnams smra bar byed /* "Logicians following Dharmakīrti propound that reality is realized through objectively gained valid cognition." As discussed in chapter 3, Jayānanda criticizes this view at length.

81 *Mahāsūtrasamuccaya, sde dge* edition 3961; the colophon lists Jayānanda, Patsab, and Khu mDo sde 'bar as translators, working in dPal ldan Ya gad at Zhogs.

82 As reported in Śākya mchog ldan (1428–1507), *dBu ma rnam par nges pa'i mdzod lung dang rigs pa'i rgya mtsho, Collected Works,* vol. 14 (Thimphu, Bhutan: Kunzang Tobgey, 1975), 518. Śākya mchog ldan's account of this debate is drawn directly from Chapa's *Compilation of the Three Mādhyamikas from the East* (*dBu ma shar gsum stong mthun*), in a section where Chapa states a number of (hypothetical) opponent's objections and his own responses. It is possible, but unlikely, that Chapa's text recounts the verbatim contents of an actual debate.

83 On Jayānanda's role, see Leonard W.J. Van der Kuijp, "Jayānanda. A Twelfth Century *Guoshi* from Kashmir Among the Tangut," *Central Asiatic Journal 37,* no. 3/4 (1993): 188–97. On the Tangut translation project generally, see E.I. Kychanov, "From the History of the Tangut Translation of the Buddhist Canon," in *Tibetan and Buddhist Studies Commemorating the 200th Anniversary of the Birth of Alexander Csoma de Kőrös,* ed. Louis Ligetti (Budapest: Akadémiai Kiadó, 1984), 377–87. And on Tibetan culture among the Tanguts, see E.I. Kychanov, "Tibetans and Tibetan Culture in the Tangut State Hsi Hsia (982–1227)," in *Proceedings of the Csoma de Kőrös Memorial Symposium, 1976,* ed. Louis Ligeti (Budapest: Akadémiai Kiadó, 1978), 205–11.

84 On Pa tshab sGom nag, see *Blue Annals,* 923–28. Given the connection between Jayānanda, Kun dga' grags, and Pa tshab sgom nag and the certainty that the former two worked together on translations in Tangut lands, one wonders whether Pa tshab sgom nag could be the collaborator of Jayānanda and Kun dga' grags known only as Poloxiansheng, who held the office of Imperial Preceptor (*dishi;* see Van der Kuijp, "Jayānanda," 189–90).

85 Jayānanda's citation of *Clear Words* is in his *Madhyamakāvatāraṭīkā, sde dge* edition 3870, *dbu ma,* vol. *ra,* 108b.6ff.

86 Van der Kuijp, "Jayānanda," 188–89.

87 Dunnell, *The Great State,* 27–50. Dunnell records four requests by the Tangut court to Song China for a copy of the Song Buddhist canon between 1031 and 1058. Kychanov ("History of the Tangut Translation," 381–82) shows the presence of Tangut translations from Tibetan at least from 1085. The Tibetan originals, however, could well have come from the Kokonor region and cannot be used as evidence for Tangut relations with Central Tibet in the late eleventh century.

88 Dunnell, *The Great State,* xxiv.

89 Helmut Tauscher, ed., *Phya pa chos kyi seṅ ge: dbu ma śar gsum gyi stoṅ thun* (Vienna: Arbeitskreis für Tibetische und Buddhistische Studien, 1999).

90 I show in chapter 3 that Chapa's portrayal of Candrakīrti presupposes knowledge of Jayānanda's ideas. It is well possible that Chapa had in mind the portrayal of Candrakīrti by his former students who abandoned his views in favor of Prāsaṅgika, particularly the writings of rMa bya byang chub brtson 'grus.

91 *Madhyamakāvatāraṭīkā, sde dge* edition 3870, *dbu ma,* vol. *ra,* 146b.5ff, commenting on stanza VI.28. This is discussed at length in chapter 4.

92 Van der Kuijp (*Contributions,* 69) notes a "massive shift in allegiance away from Phya-pa."

93 In the writings of Jayānanda, Mabja Jangchub Tsondru, and Chapa's student Sonam Tsemo (who is discussed below).

94 *gTsang nag pa brTson 'grus seng ge,* d. 1171. See David Jackson, "Madhyamaka Studies Among the Early Sa-skya-pas," *Tibet Journal* 10, no. 2 (1985): 24. Several of gTsang nag pa's works are now available in the *bKa' gdams gsung 'bum,* including his commentary to Śāntideva's *Bodhicaryāvatāra.*

95 *rMa bya Byang chub brtson 'grus,* d. 1185. See Jackson, "Madhyamaka Studies," 24, and Leonard W.J. van der Kuijp, "Notes on the Transmission of Nāgārjuna's *Ratnāvali* in Tibet," *Tibet Journal* 10, no. 2 (1985): 8. Two brief texts of rMa bya's are included in the *bKa' gdams gsung 'bum,* both surveying Nāgārjuna's corpus; the lengthier is a 34 folio work, *dbu rig pa'i tshogs kyi rgyan de nyid snang ba.*

96 *mTshur gZhon nu seng ge.* See Jackson, "Madhyamaka Studies," 24 and van der Kuijp, "Notes on the Transmission," 8. One of Tsur's valid cognition texts is available: Pascale Hugon, *mTshur ston gZhon nu seng ge, Tshad ma shes rab sgron ma* (Vienna: Arbeitskreis für Tibetische und Buddhistische Studien Universität Wien, 2004).

97 *Blue Annals,* 343.

98 Jackson, "Madhyamaka Studies," 24.

99 Williams notes that Mabja refers readers of his *'Thad pa'i rgyan* to an *dBu ma'i de kho na nyid gtan la dbab pa* for his own more thorough discussion of these issues. Williams suspects that this was the subtitle to Mabja's *Hammer of Logic* commentary; Williams takes as the main title that used by the Eighth Karmapa, Mi bskyod rdo rje, to refer to Mabja's commentary, *Rigs rgyan snang ba.* See Paul Williams, "rMa bya pa Byang chub brtson 'grus on Madhyamaka Method," *Journal of Indian Philosophy* 13 (1985): 207 and 220, nn. 7 and 8. The (sub)title bears a close similarity to the alternative title Chapa gave to his *Compilation of the Three Mādhyamikas from the East,* namely, *dbu ma de kho na nyid kyi snying po.* Given this similarity, Mabja could

instead be referring to his independent work, *dBu ma stong mthun* (*Compilation of Madhyamaka*).

100 This link is reported in van der Kuijp, "Notes on the Transmission," 8. Van der Kuijp further reports that Tibetan historians disagree as to whether Mabja Jangchub Tsondru studied with Patsab directly or with one of Patsab's students, Mabja Jangchub Yeshe (*rMa bya Byang chub ye shes*). Mabja Jangchub Tsondru's study with Jayānanda makes it more likely that he would have studied with Patsab's student, rather than Patsab.

101 gTsang nag pa, *Tshad ma rnam par nges pa'i ṭīkā Legs bshad bsdus pa,* Otani University Tibetan Works Series, 2 (Kyōto: Otani University, 1989).

102 rMa bya pa Byang chub brtson 'grus, *dBu ma rtsa ba shes rab kyi 'grel pa 'Thad pa'i rgyan* (Rumtek, Sikkim: Dharma Chakra Center, 1975).

103 Ruegg, *Three Studies,* 164; Williams, "rMa bya pa," 205–8; and rMa bya, *'Thad pa'i rgyan,* 41–42.

104 Ruegg, *Three Studies,* 159–62. Ruegg points out that we do not know whether Patsab's view is here stated from an ultimate or conventional vantage point. Additionally, Mabja criticizes a third position, similar to that purportedly held by Khu Dodebar, that a Mādhyamika negates only with respect to the opponent's position and so does not have a negative thesis. This is regarded as Mabja Jangchub Yeshe's position. See Ruegg, *Three Studies,* 166–67. While Mabja Jangchub Tsondru reports these positions, he does not identify who held them; rather, this information is supplied by much later authors. As noted in the introduction to this book, the recent publications of eleventh- and twelfth-century Tibetan philosophical literature allows us to begin evaluating the accounts that later Tibetan authors gave of these earlier scholars and, as noted there, the results are mixed: we see portrayals of, for instance, Chapa's views that seem to be entirely off base.

105 In *'Thad pa'i rgyan* (p. 41ff) Mabja argues against "objectively gained [valid cognition]" (*dngos po'i stobs kyis zhugs*) or "valid cognition with an unmistaken mode of apprehension" (*'dzin stangs mi 'khrul pa'i tshad ma*) in favor of "valid cognition renowned in the world" (*'jig rten la grags pa'i tshad ma*), noting that the latter category includes the four types of valid cognition that were accepted in non-Buddhist schools, the same four types that Candrakīrti also accepted in the "worldly renown" context: direct perception, inference, analogy, and testimony. More on this topic is found in chapter 3.

106 Ruegg (*Three Studies,* 167–68) notes Mabja's argument against *sgrub byed 'phen pa'i thal 'gyur* ("consequences that imply proof") in his *'Thad pa'i rgyan* (Thimpu edition, 21a; Rumtek edition, 44). I discuss Mabja's arguments in detail in chapter 3.

107 For a discussion of bSod nams rtse mo's life see Davidson, *Tibetan Renaissance,* 338–43.

108 bSod nams rtse mo, *Byang chub sems dpa'i spyod pa la 'jug pa'i 'grel pa,* in *Sa skya pa'i bka' 'bum,* vol. 2 (Tokyo: Toyo Bunko, 1968), 515.2.5–6 (vol. *ca,* 335a.5–6). It will be interesting to evaluate this claim and the development of Sangpu exegesis of Śāntideva's text with recourse to the several early Kadampa commentaries now available.

109 bSod nams rtse mo, *sPyod pa la 'jug pa'i 'grel pa,* 495.4.1–496.1.3 (vol. *ca,* 296a.1–296b.3).

110 bSod nams rtse mo, *sPyod pa la 'jug pa'i 'grel pa,* 495.4.5–6 (vol. *ca,* 296a.5–6).

111 bSod nams rtse mo, *sPyod pa la 'jug pa'i 'grel pa,* 511.2.2–511.4.2 (vol. *ca,* 327a.2–328a.2).

112 For a discussion of Grags pa rgyal mtshan's life, see Davidson, *Tibetan Renaissance,* 343–52.

113 Grags pa rgyal mtshan's *rGyud kyi mngon par rtogs pa rin po che'i ljong shing* (in *Sa skya pa'i bka' 'bum,* vol. 3 [Tokyo: Toyo Bunko, 1968], 15.3.2 [vol. *cha,* 30a.2]) makes this five-fold division into: *'jig rten grags sde pa, bye brag smra ba dang tshul mtshungs pa* ("Mādhyamikas similar to Vaibhāṣikas"), *sgyu ma pa* ("Illusion-[like] Mādhyamikas"), *mdo sde spyod pa* ("Sautrāntika Mādhyamikas"), and *rnal 'byor spyod pa'i dbu ma pa* ("Yogic Practice Mādhyamikas"). The connection between Mādhyamikas of Worldly Renown and Prāsaṅgika is not made overtly by Drakpa Gyeltsen but by his later commentators.

114 When listing the four views in *Rin po che'i ljon shing,* 21.3.6–21.4.1, Drakpa calls the third and fourth *rgyun chad rab tu mi gnas pa* (perhaps "[Mental] Continuum Cutting Thoroughly Non-Abiding [Mādhyamikas]") and *zung 'jug rab tu mi gnas pa* (perhaps "Union Thoroughly Non-Abiding [Mādhyamikas]"), respectively. However, when discussing these, the third is called *dbu ma thal 'gyur ba* ("Prāsaṅgika Madhyamaka," 21.4.5) and the fourth is called *dbu ma rang rgyud pa* ("Svātantrika Madhyamaka," 22.1.1).

115 The three views seem to be varying ways of separating Madhyamaka from Yogācāra; the first two views—Yogācāra-Madhyamaka and, I believe, Prāsaṅgika—state how the Madhyamaka presentation of nirvāṇa differs from the Yogācāra position. The third view, claiming no essential difference between Yogācāra and Madhyamaka, does not discuss nirvāṇa directly. The Yogācāra-Madhyamaka view concludes on Grags pa, *Rin po che'i ljong shing,* 15.4.4 while the second view, introduced only by "certain Mādhyamikas" (*dbu ma pa kha cig*), is at 15.4.4–16.1.2.

116 Grags pa, *Rin po che'i ljong shing,* 21.4.6, pronounces that the Prāsaṅgika position "is not correct." The same text at 22.1.1–4 presents the Svātantrika view that allows for non-abiding nirvāṇa, allowing for a Buddha to be both always in meditative equipoise and able to aid sentient beings.

117 Grags pa, *Rin po che'i ljong shing,* 21.3.2–23.2.5–6.

118 Grags pa, *Rin po che'i ljong shing,* 22.4.6: *de ltar du da lta bod kyi dbu ma pa phal cher yang 'dod do / / yang dag pa ma yin te* ("Most contemporary Tibetan Mādhyamikas assert this. It is not correct") and 21.4.6–22.1.1: *slob dpon zla grags nyid kyis kyang / rigs pa drug cu pa'i 'grel pa las / bden pa gnyis su 'jog pa ni / 'jig rten pa'i blo la ltos te 'jog go zhes dam bcas pa 'gal bar 'gyur pa'i skyod yod do/* ("Also, [this view] has the fault of contradicting the master Candrakīrti's assertion, in his *Commentary on [Nāgārjuna's] Sixty Stanzas on Reasoning,* 'Truths are posited as two from the perspective of worldly awareness'"). I have not been able to locate this quote in Candrakīrti's commentary and assume it is Drakpa Gyeltsen's paraphrase.

119 Grags pa, *Rin po che'i ljong shing,* 16.1.4–5: *dbu ma la mos pa rnams la spyod pa dang bcas par sbyar ba ni gtam bya rin chen phreng ba dang / spyod pa la 'jug pa dang / dbu ma la 'jug pa la sogs pa yin pas de don du gnyer bas de dag la bslab par bya'o/.*

120 Grags pa, *Rin po che'i ljong shing,* 26.3.4: *zung 'jug gi tshul gyis nyams su blang ba.*

121 Drakpa Gyeltsen cites Asaṅga's *Mahāyānasūtrālaṃkāra,* the *Hevajra Tantra,* and the *Saṃpuṭa Tantra.*

122 Jackson, "Madhyamaka Studies," 27, discusses Sapaṇ's methodology for distinguishing Svātantrika and Prāsaṅgika and his reasons for holding the latter to be superior. It should be noted that Jackson's equating Sapaṇ's study of Candrakīrti's *Clear Words* with the birth of Sakya Prāsaṅgika study (p. 24) needs to be revised in light of the above discussion of Drakpa Gyeltsen's interest in Candrakīrti's *Entrance to the Middle.*

123 Jackson, "Madhyamaka Studies," 24, and van der Kuijp, "Notes on the Transmission," 8–9.

124 *Kar ma pa I, Dus gsum mkhyen pa* (1110–93), who had also studied Madhyamaka with Chapa (van der Kuijp, *Contributions,* 60). Elliot Sperling ("Lama to the King of Hsia," *The Journal of the Tibet Society* 7 [1987]: 32–33) points out that Dusum Kyenpa sent his student, Konchog Sengé (*gTsang po pa dKon mchog seng ge*), to the Tangut court, in whose service the latter died in 1218/1219. Upon his death, the "imperial preceptor" (*ti shih*) post was filled by Tishri Repa (*Ti shri Sangs rgyas ras chen,* 1164/1165–1236), who seems to have held the post up until the collapse of the Tangut state in 1227 (Sperling, p. 34, notes that he returned to Tibet at age sixty-three).

125 *'Jig rten mgon po;* Sperling, "Lama to the King," 32.

126 Sperling strongly suggests that the pattern of religious advisor established by Tibetans and Tanguts provided the model for Tibetan and Mongol relations; see Elliot Sperling, "Rtsa-mi lo-tsā-ba Sangs-rgyas grags-pa and the Tangut Background to Early Mongol-Tibetan Relations," in *Tibetan Studies: Proceedings of the 6th Seminar of the International Association for Tibetan Studies, Fagernes, 1992,* ed. Per Kvaerne (Oslo: Institute for Comparative Research in Human Culture, 1994), 801–24.

127 See for instance Tagtsang's (*sTag tshang lo tsa ba Shes rab rin chen,* b. 1405) lengthy criticism of Tsongkhapa's Prāsaṅgika, charging that his position is, in fact, Svātantrika, in Jeffrey Hopkins, *Maps of the Profound* (Ithaca, NY: Snow Lion Publications, 2003), 527–75.

Notes to Chapter 3

1 This discounts the possibility that Dharmakīrti *was* a Mādhyamika. Some Indian and Tibetan thinkers who blended Middle Way ontology with epistemological developments considered Dharmakīrti to be a proponent of the Middle Way. See Ernst Steinkellner, "Is Dharmakīrti a Mādhyamika?" in *Earliest Buddhism and Madhyamaka,* ed. David Seyfort Ruegg and Lambert Schmithausen (Leiden: E.J. Brill, 1990), 72–90.

2 Dharmakīrti is typically dated c. 600–660; however, Kimura detects some knowledge of Dharmakīrti's writings in Dharmapāla's work and dates the latter to c. 550–620. Kimura suggests Dharmakīrti is the elder of the two. See T. Kimura, "A New Chronology of Dharmakīrti," in *Dharmakīrti's Thought and Its Impact on Indian and Tibetan Philosophy,* ed. S. Katsura (Vienna: Österreichischen Akademie der Wissenschaften, 1999), 209–14.

3 In his *Pramāṇavārttika*, stanza II.1ab, we read: *pramāṇam avisaṃvādi jñānam arthakriyāsthitiḥ* / (Yūsho Miyasaka, "*Pramāṇavārttika-Kārikā* [Sanskrit and Tibetan]," *Acta Indologica* 2 [1971–72]: 2). At stanza II.5c, again characterizing valid cognition, he writes: *ajñātārthaprakāśo vā* / (Miyasaka, "*Pramāṇavārttika,*" 2). Dreyfus (Georges B.J. Dreyfus, *Recognizing Reality* [Albany, NY: State University of New York Press, 1997], 289) translates the first "Valid cognition is that cognition [which is] nondeceptive. [Nondeceptiveness consists] in the readiness [for the object] to perform a function." The second passage Dreyfus (*Recognizing Reality,* 290) translates "Or, [i.e., another explanation is that *pramāṇa*] is the revealing of a [yet] unknown thing." Considerable debate has focused on whether Dharmakīrti intended this second passage to define "valid cognition" and if so, whether it is to be taken in conjunction with the previous statement or as an alternative to it. Dharmakīrti gives a further definition of "valid cognition" in his *Pramāṇaviniścaya,* written later than his *Pramāṇavārttika,* stating that perception and inference are valid cognitions "because they are nondeceptive with respect to the purpose [of the action] in the application [toward an object] after having determined it" (Dreyfus, *Recognizing Reality,* 291).

Eli Franco (*Dharmakīrti on Compassion and Rebirth* [Vienna: Arbeitskreis für Tibetische und Buddhistische Studien Universität Wien, 1997], chapter 2, which is a reprint of his "The Disjunction in *Pramāṇavārttika, Pramāṇasiddhi* Chapter 5c," in *Studies in the Buddhist Epistemological Tradition* [Vienna: Österreichischen Akademie der Wissenschaften, 1991], 39–51), argues that in the opening verses of the *Pramāṇasiddhi* chapter, Dharmakīrti does not intend to define valid cognition such that he may then prove that the Buddha meets the definition but rather intends only to prove that the Buddha is valid (p. 57) using notions of validity known and accepted by Buddhists and non-Buddhists alike (64–66). Franco's argument does not harm my contention that Dharmakīrti regarded some cognitions—perception and inference—to be valid and not delusive. Furthermore, Franco's project of recovering Dharmakīrti's intention amid the "skillful but cunning commentators' tricks" (p. 54) is much the opposite of my present purpose, which is to show that the issue of what constitutes validity was hotly debated and developed by Dharmakīrti's commentators and that this debate was picked up by Mādhyamikas in the eleventh- and twelfth-century, who argued over whether any human cognition could be considered valid. If, as Franco holds (p. 60), Dharmottara represents a new turn in the Indian Buddhist epistemological tradition toward deep consideration of the notion of validity, the concern to define validity arose among epistemologists at roughly the same time as it arose amid Mādhyamikas, as Kamalaśīla's Madhyamaka-epistemology writings show. A rejoinder to Franco and an alternate interpretation of the same passage is found in Claus Oetke, "The Disjunction in the Pramāṇasiddhi," in *Dharmakīrti's Thought and its Impact on Indian and Tibetan Philosophy,* ed. Shoryu Katsura (Vienna: Österreichischen Akademie der Wissenschaften, 1999), 243–51.

4 A thorough discussion of Dharmakīrti's exploration of the two types of valid cognition and the corresponding two types of knowable objects, as well as the broader Indian background of these notions, is found in John D. Dunne, *Foundations of Dharmakīrti's Philosophy* (Boston: Wisdom Publications, 2004), 22ff and 79ff.

5 *Pramāṇasamuccaya,* stanzas I.3c and I.7cd; Hattori, *Dignāga,* 28, 176–77, and 180–81. Stanza I.8ab continues the list of what is not perception, including memory, desire, and perceptions made with faulty sense faculties. Surely Dreyfus (*Recognizing Reality,* 531, n. 16) is correct in stating that Dharmakīrti did not intend "cognitions of the conventional" to include inference. Dignāga here very clearly does not wish to include inference within cognitions of the conventional either, as he lists inference immediately after cognitions of the conventional in his list of pseudo-perceptions. However, this very listing casts aspersions on the status of inference in Dignāga's system; it does not follow that inference, not being included among cognitions of the conventional, must therefore be unproblematically valid, but instead suggests that cognitions of the conventional and inference share in a problematic status, that of pseudo-perceptions.

6 See Devendrabuddhi's comments in Vittorio A. van Bijlert, *Epistemology and Spiritual Authority* (Vienna: Arbeitskreis für Tibetische und Buddhistische Studien Universität Wien, 1989), 125.

7 Devendrabuddhi's *Pramāṇavārttikapañjikā,* ad II.6bc; Peking 5717, p. 6b.8–7a.2; van Bijlert, *Epistemology,* 156: *khyad par dang bcas pa'i mtshan nyid bshad pas spyi shes pa ni tshad ma ma yin no //.*

8 Stanza III.56ab on *anumānasiddhiḥ*; Miyasaka, "*Pramāṇavārttika,*" 48–49: *abhiprāyāvisaṃvādād api bhrānteḥ pramāṇatā /; / bsam pa la ni bslu med phyir // 'khrul pa yin yang tshad ma nyid /* "Since that mind is non-deceptive, it is just valid cognition even though it is mistaken." I adopt Ernst Steinkellner's emendation to the Tibetan from his *Verse-Index of Dharmakīrti's Works* (Vienna: Arbeitskreis für Tibetische und Buddhistische Studien Universität Wien, 1977), Appendix I, p. 219: *bslu : bsul.*

9 *Nyāyabinduṭīkā,* ad I.4; Stcherbatsky ed., 7.12–13: *bhrāntam hy anumāṇam / svapratibhāso 'narthe 'rthādhyavasāyena pravṛttatvāt /.*

10 Devendrabuddhi (in his *Pramāṇavārttikapañjikā,* ad II.1b; Peking 5717, p.2b.3–5; van Bijlert, *Epistemology,* 127), writing earlier than Dharmottara, likewise distinguishes inference as non-deceptive but mistaken, but without the further rationale for this distinction that Dharmottara provides. Inference's status as a second-class valid cognition leads Tillemans to adopt "incongruent," rather than "mistaken," to translate *bhrānta* as it applies to inference; thus, inference may be said to be "incongruent" but still "true," a more felicitous English than my calling inference "mistaken" but "non-deceptive." See Tom J.F. Tillemans, *Scripture, Logic, Language: Essays on Dharmakīrti and His Tibetan Successors* (Boston: Wisdom Publications, 1999), 8–11.

11 Toru Funayama, "Kamalaśīla's Interpretation of 'Non-Erroneous' in the Definition of Direct Perception and Related Problems," in *Dharmakīrti's Thought,* 80. As Funayama points out (p. 82, n. 42), there is some evidence in Dharmakīrti's *Pramāṇaviniścaya,* stanza I.33, for equating "unmistaken" and "nondeceptive."

12 *Pramāṇavārttika,* I.215; Miyasaka, "*Pramāṇavārttika,*" 146.

13 Steinkellner concludes that Karṇakagomin must have written after Dharmottara's *Pramāṇaviniścayaṭīkā* and consequently assigns him to around 800; Ernst Steinkellner, "Miszellen zur Erkenntnistheoretisch-Logischen Schule des Buddhismus," *Wiener Zeitschrift für die Kunde Südasiens* 23 (1979): 148–49.

14 Rahula Sankrityayana, *Karṇakagomin's Commentary on the Pramāṇavārttikavṛtti of Dharmakīrti* (Kyoto: Rinsen, 1982), 392.14–15: *anumānena ca dvividhena vastubalapravṛttenāgamāśritena.*

15 For a further discussion, see Tom J.F. Tillemans, *Materials for the Study of Āryadeva, Dharmapāla and Candrakīrti,* vol. 1 (Vienna: Arbeitskreis für Tibetische und Buddhistische Studien Universität Wien, 1990), 24–35.

16 Whether this rejection of the scope of logic entails a concomitant reliance on Buddhist scripture on the part of Candrakīrti's early supporters remains to be seen.

17 Sara L. McClintock, "The Role of the 'Given' in the Classification of Śāntarakṣita and Kamalaśīla as Svātantrika-Mādhyamikas," in *The Svātantrika-Prāsaṅgika Distinction,* ed. Georges B.J. Dreyfus and Sara L. McClintock (Boston: Wisdom Publications, 2002), 125–71, particularly her conclusion on p. 151. McClintock rejects Tillemans's conclusion that Śāntarakṣita and Kamalaśīla are quasi-realists. Tillemans concludes that Śāntarakṣita's and Kamalaśīla's reliance on the Epistemological tradition indicates "a version of the ideas of deference [to an objective world] and self-assurance [in the ability to know that world] that we have taken to be central to realism." See Tom J.F. Tillemans, "Metaphysics for Mādhyamikas," in *The Svātantrika-Prāsaṅgika Distinction,* 111. Both authors utilize Sellars's notion of the epistemological "given" as a means for evaluating Śāntarakṣita's and Kamalaśīla's views. See Wilfrid Sellars, *Empiricism and the Philosophy of Mind* (Cambridge: Harvard University Press, 1997), particularly pp. 68–69.

18 McClintock, "The Role of the 'Given,'" 143; Śāntarakṣita's *Tattvasaṃgraha,* 2041–43 and Kamalaśīla's *Pañjikā* thereon. It is interesting to note that Kamalaśīla equates, per Vinītadeva, "unmistaken" and "non-deceptive." That Kamalaśīla wrote later than Vinītadeva is established in Krasser, "On the Relationship," 151–58. Funayama ("Kamalaśīla's Interpretation," 81) notes that Kamalaśīla's adoption of Vinītadeva's equation runs overtly counter to Dharmottara's criticism, discussed above, of Vinītadeva.

19 McClintock, "The Role of the 'Given,'" 146 and 170, n. 88, referring to Kamalaśīla's *Tattvasaṃgrahapañjikā, ad* 586–87.

20 McClintock, "The Role of the 'Given,'" 150 and 171, n. 102, referring to Kamalaśīla's *Tattvasaṃgrahapañjikā, ad* 3338.

21 Nāgārjuna's text, stanza XXIV.8, reads: "Buddhas teach the Dharma in dependence on two truths: Worldly, conventional truth and ultimate truth"; de Jong, *Mūlamadhyamakakārikāḥ,* 34: *dve satye samupāśritya buddhānāṃ dharmadeśanā / lokasaṃvṛtisatyaṃ ca satyaṃ ca paramārthataḥ //.*

22 Tillemans, *Materials,* 44, 48–51.

23 *Madhyamakāvatāra,* stanza VI.23cd; Louis de la Vallée Poussin, *Madhyamakāvatāra par Candrakīrti,* Bibliotheca Buddhica, 9 (Osnabrück, Germany: Biblio Verlag, 1970), 102.10–11: *yang dag mthong yul gang de de nyid de / mthong ba brdzun pa kun rdzob bden par gsungs /;* Sanskrit preserved in Louis de la Vallée Poussin, *Bodhicaryāvatārapañjikā, Prajñākaramati's Commentary to the Bodhicaryāvatāra of Çāntideva,* Bibiotheca Indica 3 (1905): 361.4: *samyagdṛśāṃ yo viṣayaḥ sa tattvaṃ mṛṣādṛśāṃ saṃvṛtisatyam uktam //.*

24 The addition of "found" (*rnyed pa*) is supported by Candrakīrti's commentary (La Vallée Pousin, *Madhyamakāvatāra,* 102.16–17): *don dam pa ni yang dag par gzigs pa*

rnams kyi ye shes kyi khyad par gyi yul nyid kyis bdag gi ngo bo rnyed pa yin / ("The ultimate is the nature found by being the very referent particular to the wisdom of those with pure vision.") and (102.20–103.1) *mthong ba rdzun pa'i stobs las bdag gi yod pa rnyed pa /* ("the existence of a self found due to the force of erroneous vision").

25 We see evidence in Abhayākaragupta's writings that Candrakīrti's two truths were also the focus of debate in India in the twelfth century. For complete references, see chapter 1, note 113.

26 *Svatantrānumāna, rang rgyud kyi rjes dpag.* This term is frequently translated as "autonomous inferences", a translation that relies on Gelukpa authors' equation (based on the Indian lexicon of Amarasiṃha, the *Amarakośa* [Peking 5787, vol. 140]) of *rang rgyud* with *rang dbang,* "own power," and *bdag dbang,* "self-powered"; see Jeffrey Hopkins, "A Tibetan Delineation of Different Views of Emptiness in the Indian Middle Way Schools," *Tibetan Journal* 14, no. 1 (1989): note 65. Such a translation allows the Gelukpa loading of this term, in which "autonomous inferences" are understood as inferences in which the "three modes"—the reason being a property of the inferential subject and the forward and reverse entailments—are established by way of their own character (*rang gi mtshan nyid kyi grub pa*). Such establishment is clearly unacceptable for a Mādhyamika and, consequently, such inferences are as well. The use of "autonomous inferences" by certain Mādhyamikas—most notably, Bhāvaviveka, Śāntarakṣita, Kamalaśīla, and Jñānagarbha—allow Gelukpa authors to categorize them as Svātantrika Mādhyamikas. However, part of what I hope to accomplish in this book is to show that the projects of later Tibetan authors' doxographies do not accurately reflect the debates of eleventh- and twelfth-century Tibet, the period in which the place of formal inference within Madhyamaka thought was seriously debated. As will be shown, it is not at all clear that Chapa understood the inferences he employed to be "established by way of their own character." Rather, he emphasizes the need to employ inferences "in one's own continuum," utilizing reasons that are acceptable to oneself. As will be seen, this runs counter to Candrakīrti's use only of inferences "renowned to others," inferences which one employs against an opponent utilizing reasons the opponent accepts to reach conclusions the opponent cannot accept.

27 Rather than "Prāsaṅgika," Chapa writes of "Candrakīrti and others"; Phya pa chos kyi seṅ ge, *dbu ma śar gsum gyi stoṅ thun,* ed. Helmut Tauscher (Vienna: Arbeitskreis für Tibetische und Buddhistische Studien Universität Wien, 1999), 58.9: *slob dpon zla ba grags pa la sogs pa.* As will be seen below, Jayānanda is among those figuring in Chapa's thinking as "others." Chapa's discussion of mistaken and unmistaken consciousness (*blo 'khrul ba dang ma 'khrul ba*) and the two truths—the "setting forth the opponent's position" (*gzhan gyi lugs dgod pa*)—immediately follows this passage.

28 Phya pa, *dbu ma shar gsum,* 58.13–15: *sa thob pa'i mnyam bzhag dang sangs rgyas kyi sa na . . . chos nyid rtogs pas yang dag pa'i blo ma 'khrul zhes gdags ste /* "The meditative absorptions of those who have attained a ground (*bhūmi*) and those on the Buddha ground, due to realizing the final nature, are considered correct, unmistaken awareness."

29 Stanza VI.24; Chapa's citation varies slightly from the Tibetan text edited by La Vallée Poussin, *Madhyamakāvatāra,* 103.11.

30 Phya pa, *dbu ma shar gsum,* 59.1: *mthong pa brdzun pa'i blo 'khrul ba.* It should be noted as well that Candrakīrti seems in this stanza to gloss "seeing" (*mthong ba*) with "consciousness" (*shes pa*), justifying Chapa's substitution (discussed just above) of "awareness" (*blo*) for "seeing."

31 Phya pa, *dbu ma shar gsum,* 59.4–7. Those with defective senses "superimpose" two moons upon one (they see two moons instead of one) or floating hairs where none exist; others "superimpose" the notion of "self" (*bdag, ātman*) due to specious reasoning and false beliefs.

32 Phya pa, *dbu ma shar gsum,* 59.1–4. Chapa here certainly draws on Candrakīrti's somewhat perverse admission—following his lengthy criticisms of Dignāga's valid cognition system and Bhāvaviveka's adoption of it in a Madhyamaka context—of all four types of valid cognition in his *Prasannapadā;* see La Vallée Poussin, *Prasannapadā,* 75.9. Chapa's framing Candrakīrti's discussion as an elaboration of the various types of mistaken consciousness is an interesting twist on a somewhat mysterious passage in the *Prasannapadā.*

33 Chapa's text (Phya pa, *dbu ma shar gsum,* 62.2) cites the final line of this stanza quite differently from La Vallée Poussin's text (La Vallée Poussin, *Madhyamakāvatāra,* 112.7) or any of the canonical editions, reading *blun po tshad mar gyur pa ga la yod /* for *blun po tshad mar rigs pa'ang ma yin no /.* The more standard edition translates: "It is not reasonable for foolishness also to be valid cognition." Chapa clearly understands *tshad ma* in this stanza to mean "valid cognition" and not simply "authority." This point is taken up in more detail in Jayānanda's discussion of the stanza below.

34 Phya pa, *dbu ma shar gsum,* 59.13: *blo 'khrul ba log pa'i mthong ba.*

35 La Vallée Poussin, *Madhyamakāvatāra,* 107.1: *gti mug rang bzhin sgrib phyir kun rdzob ste /;* la Vallée Poussin, *Bodhicaryāvatārapañjikā* (1905), 353.3: *mohaḥ svabhāvāvaraṇāddhi saṃvṛtiḥ.*

36 *Laṅkāvatārasūtra,* stanza X.429; Sanskrit text in Bunyiu Nanjio, *The Laṇkāvatāra Sūtra,* Bibliotheca Otaniensis, vol. 1 (Kyoto: Otani University Press, 1923), 319: *bhāvā vidyanti saṃvṛtyā paramārthe na bhāvakāḥ / niḥsvabhāveṣu yā bhrāntistatsatyaṃ saṃvṛtirbhavet //;* "The production of things [is so] conventionally; it is not so ultimately. That [consciousness] which is mistaken regarding naturelessness is asserted as the obscurer of truth." Note that the sūtra's use of *bhrānti* lends more credence to Chapa's equation of delusion, obscuration, and mistake.

37 Phya pa, *dbu ma shar gsum,* 60.4–5: *blo'i 'jug pa zhi ba la sgrib pa'i gti' mug gi rang bzhin kun rdzob kyi blo'i yul du bden par brtags pas kun rdzob kyi bden pa ste /.*

38 Phya pa, *dbu ma shar gsum,* 59.14: *ci'ang bltar med pa.*

39 Phya pa, *dbu ma shar gsum,* 60.16: *'phags pa'i mnyam bzhag 'khrul pa zad pas cir yang dmigs par byar med pa.*

40 Phya pa, *dbu ma shar gsum,* 58.13–15.

41 La Vallée Poussin, *Madhyamakāvatāra,* 109.6.

42 La Vallée Poussin, *Madhyamakāvatāra,* 357.20.

43 Chapa's critique of Prāsaṅgikas' denial that Buddhas have consciousnesses "with appearance" (*snang bcas*) is taken up in chapter 5.

44 We could posit consciousnesses arising from Candrakīrti's "clear faculties" to qualify for "conventional valid cognition" (*tha snyad pa'i tshad ma*), a status that would fall far short of realization of the ultimate but still bear validity in the world.

45 Candrakīrti writes: "Because it obstructs (*rmongs par byed pa*) sentient beings from viewing the entity just as it abides, it is delusion (*moha, gti mug*); it is the ignorance (*avidyā, ma rig pa*) that reifies the non-existent nature of entities and has the character of obscuring (*sgrib pa*) perception of the nature" (La Vallée Poussin, *Madhyamakāvatāra,* 107.5–8: *de la 'dis sems can rnams ji ltar gnas pa'i dngos po lta ba la rmongs par byed pas na gti mug ste / ma rig pa dnogs po'i rang gi ngo bo yod pa ma yin pa sgro 'dogs par byed pa rang bzhin mthong ba la sgrib pa'i bdag nyid can ni kun rdzob bo /*).

46 La Vallée Poussin, *Madhyamakāvatāra,* 107.15–16: *rang bzhin ni ma rig pa dang ldan pa rnams la rnam pa thams cad du mi snang ngo /.*

47 Jayānanda, *Madhyamakāvatāraṭīkā, sde dge* edition 3870, *dbu ma,* vol. *ra,* 144a.4: *gti mug gi stobs kyis yod pa dang med pa la sogs pa dang bral ba'i de kho na nyid mi snang ba* ("Through the power of delusion, suchness—free from existence, non-existence, and so forth—does not appear") and 144b.3: *ji ltar gnas pa'i dngos po lta ba la zhes bya ba ni stong pa nyid kyi dngos po mthong ba la'o /* ("[Candrakīrti writes] 'from viewing the entity just as it abides' [meaning] from seeing the entity of emptiness"). This latter passage expands upon Candrakīrti's autocommentary, translated in note 45. Jayānanda interprets *ji ltar gnas pa* as emptiness; thus, in his view, delusion obstructs one from viewing emptiness, contrary to Huntington's interpretation (*The Emptiness of Emptiness: An Introduction to Early Indian Mādhyamika* [Honolulu: University of Hawaii Press, 1989], 232, n. 47) that delusion "causes sentient beings to become muddled in the view of entities as they are [in the full context of everyday experience]" and La Vallée Poussin's interpretation (*Muséon* 11 [1910], 303) that "les creatures se trompent [*mohayati*] dans la vue des choses comme elles sont."

48 Jayānanda, *Madhyamakāvatāraṭīkā,* 144a.4: *gti mug gi rang bzhin can gyi kun rdzob.*

49 La Vallée Poussin, *Madhyamakāvatāra,* 107.10: *'jig rten phyin ci log tu gyur pa'i kun rdzob tu bden pa.*

50 Jayānanda, *Madhyamakāvatāraṭīkā,* 142b.6: *'jig rten pas phyin ci log nyid du shes pa yin no.*

51 Jayānanda, *Madhyamakāvatāraṭīkā,* 146b.2–3: *'dir sgrib pa ni rnam pa gnyis te / nyon mongs pa can gyi dang / nyon mongs pa can ma yin par ma rig pa'o / / de la nyon mongs pa can gyi ma rig pa ni 'khor ba'i rgyun 'jug pa'i rgyu yin la / nyon mongs pa can ma yin pa'i ma rig pa ni gzugs la sogs pa snang ba'i rgyu yin no/ / bcom ldan 'das rnams la ni sgrib pa gnyis ka mi mnga' bas rgyu med pas 'bras bu med pa'i phyir 'khor ba dang gzugs la sogs pa dag snang ba med pa'i phyir ji ltar kun rdzob tsam snang bar 'gyur /.*

52 Candrakīrti likewise posits distinctions between obscurational truths and mere conventionalities. In his autocommentary to stanza VI.28, he writes, "That [ultimate truth] and anything considered erroneous even conventionally are not obscurational truths" (La Vallée Poussin, *Madhyamakāvatāra,* 107.16–17: *de dang gang zhig kun rdzob tu yang rdzun pa ni kun rdzob kyi bden pa ma yin no*). This dispenses with one type of "mere conventionality," those things not considered true even in the world. Candrakīrti continues, separating out from obscurational truths the appearances to realized beings, demarcating a second class of mere conventionalities: "Obscurational truths are posited through the force of afflictive ignorance. For those Hearers, Solitary Realizers, and Bodhisattvas who have dispelled

afflictive ignorance, who see composite phenomena as similar to the existence of a reflection and so forth, those [obscurational truths] have a fabricated nature; they are not true because [these beings] do not exaggerate these as true. [Obscurational truths] deceive fools. However, these are mere conventionalities to the others, since [these appear as] just illusion-like dependent arisings" (La Vallée Poussin, *Madhyamakāvatāra,* 107.18–108.6: *nyon mongs pa can gyi ma rig pa'i dbang gis kun rdzob kyi bden pa rnam par bzhag go / de yang nyan thos dang rang sangs rgyas dang byang chub sems dpa' nyon mongs pa can gyi ma rig pa spangs pa / 'du byed gzugs brnyan la sogs pa'i yod pa nyid dang 'dra bar gzigs pa rnams la ni bcos ma'i rang bzhin* yin gyi / bden pa ni ma yin te / bden par mngon par rlom pa med pa'i phyir ro / / byis pa rnams la ni bslu bar byed pa yin la / de las gzhan pa rnams la ni sgyu ma la sogs pa ltar rten cing 'brel bar 'byung ba nyid kyis kun rdzob tsam du 'gyur ro /* * Jayānanda here reads *rang bzhin can,* which I adopt in my translation).

Jayānanda (*Madhyamakāvatāraṭīkā,* 145b.6) reads *de las gzhan* as referring to people: Hearers, Solitary Realizers, and Bodhisattvas. This differs from Huntington's translation, "other things" (*Emptiness of Emptiness,* 233, n. 47). Jayānanda further reads Candrakīrti's *sgyu ma la sogs pa ltar rten cing 'brel bar 'byung ba nyid kyis* ("since [these appear as] just illusion-like dependent arisings") as *sgyu ma la sogs pa ltar rten cing 'brel bar 'byung ba nyid du snang bas* ("since these appear as just illusion-like dependent arisings"), making it clear that what are obscurational truths for ordinary people appear to these more realized beings as dependent arisings, without the conception that these appearances are true. It should be noted that Tsong kha pa, in his *dGongs pa rab gsal,* argues at length against the idea that "mere conventionalities" are not also obscurational truths.

53 Jayānanda, *Madhyamakāvatāraṭīkā,* 146a.2–4.

54 Jayānanda, *Madhyamakāvatāraṭīkā,* 145b.6.

55 Candrakīrti states (La Vallée Poussin, *Madhyamakāvatāra,* 108.6–9) *de yang shes bya'i sgrib pa'i mtshan nyid can ma rig pa tsam kun tu spyod pa'i phyir / snang ba dang bcas pa'i spyod yul can gyi 'phags pa rnams la snang gi / snang ba med pa'i spyod yul mnga' ba rnams la ni ma yin no /* ("These, also, due to the activity of mere ignorance that has the character of staining the object of knowledge, appear to those āryas whose sphere of activities has appearances but do not [appear] to those lords whose sphere of activities is without appearance"). Jayānanda (*Madhyamakāvatāraṭīkā,* 145b.7–146a.1) reads *de yang zhes bya ba ni sgyu ma la sogs pa ltar rten cing 'brel par 'byung ba nyid du snang ba gang yin pa'o / / shes bya'i sgrib pa'i mtshan nyid can ma rig pa tsam kun tu spyod pa'i phyir zhes bya ba ni yod pa dang med pa la sogs pa dang bral ba'i de kho na nyid ni shes bya yin la / de'i sgrib pa ni gang gis de mi snang bar byed pa'o /* ("[Candrakīrti writes] 'These, also,': all that appears as illusion-like dependent arisings. [He writes] 'Due to the activity of mere ignorance that has the character of staining the object of knowledge': suchness which is free from existence, non-existence, and so forth is the object of knowledge. That which stains that [suchness] causes it not to appear"). Thus, Jayānanda understands this level of ignorance that causes ordinary appearances to obstruct knowledge of emptiness: *shes bya'i sgrib* is understood to mean "obstructs the object of knowledge [that is, emptiness]" rather than "obstructs [knowledge of all] objects of knowledge" or "obstructions to omniscience" as is the Gelukpa reading.

56 In doing so, Jayānanda takes a very straightforward reading of Candrakīrti's statement, noted just above (La Vallée Poussin, *Madhyamakāvatāra,* 108.7–9), *snang ba dang bcas pa'i spyod yul can gyi 'phags pa rnams la snang gi / snang ba med pa'i spyod yul mnga' ba rnams la ni ma yin no /* ("[These things] appear to those āryas whose sphere of activities has appearances but do not [appear] to those lords whose sphere of activities is without appearance."), in which Candrakīrti separates a certain class of āryas from Buddhas. This will be discussed further below and in chapter 5.

57 La Vallée Poussin, *Madhyamakāvatāra,* 108.3–4: *byis pa rnams la ni bslu bar byed pa yin la /.*

58 Jayānanda, *Madhyamakāvatāraṭīkā,* 145a.7–145b.5, especially 145b.4: *byis pa rnams la bden pa ma yin pa la bden par zhen pas slu bar byed pa yin.*

59 One could well interpret Candrakīrti's statement as opposing ordinary valid cognition, as well. However, to see it as opposing a technical usage of valid cognition, one would need to find an equation of "valid cognition" and "non-deceptive" in the writings of Dignāga, Vasubandhu, or Dharmapāla or attempt to show Candrakīrti's familiarity with Dharmakīrti's corpus. On the other hand, one could argue that Candrakīrti does not intend to implicate valid cognition in this statement and that Jayānanda simply adopts Candrakīrti's "deceive," also without intending to criticize the Dharmakīrti tradition. However, as we will see below, Jayānanda explicitly addresses some of his criticism to Dharmakīrti and his followers.

60 Commenting on stanza VI.29; Jayānanda, *Madhyamakāvatāraṭīkā,* 149b.1–6, especially 149b.6: *nyon mongs pa can ma yin pa'i ma rig pas phung po la sogs pa snang ba'i 'khrul pa yod pas so.*

61 In chapter 5, I examine at length Jayānanda's exposition of Candrakīrti's claim that mind and mental factors cease upon buddhahood. That claim makes quite clear that all notions of subject and object, in which common perception is mired, are rejected. In his comments on stanza VI.29, Jayānanda notes that "Due to the cessation of all conceptuality, the nature [that is, the emptiness] of the aggregates and so forth is realized" (Jayānanda, *Madhyamakāvatāraṭīkā,* 149b.7–150a.1: *de'i tshe rnam par rtog pa thams cad log pas phung po la sogs pa rnams kyi rang bzhin rtogs pa yin no /*). Conceptuality opposes realization of emptiness. He further explains that this nature is ultimate truth and one who realizes this nature possesses "the complete cessation of the movement of mind and mental factors."

62 Commenting on stanza VI.30; Jayānanda, *Madhyamakāvatāraṭīkā,* 151a.6–7: *'di'i don ni 'dir mi slu ba nyid yin par 'gyur na tshad ma nyid du 'gyur ba yin la /.*

63 When translating Candrakīrti's stanzas and autocommentary, the first line of this stanza would then more comfortably translate as "If the world were authoritative, the world would see suchness." Elsewhere, in commenting on Candrakīrti's stanza VI.3, Jayānanda echoes Candrakīrti in calling Nāgārjuna an "authoritative person" (*tshad mar gyur pa'i skyes bu*); see *Madhyamakāvatāraṭīkā,* 112a.6–112b.3. Interpreting Candrakīrti as referring to authoritative persons as separate from "the world" allows for the possibility that Candrakīrti accepts that valid cognition (as a mental state) exists within the world. Jayānanda's interpretation here does not allow that reading.

64 Jayānanda, *Madhyamakāvatāraṭīkā,* 151a.7–151b.1: *mi slu ba nyid kyang dngos po ji lta ba bzhin du gnas pa yong su shes pa'i rgyu mtshan can yin la / yongs su shes pa de yang yod pa dang med pa dang bral ba'i dngos po yongs su shes pa yin no zhes pa'o / / des na*

'jig rten pas de kho na nyid mthong bar 'gyur la / de'i phyir ma rig pa spangs par 'gyur ro /. Candrakīrti likewise equates "authority," "seeing suchness," and "having dispelled ignorance" in his comments on this stanza; La Vallée Poussin, *Madhyamakāvatāra,* 112.8–10.

65 Jayānanda, *Madhyamakāvatāraṭīkā,* 151b.1–2: *dngos po ci lta ba bzhin du gnas pa yongs su ma shes pa dang / yod pa dang med pa nyid la sogs pa'i phyin ci log gi dngos por sgro btags pa la blun po zhes bya la /.*

66 La Vallée Poussin, *Madhyamakāvatāra,* 111.18–19: *de kho na nyid bsam pa la 'phags pa rnams kho na tshad ma yin* ("In considering suchness, āryas are the only authorities").

67 Jayānanda, *Madhyamakāvatāraṭīkā,* 151b.6: *'phags pa'i lam khong du chud par zhes bya ba ni mthong ba'i lam khong du chud par bya ba'i phyir ro /* ("[Candrakīrti writes] 'Realizing the āryas' path' [meaning] for the sake of realizing the path of seeing").

68 Jayānanda, *Tarkamudgara,* stanza 1; Toh. 3869, *sde dge bstan 'gyur, dbu ma,* vol. *ya,* 374b.3–4: */ yul dngos stobs kyis zhugs pa yi / / tshad mas de nyid rtogs so zhes / / chos kyi grags pa'i rjes 'brang ba'i / / rtog ge ba rnams smra bar byed /.*

69 See Tillemans, *Metaphysics for Mādhyamikas,* 111, and above, note 17.

70 Justification for this move might be found in Dharmakīrti's *Pramāṇaviniścaya,* Toh. 4211, *sde dge* edition, 197a.5ff.

71 I think it clear that Jayānanda intends to include his "Svātantrika" opponents among "Logicians following Dharmakīrti" at the opening of his *Tarkamudgara.*

72 Jayānanda, *Tarkamudgara,* stanza 2, 374b.4: */ blo gang bcad don thob byed pa / / tshad ma yin zhes kha cig smra / / la la ma rtogs don gsal 'dod / / gzhan dag bden pa'i don rtogs smra /* ("Some say that the awareness that reaches an identified object is valid cognition. Some assert that [valid cognition] reveals a [previously] unknown object. Other say [valid cognition] knows a true object"). Williams notes that Śākya mchog ldan's citation of a passage attributed to rMa bya byang chub brtson 'grus bears a close resemblance to this stanza. The reading is consistent with rMa bya's views, discussed below, and adds clarity to Jayānanda's stanza; it reads: *bcad don thob byed nus pa mi slu ba / tshad ma'i mtshan nyid yin zhes kha cig zer / ma rtogs yul la 'dzin pa ma 'khrul bas / sgro 'dogs sel ba'i don ldog kha cig 'dod /* ("Some say the definition of valid cognition is 'non-deceptive, able to reach an identified object.' Some assert that [valid cognition] has the meaning of removing superimposition upon a [previously] unknown object by way of an unmistaken apprehension"). See Paul Williams, "rMa bya pa Byang chub brtson 'grus on Madhyamaka Method," *Journal of Indian Philosophy* 13 (1985): 220–221, n. 11. rMa bya makes clear that "able to reach an identified object" marks a cognition as "non-deceptive" and that this status is the opponent's litmus of valid cognition. His addition of "by way of an unmistaken apprehension" would seem to be his own addition, which he attributes to a second opponent (much as Jayānanda attributes the views in this stanza to three different sources). One is reminded of the Vinītadeva-Kamalaśīla tradition of redefining valid cognition as "unmistaken." rMa bya's clarifications and additions reveal both development of Jayānanda's ideas and the facility of Tibetan composition.

73 Jayānanda, *Tarkamudgara,* stanza 8, 374b.7: */ smig rgyu la ni chu bzhin du / / rdzas ldog rdzas su 'thad ma yin / / de lta yin na tshad ma ni / / dngos po'i yul can ma yin zhing /* ("Similar to water in a mirage, substance [from among] substance and isolate is not feasible. If that is so, valid cognition is not a consciousness of an entity").

74 Jayānanda, *Tarkamudgara,* stanza 11cd 12ab, 375a.2: */ bden don rtogs pa tshad ma yi / / mtshan nyid min te gang gi phyir / / bden nyid grub pa med phyir dang / / tshad min tshad mar 'gyur phyir ro /* ("Knowing a true object is not the definition of valid cognition. Why? Because truthfulness is not established and because invalid cognition would become valid cognition").

75 Jayānanda, *Tarkamudgara,* stanza 13ab, 375a.2–3: */ yul bden yin par 'gyur zhig grang / / log shes tshad mar 'gyur pa'i phyir/* ("Counting [appearances] as true objects would make wrong consciousness become valid cognition").

76 Candrakīrti also seems to pit his reading of the two truths against the possibility of worldly valid cognition although, as noted above, understanding *Entrance to the Middle* VI.30 as denying that the world are authoritative persons allows for the possibility that valid cognition (the mental state) exists in the world.

77 Phya pa, *dbu ma shar gsum,* 1.18–20: *mthar thug dpyod pa'i tshad mas gtan la phab pa don dam pa'i bden pa dang / mthar thug mi dpyod pa'i tshad mas gtan la phab pa kun rdzob kyi bden pa gnyis su dbye'o //* ("The two-fold division is ultimate truth, delineated by the valid cognition of final analysis, and obscurational truths, delineated by the valid cognition of non-final analysis").

78 Chapa makes this point clearly, stating that "All grounds of objects of knowledge do not surpass [that is, are encompassed within] the two truths"; Phya pa, *dbu ma shar gsum,* 1.12–13: *shes bya'i sa thams cad bden pa gnyis las ma 'das pas.* An additional outflow of this point, discussed at length in chapter 4, is that ultimate truth is an object of knowledge, which is a claim Candrakīrti, Śāntideva, Jayānanda, Mabja, and even Ngok Lotsawa reject.

79 Chapa states that "All consciousnesses that do not comprehend finality are called *saṃvṛti;* because they veil the meaning of reality, they are obscurational"; Phya pa, *dbu ma shar gsum,* 14.16–17: *mthar thug mi 'jal ba'i blo thams cad ni saṃ bhri ti zhes pa yang dag pa'i don la sgrib pas kun rdzob po //.* He notes that worldly consciousnesses (*khams gsum pa'i blo*) and those of Hearers and others (realized beings who are yet not Buddhas) share in the etymology (*sgra bshad*) but are not "the bases of engagement" (*'jug pa'i gzhi*) of the term, while consciousnesses of Buddhas having appearances are the bases of engagement but do not share in the etymology.

80 Phya pa, *dbu ma shar gsum,* 15.1–2: *de'i yul dpyad mi bzod pa'i snang ba grub pa thams cad ni 'khrul pa'i bsam ngor bden pas kun rdzob kyi bden pa'o //.* To express the difference between "truth" in "obscurational truth" and what is "really" true, Chapa cites Nāgārjuna's famous dictum that "only nirvāṇa is true" from *Yuktiṣaṣṭikā,* stanza 35. For Candrakīrti's comments on that stanza, see Cristina Anna Scherrer-Schaub, *Yuktiṣaṣṭikāvṛtti. Commentaire à la soixantaine sur le raisonnement ou Du vrai enseignement de la causalité par le Maitre indien Candrakīrti,* Mélanges chinois et bouddhiques, 25 (Bruselles: Institut belge des hautes etudes chinoises, 1991), 75–76 and 263.

81 Phya pa, *dbu ma shar gsum,* 16.4: *mthar thug 'jal ba'i yul du mi bden la ma dpyad pa'i bsam ngor bden pa kun rdzob kyi bden pa'i mtshan nyid do //* ("The definition of obscurational truth is that which is not true as an object of cognition of finality but is true in the perspective of non-analytical thinking"). This is Chapa's definition of obscurational truths, rather than the etymology given just above.

82 Phya pa, *dbu ma shar gsum,* 16.20–22: *don dam pa'i bden pa'i mtshan nyid ni mthar*

thug 'jal ba'i tshad ma'i yul du bden pa ste / ldog pa 'ga' zhig la khyad par dpyad pas bden pa'i zhen pa bzlog du myed pa ni dpyad bzod pa yin la de 'jal ba ni mthar thug 'jal ba'i tshad ma yin la de'i gzhal byar bden pa don dam pa'i bden pa'o // ("The definition of ultimate truth is that which is true as the referent of a valid cognition that cognizes finality. The unreversibility of the conception of truth through analyzing attributes in a specific isolate is "bearing analysis." The cognition of that is the valid cognition comprehending finality. Being true as the object of that comprehension is ultimate truth"). Chapa, in contradistinction to most Tibetan scholars of his day and later, holds that ultimate truth bears analysis because when analyzed, one's conception of its truth is not reversed.

83 Phya pa, *dbu ma shar gsum,* 18.2–3: *mthar thug mi 'jal ba'i yul 'khrul pa'i gzung yul ma yin pa ni yang dag pa'i kun rdzob po //.*

84 Phya pa, *dbu ma shar gsum,* 15.8–12: *rtag pa'i dngos por zhen pa lta bu shes bya la mi srid pa la srid par zhen pa'i 'khrul pa dang zla ba gnyis dang don spyi lasogs par snang ba lta bu don byed pas stong ba gzung yul du byed pa'i 'khrul pa la sgrib pas khyab kyang de sangs rgyas la mi mnga' bas sgrib pa dang bcas par thal ba'i skyon brjod na gtan tshigs ma grub pa yin la / dpyad mi bzod pa'i yul can gyi 'khrul pa mnga' ba'i phyir sgrib pa dang bcas par 'gyur ro zhe na khyab pa ma grub pa yin no //.* This passage is discussed again in chapter 5, on the topic of how Buddhas perceive ordinary appearances. As I state there, the passage indicates three levels of mistake: the mistake that binds us in cyclic existence, the useful mistake that allows us to utilize concepts (here grouped with the perceptual mistake of those with faulty sense faculties—a common Madhyamaka metaphor for how we perceive the ordinary world), and the mistake that allows even Buddhas to perceive appearances.

85 *rMa bya Byang chub brtson 'grus,* d. 1185.

86 Williams ("Madhyamaka Method," 207 and 220, nn. 7 and 8) suspects that the primary locus for Mabja's views on these issues may be lost. He notes that Mabja refers readers of his *'Thad pa'i rgyan* to his *dBu ma'i de kho na nyid gtan la dbab pa* for a more thorough discussion of these issues. Williams suspects that the latter was the subtitle to Mabja's commentary to Jayānanda's *Hammer of Logic;* Williams takes as the main title that used by the Eighth Karmapa, Mi bskyod rdo rje, to refer to Mabja's commentary, *Rigs rgyan snang ba.*

87 rMa bya pa Byang chub brtson 'grus, *dBu ma rtsa ba shes rab kyi 'grel pa 'Thad pa'i rgyan* (Rumtek, Sikkim: Dharma Chakra Center, 1975), 41.4–5: *rang rgyud du smra ba'i dbu ma pa dag rgol phyir rgol gnyi ga la grags pa'i dngos po'i stobs kyis zhugs pa'am / 'dzin stangs mi 'khrul ba'i tshad ma nyid kyis nges pa yin no zhes zer ro /.* The *bKa' gdams gsung 'bum* collection contains two of Mabja's texts, both discussions of Nāgārjuna's "Collection of Reasoning" (*rig tshogs*), one in two folios, the other in thirty-four folios.

88 rMa bya, *'Thad pa'i rgyan,* 42.5–6: *pha rol 'am 'jig rten la grags pa'i tshad ma tsam.* Williams's conjecture ("Madhyamaka Method," 222, n. 26) that the following *las ma blangs* must be emended to *khas ma blangs* is supported by the Thimpu edition of rMa bya's text.

89 rMa bya, *'Thad pa'i rgyan,* 44.4–5: *dngos po stobs zhugs kyis grub pa'i mtha' gcig tu nges pa dang / bzlog pa 'phangs pa ni kun rdzob tu yang med pas rang rgyud dang sgrub byed 'phen pa'i thal 'gyur du mi 'gyur bar shes par bya'o //.*

90 rMa bya, *'Thad pa'i rgyan,* 45.4–5: *snang bcas kyi blo'i yul thams cad brdzun pa sgyu ma lta bu dang / blo 'khrul bar grub par mtshan gzhi shes bya tsam kun rdzob kyi mtshan nyid tha snyad kyi shes pa 'khrul pa'i yul du bden pa dang ldan par nges pa yin no/* ("All referents of consciousness having appearance, which are like false illusions, and mere objects of knowledge—illustrations that are established for a mistaken consciousness—are ascertained as being true as referents of conventional, mistaken consciousness, having the character of obscuration").

91 The exception that both sides would agree upon is "yogic direct perception," the meditative perception of emptiness. Mabja rejects the Dharmakīrtian notion that ordinary perception is unmistaken and the Vinītadeva notion that all valid cognition is unmistaken, siding with Jayānanda that only direct perception of emptiness is valid cognition.

92 Within "mistaken consciousnesses" lie āryas' consciousnesses having appearance, the appearances to which Mabja calls a second kind of obscurational truth (*'Thad pa'i rgyan,* 38.4: *nyon mongs can ma yin pa'i ma rig pas 'khrul par byas pa snang ba dang bcas pa'i 'phags pa gsum gyi rjes kyi shes pa 'khrul pa'i yul du grub pa 'phags pa'i kun rdzob kyi bden pa gnyis yin la /* "[Those which are] established as referents of the mistaken consciousnesses subsequent [to meditative absorption] of the three āryas who [have consciousnesses] having appearance, which are held to be mistaken due to non-afflictive ignorance, are the second, āryas' obscurational truths"). Thus, like Jayānanda, he equates appearance and mistake. Unlike Jayānanda—who equates obscurational truths with the belief in the truth of appearances—Mabja considers all appearances to be obscurational truths, although he does (40.1–2) state that āryas' obscurational truths are also called mere conventionalities (per Jayānanda). Mabja additionally states that "illustrations of obscurational truths" (*kun rdzob bden pa'i mtshan gzhi*) are "all the variety of knowable phenomena, referents of mind having appearance" (*'Thad pa'i rgyan,* 38.3: *snang bcas kyi blo'i yul shes bya'i chos gang ji snyed pa thams cad do /*). Mabja accounts for all phenomena (if we can say emptiness is a phenomenon, which Mabja would not seem to do) within the two truths, whereas Jayānanda must posit two kinds of mere conventionalities outside of the two truths. Both Mabja and Jayānanda hold that emptiness is not an object of knowledge and so deny that objects of knowledge are the basis of division of the two truths.

93 *'Thad pa'i rgyan,* 37.6–38.1 presents Mabja's primary delineation of the two truths as the objects of mistaken and unmistaken consciousnesses; obscurational truths are "true as referents of conventional, mistaken consciousness" (*tha snyad pa'i shes pa 'khrul pa'i yul du bden pa yin*) while ultimate truth is "true as a referent of unmistaken consciousness" (*blo ma 'khrul pa'i yul du bden pa*). At 38.4–5, Mabja divides afflicted obscurational truths into real and unreal on the basis of being cognized by unmistaken or mistaken worldly consciousnesses.

94 rMa bya, *'Thad pa'i rgyan,* 38.1–2: *blo ma 'khrul pa'i yul du bden pa ste 'phags pa'i mnyam gzhag mi rtog pa'i ye shes sam / tshul gsum pa'i rtags las mthar thug de kho na nyid dpyod pa rigs pa'i shes pa'i ngor bden pa'o /.*

95 Candrakīrti's *Prasannapadā,* following a lengthy critique of Dignāga's notions of valid cognition and perception, adopts a four-fold model of validity (*pramāṇacatuṣṭaya*) for worldly knowledge, in which valid cognition and its object are established in mutual dependence and not established in their own natures (*svābhāvikī siddhiḥ*);

see La Vallée Poussin, *Prasannapadā,* 75.6–9; David Seyfort Ruegg, *Two Prolegomena to Madhyamaka Philosophy, Studies in Indian and Tibetan Madhyamaka Thought, Part II* (Vienna: Arbeitskreis für Tibetische und Buddhistische Studien Universität Wien, 2002), 132–35; and Dan Arnold, *Buddhists, Brahmins, and Belief* (New York: Columbia University Press, 2005), 151ff.

96 rMa bya, *'Thad pa'i rgyan,* 42.6: *'jig rten la grags pa'i tshad ma bzhi.* This usage subtly shifts Candrakīrti's wording.

97 rMa bya, *'Thad pa'i rgyan,* 40.2–3: *dbu ma pa rnams kyis kyang dngos po la de kho na ltar snang bcas kyi blo'i yul thams cad brdzun pa dang blo thams cad 'khrul bar 'dod pa.*

98 All of the passages quoted herein from Mabja's *'Thad pa'i rgyan* are found in a section discussing "the nature of the two truths" (37.5: *bden pa gnyis kyi rang bzhin*). In delineating the two truths' definitions and illustrations (the first two of three subsections into which "the nature of the two truths" is divided), Mabja cites Candrakīrti's "two truths" section of *Entrance to the Middle* six times (stanzas VI.23–26, 28–29: the same stanzas Chapa cites when setting up Candrakīrti's division of consciousnesses and their referents) and Śāntideva's declaration of the two truths in stanza IX.2 of *Engaging in the Bodhisattva's Deeds.* Mabja's critique of "objectively gained valid cognition" and his discussion of "worldly valid cognition" occurs in the third subsection of "the nature of the two truths," "the valid cognition that ascertains the definitions within the illustrations" (37.6 and 41.2). This three-fold discussion of the two truths mirrors closely Chapa's formulation in *dBu ma shar gsum gyi stong mthun,* in which a five part presentation is given: *bden pa gnyis kyi so so'i mtshan nyid* ("Definitions of the individual two truths"), *mtshan nyid gnas pa'i rten mtshan gzhi* ("Illustrations that are the bases where the definitions abide"), *mtshan gzhi la brtsad pa spang pa* ("Dispelling objections to our illustrations"), *mtshan gzhi nges byed kyi tshad ma* ("The valid cognitions that ascertain the illustrations"), *de la mtshan nyid rten par nges byed kyi tshad ma* ("The valid cognitions that ascertain that the definitions are supported in those [illustrations]").

99 rMa bya, *'Thad pa'i rgyan,* 41.4.

100 Chapa (*dBu ma shar gsum,* 73.1–3 and 75.14ff) accuses the Prāsaṅgika of adopting the Indian Cārvāka system, in which death is held to terminate living beings entirely without the possibility of afterlife or rebirth, or of holding a "nirvāṇa without remainder" position, in which the Buddhist path culminates in an extinction that does not allow for the compassionate aid of sentient beings deemed central to Mahāyāna notions of buddhahood.

101 Jayānanda here (*Madhyamakāvatāraṭīkā,* 151b) comments on Candrakīrti's rhetorical question in *Madhyamakāvatāra* stanza VI.30, "What need would there be for the others, the Superiors, and what would be the use of the Superior path?"; La Vallée Pousin, *Madhyamakāvatāra,* 112.5–6: *'phags gzhan gyis // ci dgos 'phags pa'i lam gyis ci zhig bya /.*

Notes to Chapter 4

1 For a stimulating discussion of dGe lugs pa approaches to the issue of ineffability, see José Ignacio Cabezón, *Buddhism and Language* (Albany, NY: State University of New York Press, 1994), 171–87.

2 Louis de la Vallée Poussin, *Madhyamakāvatāra par Candrakīrti,* Bibiotheca Buddhica, 9 (Osnabrück, Germany: Biblio Verlag, 1970), 109.2–3: *don dam pa'i bden pa bstan par 'dod pas de ni brjod du med pa'i phyir dang shes pa'i yul ma yin pa nyid kyi phyir dngos su bstan par mi nus pas* ("One wishing to teach ultimate truth cannot teach explicitly for it is ineffable and just not a referent of consciousness").

3 Jayānanda, *Madhyamakāvatāraṭīkā,* Toh. 3870, *sde dge* edition, *dbu ma,* vol. *ra,* 147b.4: *rnam par rtog pa'i shes pa'i yul ma yin pa'i phyir te'o/ /de rnams yod pa dang med pa la sogs pa'i yul la 'jug pas so/.*

4 Stanza IX.2; Louis de la Vallée Poussin, *Prajñākaramati's Commentary to the Bodhicaryāvatāra of Çāntideva,* Bibliotheca Indica (Calcutta: Asiatic Society of Bengal, 1905), 352: *saṃvṛtiḥ paramārthaś ca satyadvayam idaṃ matam / buddher agocaras tattvaṃ buddhiḥ saṃvṛtir ucyate //.* The Tibetan of pāda cd (D3871, vol. *ya,* 31a.1) reads: *don dam blo yi spyod yul min / blo ni kun rdzob yin par brjod //.*

Saito ("Śāntideva in the History of Mādhyamika," 261, n. 3) reports that the Dunhuang version for pāda d reads: *blo dang sgra ni kun rdzob yin //* (= *buddhiḥ śabdaś ca saṃvṛtiḥ*). I have translated pāda c in accordance with the canonical Tibetan; however, in accordance with the Sanskrit, it could be translated just as well—and with the same meaning—as "Reality is not a referent of awareness." The Dunhuang version of pāda d declares the both "awareness and speech are obscurational." This reading would mirror Candrakīrti's declaration more closely than the Sanskrit or Tibetan canonical readings.

For a discussion of later Tibetan debates over the meaning of Śāntideva's stanza, see Michael Sweet, "*Bodhicaryāvatāra* (IX,2) as a Focus for Tibetan Interpretations of the Two Truths in the Prāsaṅgika Mādhyamika," *Journal of the International Association of Buddhist Studies* 2 (1979): 79–89.

5 Prajñākaramati cites *Madhyamakāvatāra,* VI.23, 25, 28, and 29, all stanzas in which Candrakīrti explicates the two truths.

6 La Vallée Poussin, *Prajñākaramati's Commentary* (1905), 366.8–9: *paramārthasya vastutaḥ sāṃvṛtajñānāviṣayatvāt //.*

7 La Vallée Poussin, *Prajñākaramati's Commentary* (1905), 363.7: *buddheḥ sarvajñānānāṃ / samatikrāntasarvajñānaviṣayatvādagocaraḥ / aviṣayaḥ / kena cit prakāreṇa tatsarvabuddhiviṣayīkartuṃ na śakyata.*

8 *bden pa gnyis la 'jug pa, satyakaparivarta;* P813, vol. 32. Cited in Candrakīrti's *Madhyamakāvatāra,* 110.15ff. Prajñākaramati cites the first paragraph, up to "It is not as expressed . . ." in his *Bodhicaryāvatārapañjikā* (1905), 366.10–16: *yadi hi devaputra parmārthataḥ paramārthasatyaṃ kāyavāṅmanasāṃ viṣayatāmupagacchet / na tatparamārthasatyamiti saṃkhyāṃ gacchet / saṃvṛtisatyam eva tad bhavet / api tu devaputra paramārthasatyaṃ sarvavyavahārasamatikrāntaṃ nirviśeṣaṃ / asamutpannamaniruddhaṃ / abhidheyābhidhānajñeyajñānavigataṃ / yāvatsarvākāravaropetasarvajñajñānaviṣayabhāvasamatikrāntaṃ paramārthasatyamiti vistaraḥ /.*

Candrakīrti's citation differs in small measure from Prajñākaramati's. I give here the full passage cited by Candrakīrti but follow Prajñākaramati's reading as far as he cites. The portion cited by Prajñākaramati is translated in Christian Lindtner, "Atiśa's Introduction to the Two Truths," *Journal of Indian Philosophy* 9 (1981): 187.

9 La Vallée Poussin, *Prajñākaramati's Commentary* (1905), 367.6–7, citing the *Pitāputrasamāgamasūtra: yaḥ punaḥ paramārthaḥ so 'nabhilāpyaḥ / anājñeyaḥ / aparijñeyaḥ / avijñeyaḥ /.*

10 La Vallée Poussin, *Prajñākaramati's Commentary* (1905), 366.2–4: *sarvā hi buddhirālambananirālambanatayā vikalpasvabhāvā / vikalpaśca sarva evāvidyāsvabhāvaḥ / avastugrāhitvāt /.*

11 La Vallée Poussin, *Prajñākaramati's Commentary* (1905), 366.17: *ata eva tad aviṣayaḥ sarvakalpanānāṃ.*

12 Jayānanda, *Madhyamakāvatāraṭīkā,* 150b.2: *sgra dang rnam par rtog pa dag gi spyod yul ma yin no zhes bya ba'i tha tshig go /.* Jayānanda adds this comment to an abbreviated citation of the sūtra passage that reads only *smra bar bya ba dang zhes bya ba la sogs pa gsungs te /* ("'object of speech and' and so forth is said"). As he cites no more of this sentence, it is safe to assume that his "and so forth" encompasses the sūtra's "speech itself, as well as object of knowledge and consciousness" and so his comment substitutes "words" for the sūtra's "object of speech and speech itself" and substitutes "conceptuality" for the sūtra's "object of knowledge and consciousness."

13 Jayānanda, *Madhyamakāvatāraṭīkā,* 150b.4: *de kho na nyid kyi sgra dang rnam par rtog pa'i yul ma yin pa'i phyir ro /.*

14 Jayānanda, *Madhyamakāvatāraṭīkā,* 150b.3–4: *mu bzhi dang bral ba la yul gyi dngos po mi rigs pa dang / gdul bya rnams kyis thams cad mkhyen pas de kho na nyid thugs su chud pa yin no zhes yul gyi dngos po brtags pa yin pas so /.*

15 Phya pa chos kyi seṅ ge, *dbu ma śar gsum gyi stoṅ thun,* ed. Helmut Tauscher (Vienna: Arbeitskreis für Tibetische und Buddhistische Studien Universität Wien, 1999), 1.17.

16 Phya pa, *dbu ma shar gsum,* 18.7–13.

17 Phya pa, *dbu ma shar gsum,* 20.4–5.

18 Phya pa, *dbu ma shar gsum,* 20.9–13.

19 Phya pa, *dbu ma shar gsum,* 1.18–20.

20 Phya pa, *dbu ma shar gsum,* 10.9: *ma grub pa nyid mthar thug dpyod pa'i gzhal byar gnas pas don dam pa'i bden pa yin.*

21 Playing with the much older Buddhist conception of phenomena as either positive (*viddhi, sgrub pa*) or negative (*pratiṣedha, dgag pa*) and, further, the division of negatives into either affirming negatives (*paryudāsapratiṣedha, ma yin dgag*) or non-affirming negatives (*prasajyapratiṣedha, med dgag*), Chapa writes "I just accept the consequence that positives are negatives because all positives are affirming negatives" (Phya pa, *dbu ma shar gsum,* 85.20: *sgrub pa dgag par thal ba ni 'dod pa nyid de sgrub pa thams cad ma yin dgag yin pa'i phyir ro //*). Defining these terms, he writes: "A positive phenomenon is that which is suitable for its own meaning generality to be conceived upon appearing as self-powered, without dependence upon its opposite's meaning generality appearing" (87.2–3: *bzlog pa'i don spyi 'char ba la ma ltos par rang nyid kyi don spyi rang dbang du shar nas zhen du rung ba rnams ni sgrub pa'i chos zhes bya'o//*). "A negative phenomenon is that

which is suitable to be conceived upon the appearance of a meaning generality which is the opposite of the object of negation in dependence on the appearance of the meaning generality of the object of negation—[for instance] emptiness of performing a function, not being produced from causes, not ceasing, and so forth" (87.3–5: *don byed pas stong ba dang rgyus bskyed pa myed pa dang 'gag pa myed pa la sogs pa dgag bya'i don spyi shar ba la ltos nas de las bzlog pa'i don spyi shar ste zhen du rung ba ni dgag pa'i chos zhes bya'o*). "The definition of non-affirming negative is that which is determined by awareness as just negative when ascertaining just the simpliciter itself" (87.10–11: *myed dgag gi mtshan nyid ni ldog pa de kha yar nges pa na dgag pa 'ba' zhig par blos zhen par bya ba yin*). "The definition of affirming negative is that which is apprehended without dispelling the positive factor when ascertaining just the simpliciter itself" (87.11–12: *ma yin dgag gi mtshan nyid ni ldog pa de kha yar nges pa na sgrub pa'i cha ma dor bar zhen par bya ba yin*).

22 Phya pa, *dbu ma shar gsum,* 17.10–13.

23 In his *Sixty Stanzas on Reasoning* (*Yuktiṣaṣṭikā*), Nāgārjuna writes: "When the Conquerors have said 'Only nirvāṇa is true,' what wise person would think 'The rest are not false'?" (stanza 35; *sde dge* 3825, *dbu ma,* vol. *tsa,* 21b.5; Christian Lindtner, *Master of Wisdom: Writings of the Buddhist Master Nāgārjuna* (Oakland: Dharma Publishing, 1986), 84. While later Tibetan scholarship debates whether nirvāṇa, here meaning the ultimate, is ultimately true in the sense of ultimately established, Chapa clearly sees it as ultimately true and bearing analysis.

24 Phya pa, *dbu ma shar gsum,* 25.19–26.1. Elsewhere (16.20), Chapa writes, "The definition of ultimate truth is that which is true as the referent of a valid cognition that cognizes finality. The cognition of that is the valid cognition comprehending finality. Being true as the object of that comprehension is ultimate truth." He also notes (17.19), "We assert that only a non-affirming negative possesses the definition of being true as the object cognized by cognitions of finality."

25 Chapa writes, "The unreversibility of the conception of truth through analyzing attributes in a specific isolate is 'bearing analysis'" (Phya pa, *dbu ma shar gsum,* 16.21: *ldog pa 'ga' zhig la khyad par dpyad pas bden pa'i zhen pa bzlog du myed pa ni dpyad bzod pa yin la*).

26 Phya pa, *dbu ma shar gsum,* 17.13–15. Chapa also writes, "Only a non-affirming negative possesses the definition of being true as the object cognized by cognitions of finality" (Phya pa, *dbu ma shar gsum,* 17.19–20).

27 Phya pa, *dbu ma shar gsum,* 17.15–19.

28 This passage has been translated by Helmut Tauscher, "Phya pa chos kyi seng ge as a Svātantrika," in *The Svātantrika-Prāsaṅgika Distinction: What Difference Does a Difference Make?* eds. Georges B.J. Dreyfus and Sara L. McClintock (Boston: Wisdom Publications, 2002), 224–225. My translation and understanding of the passage differ slightly from what he presents there. Tauscher suggests (p. 224) that this passage "would clearly indicate Phya pa's ontological position and, in addition, establish him as a proponent of Madhyamaka and as being under the very strong influence of Yogācāra philosophy, yet only if one takes the introductory question to reflect Phya pa's opinion." The difficulty of this passage warrants Tauscher's qualification, "only if," or, alternatively, a lengthy footnote qualifying one's understanding. I believe that

the opening question must be Chapa introducing a hypothetical opponent, not a Prāsaṅgika and not himself, who holds that a consciousness that is established by experience—the Prāsaṅgika's own mode of conventional establishment—exists ultimately. Chapa nowhere else in this text claims that mind is the ultimate. His point in introducing the imagined opponent's position is to bait the Prāsaṅgika into taking a stand: how can the Prāsaṅgika argue with his own "worldly renown" even when it is used to justify the ultimate existence of mind? Chapa only states his own position in the fifth sentence, where he writes, "We, also, do not assert any distinction regarding the ultimate." As shown above, Chapa argues for an ultimate without distinctions in several places. One weakness of my interpretation is the presence of "clear" (*gsal ba*) in this fifth sentence, which would seem to refer to the "clear awareness" in the first sentence. Rather than have Chapa claim "clear awareness" as his own ultimate, I twist the passage around to have just the one word, "clear," indicate the hypothetical opponent's idea of the ultimate. Tauscher's translation avoids this problem. Another way to interpret the sentence would be that Chapa merely pretends to adopt "clear awareness" as his ultimate in order to cause problems for his Prāsaṅgika opponent and does not, even in this fifth sentence, state his own position. Yet another possibility is to read the fifth sentences' *gsal ba* as "predicate" of a formal inference (that which clarifies the subject of the inference) rather than "clear." This interpretation is attractive because so much of Chapa's text aims at showing the proper way to realize emptiness inferentially—emptiness is the predicate of all phenomena. It is just barely possible to read the *gsal ba* in the first sentence of this passage in the same way: ". . . proponents of existence [who hold] the thesis that an awareness that is singularly established by experience has the predicate, 'only exists ultimately.'" However, this reading of *gsal ba* goes against the common usage of *blo gsal ba* as "clear awareness." Also, in the only other usage of *gsal ba* that I find in Chapa's text (Phya pa, *dbu ma shar gsum,* 94.8–10) the term definitely refers to a broad quality of consciousness, "clarity," rather than a part of formal inference, as Chapa speaks to a feature of a direct perception in that passage.

Additionally, due to my understanding of the first sentence of this passage, I do not accept the emendation to Chapa's text that Tauscher tentatively adopts (Phya pa, *dbu ma shar gsum,* 67.4). Chapa's heading to this passage reads "[In the absence of theses, the Prāsaṅgika] would be unable to refute a mere consciousness that bears analysis" (*dpyad bzod pa'i shes pa tsam dgag mi nus pa*). In citing this passage, Śākya Chokden (Śākya mchog ldan, *Lung rigs rgya mtsho,* vol. 14, 519.2) reads ". . . a mere consciousness that does *not* bear analysis" (*dpyad mi bzod . . .*). In his edition of Chapa's text and in his translation of this passage (p. 224), Tauscher tentatively adopts Śākya Chokden's reading. My understanding is that the heading to the passage directly introduces the first sentence, the hypothetical position of a clear awareness that exists ultimately. In the heading, "a mere consciousness that bears analysis" refers to this clear awareness that exists ultimately. If we emend the text per Śākya Chokden, the reading ". . . a mere consciousness that does *not* bear analysis" would have to refer to something else, perhaps to a position that Śākya Chokden believes Chapa to hold.

29 For more on "explicit contradictories" and other classes of contradictories, see Birgit Kellner, "Types of Incompatibility (*'gal ba*) and Types of Non-Cognition (*ma/mi dmigs*) in Early Tibetan *tshad ma* Literature," *Tibetan Studies: Proceedings of the 7th*

Seminar of the International Association for Tibetan Studies, particularly pp. 499–500.

30 Phya pa, *dbu ma shar gsum,* 66.7ff.

31 In one important case (Phya pa, *dbu ma shar gsum,* 73.1ff), Chapa shows that any argument the Prāsaṅgika could make against the Hedonist (*Cārvāka, tshu rol mdzes pa ba*) rejection of future rebirth can apply equally to their own rejection of mind and mental factors upon buddhahood. In this example, we can be certain that Chapa does not intend to defend the Hedonist position as his own.

32 In his *Refutation of Objections;* E.H. Johnston, A. Kunst, K. Bhattacharya, *The Dialectical Method of Nāgārjuna: Vigrahavyāvartanī* (Delhi: Motilal Banarsidass, 1998), 14, 61: *yadi kācana pratijñā syānme tata eṣa me bhaveddoṣaḥ / nāsti ca mama pratijñā tasmānnaivāsti me doṣaḥ //.*

33 Phya pa, *dbu ma shar gsum,* 77.7–10.

34 I only find Chapa using the phrase *don dam du yod pa* once, in the passage (Phya pa, *dbu ma shar gsum,* 67.5: *blo gsal ba don dam du yod pa*), discussed above, in which Chapa challenges the Prāsaṅgika to refute one who holds that "clear awareness ultimately exists." He uses the phrase *don dam par* more frequently. In several places, the phrase clearly means "ultimately": "ultimately, proliferations are negated" (74.19: *don dam par spros pa bkag pa*); "conventionally, not ultimately" (77.13: *kun rdzob du yin gyi don dam par ma yin no*); an opponent asks how he "negates the convention, ultimately existent (88.17: *don dam par yod pa'i tha snyad bkag pa*). Elsewhere, *don dam par* could mean "as the ultimate" particularly where the words are placed in an opponent's mouth; for instance, he argues against the Prāsaṅgika who "makes no assertion at all ultimately/as the ultimate" (69.18: *don dam par ci yang khas mi len pa'i dbu ma*). Twice (71.8–9) he uses *don dam gyi* for "ultimately."

35 Phya pa, *dbu ma shar gsum,* 77.18–20: *de bzhin nyid cir yang ma grub pa la don dam par gzhal bya la sogs pa'i chos myed kyang tha snyad du rnal 'byor gyi mngon sum la ltos nas gzhal bya mngon gyur dang spros pa gcod pa'i rjes dpag la ltos na[s] gzhal bya lkog gyur yin pa'i chos kyang gnas pa.*

36 Donald S. Lopez (*A Study of Svātantrika* [Ithaca, NY: Snow Lion Publications, 1987], 143) correctly reports that Chapa holds that the ultimate bears analysis and, perhaps less correctly, that the ultimate exists ultimately. The Gelukpa scholars whom Lopez represents equate "bearing analysis" and "ultimately existing" (much more precisely, Lopez writes "to not exist ultimately is to not be established as capable of bearing analysis by a conceptual reasoning consciousness which properly analyzes the mode of being of phenomena") but Chapa, it seems, does not.

37 As will be shown below, the topic of concordant ultimates is much older than Chapa, running at least as far back as eighth-century India. It is developed in the works of Jñānagarbha, Śāntarakṣita, and Kamalaśīla and in certain writings of Bhāvaviveka. The place of concordant ultimates in Bhāvaviveka's thought is unclear, particularly whether the sixth-century Bhāvaviveka developed the idea or whether later authors writing under the name, Bhāvaviveka, developed it. I discuss this in more detail in chapter 1.

38 The opponent's objection runs Phya pa, *dbu ma shar gsum,* 7.19–8.2.

39 Phya pa, *dbu ma shar gsum,* 8.3–4: *de ltar na snang ba'i dngos po don dam pa'i dngos por zhen pa'i log shes dang don dam pa'i bden pa cir yang ma grub par rtogs pa'i tshad mas gnod bya gnod byed ma yin par 'gyur te gzhi tha dad la 'jug pa'i phyir /* ("If that is

so, the wrong consciousness that conceives appearing entities to be ultimate entities and the valid cognition that realizes appearing entities to be utterly unestablished—ultimate truth—would not be invalidated and invalidator [respectively] because of engaging different bases").

40 Phya pa, *dbu ma shar gsum,* 26.9–10.

41 Here (Phya pa, *dbu ma shar gsum,* 26.9), Chapa uses *bye brag,* which he uses interchangably with *khyad par.*

42 Phya pa, *dbu ma shar gsum,* 26.10–12.

43 Phya pa, *dbu ma shar gsum,* 26.12–14: *dgag pa de gzhi dang 'brel pa'am dgag bya bsal pa'i rnam par rtog pa la snang ba ma yin dgag dag kun rdzob pa'i ngo bo yin yang / dgag byas stong ba'i chas myed dgag dang 'dra bas mthun pa'i don dam du bshad pa yin gyi myed dgag mthun pa'i don dam du bshad pa ma yin no //.*

44 Phya pa, *dbu ma shar gsum,* 27.21: *snang ba dang rang bzhin myed pa'i tshogs pa.*

45 Phya pa, *dbu ma shar gsum,* 27.21–28.4.

46 Phya pa, *dbu ma shar gsum,* 28.11–13.

47 Phya pa, *dbu ma shar gsum,* 87.16–18.

48 Phya pa, *dbu ma shar gsum,* 87.15. Chapa's Perfection of Wisdom teacher and elder at Sangpu, Gro lung pa bLo gros 'byung gnas, argued at length that the illusion-like nature is not ultimate truth and is not found by a reasoning consciousness. See José Ignacio Cabezón, "The Madhyamaka in Gro lung pa's *Bstan Rim chen mo,*" *Proceedings of the 11th Seminar of the International Association of Tibetan Studies 2006* (forthcoming). While Chapa differs from Drolungpa on several important issues, this is one point of harmony in their views.

49 *Tsong kha pa bLo bzang grags pa,* 1357–1419.

50 Tsong kha pa bLo bzang grags pa, *sKyes bu gsum gyi nyams su blang ba'i byang chub lam gyi rim pa / Lam rim 'bring* (Mundgod, India: dga' ldan shar rtse, n.d.), 484.3–485.1; translated in Jeffrey Hopkins, *Tsong-kha-pa's Final Exposition of Wisdom* (Ithaca, NY: Snow Lion Publications, 2008), 200–201. Tsongkhapa's and other Gelukpa scholars' views on illusion-like nature are also discussed in David Seyfort Ruegg, *Three Studies in the History of Indian and Tibetan Madhyamaka Philosophy, Studies in Indian and Tibetan Madhyamaka Thought, Part I* (Vienna: Arbeitskreis für Tibetische und Buddhistische Studien Universität Wien, 2000), 96–101.

51 Elizabeth Napper, *Dependent-Arising and Emptiness* (Boston: Wisdom Publications, 1989), 403–40 (Appendix I: The Division of Mādhyamikas Into Reason-Established Illusionists and Proponents of Thorough Non-Abiding); Cabezón, "The Madhyamaka in Gro lung pa"; Ruegg, *Three Studies,* 96ff.

52 As Napper shows (*Dependent-Arising and Emptiness,* 403–4), Tsongkhapa seems to indicate that some earlier scholars divide Madhyamaka into those who accept that the illusion-like nature is established by reasoning and those who hold "thorough non-abiding" (*rab tu mi gnas pa*) to be the ultimate. Cabezón, "The Madhyamaka in Gro lung pa," shows that Gro lung pa argued against this division of Madhyamaka. Ruegg (*Three Studies,* 35, footnote 60) points out that such a division is found in a work of Gampopa (*sGam po pa bSod nams rin chen,* 1079–1153) and that the latter category—proponents of throrough non-abiding—is further subdivided into "Union Thoroughly Non-Abiding" (*zung 'jug rab tu mi gnas pa*) and "Continuum Cutting Thoroughly Non-Abiding" (*rgyun chad rab tu mi gnas pa*) branches (the

translations of these names is mine, based on usage examined below). These latter terms are adopted by Drakpa Gyeltsen, who equates them with Svātantrikas and Prāsaṅgikas. This is discussed in detail below. Thus, in Drakpa Gyeltsen's usage, those who accept that the illusion-like nature is the ultimate—whoever they may be—are neither Svātantrikas nor Prāsaṅgikas.

53 This is the thrust of Chapa's arguments spanning Phya pa, *dbu ma shar gsum,* 93.14–97.14; see especially 94.14–18.

54 *Madhyamakāloka;* Toh. 3887, *bstan 'gyur, sde dge* edition, *dbu ma,* vol. *sa,* 149a.5: "Because this absence of production also accords with the ultimate, it is called an 'ultimate,' but it is not actually so because actually the ultimate is beyond all proliferations."

55 *dbu ma rgyan, madhyamakālaṃkāra,* stanza 70; Toh. 3884, *bstan 'gyur, sde dge* edition, *dbu ma,* vol. *sa,* 55b.2; edited Tibetan in Masamichi Ichigō, "Śāntarakṣita's Madhyamakālaṃkāra," in *Studies in the Literature of the Great Vehicle,* Michigan Studies in Buddhist Literature, no. 1, eds. Luis O. Gómez and Jonathan A. Silk (Ann Arbor: Collegiate Institute for the Study of Buddhist Literature and Center for South and Southeast Asian Studies, University of Michigan, 1989), 214. The stanza reads "Because of according with the ultimate, this is called an 'ultimate.' In reality [the ultimate] is free from all the collections of proliferations." Ichigō's English translation is found on p. 215.

56 Tsong kha pa, *lam rim 'bring,* 482.2; Hopkins, *Tsong-kha-pa's Final Exposition of Wisdom,* 198.

57 Tsong kha pa, *lam rim 'bring,* 483.6ff; Hopkins, *Tsong-kha-pa's Final Exposition of Wisdom,* 199ff.

58 Tsong kha pa, *lam rim 'bring,* 486.6; Hopkins, *Tsong-kha-pa's Final Exposition of Wisdom,* 203–4.

59 Indeed, the title of Chapa's text, *dBu ma shar gsum gyi stong mthun* ("Compilation of the Three Mādhyamikas from the East"), refers to the main Madhyamaka treatises of these three authors.

60 This assessment is only provisional; as more of Chapa's writings come to light, we may find his own discussion of subjective concordant ultimates.

61 Tsongkhapa's passage, with its many citations of Indian sources, is found in Tsong kha pa, *lam rim 'bring,* 482.3–487.6 and translated in Hopkins, *Tsong-kha-pa's Final Exposition of Wisdom,* 198–204.

62 Tsong kha pa, *lam rim 'bring,* 481.3; Hopkins, *Tsong-kha-pa's Final Exposition of Wisdom,* 197.

63 Tsongkhapa never states that the topic of concordant ultimates is a Svātantrika notion nor that Prāsaṅgikas rejected the idea of concordant ultimates.

64 Grags pa rgyal mtshan, *rGyud kyi mngon par rtogs pa rin po che'i ljong shing,* in *Sa skya pa'i bka' 'bum,* vol. 3 (Tokyo: Toyo Bunko, 1968), 22.1.1–4.

65 Grags pa, *Rin po che'i ljon shing,* 21.3.6–22.1.4. Having stated that all awareness can be divided into conventional and ultimate, Drakpa Gyeltsen asks, "What persons have the second awareness [ultimate awareness] in their continuums?" He then lists four positions on this issue: the Hearer's assertion (*nyan thos kyi 'dod tshul*), the Yogic Practice assertion (*rnal 'byor spyod pa'i 'dod tshul*), the "Continuum Cutting Thoroughly Non-Abiding [Mādhyamika]" assertion (*rgyun chad rab tu mi gnas pa'i 'dod tshul*), and the "Union Thoroughly Non-Abiding [Mādhyamika]" assertion (*zung

'jug rab tu mi gnas pa'i 'dod tshul). When discussing the third and fourth groups, he terms them Prāsaṅgikas (21.4.5: *dbu ma thal 'gyur ba*) and Svātantrikas (22.1.1: *dbu ma rang rgyud pa*), respectively. The question of "who has ultimate awareness?" becomes additionally the question of "what, if any, awarenesses do Buddhas have?" Drakpa Gyeltsen tells us (23.4.2–4), "Hearer's hold that ordinary beings (*so so skye bo*) have only conventional awarenesses, āryas have both [conventional and ultimate] awarenesses, and those entering nirvāṇa without remainder have no awareness at all. . . . Yogic Practitioners [in accordance with their view of three natures (*trisvabhāva*)] hold that imputational awareness (*kun brtags kyi blo*) is conventional while the dependent and thoroughly established [natures/awarenesses] are ultimate. Consequently, ordinary beings' awarenesses include both [conventional and ultimate awarenesses]. The three classes of āryas have mere conventionalities, which are not conventional truths, and so also have both [kinds of awareness]. Since Buddhas are devoid of imputation, they only have ultimate [awareness]."

66 Grags pa, *Rin po che'i ljon shing,* 21.4.5–22.1.1. I have not located this passage in Candrakīrti's *Commentary on [Nāgārjuna's] Sixty Stanzas on Reasoning* (*Yuktiṣaṣṭikāvṛtti* [*rigs pa drug cu pa'i 'grel pa*], Toh. 3864, *bstan 'gyur, sde dge* edition, *dbu ma,* vol. *ya*; Cristina Anna Scherrer-Schaub, *Yuktiṣaṣṭikāvṛtti. Commentaire à la soixantaine sur le raisonnement ou Du vrai enseignement de la causalité par le Maitre indien Candrakīrti,* Mélanges chinois et bouddhiques, 25 [Bruselles: Institut belge des hautes etudes chinoises, 1991]). It could well be that the passage Drakpa Gyeltsen refers to was translated quite differently in the canonical editions of Candrakīrti's texts or that Drakpa Gyeltsen is paraphrasing. In one passage of his *Commentary* (7b.6–8a.2; Scherrer-Schaub, *Yuktiṣaṣṭikāvṛtti,* 36ff), on stanza 5cd, Candrakīrti explains that the four noble truths are posited as the two truths in accordance with the world: Nirvāṇa, the noble truth of cessation, "by worldly conventions is called ultimate truth because it does not deceive the world. . . . The [other] three truths, due to having the character of compositional things and appearing to exist as their own entities (*ngo bo nyid*), deceive fools. Therefore, they are posited as conventional truths. . . . Nirvāṇa always abides as just nirvāṇa; by worldly conventions it is explained to be ultimate truth." This passage could be interpreted as Candrakīrti positing the division of two truths in terms of the world and could be what Drakpa Gyeltsen paraphrases, especially so because soon after the paragraph translated, Drakpa Gyeltsen (at 23.1.5) quotes Nāgārjuna's stanza 5cd, the stanza upon which Candrakīrti here comments.

67 Grags pa, *Rin po che'i ljon shing,* 22.3.6: *don dam pa'i bden pa de blo gang gi 'ang yul ma yin no zhe na / 'o na de smos pa don med par yang 'gyur la /.*

68 Grags pa, *Rin po che'i ljon shing,* 22.1.6: *dbye ba'i gzhi 'jig rten pa'i blo nyid de /.*

69 Grags pa, *Rin po che'i ljon shing,* 22.1.6ff. The first passage he cites from the *Hevajra Tantra* reads "Just this is called cyclic existence; just this is just nirvāṇa. Other than the abandonment of cyclic existence, there is no realization of nirvāṇa" (*'di nyid 'khor ba zhes bya ste / / 'di nyid mya ngan 'das pa nyid / / 'khor ba spangs nas gzhan du ni / / mya ngan 'das pa rtogs mi 'gyur /*).

70 Grags pa, *Rin po che'i ljon shing,* 22.2.6: *blo phyin ci ma log pa'o / de'i yul bden pa ni 'khor ba dag pa ste / mya ngan las 'das pa zhes bya ba'i don to /.*

71 Grags pa, *Rin po che'i ljon shing,* 22.2.1–2: *blo de nyid la kun rdzob sgrub la don dam 'gegs pa'i tshul gyis dbye gzhir byed pa'i tshul lo /.*

72 Grags pa, *Rin po che'i ljon shing,* 22.1.1–4.

73 Grags pa, *Rin po che'i ljon shing,* 22.4.1–2: *so so skye bo'i blos brtags pa'i stong pa nyid dang skye med la sogs pa de don dam pa'i bden pa ma yin te / . . . /de'ang 'on kyang don dam pa skye ba'i rgyu yin pas / rnam grangs kyi don dam pa'o /.*

74 *Tarkajvāla,* Toh. 3856, *sde dge* edition, *dbu ma,* vol. *dza,* 60b.4–5. As discussed in chapter 1, it is difficult to know if this passage was written by the sixth-century Bhāvaviveka or by a later author writing under the same name, who expanded *Blaze of Reasoning.* The passage, in context, seems to answers a critic who claims that the Madhyamaka understanding of emptiness would invalidate attempts to prove that phenomena are empty. In response, Bhāvaviveka explains that "pure worldly wisdom" can perceive phenomena and so can attempt to demonstrate their emptiness. The criticism itself could come from Candrakīrti, who makes just such a criticism of the use of inference to prove that phenomena are empty, or it could come from a Yogācāra critic, for whom the seeming incompatibility of inference and Madhyamaka emptiness entails not the jettisoning of formal inference, as it did for Candrakīrti, but the incorrectness of the Madhyamaka view. Thus, one can see the sixth-century Bhāvaviveka here answering a Yogācāra critic or one can see an eighth-century (or later) Bhāvaviveka answering Candrakīrti. In either case, the passage is the likely inspiration for Drakpa Gyeltsen's discussion of "pure worldly wisdom."

75 As discussed in chapter 1, this Bhāvaviveka is not the same as the sixth-century author of *Heart of the Middle.* This Bhāvaviveka may have added to *Blaze of Reasoning,* the core of which was written by the sixth-century author. Thus, the passage of *Blaze of Reasoning* discussed immediately above could have been written by the author of the *Compendium of Meanings of the Middle.* In the paragraphs that follow, I refer to the author of the *Compendium of Meanings* simply as "Bhāvaviveka," but understand the author to be a different person, living some two hundred years later, than the sixth-century figure.

76 *Madhyamakārthasaṃgraha,* stanza seven; Yasunori Ejima, *Chūgan-shisō no tenkai—Bhāvaviveka kenkyū* (Tokyo: Shunjūsha, 1980), 19–20: *spros pa thams cad kyis stong pa / / de ni rnam grangs ma yin pa'i / / dam pa'i don du shes par bya /.* Stanza four declares the ultimate to be of two varieties.

77 *Madhyamakārthasaṃgraha,* stanzas 5–6; Ejima, *Bhāvaviveka kenkyū,* 19: *dang po de yang gnyis yin te / / rigs pa rnam grangs don dam dang / / skye ba bkag pa'i don dam mo / / mu bzhi skye 'gog la sogs pa'i / / gtan tshigs bzhi yi rigs pa de / / snang ba'i dngos po thams cad kyang / / skye ba bkag pa'i don dam mo /.*

78 Chapa and Drakpa Gyeltsen were part of the early Svātantrika movement. Bhāvaviveka, Jñānagarbha, Śāntarakṣita, and Kamalaśīla can only be regarded thematically as Svātantrika, as they lived centuries before the Svātantrika interpretation of Madhyamaka was formalized. However, their writings formed the textual basis for Svātantrika. The reasons why Tsongkhapa so vehemently argued for the superiority of Prāsaṅgika, when so much of his system accords with that of Svātantrika authors, remains a great mystery only partially solved by his followers' defense of his system from Tagtsang Lotsawa's (*sTag tshang lo tsā ba shes rab rin chen*) charge that Tsongkhapa really was a Svātantrika; see Jeffrey Hopkins, *Maps of the Profound* (Ithaca, NY: Snow Lion Publications, 2003), 527–75.

79 *Satyadvayāvatāra,* stanza 4ab; Toh. 3902, *bstan 'gyur sde dge* edition, *dbu ma,* vol. *a*; Christian Lindtner, "Atiśa's Introduction to the Two Truths," *Journal of Indian Philosophy* 9 (1981): 190: *dam pa'i don ni gcig nyid de / gzhan dag rnam pa gnyis su 'dod /.* Atiśa's preference for Candrakīrti's interpretation of Madhyamaka is discussed in chapter 1.

80 Grags pa, *Rin po che'i ljon shing,* 22.4.1–2; Drakpa Gyeltsen there addresses a passage, discussed above, on concordant ultimates to an opponent who claims that Drakpa's view of the ultimate runs counter to Nāgārjuna's statement that "Only nirvāṇa is true." Chapa (Phya pa, *dbu ma shar gsum,* 15.7ff) likewise addresses Nāgārjuna's statement.

Notes to Chapter 5

1 For an excellent treatment of the tensions at work in this classical Mahāyāna doctrine, see John J. Makransky, *Buddhahood Embodied* (Albany, NY: State University of New York Press, 1997), especially 85–108.

2 The Prāsaṅgika rejection of ordinary valid cognition in realizing the ultimate extends the Prāsaṅgika ideas, examined in chapter 3, that no ordinary cognition can be considered valid.

3 *Satyadvayāvatāra,* stanza 10cd; Toh. 3902, *bstan 'gyur sde dge* edition, *dbu ma,* vol. *a*; Christian Lindtner, "Atiśa's Introduction to the Two Truths," *Journal of Indian Philosophy* 9 (1981): 191: *gnyis pos stong nyid rtogs so zhes / tshu rol mthong ba'i rmongs pa smra /.* My bracketed addition is drawn from stanza 10ab. Stanzas 10–13 examine both forms of valid cognition in more detail. Additionally, we saw in chapter 1 that the author of the *Jewel Lamp of the Middle* (*Madhyamakaratnapradīpa*) firmly rejected the applicability of valid cognition and either conceptual or non-conceptual consciousness to the realization of the ultimate, writing "Both conceptual and non-conceptual consciousnesses do not realize this [ultimate truth]. The conventions of words and valid cognition are useless in meditating on that meaning."

4 Stanza 6cd; Lindtner, "Atiśa's Introduction," 190: *rtogs med tshul gyis rtogs pas na // stong nyid mthong zhes tha snyad gdags /.*

5 This interpretation of Atiśa's thought puts it in line with Dunne's understanding of Candrakīrti (John D. Dunne, "Thoughtless Buddha, Passionate Buddha," *Journal of the American Academy of Religion* LXIV/3 [1996]: 525–57). Dunne (p. 542) sees Candrakīrti holding that ordinary perception is "in some sense conceptual" and (p. 544) that Candrakīrti's denial of appearances to Buddhas is due to his unique understanding of "conceptual" perception—Buddhas do not perceive appearances because they have dispelled all forms of conceptuality.

6 Candrakīrti's metaphoric knowing is discussed in Dunne, "Thoughtless Buddha," 546–48.

7 Jayānanda labels Candrakīrti's model "Sautrāntika" at *Madhyamakāvatāraṭīkā,* 325a.4–5.

8 Louis de la Vallée Poussin, *Madhyamakāvatāra par Candrakīrti,* Bibiotheca Buddhica, 9 (Osnabrück, Germany: Biblio Verlag, 1970), stanza XII.4, pp. 357–58: *gang tshe skye med de nyid yin zhing blo yang skye ba dang 'bral ba / / de tshe de rnam rten las de yis de nyid rtogs pa lta bu ste / / ji ltar sems ni gang gi rnam pa can du 'gyur ba de yis yul / / de yongs shes pa de bzhin tha snyad nye bar rten nas rig pa yin /.*

9 Jayānanda takes up a term, "non-observation," that had wide use in Madhyamaka circles but that had first gained currency in Yogācāra texts. As discussed by Makransky (*Buddhahood Embodied,* 47–49), the *Ornament for Mahāyāna Sūtras* (*Mahāyānasūtrālaṃkāra*), stanza IX.78, states that "Utter non-perception is the highest perception" (*sarvathā 'nupalambhaśca upalambhaḥ paro mataḥ //.* Makransky translation, p. 47, Sanskrit from Sylvan Levi's edition, cited in Makransky, p. 380, n. 25). Sthiramati explains that "non-perception" indicates not perceiving false conceptually constructed duality (the "imagined nature" [*parikalpitasvabhāva*] of the Yogācāra "three natures" ontology) and that when duality is not seen, the "perfected nature" (*pariniṣpannasvabhāva*) is realized (Makransky, pp. 48–49). As will be discussed below, Jayānanda's use of "non-observation" is quite different, as he does not posit any "perfected nature" that is perceived when duality is negated, but instead holds to the interpretation that "realization" is simply a term tagged onto utter non-observation.

10 Jayānanda, *Madhyamakāvatāraṭīkā,* Toh. 3870, *sde dge* edition, *dbu ma,* vol. *ra,* 325a.3–4: *blo yang skye ba med pa'i rnam pa can yin pas blo des skye ba med pa'i rang bzhin can gyi de kho na nyid rtogs pa lta bu yin te / . . . de la gsal bar byed pa dang gsal bar bya ba dag ni yod pa ma yin no zhes pa'o / . . . / de bzhin tha snyad brten nas rig pa yin / / zhes bya ba ni sngon po yongs su shes pa bzhin du tha snyad la brten nas de kho na nyid thugs su chud par brjod pa yin gyi don dam par ni ma yin no / . . . des na dngos po gang yang rung mi dmigs pa de nyid de kho na nyid thugs su chud pa yin no /.*

11 La Vallée Poussin, *Madhyamakāvatāra,* 108.9–11: *sangs rgyas rnams la ni chos thams cad rnam pa thams cad du mngon par rdzogs par byang chub pa'i phyir / sems dang sems las byung ba'i rgyu ba gtan log par 'dod pa yin no /;* "We assert that for Buddhas, due to being manifestly and completely enlightened to all phenomena in all aspects, the movement of mind and mental factors has entirely ceased." This passage is also examined in Dunne, "Thoughtless Buddha," 544. While this passage is drawn from his discussion of the two truths, Candrakīrti makes similar statements in his discussion of buddhahood, particularly in his autocommentary to stanzas XII.8–9.

12 For a concise overview of the classical Yogācāra understanding of "transformation of the basis" (*āśrayaparivṛtti/-parāvṛtti*), see Makransky, *Buddhahood Embodied,* 63–83. For a lengthier treatment, see Ronald Mark Davidson, *Buddhist Systems of Transformation:* Āśraya-parivṛtti-parāvṛtti *Among the Yogācāra* (Ph.D. dissertation, University of California, Berkeley, 1985), 160–259.

13 Jayānanda, *Madhyamakāvatāraṭīkā,* 146a.7–146b.1: *ci yang thugs su chud pa med pa'i sgo nas byang chub pa'i phyir sems dang sems las byung ba'i rgyu ba gtan log par 'dod pa yin te nyams su myong ba'i mtshan nyid can gyi sems dang tshor ba la sogs pa sems las byung ba rnams kyi kun du spyod pa ste 'jug pa log par 'dod pa yin te / sems dang sems las byung ba rnams 'jug pa ma yin no zhes pa'o / / des na ci yang snang ba med pa yin no zhes pa'i tha tshig ste / rnam par rtog pa thams cad 'gag pa'i phyir ro /.* The last sentence is translated in Dunne, "Thoughtless Buddha," 545.

14 Jayānanda, *Madhyamakāvatāraṭīkā,* 144a.2ff., commenting on stanza VI.28. Jayānanda also explains that those things regarded as false "even in the world" are mere conventionalities and not conventional truths because the world does not regard them to be true. Thus, he posits two types of mere conventionalities.

15 Jayānanda, *Madhyamakāvatāraṭīkā,* 146a.5: *sngon po la sogs pa'i rnam pa dang bcas pa'i shes pa nyams su myong ba mi mnga' ba'i sangs rgyas bcom ldan 'das rnams la ni kun rdzob tsam snang ba med pa'o/.*

16 Jayānanda, *Madhyamakāvatāraṭīkā,* 146b.5–147a.2 (at the two points where the *sde dge* edition reading is marked incorrect, the correct reading is found in both the Peking and Narthang editions): */gal te bcom ldan 'das rnams kyi sems dang sems byung log par 'dod na sku gsum dang sems can gyi don gyi rnam gzhag byed pa mi 'thad de / 'di ltar bcom ldan 'das rnams kyi* (D: *kyis*) *rnam pa thams cad du sems dang sems las byung ba'i rgyu ba log pas lhag ma 'ga' zhig kyang med pas chos kyi sku mi 'thad de/ de la chos ni stobs dang / mi 'jigs pa la sogs pa'i yon tan rnams yin la / sku ni rang bzhin te/ stong pa nyid yin pas chos med pas rang bzhin med pa'i phyir chos sku yod pa ma yin no / / de bzhin du sems dang sems las byung ba dag log pas rgyun ma chad par chos kyi bdud rtsi la longs spyod pa med pas longs spyod rdzogs pa'i sku yang mi rigs so / / de bzhin du sems dang sems las byung ba log pas sprul pa med pa'i phyir sprul pa'i sku yang ji ltar rigs/ de bzhin du chos ston pa'i rgyu ye shes med pa'i phyir sems can gyi don gyi rnam gzhag kyang med pas bcom ldan 'das rnams kyi sems dang sems las byung ba'i rgyu ba log par* (D: *log pa*) *ci ltar 'dod ce na/ de la lan ni sangs rgyas kyi sar bcom ldan 'das la sku gsum gyi bstod pa'i gnas skabs su slob dpon rang nyid kyis 'chad par 'gyur bas 'dir ma brjod do / /.* This passage is summarized and a portion translated in Dunne, "Thoughtless Buddha," 545.

17 Candrakīrti explains the three bodies in *Madhyamakāvatāra* stanzas XII.5–18 and treats the ten powers of a Buddha in stanzas XII.19–31.

18 This is the number of folios separating the objection and Jayānanda's answer in the *sde dge* edition of the Tibetan translation of Jayānanda's text (the objection begins at 146b.5, while his answer starts at 326a.5). In forging such a wide-ranging link, Jayānanda draws a strong connection between Candrakīrti's presentation of the two truths and his presentation of buddhahood.

19 Jayānanda, *Madhyamakāvatāraṭīkā,* 326a.5: *ye shes lnga po 'di rnams ni sku gsum gyis bsdus pa ste /.* Jayānanda then cites Candragomin at length, giving his own prose explanation of Candragomin's stanzas.

20 Makransky (*Buddhahood Embodied,* 63–64) shows that in most classical Yogācāra presentations, buddhahood is defined by the twin notions of "purified thusness" (*tathatāviśuddhi*) and "non-conceptual wisdom [realizing it]" (*nirvikalpajñāna*) and that these twin notions are sometimes merged into a single term, "purified sphere of reality" (*dharmadhātuviśuddha*). Here, Jayānanda blends the two notions but retains the term, "wisdom."

21 Jayānanda, *Madhyamakāvatāraṭīkā,* 326a.1: *bag chags dang bcas pa'i sgrib pa gnyis dang bral ba'i snying rje dang shes rab gnyis su med pa'o spangs pa dang rtogs pa phun sum tshogs pa mnga' ba de kho na nyid bsgom pa rab kyi mthar gyur pa.*

22 Jayānanda, *Madhyamakāvatāraṭīkā,* 326a.4: *so sor rtog pa'i ye shes ni gang gis bcom ldan 'das de ltar mnyam par bzhag pas rnam par mi rtog pa kho na yin du zin kyang / sngon gyi smon lam dang / sems can rnams kyi bsod nams kyi dbang gis sems can rnams kyi spyod pa so sor rtog pa'o /.*

23 Candrakīrti structures *Entrance to the Middle* on the ten grounds of the bodhisattva's progress to buddhahood, frequently citing the *Sūtra on the Ten Grounds* (*Daśabhūmikāsūtra;* Peking 761.31, vol. 25).

24 Makransky (*Buddhahood Embodied,* 379–380, n. 24) shows that commentarial evidence recommends that Levi's edition (p. 48) be emended from *Buddhatvopāyapraveśe* "Entry into the method of buddhahood" to *Buddhatvapraveśopāye,* "The method of entry into buddhahood" in the introduction to stanza IX.78 of *Ornament for the Great Vehicle Sūtras,* the stanza that declares "Utter nonperception is the highest perception." For complete reference to this stanza, see above, note 9.

25 Translated in Makransky, *Buddhahood Embodied,* 48.

26 La Vallée Poussin, *Madhyamakāvatāra,* stanza XII.8, 361.11–14: *shes bya'i bud shing skam po ma lus pa / / bsregs pas zhi ste . . . sems 'gags pas de sku yis mngon sum mdzad /.* Let no one attribute Candrakīrti's lack of success in his lifetime to want for śāstric wit.

27 La Vallée Poussin, *Madhyamakāvatāra,* 362.7–9: *de ltar na ye shes kyi yul de kho na nyid la rnam pa thams cad du de'i yul na sems dang sems las byung ba rnams mi 'jug pas sku kho nas mngon sum du mdzad par kun rdzob tu rnam par bzhag go /.* The passage in full reads "In that way [previously discussed], concerning the referent of wisdom, suchness, if it is a referent of that [wisdom] in all aspects, since mind and mental factors do not engage, we conventionally posit that [suchness] is made manifest by only the body." Having denied that the inherently dualistic mind operates in realizing suchness, here Candrakīrti uses the language of conventional cognition for realization of suchness, speaking of suchness as the referent (*viṣaya, yul*) of wisdom.

28 Jayānanda, *Madhyamakāvatāraṭīkā,* 333a.1: *zhi zhes bya ba ni sems dang sems las byung ba dag dang bral bas so /.*

29 Jayānanda, *Madhyamakāvatāraṭīkā,* 333a.1–2: *sems dang sems las byung ba dag log pas zhi ba'i bdag nyid can gyis de kho na nyid kyi rang bzhin brnyes pa gang yin pa'o /.*

30 Jayānanda, *Madhyamakāvatāraṭīkā,* 333a.2–4: *'o na sems dang sems las byung ba 'gags na chos kyi sku ji ltar mngon du mdzad ce na / de la lan ni / sems 'gag pa de sku yis mngon sum mdzad / / ces bya ba gsungs te / spros pa'i rang bzhin gyis* [read: *gyi*] *sems 'gags pas longs spyod rdzogs pa'i skus ma gzigs pa'i tshul gyis mngon sum du mdzad pa'i sgo nas brnyes pas skus mngon sum du mdzad pa yin no zhes rnam par 'jog pa'o /.*

31 As Cabezón elucidates, Chapa's Perfection of Wisdom Teacher, Gro lung pa, similarly speaks of the ultimate (or *dharmadhātu*) as "manifesting" (*mngon du gyur pa*) for a practitioner, rather than using the stronger language of "realizing" or "knowing" the ultimate. Gro lung pa, like Candrakīrti, Jayānanda, and his own teacher rNgog bLo ldan shes rab, holds that the ultimate is not an object of consciousness but contra Candrakīrti and Jayānanda (and like rNgog and Phya pa) holds that inference brings one to the ultimate; inference induces the ultimate to "manifest." See José Ignacio Cabezón, "The Madhyamaka in Gron lung pa's *Bstan Rim chen mo*," *Proceedings of the 11th Seminar of the International Association of Tibetan Studies 2006* (forthcoming).

32 Jayānanda, *Madhyamakāvatāraṭīkā,* 326a.5–6: *slob dpon tsan dra go mis / nyon mongs yid ni gnas gyur la / / mnyam nyid ye shes zhes ni brjod / / yid kyi rnam shes gang yin de / / so sor rtog pa'i ye shes yin /.* He declares that they are the Complete Enjoyment Body at 326b.4.

33 Jayānanda, *Madhyamakāvatāraṭīkā,* 326b.3: *gnas gyur pa ni bag chags dang bcas pa'i nyon mongs pa dang shes bya'i sgrib pa spangs pa'i phyir bdag tu lta ba la sogs pa dang bral ba bdag dang gzhan mnyam pa nyid kyi ye shes brnyes pa'o/.*

34 Hugh B. Urban and Paul J. Griffiths, "What Else Remains in Śūnyatā? An Investigation of Terms for Mental Imagery in the *Madhyāntavibhāga*-Corpus," *Journal of the International Association of Buddhist Studies* 17/1 (1994): 1–25. On pp. 19–21, the authors critique the possibility of a "pure" consciousness without dualistic notions of conceptuality.

35 These points work against Griffiths's contention, elsewhere, that Indian Mahāyāna presentations of buddhahood "do not disagree significantly as to which properties should be predicated of Buddha's awareness." See Paul J. Griffiths, *On Being Buddha: The Classical Doctrine of Buddhahood* (Albany, NY: State University of New York Press, 1994), 157. Griffiths lumps together disparate doctrinal and philosophical works, including classical Yogācāra treatises (the *Madhyāntavibhāga* texts, the *Mahāyānasūtrālaṃkāra* texts, the *Mahāyānasaṃgraha* texts, and the *Abhidharmasamuccaya* texts), Candrakīrti's *Entrance to the Middle,* and occasionally the classic of non-Mahāyāna Buddhist philosophy, the *Treasury of Manifest Knowledge* (*Abhidharmakośa*) into his category, "doctrinal digests." For his rationale, see particularly pp. 27–46. From these "digests," he draws a picture of Mahāyāna buddhahood that forms a basis for his "doctrinal criticism," in which he argues against the logical possibility of an omniscient Buddha (pp. 181–202). While discussing what qualities the "digests" predicate to a Buddha's consciousness, he notes (p. 157), "it isn't difficult to find places in the digests where it is explicitly denied that Buddha's awareness involves the operations of the mind and its concomitants"; his footnote (p. 222, n. 17) indicates only the passage in Candrakīrti's *Entrance to the Middle* discussed above, in which Candrakīrti states, "[suchness] is made manifest by only the body." Griffiths's comment belies the rarity of such a proclamation in Indian Buddhist sources and obscures the important differences between Candrakīrti's and Jayānanda's understanding of transformation and buddhahood, on the one hand, and Yogācāra conceptions, on the other. Griffiths's sense that (p. 157) "The issue, in the end, is one of where to draw a definitional line" is certainly accurate, as the variety of Mahāyāna philosophical commitments forces lines to be drawn in very different places.

36 La Vallée Poussin, *Madhyamakāvatāra,* 361.1–3: *sems can gyi don sgrub pa lhur mdzad cing chos kyi dbyings las skad cig kyang mi bskyod la /.*

37 The triumph of Madhyamaka over Yogācāra for the ontological imagination of Mahāyāna Buddhists in Tibet and perhaps also in India poses a number of difficulties for Mādhyamikas, including how to align buddhahood with the doctrine of two truths and, for many, how to graft a Madhyamaka explanation onto tantra. The early Tibetan "Svātantrika" conception of a plausible model of buddhahood will be examined below. Prāsaṅgika authors would take longer to develop satisfying answers, coming, by the fourteenth and fifteenth centuries, to adopt positions similar to those held by twelfth-century Svātantrikas.

38 Griffiths's (*On Being Buddha,* 58–60 and 182–83) insights that Mahāyāna conceptions of buddhahood are founded on the notion of "maximal greatness"—that doctrinal authors ascribe qualities to buddhahood that would make a Buddha the

greatest possible being—and that the principle of maximal greatness leads doctrinal authors to prioritize "great-making" qualities is helpful in understanding Jayānanda's work on buddhahood. Jayānanda certainly is forced to make choices between his Prāsaṅgika notion of buddhahood and the Yogācāra model and between the two poles of buddhahood, pristine wisdom and compassionate activity.

39 The three are "mirror-like wisdom" (*ādarśajñāna*), responsible for "reflecting" all objects; the "wisdom of individual attention" (*pratyavekṣājñāna*), allowing a Buddha to attend to each beings' aid; and the "wisdom that accomplishes activities" (*kṛtyasādhanajñāna*), which, based on the wisdom of individual attention, accomplishes the welfare of sentient beings. In discussing mirror-like wisdom, Jayānanda seems to regard it as sufficient explanation for a Buddha's perception (while his metaphor here would seem to belie this interpretation). He cites the *Ornament for Great Vehicle Sūtras* (*Mahāyānasūtrālaṃkāra*), which states, "Mirror-like wisdom is unwavering," and concludes, "Since that [mirror-like wisdom], too, is of the same taste as the Dharma Body, [the explanation that mirror-like wisdom is the Dharma Body] is feasible. Due to just that [mirror-like wisdom], Supramundane Victors have knowledge (*vidyā, rig*) that lacks the capacity of memory or forgetting since all entities appear as though in a mirror at all times." Jayānanda, *Madhyamakāvatāraṭīkā,* 327a.1: *mdo sde rgyan las / me long ye shes g.yo ba med / / ces gsungs so / / de yang chos kyi sku dang ro gcig ba'i phyir 'thad pa yin no zhes bya ba / de nyid kyi phyir bcom ldan 'das rnams la dran pa nyams pa mi mnga' ba rig pa yin te / dus thams cad du dngos po thams cad me long bzhin du snang bas so /.*

40 This correlation was discussed in chapter 3. Jayānanda (*Madhyamakāvatāraṭīkā,* 146b.2–4) neatly summarizes his position as follows: "Here, stain (*sgrib pa*) has two aspects: afflictive ignorance and non-afflictive ignorance. Of those, afflictive ignorance is the cause of one continually engaging cyclic existence. Non-afflictive ignorance is the cause of the appearance of form and so forth. Supramundane Victors have no capacity for either stain and hence, the absence of the causes [that is, the absence of both afflictive and non-afflictive ignorance] results in the absence of effects [that is, cyclic existence and appearance]. Therefore, there is no cyclic existence and no appearance of form and so forth; how could mere conventionalities appear? Therefore, we assert that mind and mental factors have ceased." Excepting the last sentence, this passage is translated in Dunne, "Thoughtless Buddha," 545.

41 I supply this because the hypothetical objector has brought up the twelve links as a reason for suggesting that the appearance of a Buddha's wisdom entails ignorance, reminding Jayānanda that "Conditioned factors are caused by ignorance; consciousness is caused by conditioned factors . . ." (Jayānanda, *Madhyamakāvatāraṭīkā,* 328a.1: *ma rig pa'i rkyen gyis 'du byed 'du byed kyi rkyen gyis rnam par shes pa zhes bya ba gsungs pa*). Jayānanda explains what the Buddha meant in this statement as his point of departure here.

42 Jayānanda, *Madhyamakāvatāraṭīkā,* 328a.1–3: *nyon mongs pa dang bcas pa'i 'khor bar gyur pa'i rnam pa shes pa la ma rig pa'i rkyen can du gsungs pa yin gyi shes pa thams cad la ni ma yin te / bcom ldan 'das kyi ye shes ni snying rje'i rgyu can yin te / snying rje'i stobs kyis bcom ldan 'das rnams 'khor ba ji srid du bzhugs pas so / / dper na mar me dang po 'bru mar gyis rgyu can yin du zin kyang 'bru mar zad nas mar blugs na mi ldog pa de bzhin du 'dir yang shes pa ma rig pa'i rgyu can yin du zin kyang ma rig pa log nas sny-*

ing rje'i stobs kyis ye shes snang bas bcom ldan 'das rnams ma rig pa dang bcas par thal bar mi 'gyur ba'o /.

43 La Vallée Poussin, *Madhyamakāvatāra,* 1 (stanza I.1cd): *snying rje'i sems dang gnyis su med blo dang / byang chub sems ni rgyal sras rnams kyi rgyu /.*

44 Jayānanda, *Madhyamakāvatāraṭīkā,* 328a.3–329b.7.

45 Jayānanda, *Madhyamakāvatāraṭīkā,* 328b.3–4: *bcom ldan 'das rnams ma rig pa spong ba'i nus pa mnga' ru zin kyang bcom ldan 'das rnams kyi thugs rje'i dbang gis ma rig pa mi spong ba yin te / gzhan du na chad par 'gyur bas so /.* Dunne ("Thoughtless Buddha," pp. 533–34 and 534, n. 7) understands Jayānanda here to report on another's view. He writes, "Some Indian Buddhists went so far as to say that Buddhas actually retain some degree of ignorance in order to interact with the world on a conceptual level." I previously took Jayānanda's report, as well as another of related position, as a statement of his own views on buddhahood (Kevin Vose, *The Birth of Prāsaṅgika: A Buddhist Movement in India and Tibet* [Ph.D. dissertation, University of Virginia, 2005]). I now feel that the identification was unwarranted. This portion of Jayānanda's text contains a host of opinions on buddhahood and requires further investigation to determine just whose opinions are advanced.

46 Jayānanda, *Madhyamakāvatāraṭīkā,* 328a-b.

47 Phya pa chos kyi seṅ ge, *dbu ma śar gsum gyi stoṅ thun,* ed. Helmut Tauscher (Vienna: Arbeitskreis für Tibetische und Buddhistische Studien Universität Wien, 1999), 58.13–16: *sa thob pa'i mnyam bzhag dang sangs rgyas kyi sa na yul shes bya gang yang ma grub pas yul can gyi 'jug pa zhi ste sems dang sems las byung ba'i 'jug pa chad pa nyid la chos nyid rtogs pas yang dag pa'i blo ma 'khrul zhes gdags ste / mdo' sde bas sngon po dang 'dra ba'i blo la sngon po rtogs zhes brjod pa ltar chos nyid skye ba myed pa dang blo skye ba dang bral ba 'dra bas chos nyid rtogs zhes bya ste /.*

48 Phya pa, *dbu ma shar gsum,* 21.1ff. In this section, Chapa argues that if the "voidness of proliferations" (*spros bral,* synonymous with emptiness) were not an object of knowledge, the continuum of a reasoning consciousness (*rigs shes*) would be cut.

49 Phya pa, *dbu ma shar gsum,* 21.20–21.21: *rnal 'byor gyi mngon sum gyis spros bral gzhal bya ma yin pa la gzhal bar rlom na blo de 'khrul pa dang bcas par 'gyur la.* "If you fancy that yogic direct perception cognizes [even] when [you claim that] voidness of proliferations is not an object of valid cognition, that awareness would be mistaken."

50 Phya pa, *dbu ma shar gsum,* 73.8: *phyi ma skyed pa'i nus pas ni blo tsam la khyab pa ma yin te sred pa dang bcas pa'i blo la khyab pa yin la / rdo rje lta bu'i dus na sred pa myed pas blo phyi ma mi 'phen no zhe na /.* "Mere awareness does not entail the power to produce later [awareness]. Awareness that is conjoined with craving entails the power to produce later [awareness]. Since there is no craving during the adamantine meditative equipoise, further awareness is not impelled."

51 Phya pa, *dbu ma shar gsum,* 73.13–14: *dag pa'i shes pa ma chags pa dang zhe sdang myed pa dang gti mug myed pa'i dge ba'i sems kyi de ma thag pa las khyang skye bar myong ngo /.*

52 Phya pa, *dbu ma shar gsum,* 75.19–20: *'phrin las 'grub pa dang snang ba 'byung pa'i nus pa gang las yod / ye shes la yod par mi 'thad de blo rgyun chad pa'i phyir ro //.* "In what does the capacity to give rise to the accomplishment of Buddha activities and appearances exist? It is not feasible that [the capacity] exists in wisdom because [for you] the continuum of awareness is cut."

53 Following immediately from the preceding passage; Phya pa, *dbu ma shar gsum,* 75.20–21: *de bzhin nyid la yod par mi 'thad de de don dam pa'i bden pa 'ba' zhig yin la des 'phrin las sgrub pa'i don byed nus na don dam pa'i dngos por grub par thal bar 'gyur ro //.* "It is not feasible that it exists in suchness because [suchness] is ultimate truth alone and if [suchness] is able to perform the function of accomplishing Buddha activities, it would follow that it is established as an ultimate entity."

54 The bulk (Phya pa, *dbu ma shar gsum,* 58.5–124.10) of Chapa's *Compilation of the Three Mādhyamikas from the East,* including most of his argument against Prāsaṅgika, is structured around the correct way to refute an ultimate entity (*yang dag pa'i dngos po*).

55 Phya pa, *dbu ma shar gsum,* 76.2–5: *tshogs dang smon lam ni 'gags nas ring du lon la 'gro ba la phan pa dus phyis 'byung bas chod pa las skye bar yang 'gyur la / tshogs sog pa dang smon lam ldebs pa byang chub sems dpa' kho na'i rgyud du gtogs pas byang chub sems dpa'i 'phrin las kho nar 'gyur gyi sangs rgyas kyi 'phrin las su gtan mi 'thad do //.* "The collections and wishes having ceased, the time for aiding transmigrating beings arises later, after a long time has passed. Hence, [aiding migrating beings] would arise upon being cut off [from the collections and prayer-wishes]. Since accumulating the collections and making prayer-wishes are included within the continuums of bodhisattvas only, these would be only bodhisattva activities; Buddha activities would be utterly unfeasible."

56 Phya pa, *dbu ma shar gsum,* 75.15–16: *nyan thos phung po lhag myed ni mar me shi ba ltar nyon mongs pa dang sdug bsngal zhi ba tsam.*

57 Phya pa, *dbu ma shar gsum,* 73.17–18: *snang bcas sgyu ma lta bur rtogs pa'i blo.* It seems clear that for Chapa, seeing the illusion-like nature is a post-realization state, as this argument occurs within his claim that Buddhas perceive appearances: if they perceive appearances, surely they perceive them as having the nature of illusion.

58 As will be seen from his following discussion, Chapa, like Jayānanda, understands *shes bya'i sgrib pa* to mean "obstructions to the object to be known [that is, emptiness]." However, overcoming this class of obstructions leads to two realizations: "knowledge of the mode of being" (*ji lta ba shes pa*), which is realization of emptiness itself, and "knowledge of the varieties" (*ji snyed pa shes pa*), which is the knowledge of all objects of knowledge (Phya pa, *dbu ma shar gsum,* 74.1–2).

59 Phya pa, *dbu ma shar gsum,* 73.19–22: *dang po ni mi 'thad de nyon mongs la nges par gang zag gi bdag 'dzin rjes su 'brel pas khyab pa yin na snang bcas kyi phung po lnga skad cig du mar shes pas rtag pa gcig pur 'dzin pa bsal la / snga ma snga ma las byung par shes pas rang dbang can du 'dzin pa bsal te gang zag gi bdag du 'dzin pa dang rjes su 'brel pa myed pa'i phyir ro.* "The first case is not feasible because, whereas afflictions entail connection with the conception of a self of persons, [an awareness] having appearance [and realizing appearances to be like illusions] (1) dispels the conception of the five aggregates as being permanent and unitary through knowing that they are momentary and multiple; and (2) dispels the conception of the five aggregates as being self-powered through knowing that they arise from earlier [causes]; and thus is not connected with the conception [of the five aggregates] as a self of persons."

60 Phya pa, *dbu ma shar gsum,* 74.5: *spros bral snang ba'i chos nyid ma yin par 'gyur ba.* "Voidness of proliferations would not be the reality of appearances." Chapa (74.5–8) also points to the reverse fallacy, that if appearances and emptiness were contradic-

tory, the experiential establishment of appearances would block the possibility that appearances are empty, which in turn would prove "the position of the proponents of [real] entities" (*dngos por smra ba'i phyogs*), the chief opponent of Madhyamaka. Additionally, Chapa (74.8–9) dismisses the idea that appearances could obstruct emptiness even without the two being contradictory; if two things could obstruct each other without being contradictory, any two non-contradictory things could be said to obstruct each other, which would be logically unfeasible.

61 One might ask Chapa if the "final nature" of the false conception of the self of persons and the self of phenomena—the false conceptions that emptiness negates, in Chapa's view—is emptiness. Realizing emptiness is contradictory with these false conceptions for Chapa, so could emptiness be the final nature of the self of persons?

62 Chapa notes that the destruction of cause and effect (*rgyu 'bras*) would lead to the Cārvākas' (*tshu rol mdzes pa ba*) system (*dbu ma shar gsum,* 75.4–5) or to the Lokāyatas' (*rgyang 'phan pa*) materialism (75.13). These two Indian philosophies are often treated together, rejecting past and future lifetimes and the workings of karma.

63 Phya pa, *dbu ma shar gsum,* 74.11–12: *ma spyad pa'i ngor snang ba grub pas ma dpyad pa'i ngor mi snang ba sel gyi dpyad na cir yang ma grub pa mi sel bas spyad na cir yang ma grub pa rtogs pa'i gegs su ji ltar 'gyur /.*

64 Two sections of Chapa's argument that mind and mental factors cannot be cut off at buddhahood are "[Consciousness] having appearance is not an obstruction and, hence, is not to be dispelled" (*dbu ma shar gsum,* 73.17: *snang bcas sgrib pa ma yin pas spang bya ma yin pa*) and "There is no antidote to that [consciousness having appearance]" (74.17: *snang bcas la gnyen po myed pa*).

65 We saw above (endnote 58) that Chapa understands overcoming obstructions to the object of knowledge to involve both realizing emptiness and "knowledge of the varieties" (*ji snyed pa shes pa*). When considering whether a consciousness perceiving the illusion-like nature could obstruct knowledge of the varieties, Chapa concludes that "it is contradictory for something to obstruct itself, realization of the varieties being the very [awareness] having appearance [and realizing appearances to be like illusions]" (*dbu ma shar gsum,* 74.13–14: *ji snyed pa rtogs pa snang bcas nyid yin pas rang nyid kyis rang la sgrib pa 'gal ba'i phyir ro //*).

66 Phya pa, *dbu ma shar gsum,* 74.14–17: *sgyu ma lta bur rtogs pa'i snang bcas dpyad mi bzod pa'i yul can yin pas 'khrul snang zhes tha snyad byed kyang sgrib pa gnyis gang yang ma yin pas de sangs rgyas kyis spong bar mi 'thad do //.*

67 Phya pa, *dbu ma shar gsum,* 15.7–12: *gal te sangs rgyas kyi snang bcas kyang 'khrul pa yin la de'i yul yang 'khrul ngor bden pa yin na sangs rgyas la 'khrul pa mnga' bas sangs rgyas sgrib pa dang bcas par 'gyur ro zhe na / rtag pa'i dngos por zhen pa lta bu shes bya la mi srid pa la srid par zhen pa'i 'khrul pa dang zla ba gnyis dang don spyi lasogs par snang ba lta bu don byed pas stong ba gzung yul du byed pa'i 'khrul pa la sgrib pas khyab kyang de sangs rgyas la mi mnga' bas sgrib pa dang bcas par thal ba'i skyon brjod na gtan tshigs ma grub pa yin la / dpyad mi bzod pa'i yul can gyi 'khrul pa mnga' ba'i phyir sgrib pa dang bcas par 'gyur ro zhe na khyab pa ma grub pa yin no //.*

68 Chapa lumps in with this type of mistake the perceptual mistake of those with faulty sense faculties. He may consider perceptual mistake to be a fourth type. The perception of two moons is a common Madhyamaka analogy for the false

way in which ordinary beings perceive the world—the dualistic manner in which we perceive the world compared to how the world truly exists is similar to the way those with faulty senses perceive what does not exist. In the present context, Chapa may be using the metaphor to refer to a discussion like Jayānanda's equation of mere ignorance and mere appearances: having overcome afflictive ignorance, the non-afflictive ignorance that causes bodhisattvas to continue seeing appearances outside of meditation can be classified along with the useful mistake of conceptuality.

69 Phya pa, *dbu ma shar gsum,* 15.14: *dpyad bzod pa la mi slu ba.*

70 Prāsaṅgika is claimed by later Tibetan exegetes to have a more subtle object of negation. On the one hand, Jayānanda claims that perception is imbued with a false status that needs to be overcome. In this sense, his may be a more subtle object of negation, an object residing in the very manner in which we perceive the world. In another sense, he needs to throw away perception altogether in his conception of full enlightenment. It is difficult to see how that can be called subtle.

71 bSod nams rtse mo, *Byang chub sems dpa'i spyod pa la 'jug pa'i 'grel pa,* in *Sa skya pa'i bka' 'bum,* vol. 2 (Tokyo: Toyo Bunko, 1968), 495.4.1–496.1.3 (vol. *ca,* 296a.1–296b.3).

72 bSod nams rtse mo, *sPyod pa la 'jug pa'i 'grel pa,* 495.4.5–6 (vol. *ca,* 296a.5–6).

73 Grags pa rgyal mtshan, *rGyud kyi mngon par rtogs pa rin po che'i ljong shing,* in *Sa skya pa'i bka' 'bum,* vol. 3 (Tokyo: Toyo Bunko, 1968), 21.4.6–22.1.4.

74 Grags pa, *Rin po che'i ljon shing,* 22.1.3: *dag pa 'jig rten pa'i ye shes.*

75 Grags pa, *Rin po che'i ljon shing,* 22.4.3–7: *de la 'phags pa rnams kyi thugs ni don dam pa yin la / de'i yul skye ba dang 'gag pa med pa spros pa dang bral ba ni don dam pa'i bden pa'o / / 'o na mdo las / don dam pa'i bden pa ni rnam pa thams cad mkhyen pa'i ye shes kyi yul las 'das pa'o zhes gsungs so zhe na / bden mod / yul dang yul can gyi tshul gyis shes pa ma yin te / slob dpon zla grags kyis / gang tshe chos nyid skye med yin zhing blo 'ang skye ba dang bral ba / / de tshe de rnams bstan la de yi de nyid rtogs pa lta bu ste / / ji ltar sems ni gang gi rnam pa can du gyur bas de yi yul / / de yongs shes pa de bzhin tha snyad brten nas shes pa yin / / zhes gsungs te / gang du 'ang ma grub pa de nyid la rtogs zhes bya'o / / de lta bu de nyid la mya ngan las 'das pa zhes bya'o / / chos nyid 'dus ma byas zhes bya'o / / de nyid la 'phags pa nyan thos dag mya ngan las 'das pa zhes bya ba zhig grub par 'dod do / de ltar du da lta bod kyi dbu ma pa phal cher yang 'dod do / / yang dag pa ma yin te sngar yang sun phyung la /.*

76 Throughout this section of his text, Drakpa Gyeltsen cites Candrakīrti in support of points he makes concerning the two truths and once cites Candrakīrti to criticize a contemporary Prāsaṅgika viewpoint. While he favors the Svātantrika notion of buddhahood, he clearly supported Candrakīrti's views and saw the need to refute common misinterpretations of these views. However, he may regard Candrakīrti's notion of metaphorical realization to be the problem here, rather than misinterpretations of that notion.

Notes to the Conclusion

1 As Drakpa Gyeltsen's divisions show, several different names for these schools were known; see the discussion in chapter 4.

2 That we see a different difference between Prāsaṅgika and Svātantrika in the twelfth century from that adduced in the fifteenth century has already been proffered by Helmut Tauscher ("Phya pa chos kyi seng ge as a Svātantrika," 235–38). Tauscher detects an "old" method and a "Gelukpa" method of dividing Prāsaṅgika from Svātantrika, with both methods based on the rejection or acceptance of *svatantra* reasoning: the old method of distinguishing the two views takes *svatantra* reasoning as a Mādhyamika holding a thesis (*pratijñā*) "of one's own" that is proved by way of formal inference in which the "three modes" (*trairūpya*) of inference are established by valid cognition; the Gelukpa method of distinguishing Prāsaṅgika from Svātantrika interprets *svatantra* reasoning as a formal inference that is "established in itself" and thereby implies the acceptance of conventional "natures" of phenomena. Both "old" and "Gelukpa" methods focus on *svatantra* reasoning but differ in their interpretation of it. Tauscher endeavors to determine whether Chapa can be classified as a Svātantrika based on either the old or Gelukpa methods, answers "yes" to the first and "not really" to the second, and shows several clear similarities between Chapa's views and those of the Geluk founder, Tsongkhapa. Tauscher stops short of suggesting what his distinctions seem to imply, that Gelukpas might very well be considered Svātantrikas according to the "old" distinction.

3 Jayānanda's discussion of these issues occurs at greatest length in his *Commentary to [Candrakīrti's] Entrance to the Middle*, on stanzas VI.3–8. There, he cites at length Candrakīrti's defense/explication in *Clear Words (Prasannapadā)* of Buddhapālita's argumentative method based on logical "consequences" *(prasaṅgas)* and Candrakīrti's criticism of Bhāvaviveka's insistence on formal inference. See Jayānanda, *Madhyamakāvatāraṭīkā*, Toh. 3870, *sde dge* edition, *dbu ma*, vol. *ra*, 138b.3ff.

4 Phya pa chos kyi seṅ ge, *dbu ma śar gsum gyi stoṅ thun*, ed. Helmut Tauscher (Vienna: Arbeitskreis für Tibetische und Buddhistische Studien Universität Wien, 1999), 58.7–124.9.

5 Helmut Tauscher, "Phya pa Chos kyi seng ge's Opinion on *Prasaṅga* in his *dbu ma'i shar gsum gyi stong thun*," in *Dharmakīrti's Thought and Its Impact on Indian and Tibetan Philosophy*, edited by Shoryu Katsura (Vienna: Österreichischen Akademie der Wissenschaften, 1999), 387–93 and Tauscher, "Phya pa chos kyi seng ge as a Svātantrika," 207–55.

6 Jayānanda, who has proven to be a quite faithful interpreter of Candrakīrti, develops a strong connection between ignorance and appearance and denies the possibility of common appearance for Mādhyamikas. In his *Clear Words (Prasannapadā)*, Candrakīrti denies the possibility that an inferential subject could appear in common to two parties in a debate on the ultimate, even when putting aside the issue of how that subject is established in the tenet systems of the two parties, giving as his reason, "falsity and non-falsity are different" (Louis de La Vallée Pousin, *Mūlamadhyamakakārikās de Nāgārjuna avec la Prasannapadā Commentaire de Candrakīrti*, Bibliotheca Buddhica

4 [Osnabrück: Biblio Verlag, 1970], 30: *bhinnau hi viparyāsāviparyāsau /*). Given Jayānanda's readings of Candrakīrti, this passage may indicate that Candrakīrti rejects "common appearance" and, consequently, formal inference due to his unique interpretation of appearances being the sole domain of ignorance.

7 My mentor Jeffrey Hopkins remarked that Candrakīrti's choice of title for his commentary on Nāgārjuna's *Mūlamadhyamakakārikāḥ, Prasannapadā* (or, *"Clear Words"*) was apt, as the work exhibits a more lucid expository style than Bhāvaviveka's commentary on the same work. Candrakīrti may be clear, but he is not easy.

Notes to the Materials

1 *dBu ma shar gsum gyi stong mthun.*

2 Phya pa chos kyi seṅ ge, *dbu ma śar gsum gyi stoṅ thun,* ed. Helmut Tauscher (Vienna: Arbeitskreis für Tibetische und Buddhistische Studien Universität Wien, 1999).

3 Corresponding to Tauscher's edition, 58.5–80.13.

4 Louis de la Vallée Poussin, *Madhyamakāvatāra par Candrakīrti,* Bibliotheca Buddhica, 9 (Osnabrück, Germany: Biblio Verlag, 1970).

5 Helmut Tauscher, "Phya pa chos kyi seng ge as a Svātantrika," in *The Svātantrika-Prāsaṅgika Distinction: What Difference Does a Difference Make?* eds. Georges B.J. Dreyfus and Sara L. McClintock (Boston: Wisdom Publications, 2002), 207–55.

6 This second part is not included in the present translation. When explaining this topic, Chapa (124.10) titles it "Refuting an ultimate affirming negative that is not an entity".

7 The Sanskrit of Candrakīrti's stanza as cited by Prajñākaramati is found in Louis de la Vallée Poussin, *Prajñākaramati's Commentary to the Bodhicaryāvatāra of Çāntideva,* Bibliotheca Indica (Calcutta: Asiatic Society of Bengal, 1905), 361.4: *samyagmṛṣādarśanalabdhabhāvaṃ rūpadvayaṃ bibhrati sarvabhāvāḥ / samyagdṛśāṃ yo viṣayaḥ sa tattvaṃ mṛṣādṛśāṃ saṃvṛtisatyam uktam //.*

In pāda a, Chapa's text reads *log pa* for *rdzun pa.* This may be significant for the manner in which Chapa construes Candrakīrti's understanding of *rdzun pa.*

8 La Vallée Poussin, *Bodhicaryāvatārapañjikā,* 353.13: *vinopaghātena yad indriyāṇāṃ saṇṇām api grāhyam avaiti lokaḥ / satyaṃ hi tal lokata evaṃ śeṣaṃ vikalpitaṃ lokata eva mithyā //.*

9 This line is translated per Chapa's reading of it, as indicated by his comments above. Such a reading seems to twist the word order and moves away from other interpretations which read "nature" as the direct object of "obscures": obscurational truth obscures the nature, emptiness. A more straightforward translation is: "Delusion is a concealer because it obscures the nature." Jayānanda's reading also contains ambiguities. This stanza draws upon a stanza in the *Laṅkāvatāra Sūtra* (*Laṅkāvatārasūtra, Lang kar gshegs pa'i mdo,* stanza X.429; Sanskrit in Bunyiu Nanjio, *The Laṅkāvatāra Sūtra,* Bibliotheca Otaniensis, vol. 1 [Kyoto: Otani University Press, 1923], 319): *bhāvā vidyanti saṃvṛtyā paramārthe na bhāvakāḥ / niḥsvabhāveṣu yā bhrāntistatsatyaṃ saṃvṛtirbhavet //.* The second part of the stanza makes it clear that, for this sūtra, "truth," that is, emptiness, is concealed by ignorance: "That [con-

sciousness] which is mistaken regarding the lack of inherent existence is asserted as the concealer of reality (*yang dag kun rdzob, satyaṃ saṃvṛti*)."

10 The translation of this line reflects both the variant readings found in Chapa's citation and Chapa's interpretation of the reading: his text reads *dngos rnams* for La Vallée Poussin's *bcos ma* and *brtags pa* for *snang de.* In explaining *kun rdzob bden pa* just prior to these citations, Chapa uses the reading *brtags pa,* stating that such entities are "imputed to be true." One can appreciate his reading of *brtags pa* at the end of pāda b, as the "b" pādas of stanzas twenty-six and twenty-nine each end with *brtags pa.*

11 Here, again, Chapa's text contains a variant, reading *bden pa* for *dngos ni.* The translation of *kun rdzob tu'o* (*saṃvṛtim*) in pāda d as "conventionalities" agrees with Jayānanda's interpretation; Chapa says nothing concerning it. Finally, the Sanskrit as found in La Vallée Poussin, *Bodhicaryāvatārapañjikā,* 353.3, which in all cases agrees with La Vallée Poussin's edition of *Entrance to the Middle* (and for the most part with Jayānanda's interpretation), reads: *mohaḥ svabhāvāvaraṇād hi saṃvṛtiḥ satyaṃ tayā khyāti yad eva kṛtrimam / jagāda tat saṃvṛtisatyam ity asau muniḥ padārthaṃ kṛtakaṃ ca saṃvṛtim //.*

12 Chapa's reading of this stanza differs slightly from La Vallée Poussin's edition: for *de nyid bdag nyid gang du* (*yenātmanā*), he reads *de'i bdag nyid gang gis.* For *mthong de de nyid,* he reads *mthong ba gang yin.* The first variant follows the Sanskrit more closely and makes little difference to the translation. The second variant is perplexing; one imagines the *gang* is intended to handle the Sanskrit correlative pronoun *tat,* handled by the first *de* in La Vallée Poussin's edition. However, without *de nyid* (*tattva*), it is unclear what the stanza's simile is intended to describe. The Sanskrit, in La Vallée Poussin, *Bodhicaryāvatāra* 365.2, reads: *vikalpitaṃ yat timiraprabhāvāt keśādirūpaṃ vitathaṃ tad eva / yenātmanā paśyati śuddhadṛṣṭis tat tattvam ity evam ihāpy avaihi //.*

13 *bsgrub bya rang gi zhe 'dod bsgrub du myed pa,* literally, "The probandum does not exist to be proved as what one desires to know." Chapa seems to have the Prāsaṅgika say that even if we allow that the inferential subject can be a "mere appearance" (which is admitted only provisionally, as the Prāsaṅgika has claimed that there can be no commonly appearing subject), the probandum does not exist; hence, no reason can prove that a "mere" subject possesses a non-existent predicate. This criticism plays on Dharmakīrti's requirement that the subject of an inference be "enquired about" (*shes 'dod, jijñāsā*) as to whether it possesses the property of the probandum.

14 The text reads *rtags tshul gsum tshad ma'i kham du tshang ba'ang bstan par byar med.* Tauscher conjectures that *kham du* may be emended to *lam du. tshad ma'i kham du* would seem meaningless; *tshad ma'i lam du* could mean "by way of valid cognition"—the three modes are cognized by perception or inference to be fulfilled.

15 Both "authoritative" and "valid cognition" translate the same word, *tshad ma* (*pramāṇa*). The first *tshad ma* must be translated as "authoritative," as Candrakīrti introduces the stanza by stating that only āryas are authoritative (*tshad ma*); non-āryas are not. However, both Chapa and Jayānanda interpret the second *tshad ma* in this stanza as a mental state, Jayānanda explaining that "the world" is not non-deceptive (*mi slu ba,* using the Dharmakīrtian definition of valid cognition) and

does not possess thorough knowledge (*yongs su shes pa*), and so does not possess "valid cognition." Furthermore, Chapa's text differs from La Vallée Poussin's edition in this fourth pāda: for *rigs pa'ang ma yin no,* it reads *gyur pa ga la yod.* Whereas La Vallée Poussin's edition and Jayānanda's reading convey the statement: "It is not reasonable for foolishness also to be valid cognition," Chapa's reading poses a rhetorical question.

16 Tauscher here indicates: "4 *akṣara* deleted or *gnyis ka* to be amended?" My provisional translation "and so forth" allows for the possibility that another word was intended in addition to "sign, pervasion," (*rtags dang khyab pa*), yet *lasogs pa,* even as conjuncted throughout the text, would not fit as 4 *akṣara.*

17 E.H. Johnston, A. Kunst, K. Bhattacharya, *The Dialectical Method of Nāgārjuna: Vigrahavyāvartanī* (Delhi: Motilal Banarsidass, 1998), 14, 61: *yadi kācana pratijñā syānme tata eṣa me bhaveddoṣaḥ / nāsti ca mama pratijñā tasmānnaivāsti me doṣaḥ //.*

18 *'gal ba sdud pa'i thal 'gyur.*

19 *'go snyom pa.*

20 In a parallel passage, Candrakīrti's *Clear Words* (Louis de la Vallée Poussin, *Mūlamadhyamakakārikās de Nāgārjuna avec la Prasannapadā Commentaire de Candrakīrti,* Bibliotheca Buddhica, 4 [Osnabrück, Germany: Biblio Verlag, 1970], 38.7) reads for the first two pādas:

gṛhyeta naiva ca jagad yadi hetuśūnyaṃ syād yadvad eva
gaganotpalavarṇagandhau /.

In the third pāda, Chapa's reading varies from La Vallée Poussin's edition: . . . *bkra 'jig rten pa yis 'dzin de'i phyir* for . . . *bkra'i 'jig rten 'dzin pa'ang yin de'i phyir.* I have translated according to La Vallée Poussin's edition of *Entrance to the Middle,* as Chapa's reading simply introduces the "apprehender," which in any case is assumed, and if used would confuse the English.

21 *phyogs chos, pakṣadharma.*

22 *ma brtags nyams dga' ba'i gang zag.*

23 While "the horns of a rabbit" and "the son of a barren woman" are common examples of things that do not exist in any manner, "a flesh eater" (*sha za*) is typically considered to exist but as a supersensory being. "The vase of a flesh eater" is utterly non-existent, as supersensory beings cannot be said to possess something that is in the range of our senses. It is possible that in Chapa's response he intends again "the vase of a flesh eater"; however, his rejoinders throughout this section posit some kind of being to whom a consequence is stated, not a phenomenon about which one may argue.

24 *phan tshun spangs 'gal.* In this type of contradiction, as explained here, establishing one entity entails the denial of its counterpart, or "mate" (*zla bo*). However, unlike explicit contradictories (immediately below), it is possible to posit a third entity, unrelated to the two contradictory "mates." For example, the conception of self (*bdag 'dzin*) and the wisdom realizing emptiness (*stong nyid rtogs pa'i shes rab*) are contradictories in the sense of mutual exclusion; an eye sense consciousness seeing blue is neither. Onoda ("Phya pa Chos kyi seng ge's Theory of *'gal ba,*" in *Tibetan Studies: Proceedings of the 5th Seminar of the International Association for Tibetan Studies,* Monograph Series of Naritasan Institute for Buddhist Studies, Occasional Papers 2, ed. Ihara Shōren and Yamaguchi Zuihō [Narita: Naritasan

Shinshōji, 1992], 197–202) has sketched out a possible framework of Chapa's understanding of "contradictories" (*'gal ba*), based on Sakya sources and on Tsangnakpa's (gTsang nag pa) *Tshad ma rnam par nges pa'i ṭi ka legs bshad bsdus pa.* It is not at all clear that the composite sketched from these sources reflects Chapa's views. It is well known that Chapa's positions were the chief target of Sakya Paṇḍita's *pramāṇa* writings and while Tsangnakpa was Chapa's disciple, he is said to have left Chapa in favor of the Prāsaṅgika position. So while a fair degree of knowledge of Chapa's views can be attributed to both, a certain amount of partisanship could distort their presentations. Furthermore, the additional Sakya sources were written at hundreds of years' distance. The composite is as follows: Chapa divides "contradictories" into "contradictory in the sense of not abiding together" (*lhan cig mi gnas 'gal*) and "contradictory in the sense of mutual exclusion." This latter is equated with "mere contradictory" (*'gal ba tsam*) and is further divided into "explicit contradictory" and "implied contradictory" (*rgyud 'gal*). Onoda (p. 201) concludes that "contradictory in the sense of not abiding together" (Onoda: "contraries where there is no [possibility of] co-existence") is of little importance for Chapa—it is not mentioned in this passage. Such a classification would seem to make "explicit contradictory" a stricter relation than "contradictory in the sense of mutual exclusion," consistent with Chapa's usage here. It is not clear that this classification would make the Prāsaṅgika's position "implied contradiction." Now that we have access to some of Chapa's epistemological writing, hopefully these issues can be cleared up.

25 *dngos 'gal.* In this type of contradictory, all entities are divided into two classes, such as permanent and impermanent; no third choice is possible. Hence, as Chapa indicates, the denial of one entails the acceptance of the other. The import here is that Chapa views the first two options of the *tetralemma* (*catuṣkoti*) as explicit contradictories: if one denies existence, one must accept non-existence. As is clear just below, Chapa accepts the first option, stating that the ultimate exists.

26 I see no reason to emend this reading from *dpyad bzod pa'i shes pa tsam dgag mi nus pa* to *dpyad mi bzod...* as Śākya mchog ldan (*Lung rigs rgya mtsho,* vol. 14, 519.2) and Tauscher have done. I believe that here Chapa introduces a hypothetical opponent holding that a consciousness that is established by experience—the Prāsaṅgika's own mode of conventional establishment—exists ultimately. Chapa's point in introducing the imagined opponent's position is to bait the Prāsaṅgika into taking a stand: how can the Prāsaṅgika argue with his own "worldly renown" even when it is used to justify ultimate existence (or existence that is claimed to bear analysis)? Chapa is not stating his own position, as will be clear from what follows, and hence there is no need to change the heading's reading to "a mere consciousness that does not bear analysis" (which runs counter to the following sentence). Admittedly, my interpretation requires some stretching, as will likewise become clear below.

27 I follow Tauscher's (67.16) emendation of *gnod byed* to *gnod med.*

28 *phyogs chos, pakṣadharma.*

29 Chapa distinguishes between "comprehend" (*'jal ba*) and "perceive" (*mthong ba*) in order to show that inference (*rjes dpag, anumāna*) is valid cognition (*tshad ma, pramāṇa*) even though it does not directly perceive the truth, in distinction to Candrakīrti's implication in the stanza above—made clear by Jayānanda's commentary—that only direct perception (*mngon sum, pratyakṣa*) of ultimate truth is valid

cognition. Chapa's statement implies that only direct perception "perceives" while both direct perception and inference "comprehend." One wishes for an explanation of how direct perception "comprehends."

30 *tshu rol mthong, avargdarśana.*

31 69.18: *tha snyad 'jal ba'i 'jig rten pa'i blo'ang don dam par ci yang khas mi len pa'i dbu ma nyid kyi rgyud du gtogs pa.* Tauscher ("Phya pa chos kyi seng ge as a Svātantrika," 227) translates: "Even worldly cognition examining conventionally belongs to the very tradition of Madhyamaka, which in an absolute sense does not affirm anything whatsoever." One appreciates reading *dbu ma nyid kyi rgyud* as referring to "the very tradition of Madhyamaka." However, this interpretation of *rgyud* seems to miss the point: the Mādhyamika employing consequences is arguing that propounding "nothing at all" does not block one's own comprehension of conventionalities, such as the reason and entailment that the opponent of the Mādhyamika holds—such comprehension is still included within one's own mental continuum. This is the very point Chapa has been making in defense of the use of inferences: asserting nothing as the ultimate does not negate conventional comprehension, and it is conventional comprehension that comprehends the features of inference.

32 *dgag bya gtan dgag mi nus pa.* Tauscher ("Phya pa chos kyi seng ge as a Svātantrika," 219) notes that construing *gtan* with *mi nus pa* makes this section's second subheading mysterious: if consequences are "utterly unable to refute the object of negation" how can Chapa then allow "even if they were able . . ."? A solution is to construe *gtan* with *dgag* as I have done here: consequences are "unable to refute *completely*," allowing that consequences have a certain effectiveness but are alone insufficient.

33 Chapa entertains the notion that the simple claim that two things are related could make them related in fact. In such a case, his simple claim that dependently arisen appearances are related with "the entity of the ultimate" (*don dam pa'i dngos pa*) would make dependent arising a valid reason to prove the ultimate.

34 Chapa assumes the consequence, "It follows that things are empty of further production because of already existing." In his analysis, such a consequence functions in the same way as a *svatantra* inference.

35 With these absurd consequences, Chapa criticizes the idea that simple assertions—independently of proving their validity—could make things true in fact. If one grants statements the power to negate, without establishing these statements to be factually true, there would be no way of holding that only true statements can negate. If one accorded wrong conceptions such ability, wrong conclusions clearly would result. In the first consequence, the assertion is only wrong from Chapa's viewpoint; his Prāsaṅgika opponent would claim that a [hypothetical] ultimate entity must be one or many. However, both Chapa and his opponent would object to the conclusion, that the ultimate is established as one or many, simply by asserting it so. The second consequence, holding that things are both permanent and "merely" existent, seems hypothetical although could resemble a view held in India. The third absurdity exemplifies clearly both a wrong statement—fire does not arise from snow—and the futility of mere words: stating "fire" does not produce warmth.

36 *gegs byed.*

37 Chapa concludes by claiming that the Prāsaṅgika is merely playing with words that are not grounded in reality. Consequences, if not operating on the same principles as infer-

ences in one's own continuum, have only the power to negate words. Chapa's portrayal of Prāsaṅgika here resembles that of contemporary interpreters; see, for instance, the comparison of Candrakīrti's and Wittgenstein's views in C.W. Huntington, Jr., "The System of the Two Truths in the *Prasannapadā* and the *Madhyamakāvatāra:* A Study in Mādhyamika Soteriology," *Journal of Indian Philosophy* 11 (1983): 77–106. However, Chapa, unlike Huntington, finds the "language game" insufficient: he maintains there are entities that need to be established and negated "in reality."

38 *ldog pa gcig kyang rdzas tha dad pa. ldog pa* is sometimes translated as "isolate"; here, the opposition is between particular consequences—distinguished from others by their ability to refute production from other—and the concept "consequence," not all of which have this ability. Both Chapa and his opponent suggest the impossibility of a single class of phenomena having contradictory characteristics. However, the problem is solved in both cases by maintaining that the commonality of the class is all members being of "the same concept," even though the members themselves are different substances.

39 Again, Chapa argues that only consequences that operate in the same manner as *svatantra* inferences are effective.

40 This seems to be a subtle criticism of the manner in which consequences are said to function: rather than prove (*sgrub*) or negate (*dgag*) as inferences do, consequences "block" (*khegs,* the intransitive form of *dgag*) without ascribing any reality to what is blocked. Chapa here plays with the term, suggesting that if production is "blocked" we would not see production. I suspect Candrakīrti would agree, given his refutation ("blocking") of production from other even in the world (*Madhyamakāvatāra,* VI.32 and auto-commentary).

41 In this consequence, no reason is stated; if a reason were stated, Chapa has argued, pervasions would be established and the consequence would amount to an inference.

42 *rdo rje lta bu'i dus*, understood as *rdo rje lta bu'i ting nge 'dzin.*

43 *tshu rol mdzes pa ba, cārvāka;* literally, in Sanskrit, the "Beautiful (*cāru*)-ites." The Tibetan adds "here" (*tshu rol*), yielding "those who hold that it is beautiful here."

44 *ji lta ba shes pa.*

45 *ji snyed pa shes pa.*

46 Chapa argues that if appearances and reality contradict each other, there can be no relationship between them: voidness of proliferations would have no relation with conventional appearances. Furthermore, the appearance of either conventionalities or reality would prohibit the other—either voidness of proliferations or conventionalities would be impossible.

47 Considering the second possibility, that appearance and reality do not contradict each other but still somehow "block" each other, Chapa brings up the "consequence" that any mental state could be said to block any other mental state: knowing blue would prevent one from knowing impermanence. Chapa's conclusion is that the reality of phenomena when analyzed does not negate the appearance of phenomena when not analyzed.

48 Whereas the previous section discussed a particular consciousness of appearances, that which realizes those appearances to be like illusions, and so picked out an example of a consciousness having appearance that disproves the broad entailment that all

such consciousnesses are obstructions, this section explains that the broad category of consciousnesses having appearance cannot be dispelled.

49 The collection of merit (*bsod nams kyi tshogs*) is said to focus body, speech, and mind on affirming negations (and yet itself is not a negation, as stated just below) because the common Buddhist list of meritorious activities are all negations (for instance, "non-harm" [*ahiṃsa*]) that stop ill-deeds and "affirm" good deeds in their stead. The collection of merit does not operate on the ultimate level—only the collection of wisdom (*ye shes kyi tshogs*) leads to the realization of the ultimate non-establishment of phenomena. Chapa's logic is that since the collection of merit operates on the conventional level, does not negate appearances but instead operates within the negation of non-virtue and the affirmation of virtue, and has definite usefulness on the Buddhist path, we can be certain that the world of appearances exists conventionally.

50 In the previous section (74.5ff), Chapa explained that if ultimate non-establishment and conventional appearance were contradictory, voidness of proliferations could not be the reality of appearances, either voidness of proliferations or conventionalities would become impossible, and illusion-like appearances would not entail utter non-establishment.

51 In a similar argument to the preceding section (74.8–12), Chapa argues that if emptiness "dispels" (*spong ba*) appearances even though it is not contradictory with appearances, any awareness—equally non-contradictory—could dispel appearances, in this case, the ascertainment of impermanence. He has the Prāsaṅgika respond that contradiction is, in fact, necessary for "dispellation," bringing us back to the first case examined here.

52 *rgyang 'phan pa, [loka-]ayata.*

53 *don dam pa'i dngos po* (75.21). The contradiction that Chapa points out is that suchness is permanent and consequently is not able to perform functions. If the Prāsaṅgika claims that suchness is able to perform the function of accomplishing Buddha activities, then a functioning thing—an entity—would be an ultimate.

54 Chapa's logic here seems to follow Kamalaśīla's understanding that the "non-observation reason" (*mi dmigs pa'i rtags, anupalabdhihetu*) used to refute a real entity is an affirming negative (*ma yin dgag, paryudāsa-pratiṣedha*); just what it affirms in Kamalaśīla's understanding is unclear (see Ryusei Keira, "Kamalaśīla's Interpretation of *Anupalabdhi* in the *Madhyamakāloka,*" in *Tibetan Studies: Proceedings of the 7th Seminar of the International Association for Tibetan Studies,* edited by Helmut Krasser, Michael Torsten Much, Ernst Steinkellner, Helmut Tauscher (Vienna: Österreichischen Akademie der Wissenschaften, 1997), 185–192. For Chapa, the inferential subject—mere object of knowledge—is affirmed, while "real entity" is negated. He wishes to be clear that this affirming negative itself is not "real."

55 Chapa distinguishes here between the category "object of knowledge" that is used as the inferential subject, or base, for proving the emptiness of proliferations and particular objects of knowledge, which are implicitly understood to be empty of proliferations. This is detailed in a subsequent section, "The mode of refuting proliferations through inference."

56 *'gal ba sdud pa'i thal ba.*

57 At 70.18–71.3, Chapa points out that if consequences function by way of contra-

dictions that are established "in the basic disposition of objects of knowledge" (*shes bya'i gshis su grub pa*), consequences amount to *svatantra* inferences. Here, again, he is making a distinction between what is true in fact and what is merely stated to be true—what is just talk.

58 The additions in this paragraph are drawn from Chapa's statement of his position in the preceding section, which the opponent here criticizes.

59 At 71.7ff, Chapa ridicules the notion that a wrong conception (*log rtog[s]*) could refute an opponent; if such a case were allowed, wrong conclusions would be reached. Furthermore, and more pertinent here, words alone—whether true or false—would have the power to establish and negate; establishing the validity of one's argument would not be necessary.

60 *dam 'cha' ba bo'i blo.*

61 *Vaidalyaprakaraṇa, Zhib mo rnam par 'thag pa,* P5226, D3826; Fernando Tola and Carmen Dragonetti, *Nāgārjuna's Refutation of Logic (Nyāya): Vaidalyaprakaraṇa* (Delhi: Motilal Banarsidass, 1995).

62 Tauscher indicates in his edition (p. 77, n. 69) that a very similar passage occurs in Kamalaśīla's *Illumination of the Middle* (*Madhyamakāloka, dBu ma snang ba,* D3886, vol. *sa,* 171a.4–5): An opponent objects that because Kamalaśīla holds the inferential reason, example, subject, and so forth do not exist ultimately, the conventions of inference and inferable do not apply (*mi 'jug pa*). Kamalaśīla responds that he agrees; he does not accept that inference and the inferable operate ultimately.

63 Here, Chapa states the thesis of the inference that proves "pervasive emptiness" (*khyab pa'i stong pa nyid*): "objects of knowledge are empty." Immediately below, Chapa discusses the reasons that prove "objects of knowledge are empty" in detail. The inferential subject cannot be a particular object of knowledge but must be "objects of knowledge" in its generality, the category itself ("all [particular] objects of knowledge" cannot literally be the inferential subject prior to omniscience; Chapa has stated in the previous section that proliferations in particular objects of knowledge are implicitly blocked by this inference). Tom Tillemans ("Formal and Semantic Aspects of Tibetan Buddhist Debate Logic" in *Scripture, Logic, Language: Essays on Dharmakīrti and his Tibetan Successors* [Boston: Wisdom Publications, 1999], 130–31) points out that confusion over what is meant by "object of knowledge" stems from the fact that Tibetan lacks definite articles and Tibetan authors rarely use indefinite articles or the abstractive particle, *nyid.* He is clearly correct that "object of knowledge" must sometimes be understood as "the quality of being an object of knowledge" (that is, *shes bya nyid*). Such an interpretation—the quality of being in the category, "object of knowledge"—is similar to how I understand the present usage: the category "object of knowledge." Furthermore, in the following discussion, "entity" (*dngos po*) substitutes for "object of knowledge" (*shes bya*) despite being (along with "non-entity" [*dngos med*]) a subset of object of knowledge; Chapa explains how this can be so below.

64 The line of reasoning followed throughout this argument calls for this phrase to read "are not ascertained in relation to entity because entity is not taken as an object at all." Chapa may regard "entity" (*dngos po*) and "existent" (*yod pa*) as mutually inclusive.

65 Here (79.20), Chapa uses *khyab byed du phyogs chos,* instead of the more common *phyogs chos.*

66 The opponent's criticism rests on the fact that "object of knowledge" (*shes bya*) is divided into "entity" (*dngos po*) and "non-entity" (*dngos med*); only "entities" are dependent arisings, and thus, the reason "dependent arising" is not entailed by the inferential subject "object of knowledge," but only by one class of objects of knowledge.

67 *dngos po dang yang dag tshogs pas mi dben pa.*

68 *khyab byed mi dmigs pa, vyāpaka-anupalabdhi.*

69 *yang dag pa'i rang bzhin.*

70 Non-entity (*dngos med*) will always be a meaning generality (*don spyi*), not an object of direct perception; voidness of one or many is a meaning generality here in the inference, as objects of inference are also always meaning generalities. In meditation, voidness of one or many can be the object of yogic direct perception. As discussed above, non-entity is the example in relation to which the entailment is initially understood: non-entity is understood to lack real nature because it lacks a real one or many. This entailment is then applied to object of knowledge, object of comprehension, appearance, and mere entity.

71 This is stated in the form of an "inference for others" (*parārthānumāna, gzhan gyi don gyi rjes dpag*), showing the "three modes" (*trairūpya, tshul gsum*) of a valid reason: the entailment is stated, then an example, followed by the fact that the reason (emptiness of a real one or many) is a property of the subject (object of knowledge, object of comprehension, appearance, and mere entity). In inference for others, the thesis is not stated; here it would be "Object of knowledge, object of comprehension, appearance, and mere entity are empty of real nature." Following this point, Chapa details the five parts of the inference that proves pervasive emptiness, giving lengthy discourses on the inferential subject (*chos can*), predicate (*bsgrub bya*), reason (*gtan tshigs*), the reason being a property of the subject (*phyogs chos*), and the pervasions (*khyab pa*).

Bibliography

Unedited Sanskrit and Tibetan Sources

A khu ching shes rab rgya mtsho. *dPe rgyun dkon pa 'ga' zhig gi tho yig don gnyer yid kyi kunda bzhad pa'i zla 'od 'bum gyi snye ma.* In *Materials for a History of Tibetan Literature*, ed. Lokesh Candra, 503–601. Kyoto: Rinsen, 1981.

Abhayākaragupta. *Munimatālaṃkāra (thub pa'i dgongs pa'i rgyan).* Toh. 3903, *bstan 'gyur, sde dge* edition, *dbu ma*, vol. *a.*

Amarasiṃha. *Amarakośa ('chi med mdzod).* Toh. 4299, *bstan 'gyur, sde dge* edition, *sgra mdo*, vol. *se.*

Atiśa. *Bodhimārgapradīpapañjikā (byang chub lam gyi sgron ma'i dka' 'grel).* Toh. 3948, *bstan 'gyur, sde dge* edition, *dbu ma*, vol. *khi.*

Avalokitavrata. *Prajñāpradīpaṭīkā (shes rab sgron me'i rgya cher 'grel pa).* Toh. 3559, *bstan 'gyur, sde dge* edition, *dbu ma*, vol. *wa.*

Bhāvaviveka. *Prajñāpradīpamūlamadhyamakavṛtti (dbu ma rtsa ba'i 'grel pa shes rab sgron ma).* Toh. 3853, *bstan 'gyur, sde dge* edition, *dbu ma*, vol. *dza.*

———. *Madhyamakaratnapradīpa (dbu ma rin po che'i sgron ma).* Toh. 3854, *bstan 'gyur, sde dge* edition, *dbu ma*, vol. *dza.*

———. *Madhyamakahṛdaya (dbu ma'i snying po).* Toh. 3855, *bstan 'gyur, sde dge* edition, *dbu ma,* vol. *dza.*

———. *Madhyamakahṛdayavṛttitarkajvālā (dbu ma'i snying po'i 'grel pa rtog ge 'bar ba).* Toh. 3856, *bstan 'gyur, sde dge* edition, *dbu ma*, vol. *dza.*

———. *Madhyamakārthasaṃgraha (dbu ma'i don bsdus pa).* Toh. 3857, *bstan 'gyur, sde dge* edition, *dbu ma*, vol. *dza.*

Candrakīrti III. *Madhyamakāvatāraprajñā (dbu ma shes rab la 'jug pa).* Toh. 3863, *bstan 'gyur, sde dge* edition, *dbu ma,* vol. *'a.*

Grags pa rgyal mtshan. *rGya bod kyi sde pa'i gyes mdo.* In *Sa skya pa'i bka' 'bum,* vol. 4. Tokyo: Toyo Bunko, 1968.

———. *rGyud kyi mngon par rtogs pa rin po che'i ljong shing.* In *Sa skya pa'i bka' 'bum*, vol. 3. Tokyo: Toyo Bunko, 1968.

Gro lung pa blo gros 'byung gnas. *bDe bar gshegs pa'i bstan pa rin po che la 'jug pa'i lam gyi rim pa rnam par bshad pa.* Patna, India: Bihar Research Society, n.d.

'Jam dbyangs bzhad pa. *dBu ma chen mo : dbu ma 'jug pa'i mtha' dpyod lung rigs gter mdzod zab don kun gsal skal bzang 'jug ngogs.* Buxaduor, India: Gomang, 1967.

Jayānanda. *Tarkamudgara (rtog ge tho ba).* Toh. 3870, *bstan 'gyur, sde dge* edition, *dbu ma,* vol. *ya.*

———. *Madhyamakāvatāraṭīkā (dbu ma la 'jug pa 'grel pa).* Toh. 3871, *bstan 'gyur, sde dge* edition, *dbu ma,* vol. *ya.*

Kamalaśīla. *Madhyamakāloka (dbu ma snang ba).* Toh. 3887, *bstan 'gyur, sde dge* edition, *dbu ma,* vol. *sa.*

bKa' gdams gsung 'bum phyogs bgrigs. Lhasa: dPal brtsegs bod yig dpe rnying zhib 'jug khang, 2006.

rMa bya Byang chub brtson 'grus. *dBu ma rtsa ba shes rab kyi 'grel pa 'thad pa'i rgyan.* Rumtek, Sikkim: rGyal ba Karma pa, 1975.

Maitrīpāda. *Tattvadaśaka (de kho na nyid bcu pa).* Toh. 2236, *bstan 'gyur, sde dge* edition, *rgyud 'grel,* vol. *wi.*

rNgog bLo ldan shes rab. *Theg chen rgyud bla ma'i don bsdus pa.* Dharamsala, India: Library of Tibetan Works and Archives, 1993.

Sahajavajra. *Tattvadaśakaṭīkā (de kho na nyid bcu pa'i rgya cher 'grel pa).* Toh. 2254, *bstan 'gyur, sde dge* edition, *rgyud 'grel,* vol. *wi.*

Śākya mchog ldan. *The Collected Works (Gsuṅ 'bum) of Gser-mdog Paṇ-chen Śākya-mchog-ldan,* vol. 14. Thimphu, Bhutan: Kunzang Topgey, 1975.

Śāntarakṣita. *Madhyamakālaṃkāra (dbu ma'i rgyan).* Toh. 3884, *bstan 'gyur, sde dge* edition, *dbu ma,* vol. *sa.*

bSod nams rtse mo. *Byang chub sems dpa'i spyod pa la 'jug pa'i 'grel pa.* In *Sa skya pa'i bka' 'bum,* vol. 2. Tokyo: Toyo Bunko, 1968.

Tsong kha pa. *Lam rim 'bring : skyes bu gsum gyi nyams su blang ba'i byang chub lam gyi rim pa.* P6002, vols. 152–53.

———. *Drang ba dang nges pa'i don rnam par phye ba'i bstan bcos legs bshad snying po.* P6142, vol. 153 and in *The Collected Works [gSuṅ 'bum] of rJe Tsoṅ-kha-pa Blo-bzaṅ-grags-pa.* New Delhi: Ngawang Gelek Demo, 1975.

———. *Lam rim chen mo : skyes bu gsum gyi nyams su blang ba'i rim pa thams cad tshang bar ston pa'i byang chub lam gyi rim pa.* P6001 and in *The Collected Works [gSuṅ 'bum] of rJe Tsoṅ-kha-pa Blo-bzaṅ-grags-pa,* vol. 19–20. New Delhi: Ngawang Gelek Demo, 1975.

gTsang nag pa. *Tshad ma rnam par nges pa'i ṭika legs bshad bsdus pa.* Otani University Tibetan Works Series, 2. Kyōto: Otani University, 1989.

Vibhūticandra, *Bodhicaryāvatāratātparyapañjikāviśeṣadyotanī (byang chub kyi spyod pa la 'jug pa'i dgongs pa'i 'grel pa khyad par gsal byed).* Toh. 3880, *bstan 'gyur, sde dge* edition, *dbu ma,* vol. *sha.*

Editions and Translations

Ames, William. "Bhāvaviveka's *Prajñāpradīpa.* A Translation of Chapter One: 'Examination of Causal Conditions' (*pratyaya*)." *Journal of Indian Philosophy* 21, no. 3 (1993): 209–59.

Bendall, Cecil. *Çikshāsamuccaya: A Compendium of Buddhistic Teaching,* Bibliotheca Buddhica I. Osnabrück, Germany: Biblio Verlag, 1970.

———. *Subhāṣitasaṃgraha. Muséon* IV (1903): 375–402 and V (1904): 5–46 and 245–74.

Dram Dul. *'Jig rten mig gcig blo ldan śes rab kyi rnam thar, Biography of Blo ldan śes rab, The Unique Eye of the World by Gro luṅ pa Blo gros 'byuṅ gnas, The Xylograph Compared with a Bhutanese Manuscript.* Vienna: Arbeitskreis für Tibetische und Buddhistische Studien Universität Wien, 2004.

Eckel, Malcolm David. *Jñānagarbha's Commentary on the Distinction between the Two Truths: An Eighth Century Handbook of Madhyamaka Philosophy.* Albany, NY: State University of New York Press, 1987.

Ejima, Y. *Chūgan-shisō no tenkai—Bhāvaviveka kenkyū.* Tokyo: Shunjūsha, 1980.

Erb, Felix. *Śūnyatāsaptativṛtti.* Stuttgart: Franz Steiner Verlag, 1997.

Garfield, Jay L. *The Fundamental Wisdom of the Middle Way.* New York: Oxford University Press, 1995.

Gnoli, Raniero. *The Pramāṇavārttikam of Dharmakīrti, The First Chapter with the Autocommentary.* Rome: Istituto Italiano per il Medio ed Estremo Oriente, 1960.

Hattori, Masaaki. *Dignāga, On Perception.* Harvard Oriental Series, 47. Cambridge, MA: Harvard University Press, 1968.

Hugon, Pascale. *mTshur ston gZhon nu seng ge, Tshad ma shes rab sgron ma.* Vienna: Arbeitskreis für Tibetische und Buddhistische Studien Universität Wien, 2004.

Huntington, C.W., Jr. *The Emptiness of Emptiness: An Introduction to Early Indian Mādhyamika.* Honolulu: University of Hawaii Press, 1989.

Ichigō, Masamichi. "Śāntarakṣita's Madhyamakālaṃkāra" in *Studies in the Literature of the Great Vehicle.* Michigan Studies in Buddhist Literature,

1, edited by Luis O. Gómez and Jonathan A. Silk, 141–240. Ann Arbor: Collegiate Institute for the Study of Buddhist Literature and Center for South and Southeast Asian Studies, The University of Michigan, 1989.

Jackson, David P. *The Entrance Gate for the Wise (Section III): Sa-skya Paṇḍita on Indian and Tibetan Traditions of Pramāṇa and Philosophical Debate.* Vienna: Arbeitskreis für Tibetische und Buddhistische Studien Universität Wien, 1987.

Jha, Ganganatha. *The Tattvasaṅgraha of Shāntarakṣita with the Commentary of Kamalashīla.* 2 vols. Delhi: Motilal Banarsidass, 1937 (1986).

Johnston, E.H., A. Kunst, and K. Bhattacharya. *The Dialectical Method of Nāgārjuna: Vigrahavyāvartanī.* Delhi: Motilal Banarsidass, 1998.

de Jong, J.W. *Nāgārjuna, Mūlamadhyamakakārikāḥ*. Madras, India: Adyar Library and Research Centre, 1977.

Kajiyama, Yuichi. *An Introduction to Buddhist Philosophy: An Annotated Translation of the Tarkabhāṣā of Mokṣākaragupta: Reprint with Corrections in the Author's Hand.* Vienna: Arbeitskreis für Tibetische und Buddhistische Studien Universität Wien, 1998.

Kano, Kazuo. *rNgog Blo-ldan-shes-rab's Summary of the* Ratnagotravibhāga. Ph.D. dissertation, Hamburg University, 2006.

Lang, Karen. *Āryadeva's Catuḥśataka: On the Bodhisattva's Cultivation of Merit and Knowledge.* Indiste Studier, 7. Copenhagen: Akademisk Forlag, 1986.

Lindtner, Christian. *Master of Wisdom: Writings of the Buddhist Master Nāgārjuna.* Oakland: Dharma Publishing, 1986.

Malvania, Dalsukhbhai. *Paṇḍita Durveka Miśra's Dharmottarapradīpa.* Patna: Kashiprasad Jayaswal Research Institute, 1971.

Mimaki, Katsumi. *Blo gsal grub mtha'.* Kyoto: Université de Kyoto, 1982.

Mimaki, Katsumi and Toru Tomabechi. *Pañcakrama: Sanskrit and Tibetan Texts Critically Edited with Verse Index and Facsimile Edition of the Sanskrit Manuscripts.* Bibliotheca Codicum Asiaticorum, 8. Tokyo: The Centre for East Asian Cultural Studies for Unesco, 1994.

Minaev, I.P. "Bodhicaryāvatāra." *Zapiski Vostočnago Otdělenija Imperatorskago Russkago Archeologičeskago Obščestva* 4 (1889), 153–228.

Miyasaka, Yūsho. "*Pramāṇavārttika-kārikā:* Sanskrit and Tibetan." *Indo Koten Kenkyu (Acta Indologica)* 2 (1971–72): 1–206.

Nagatomi, Masatoshi. *A Study of Dharmakīrti's Pramāṇavārttika: An English Translation and Annotation of the Pramāṇavārttika, Book I.* Ph.D. dissertation, Harvard University, 1957.

Nanjio, Bunyiu. *The Laṅkāvatāra Sūtra*. Bibliotheca Otaniensis, vol. 1. Kyoto: Otani University Press, 1923.

Roerich, George N., trans. *The Blue Annals*. Delhi: Motilal Banarsidass, 1949 (1996).

Sankrityayana, Rahula. *Karṇakagomin's Commentary on the Pramāṇavārttikavṛtti of Dharmakīrti*. Kyoto: Rinsen Book Company. 1982.

Scherrer-Schaub, Cristina Anna. *Yuktiṣaṣṭikāvṛtti. Commentaire à la soixantaine sur le raisonnement ou Du vrai enseignement de la causalité par le Maitre indien Candrakīrti*. Mélanges chinois et bouddhiques, 25. Bruselles: Institut belge des hautes etudes chinoises, 1991.

Schoening, Jeffrey D. *The Śālistamba Sūtra and its Indian Commentaries*. Vienna: Arbeitskreis für Tibetische und Buddhistische Studien Universität Wien, 1995.

Shastri, Swami Dwarkidas, ed. *Tattvasaṃgraha with Kamalaśīla's Pañjikā*. Varanasi: Bauddha Bharati, 1968.

Sherburne, Richard. *The Complete Works of Atiśa*. New Delhi: Aditya Prakashan, 2000.

Sorensen, Per K. *Triśaraṇasaptati: The Septuagint on the Three Refuges*. Vienna: Arbeitskreis für Tibetische und Buddhistische Studien Universität Wien, 1986.

Suzuki, Koshin. "A Transliteration of the Sanskrit Notes on the *Catuḥśatakaṭīkā* in the **Lakṣaṇaṭīkā*." In *Gedenkschrift J. W. de Jong*, ed. H.W. Bodewitz and Minoru Hara, 189–206. Tokyo: The International Institute for Buddhist Studies of The International College for Advanced Buddhist Studies, 2004.

von Staël-Holstein, Alexander. *Kāçyapaparivarta: A Mahāyanasūtra of the Ratnakūṭa Class*. Shanghai: Commercial Press, 1926.

Stcherbatsky, Theodore. *Nyāyabindu*. Bibliotheca Buddhica, 7. Osnabrück, Germany: Biblio Verlag, 1970.

Tauscher, Helmut. *Candrakīrti-Madhyamakāvatāraḥ und Madhyamakāvatārabhāṣyam*. Wiener Studien zur Tibetologie und Buddhismuskunde, 5. Vienna: Arbeitskreis für Tibetische und Buddhistische Studien Universität Wien, 1981.

———, ed. *Phya pa chos kyi seṅ ge: dbu ma śar gsum gyi stoṅ thun*. Vienna: Arbeitskreis für Tibetische und Buddhistische Studien Universität Wien, 1999.

Tillemans, Tom J.F. *Dharmakīrti's Pramāṇavārttika: An Annotated Translation of the Fourth Chapter (parārthānumāna)*, vol. 1 (k. 1–148). Vienna: Österreichischen Akademie der Wissenschaften, 2000.

Tola, Fermando and Carmen Dragonetti. *Nāgārjuna's Refutation of Logic (Nyāya) Vaidalyaprakaraṇa.* Delhi: Motilal Banarsidass, 1995.

Tomabechi, Toru. *Étude du Pañcakrama. Introduction et traduction annotée.* Thèse de doctorat, Faculté des Lettres, Université de Lausanne, 2006.

la Vallée Poussin, Louis de. *Mūlamadhyamakakārikās de Nāgārjuna avec la Prasannapadā commentaire de Candrakīrti.* Bibliotheca Buddhica, 4. Osnabrück, Germany: Biblio Verlag, 1970.

———. *Madhyamakāvatāra par Candrakīrti.* Bibliotheca Buddhica, 9. Osnabrück, Germany: Biblio Verlag, 1970.

———. "*Madhyamakāvatāra.* Introduction au traité du milieu de l'ācārya Candrakīrti avec le commentaire de l'auteur," *Muséon* 8 (1907): 249–317; *Muséon* 11 (1910): 271–358; *Muséon* 12 (1911): 235–328.

———. *Prajñākaramati's Commentary to the Bodhicaryāvatāra of Çāntideva.* Bibliotheca Indica. Calcutta: Asiatic Society of Bengal, 1902–14.

Vetter, Tillman. *Dharmakīrti's Pramāṇaviniścayaḥ, I., Kapitel: Pratyakṣam.* Vienna: Österreichischen Akademie der Wissenschaften, 1966.

Walleser, Max. *dBu ma rca ba'i 'grel pa Buddha pā li ta (Buddhapālita-Mūlamadhyamakavṛtti) Chapters i–xii.* Bibliotheca Buddhica, 16. Osnabrück, Germany: Biblio Verlag, 1970.

Wedemeyer, Christian K. *Āryadeva's Lamp That Integrates The Practices (Caryāmelāpakapradīpa): The Gradual Path of Vajrayāna Buddhism according to the Esoteric Communion Noble Tradition.* New York: Columbia University Press, 2007.

Wogihara, Unrai. *Abhisamayālaṃkārālokā Prajñāpāramitāvyākhyā.* Tokyo: Toyo Bunko, 1932–35.

Yonezawa, Yoshiyasu. "Sanskrit notes on the *Madhyamakāvatārabhāṣya* Chapter I in the **Lakṣaṇaṭīkā.*" *Journal of Indian and Buddhist Studies (Indobukkyogaku Kenkyu)* 49, no. 2 (2001): 47–49.

———. "**Lakṣaṇaṭīkā.* Sanskrit notes on the *Prasannapadā* (1)." *Journal of the Naritasan Institute for Buddhist Studies* 27 (2004): 115–154.

———. "**Lakṣaṇaṭīkā.* Sanskrit notes on the *Prasannapadā* (2)", *Journal of the Naritasan Institute for Buddhist Studies* 28 (2005): 159–79.

———. "**Lakṣaṇaṭīkā.* Sanskrit notes on the *Prasannapadā* (3)", *Journal of the Naritasan Institute for Buddhist Studies* 29 (2006): 135–63.

Secondary Sources

Ames, William. "Bhāvaviveka's Own View of His Differences with Buddhapālita." In *The Svātantrika-Prāsaṅgika Distinction: What Difference Does a Difference Make?* edited by Georges B.J. Dreyfus and Sara L. McClintock, 41–66. Boston: Wisdom Publications, 2002.

Arnold, Dan. *Buddhists, Brahmins, and Belief: Epistemology in South Asian Philosophy of Religion.* New York: Columbia University Press, 2005.

van Bijlert, Vittorio A. *Epistemology and Spiritual Authority.* Vienna: Arbeitskreis für Tibetische und Buddhistische Studien Universität Wien, 1989.

Blackburn, Anne M. *Buddhist Learning and Textual Practice in Eighteenth-Century Lankan Monastic Culture.* Princeton: Princeton University Press, 2001.

Cabezón, José Ignacio. "The Prāsaṅgika's View on Logic: Tibetan dGe lugs pa Exegesis on the Question of Svatantras." *Journal of Indian Philosophy* 16, no. 3 (1988): 217–224.

———. "The Canonization of Philosophy and the Rhetoric of Siddhānta in Tibetan Buddhism." In *Buddha Nature: A Festschrift in Honor of Minoru Kiyota,* edited by Paul J. Griffiths and John P. Keenan, 7–26. Tokyo: Buddhist Books International, 1990.

———. *A Dose of Emptiness.* Albany, NY: State University of New York Press, 1992.

———. *Buddhism and Language: A Study of Indo-Tibetan Scholasticism.* Albany, NY: State University of New York Press, 1994.

———. "Rong ston Shākya rgyal mtshan on Mādhyamika Thesislessness." In *Tibetan Studies: Proceedings of the 7th Seminar of the International Association for Tibetan Studies,* edited by Helmut Krasser, Michael Torsten Much, Ernst Steinkellner, Helmut Tauscher, 97–106. Vienna: Österreichischen Akademie der Wissenschaften, 1997.

———. *Scholasticism: Cross-Cultural and Comparative Perspectives.* Albany, NY: State University of New York Press, 1998.

———. "Two Views on the Svātantrika-Prāsaṅgika Distinction in Fourteenth-Century Tibet." In *The Svātantrika-Prāsaṅgika Distinction: What Difference Does a Difference Make?* edited by Georges B.J. Dreyfus and Sara L. McClintock, 289–315. Boston: Wisdom Publications, 2002.

———. "The Madhyamaka in Gro lung pa's *Bstan Rim chen mo,*" *Proceedings of the 11th Seminar of the International Association of Tibetan Studies 2006.* Forthcoming.

Cabezón, José Ignacio and Geshe Lobsang Dargyay. *Freedom from Extremes: Gorampa's "Distinguishing the Views" and the Polemics of Emptiness.* Boston: Wisdom Publications, 2006.

Chu, Junjie. "The Ontological Problem in Tsoṅ kha pa's *prasaṅga* Theory: The Establishment or Unestablishment of the Subject (*dharmin*) of an Argument." In *Tibetan Studies: Proceedings of the 7th Seminar of the International Association for Tibetan Studies,* edited by Helmut Krasser, Michael Torsten Much, Ernst Steinkellner, Helmut Tauscher, 157–78. Vienna: Österreichischen Akademie der Wissenschaften, 1997.

Copeland, Rita. *Rhetoric, Hermeneutics, and Translation in the Middle Ages.* Cambridge: Cambridge University Press, 1991.

Cox, Collett. *Disputed Dharmas: Early Buddhist Theories on Existence.* Tokyo: International Institute for Buddhist Studies, 1995.

Dagenais, John. *The Ethics of Reading in Manuscript Culture: Glossing the 'Libro de buen amor'.* Princeton: Princeton University Press, 1994.

Dalton, Jacob. *Uses of the* Dgongs pa 'dus pa'i mdo *in the Development of the* Rnying-ma *School.* Ph.D. dissertation, University of Michigan, 2002.

Davidson, Ronald Mark. *Buddhist Systems of Transformation:* Āśraya-parivṛtti-parāvṛtti *Among the Yogācāra.* Ph.D. dissertation, University of California, Berkeley, 1985.

———. "Reflections on the Maheśvara Subjugation Myth: Indic Materials, Sa-skya-pa Apologetics, and the Birth of the Heruka." *Journal of the International Association of Buddhist Studies* 14, no. 2 (1991): 197–235.

———. "Masquerading as *Pramāṇa:* Esoteric Buddhism and Epistemological Nomenclature." In *Dharmakīrti's Thought and Its Impact on Indian and Tibetan Philosophy,* edited by S. Katsura, 25–35. Vienna: Österreichischen Akademie der Wissenschaften, 1999.

———. *Indian Esoteric Buddhism: A Social History of the Tantric Movement.* New York: Columbia University Press, 2002.

———. *Tibetan Renaissance: Tantric Buddhism in the Rebirth of Tibetan Culture.* New York: Columbia University Press, 2005.

Demiéville, Paul. *Le concile de Lhasa.* Paris: Imprimerie nationale de France, 1952.

Dreyfus, Georges B.J. *Recognizing Reality: Dharmakīrti's Philosophy and its Tibetan Interpretations.* Albany, NY: State University of New York Press, 1997.

———. *The Sound of Two Hands Clapping: The Education of a Tibetan Buddhist Monk.* Berkeley, CA: University of California Press, 2003.

———. "Where Do Commentarial Schools Come From? Reflections on the History of Tibetan Scholasticism." *Journal of the International Association of Buddhist Studies* 28, no. 2 (2005): 273–97.

Dreyfus, Georges B.J. and Sara L. McClintock. *The Svātantrika-Prāsaṅgika Distinction: What Difference Does a Difference Make?* Boston: Wisdom Publications, 2002.

Dunne, John D. "Thoughtless Buddha, Passionate Buddha." *Journal of the American Academy of Religion* LXIV/3 (1996): 525–57.

———. *Foundations of Dharmakīrti's Philosophy.* Boston: Wisdom Publications, 2004.

Dunnell, Ruth W. *The Great State of White and High.* Honolulu: University of Hawaii Press, 1996.

Fanwen, Li. "The Influence of Tibetan Buddhism on Xixia." In *Tibetan Studies: Proceedings of the 7th Seminar of the International Association for Tibetan Studies,* edited by Helmut Krasser, Michael Torsten Much, Ernst Steinkellner, Helmut Tauscher, 559–72. Vienna: Österreichischen Akademie der Wissenschaften, 1997.

Fehér, Judit. "Buddhapālita's *Mūlamadhyamakavṛtti*—Arrival and Spread of Prāsaṅgika-Mādhyamika Literature in Tibet." In *Tibetan and Buddhist Studies Commemorating the 200th Anniversary of the Birth of Alexander Csoma de Kőrös*, vol. 1, edited by Louis Ligeti, 211–40. Budapest: Akadémiai Kiadó, 1984.

Franco, Eli. "The Disjunction in *Pramāṇavārttika, Pramāṇasiddhi* Chapter 5c." In *Studies in the Buddhist Epistemological Tradition*, 39–51. Vienna: Österreichischen Akademie der Wissenschaften, 1991.

———. *Dharmakīrti on Compassion and Rebirth.* Vienna: Arbeitskreis für Tibetische und Buddhistische Studien Universität Wien, 1997.

Funayama, Toru. "Kamalaśīla's Interpretation of 'Non-Erroneous' in the Definition of Direct Perception and Related Problems." In *Dharmakīrti's Thought and its Impact on Indian and Tibetan Philosophy,* ed. Shoryu Katsura. Vienna: Österreichischen Akademie der Wissenschaften, 1999.

Griffiths, Paul J. *On Being Buddha.* Albany, NY: State University of New York Press, 1994.

———. "Scholasticism: The Possible Recovery of an Intellectual Practice." In *Scholasticism: Cross-Cultural and Comparative Perspectives,* edited by José Ignacio Cabezón, 206–8. Albany, NY: State University of New York Press, 1998.

Halbfass, Wilhelm. *Tradition and Reflection: Explorations in Indian Thought.* Albany, NY: State University of New York Press, 1991.

Hobsbawn, Eric and Terrence Ranger, eds. *The Invention of Tradition.* Cambridge: Cambridge University Press, 1983.

Hopkins, Jeffrey. *Meditation on Emptiness.* London: Wisdom, 1983; rev. ed., Boston: Wisdom Publications, 1996.

———. "A Tibetan Delineation of Different Views of Emptiness in the Indian Middle Way School: Dzong-ka-ba's Two Interpretations of the *Locus Classicus* in Chandrakīrti's *Clear Words* Showing Bhāvaviveka's Assertion of Commonly Appearing Subjects and Inherent Existence." *Tibet Journal* 14, no. 1 (1989): 10–43.

———. *Emptiness Yoga.* Ithaca, NY: Snow Lion Publications, 1987.

———. *Emptiness in the Mind-Only School of Buddhism.* Berkeley, CA: University of California Press, 1999.

———. *Maps of the Profound.* Ithaca, NY: Snow Lion Publications, 2003.

Huntington, C.W., Jr. "The System of the Two Truths in the *Prasannapadā* and the *Madhyamakāvatāra*: A Study in Mādhyamika Soteriology." *Journal of Indian Philosophy* 11 (1983): 77–106.

———. "Was Candrakīrti a Prāsaṅgika?" In *The Svātantrika-Prāsaṅgika Distinction: What Difference Does a Difference Make?* edited by Georges B.J. Dreyfus and Sara L. McClintock, 67–91. Boston: Wisdom Publications, 2002.

Ichigō, Masamichi. "Śāntarakṣita and Bhāvaviveka as Opponents of the Mādhyamika in the *Madhyamakāloka*." In *Wisdom, Compassion, and the Search for Understanding: The Buddhist Studies Legacy of Gadjin M. Nagao,* edited by Jonathan A. Silk, 147–170. Honolulu: University of Hawai'i Press, 2000.

Iida, Shōtarō. *Reason and Emptiness.* Tokyo: Hokuseido, 1980.

Irvine, Martin. *The Making of Textual Culture.* Cambridge: Cambridge University Press, 1994.

Isaacson, Harunaga. "Ratnākaraśānti's *Hevajrasahajasadyoga* (Studies in Ratnākaraśānti's Tantric Works I)." In *Le Parole e i Marmi: studi in onore di Raniero Gnoli nel suo 70° compleanno.* Serie Orientale Roma, XCII, ed. Raffaele Torella. Roma: Istituto Italiano per l'Africa e l'Oriente, 2001.

Iwasaki, Tsutomu. "The Tibetan Tribes of Ho-hsi and Buddhism During the Northern Sung Period." *Acta Asiatica* 64 (1993): 17–37.

Iwata, Takashi. *Prasaṅga und Prasaṅgaviparyaya bei Dharmakīrti und Seinen Kommentatoren.* Vienna: Arbeitskreis für Tibetische und Buddhistische Studien Universität Wien, 1993.

———. "On *prasaṅgaviparyaya* in Dharmakīrti's Tradition—Prajñākaragupta and gTsaṅ nag pa." In *Tibetan Studies: Proceedings of the 7th Seminar of the*

International Association for Tibetan Studies, edited by Helmut Krasser, Michael Torsten Much, Ernst Steinkellner, Helmut Tauscher, 427–437. Vienna: Österreichischen Akademie der Wissenschaften, 1997.

Jackson, David P. "Madhyamaka Studies Among the Early Sa-skya-pas." *Tibet Journal* 10, no. 2 (1985): 20–34.

———. "An Early Biography of rNgog Lo-tsā-ba bLo ldan shes rab." In *Tibetan Studies: Proceedings of the 6th Seminar of the International Association for Tibetan Studies,* edited by Per Kvaerne, 372–392. Oslo: The Institute for Comparative Research in Human Culture, 1994.

———. *Enlightenment by a Single Means: Tibetan Controversies on the "Self-Sufficient White Remedy" (dkar po chig thub).* Vienna: Österreichischen Akademie der Wissenschaften, 1994.

———. "rNgog Lo-tsā-ba's Commentary on the Ratnagotravibhāga: An Early–20th-Century Lhasa Printed Edition." In *Tibetan Studies: Proceedings of the 7th Seminar of the International Association for Tibetan Studies,* edited by Helmut Krasser, Michael Torsten Much, Ernst Steinkellner, Helmut Tauscher, 438–56. Vienna: Österreichischen Akademie der Wissenschaften, 1997.

de Jong, J.W. "La légende de Śāntideva." *Indo-Iranian Journal* 16 (1975): 161–82.

———. "Text-critical Notes on the *Prassanapadā.*" *Indo-Iranian Journal* 20, nos. 1/2 (1978): 25–59, nos. 3/4 (1978): 217–52.

Kapstein, Matthew. *The Tibetan Assimilation of Buddhism: Conversion, Contestation, and Memory.* New York: Oxford University Press, 2000.

———. *Reason's Traces: Identity and Interpretation in Indian and Tibetan Buddhist Thought.* Boston: Wisdom Publications, 2001.

Katsura, Shōryū. "Nāgārjuna and the Tetralemma (*Catuṣkoṭi*)." In *Wisdom, Compassion, and the Search for Understanding: The Buddhist Studies Legacy of Gadjin M. Nagao,* edited by Jonathan A. Silk, 201–20. Honolulu: University of Hawai'i Press, 2000.

Keira, Ryusei. "Kamalaśīla's Interpretation of *Anupalabdhi* in the *Madhyamakāloka.*" In *Tibetan Studies: Proceedings of the 7th Seminar of the International Association for Tibetan Studies,* edited by Helmut Krasser, Michael Torsten Much, Ernst Steinkellner, Helmut Tauscher, 185–92. Vienna: Österreichischen Akademie der Wissenschaften, 1997.

Kellner, Birgit. "Types of Incompatibility (*'gal ba*) and Types of Non-Cognition (*ma/mi dmigs*) in Early Tibetan *tshad ma* Literature." In *Tibetan Studies: Proceedings of the 7th Seminar of the International Association for Tibetan Studies,* edited by Helmut Krasser, Michael Torsten Much,

Ernst Steinkellner, Helmut Tauscher, 495–510. Vienna: Österreichischen Akademie der Wissenschaften, 1997.

Kimura, Toshihiko, "A New Chronology of Dharmakīrti." In *Dharmakīrti's Thought and Its Impact on Indian and Tibetan Philosophy,* edited by Shoryu Katsura, 209–14. Vienna: Österreichischen Akademie der Wissenschaften, 1999.

Krasser, Helmut. "On the Relationship between Dharmottara, Śāntarakṣita and Kamalaśīla." In *Tibetan Studies: Proceedings of the 5th Seminar of the International Association for Tibetan Studies,* Monograph Series of Naritasan Institute for Buddhist Studies: Occasional Papers 2, edited by Ihara Shōren and Yamaguchi Zuihō, 151–58. Narita: Naritasan Shinshōji, 1992.

van der Kuijp, Leonard W. J. "Phya-pa Chos kyi Seng ge's Impact on Tibetan Epistemological Theory." *Journal of Indian Philosophy* 5 (1978): 355–69.

———. *Contributions to the Development of Tibetan Buddhist Epistemology, from the Eleventh to the Thirteenth Century.* Wiesbaden: Franz Steiner, 1983.

———. "Notes on the Transmission of Nāgārjuna's *Ratnāvali* in Tibet." *Tibet Journal* 10, no. 2 (1985): 3–19.

———. "The Monastery of Gsang-phu ne'u-thog and Its Abbatial Succession from ca. 1073 to 1250." *Berliner Indologische Studien* 3 (1987): 103–27.

———. "Jayānanda. A Twelfth Century *Guoshi* from Kashmir Among the Tangut." *Central Asiatic Journal* 37, no. 3/4 (1993): 188–97.

E.I. Kychanov, "Tibetans and Tibetan Culture in the Tangut State Hsi Hsia (982–1227)." In *Proceedings of the Csoma de Kőrös Memorial Symposium, 1976,* edited by Louis Ligeti, 205–211. Budapest: Akadémiai Kiadó, 1978.

———. "From the History of the Tangut Translation of the Buddhist Canon." In *Tibetan and Buddhist Studies Commemorating the 200th Anniversary of the Birth of Alexander Csoma de Kőrös,* edited by Louis Ligetti, 377–87. Budapest: Akadémiai Kiadó, 1984.

Lalou, Marcelle. "Les textes Bouddhiques au temps du roi khri-srong-lde-bcan." *Journal Asiatique* 241 (1953): 313–53.

Lang, Karen. "Spa-tshab Nyi-ma-grags and the Introduction of Prāsaṅgika Madhyamaka into Tibet." In *Reflections on Tibetan Culture: Essays in Memory of Turrell V. Wylie,* edited by Lawrence Epstein and Richard F. Sherbourne. Lewiston, NY: E. Mellon Press, 1990.

Larson, Gerald James and Ram Shankar Bhattacharya. *Sāṃkhya: A Dualist Tradition in Indian Philosophy.* Encyclopedia of Indian Philosophies, 4. Princeton, NJ: Princeton University Press, 1987.

Lindtner, Christian. "Atiśa's Introduction to the Two Truths, and Its Sources." *Journal of Indian Philosophy* 9 (1981), 161–214.

———. "Buddhapālita on Emptiness." *Indo-Iranian Journal* 23 (1981): 187–217.

Lopez, Donald S. Jr. *A Study of Svātantrika.* Ithaca, NY: Snow Lion Publications, 1987.

MacDonald, Anne. "The *Prasannapadā: More Manuscripts from Nepal.*" *Wiener Zeitschrift für die Kunde Südasiens* 44 (2000): 165–81.

———. "Interpreting *Prasannapadā* 19.3–7 in Context: A Response to Claus Oetke." *Wiener Zeitschrift für die Kunde Südasiens* 47 (2003): 143–95.

Makransky, John. *Buddhahood Embodied: Sources of Controversy in India and Tibet.* Albany, NY: State University of New York Press, 1997.

Martin, Daniel. "A Twelfth-century Tibetan Classic of Mahamudra, The Path of Ultimate Profundity: The Great Seal Instructions of Zhang." *Journal of the International Association of Buddhist Studies* 15, no. 2 (1992): 243–319.

———. "The 'Star King' and the Four Children of Pehar: Popular Religious Movements of 11th to 12th Century Tibet." *Acta Orientalia Academiae Scientiarum Hungarium* 49, no. 1–2 (1996): 171–95.

Matilal, Bimal Krishna. *Perception: An Essay on Classical Indian Theories of Knowledge.* Oxford: Clarendon Press, 1986.

———. *The Character of Logic in India.* Albany, NY: State University of New York Press, 1998.

McClintock, Sara L. "The Role of the 'Given' in the Classification of Śāntarakṣita and Kamalaśīla as Svātantrika-Mādhyamikas." In *The Svātantrika-Prāsaṅgika Distinction,* edited by Georges B.J. Dreyfus and Sara L. McClintock, 125–71. Boston: Wisdom Publications, 2003.

Mejor, Marek. "On the Date of the Tibetan Translations of the *Pramāṇasamuccaya* and the *Pramāṇavārttika.*" In *Studies in the Buddhist Epistemological Tradition,* ed. Ernst Steinkellner, 175–97. Vienna: Österreichischen Akademie der Wissenschaften, 1991.

Mimaki, Katsumi. "The *Blo gsal grub mtha'*, and the Mādhyamika Classification in Tibetan *grub mtha'* Literature." In *Contributions on Tibetan and Buddhist Religion and Philosophy,* edited by Ernst Steinkellner and Helmut Tauscher, 161–67. Vienna: Arbeitskreis für Tibetische und Buddhistische Studien, 1983.

———. "*Jñānasārasamuccaya* kk. 20–28: *Mise au point* with a Sanskrit Manuscript." In *Wisdom, Compassion, and the Search for Understanding: The*

Buddhist Studies Legacy of Gadjin M. Nagao, edited by Jonathan A. Silk, 233–244. Honolulu: University of Hawai'i Press, 2000.

Napper, Elizabeth. *Dependent-Arising and Emptiness.* London: Wisdom Publications, 1989.

Newland, Guy. *The Two Truths.* Ithaca, NY: Snow Lion Publications, 1992.

Newman, John. "Buddhist Siddhānta in the Kālacakra Tantra." *Wiener Zeitschrift für die Kunde Südasiens* 36 (1992): 227–34.

Naudou, Jean. *Buddhists of Kaśmīr.* Delhi: Agam Kala Prakashan, 1980.

Oetke, Claus. "The Disjunction in the Pramāṇasiddhi." In *Dharmakīrti's Thought and its Impact on Indian and Tibetan Philosophy,* ed. Shoryu Katsura, 243–51. Vienna: Österreichischen Akademie der Wissenschaften, 1999.

———. "*Prasannapadā* 19.3–7 and Its Context." *Wiener Zeitschrift für die Kunde Südasiens* 47 (2003): 111–42.

Ono, Motoi. *Prajñākaragupta's Erklarung der Definition Gultiger Erkenntnis (Pramāṇavārttikālaṃkāra zu Pramāṇavārttika II 1–7).* Vienna: Österreichischen Akademie der Wissenschaften, 2000.

Onoda, Shunzu. "Phya pa Chos kyi seng ge's Classification of Thal 'gyur." *Berliner Indologische Studien* 2 (1986): 341–46.

———. "On the Tibetan Controversy Concerning the Various Ways of Relying to Prasaṅgas." *Tibet Journal* 13, no. 2 (1988): 36–41.

———. "Abbatial Successions of the Colleges of gSang phu sne'u thog Monastery." *Bulletin of the National Museum of Ethnology* 15, no. 4 (1990): 1049–71.

———. *Monastic Debate in Tibet: A Study on the History and Structures of bsdus grwa Logic.* Vienna: Arbeitskreis für Tibetische und Buddhistische Studien Universität Wien, 1992.

———. "Phya pa Chos kyi seng ge's Theory of *'gal ba.*" In *Tibetan Studies: Proceedings of the 5th Seminar of the International Association for Tibetan Studies.* Monograph Series of Naritasan Institute for Buddhist Studies: Occasional Papers 2, edited by Ihara Shōnen and Yamaguchi Zuihō, 197–202. Narita: Naritasan Shinshōji, 1992.

Pollack, Sheldon. "The Sanskrit Cosmopolis, 300–1300 CE: Transculturation, Vernacularization, and the Question of Ideology." In *Ideology and Status of Sanskrit: Contributions to the History of the Sanskrit Language,* ed. Jan E.M. Houben, 197–247. Leiden: E.J. Brill, 1996.

Richardson, Hugh. "A Tibetan Inscription from Rgyal Lha-khaṅ; and a Note on Tibetan Chronology from A.D. 841 to A.D. 1042." *Journal of the Royal Asiatic Society* (April 1957): 56–78.

Ruegg, David Seyfort. "The Use of the Four Positions of the Catuṣkoṭi and Problem of the Description of Reality in Mahāyāna Buddhism." *Journal of Indian Philosophy* 5 (1977): 1–71.

———. *The Literature of the Madhyamaka School of Philosophy in India.* Wiesbaden: Otto Harrasowitz, 1981.

———. "A Kar Ma bKa' brGyud Work on the Lineages and Traditions of the Indo-Tibetan dBu ma (Madhyamaka)." In *Orientalia Iosephi Tucci memoriae dicata,* edited by G. Gnoli and L. Lanciotti. Rome: Istituto italiano per il Medio ed Estremo Oriente, 1985.

———. "On the authorship of some works ascribed to Bhāvaviveka/Bhavya." In *Earliest Buddhism and Madhyamaka,* ed. David Seyfort Ruegg and Lambert Schmithausen, 59–71. Leiden: E.J. Brill, 1990.

———. "The Preceptor-Donor (*yon mchod*) Relation in Thirteenth Century Tibetan Society and Polity, its Inner Asian Precursors and Indian Models." In *Tibetan Studies: Proceedings of the 7th Seminar of the International Association for Tibetan Studies,* edited by Helmut Krasser, Michael Torsten Much, Ernst Steinkellner, Helmut Tauscher, 857–82. Vienna: Österreichischen Akademie der Wissenschaften, 1997.

———. *Three Studies in the History of Indian and Tibetan Madhyamaka Philosophy, Studies in Indian and Tibetan Madhyamaka Thought, Part 1.* Vienna: Arbeitskreis für Tibetische und Buddhistische Studien Universitat Wien, 2000.

———. *Two Prolegomena to Madhyamaka Philosophy, Studies in Indian and Tibetan Madhyamaka Thought, Part II.* Vienna: Arbeitskreis für Tibetische und Buddhistische Studien Universität Wien, 2002.

Saito, Akira. "Problems in Translating the *Mūlamadhyamakakārikā* as Cited in its Commentaries." In *Buddhist Translations: Problems and Perspectives,* ed. Doboom Tulku, 87–96. New Delhi: Manohar, 1995.

———. "Śāntideva in the History of Mādhyamika Philosophy." In *Buddhism in India and Abroad,* ed. Kalpakam Sankarnarayan, Motohiro Yoritomi, and Shubhada A. Joshi. Mumbai and New Delhi: Somaiya Publications, 1996.

Sellars, Wilfrid. *Empiricism and the Philosophy of Mind.* Cambridge: Harvard University Press, 1997.

Shastri, Lobsang. "The Fire Dragon *Chos 'khor* (1076 AD)." In *Tibetan Studies: Proceedings of the 7th Seminar of the International Association for Tibetan Studies,* edited by Helmut Krasser, Michael Torsten Much, Ernst Steinkellner, Helmut Tauscher, 873–82. Vienna: Österreichischen Akademie der Wissenschaften, 1997.

Sopa, Geshe Lhundup and Jeffrey Hopkins. *Cutting through Appearances: The Practice and Theory of Tibetan Buddhism.* Ithaca, NY: Snow Lion, 1989.

Sperling, Eliot. "Lama to the King of Hsia." *Journal of the Tibet Society* 7 (1987): 31–50.

———. "Rtsa-mi lo-tsā-ba Sangs-rgyas grags-pa and the Tangut Background to Mongol-Tibetan Relations." In *Tibetan Studies: Proceedings of the 6th Seminar of the International Association for Tibetan Studies, Fagernes, 1992,* edited by Per Kvaerne, 801–24. Oslo: Institute for Comparative Research in Human Culture, 1994.

Steinkellner, Ernst. *Verse-Index of Dharmakīrti's Works.* Vienna: Arbeitskreis für Tibetische und Buddhistische Studien Universität Wien, 1977.

———. "Miszellen zur Erkenntnistheoretisch-Logischen Schule des Buddhismus I. I. Zur Datierung Karṇakogomins." *Wiener Zeitschrift für die Kunde Südasiens* 23 (1979): 141–50.

———. "Was Dharmakīrti a Mādhyamika?" In *Earliest Buddhism and Madhyamaka,* ed. David Seyfort Ruegg and Lambert Schmithausen, 72–90. Leiden: E.J. Brill, 1990.

———. "Early Tibetan Ideas on the Ascertainment of Validity (*nges byed kyi tshad ma*)." In *Tibetan Studies: Proceedings of the 5th Seminar of the International Association for Tibetan Studies.* Monograph Series of Naritasan Institute for Buddhist Studies: Occasional Papers 2, edited by Ihara Shōnen and Yamaguchi Zuihō, 257–73. Narita: Naritasan Shinshōji, 1992.

———. "Yogic Cognition, Tantric Goal, and Other Methodological Applications of Dharmakīrti's *Kāryānumāna* Theorem." In *Dharmakīrti's Thought and Its Impact on Indian and Tibetan Philosophy,* edited by S. Katsura, 349–62. Vienna: Österreichischen Akademie der Wissenschaften, 1999.

Stock, Brian. *The Implications of Literacy: Written Language and Models of Interpretation in the Eleventh and Twelfth Centuries.* Princeton: Princeton University Press, 1983.

———. *Listening for the Text: On the Uses of the Past.* Philadelphia: University of Pennsylvania Press, 1996.

Tanselle, G. Thomas. *A Rationale of Textual Criticism.* Philadelphia, University of Pennsylvania Press, 1989.

Tatz, Mark. "Maitrī-pa and Atiśa." In *Tibetan Studies: Proceedings of the 4th Seminar of the International Association for Tibetan Studies,* edited by Helga Uebach and Jampa L. Panglung, 473–82. Munchen: Kommission für Zentralasiatische Studien Bayerische Akademie der Wissenschaften, 1988.

Tauscher, Helmut. "Some Problems of Textual History in Connection with the Tibetan Translations of the *Madhyamakāvatāra* and its Commentary." In *Contributions on Tibetan and Buddhist Religion and Philosophy,* edited by Ernst Steinkellner and Helmut Tauscher, 293–303. Vienna: Arbeitskreis für Tibetische und Buddhistische Studien, 1983.

———. "Phya pa chos kyi seng ge's opinion on *prasaṅga* in his *dBu ma'i shar gsum gyi stong thun.*" In *Dharmakīrti's Thought and its Impact on Indian and Tibetan Philosophy,* edited by Shoryu Katsura, 387–93. Vienna: Österreichischen Akademie der Wissenschaften, 1999.

———. "Phya pa chos kyi seng ge as a Svātantrika." In *The Svātantrika-Prāsaṅgika Distinction: What Difference Does a Difference Make?* edited by Georges B.J. Dreyfus and Sara L. McClintock, 207–55. Boston: Wisdom Publications, 2002.

Tillemans, Tom J.F. "The Neither One nor Many Argument for Śūnyatā, and Tibetan Interpretations: Background Information and Source Materials." *Études de Letters, Université de Lausanne* 3 (1982): 103–28.

———. *Materials for the Study of Āryadeva, Dharmapāla and Candrakīrti.* Vienna: Arbeitskreis für Tibetische und Buddhistische Studien Universität Wien, 1990.

———. "Tsong kha pa *et al.* on the Bhāvaviveka-Candrakīrti Debate" in *Tibetan Studies: Proceedings of the 5th Seminar of the International Association for Tibetan Studies.* Monograph Series of Naritasan Institute for Buddhist Studies: Occasional Papers 2, edited by Ihara Shōnen and Yamaguchi Zuihō. Narita: Naritasan Shinshōji, 1992.

———. *Scripture, Logic, Language: Essays on Dharmakīrti and His Tibetan Successors.* Boston: Wisdom Publications, 1999.

———. "Metaphysics for Mādhyamikas." In *The Svātantrika-Prāsaṅgika Distinction,* ed. Georges B.J. Dreyfus and Sara L. McClintock, 93–123. Boston: Wisdom Publications, 2003.

Urban, Hugh B. and Paul J. Griffiths. "What Else Remains in Śūnyatā? An Investigation of Terms for Mental Imagery in the *Madhyāntavibhāga*-Corpus." *Journal of the International Association of Buddhist Studies* 17/1 (1994): 1–25.

Vitali, Roberto. *Early Temples of Central Tibet.* London: Serindia Publications, 1990.

———. *The Kingdoms of Gu.ge Pu.hrang According to mNga'.ris rgyal.rabs by Gu.ge mkhan.chen Ngag.dbang.grags.pa.* Dharamsala, India: Library of Tibetan Works and Archives, 1996.

Vose, Kevin *The Birth of Prāsaṅgika: A Buddhist Movement in India and Tibet.* Ph.D. dissertation, University of Virginia, 2005.

Watson, Craig Earl. "The Second Propagation of Buddhism from Eastern Tibet." *Central Asiatic Journal* 22, nos. 3–4 (1978): 263–85.

———. "The Introduction of the Second Propagation of Buddhism in Tibet According to R.A. Stein's Edition of the Sba-bzhed." *Tibet Journal* 5, no. 4 (1980): 20–27.

Wayman, Alex. *Yoga of the Guhyasamājatantra.* Delhi: Motilal Banarsidass, 1977.

Williams, Paul. "rMa bya pa Byang chub brtson 'grus on Madhyamaka Method." *Journal of Indian Philosophy* 13 (1985): 205–25.

———. *The Reflexive Nature of Awareness.* London: Curzon Press, 1998.

Yonezawa, Yoshiyasu. "*Lakṣaṇaṭīkā:* A Sanskrit Manuscript of an Anonymous Commentary on the *Prasannapadā.*" *Journal of Indian and Buddhist Studies* 47, no. 2 (1999): 1024–1022.

———. *Introduction to the Facsimile Edition of a Collection of Sanskrit Palm-leaf Manuscripts in Tibetan* dBu med *Script.* Tokyo: The Institute for Comprehensive Studies of Buddhism, Taishō University, 2001.

Yoshimizu, Chizuko. "Tsong kha pa's Reevaluation of Candrakīrti's Criticism of Autonomous Inference." In *The Svātantrika-Prāsaṅgika Distinction: What Difference Does a Difference Make?* edited by Georges B.J. Dreyfus and Sara L. McClintock, 257–88. Boston: Wisdom Publications, 2002.

Yotsuya, Kodo. *The Critique of Svatantra Reasoning by Candrakīrti and Tsong-kha-pa: A Study of Philosophical Proof According to Two Prāsaṅgika Madhyamaka Traditions of India and Tibet.* Tibetan and Indo-Tibetan Studies, 8. Stuttgart: Franz Steiner Verlag, 1999.

Yün-hua, Jan. "Buddhist Relations between India and Sung China." Parts 1 and 2. *History of Religions* 6, no. 1 (August 1966): 24–42 and 6, no. 2 (November 1966): 135–68.

Index

About the Author

Kevin A. Vose is a professor of religious studies at the College of William and Mary in Williamsburg, Virginia. He received his Ph.D. in Buddhist Studies from the University of Virginia, where he received an American Institute of Indian Studies fellowship to study with Tibetan scholars in India. His research examines the interplay of late-Indian and early-Tibetan Madhyamaka and the formation of Tibetan scholasticism.

About Wisdom Publications

WISDOM PUBLICATIONS is dedicated to making available authentic Buddhist works for the benefit of all. We publish translations of the sutras and tantras, commentaries and teachings of past and contemporary Buddhist masters, and original works by the world's leading Buddhist scholars. We publish our titles with the appreciation of Buddhism as a living philosophy and with the special commitment to preserve and transmit important works from all the major Buddhist traditions.

Wisdom Publications
199 Elm Street
Somerville, Massachusetts 02144 USA
Telephone: 617-776-7416
Fax: 617-776-7841
Email: info@wisdompubs.org
www.wisdompubs.org

Wisdom is a nonprofit, charitable 501(c)(3) organization affiliated with the Foundation for the Preservation of the Mahayana Tradition (FPMT).